PSYCHOLOGICAL ANALYSIS AND THE PHILOSOPHY OF JOHN STUART MILL

Psychological Analysis and the Philosophy of John Stuart Mill

FRED WILSON

UNIVERSITY OF TORONTO PRESS

Toronto Buffalo London

© University of Toronto Press 1990
Toronto Buffalo London
Printed in Canada

ISBN 0-8020-2714-8

Printed on acid-free paper

Canadian Cataloguing in Publication Data

Wilson, Fred, 1937–
Psychological analysis and the philosophy of
John Stuart Mill

ISBN 0-8020-2714-8

1. Mill, John Stuart, 1806–1873 – Contributions in
psychology. 2. Mill, John Stuart, 1806–1873.
3. Mill, James, 1773–1836 – Contributions in
psychology. 4. Mill, James, 1773–1836. I. Title.

B1608.P7W55 1990   192   c89-090631-9

This book has been published with the help of a grant from the
Canadian Federation for the Humanities, using funds provided by the
Social Sciences and Humanities Research Council of Canada.

TO MY PARENTS

Contents

Preface

The aim of this essay is to discuss the theory of classical or introspective psychology as found in the works of James Mill and of John Stuart Mill. Specifically, the intention is to discuss it as theory, in its own right, with respect to our capacities to discriminate relations and to perceive things at a distance, and, in its applications, with respect to classical economics and to the moral philosophy of the utilitarians.

I first became aware of the connections that this book attempts to trace while a graduate student in Gustav Bergmann's lectures on the history and systems of psychology. Over the years I have discussed the ideas with various people; such encounters with Wendy Donner have been especially useful. Some of the main points regarding John Stuart Mill's modifications to his father's theory of psychology were presented as a public lecture during the annual Symposium at University College at the University of Toronto in January 1984; Hans de Groot is to be thanked for providing the occasion and for some stimulating discussion of the lecture in which my ideas were often reduced by condensation, I think, to the point of being nothing more than cryptic.

The final version of the manuscript was completed during sabbatical leave from the University of Toronto in 1986–7. The University of Toronto Faculty Association deserves many thanks for securing me the right to sabbatical leaves at only a modest reduction in salary.

My wife and family, as usual, must be thanked for their tolerance; their role is not quite that of Harriet Taylor, but it is equally indispensable.

FW

PSYCHOLOGICAL ANALYSIS AND THE

PHILOSOPHY OF JOHN STUART MILL

Introduction

Classical economics as formulated by Adam Smith and David Ricardo provided the outline of the first systematic theory in economics. This theory began with certain assumptions, and deduced theorems therefrom. Crucial among the assumptions was the thesis that *in the area of economic phenomena, the only motive that moves persons to action is the desire to maximize one's own pleasures.* If psychological egoism is the thesis that persons seek only to maximize their own pleasure, then the classical economists assumed that psychological egoism held for the area of economic behaviour. This initial assumption is certainly not true a priori nor can it be accepted as empirically true without serious qualifications; but, suitably qualified, it is, and remains, a plausible starting-point for economics. The theorems that were deduced from the initial axioms, including the psychological-egoist assumption, had a certain amount of independent empirical support. It was not Newtonian mechanics by any means, but it was not a bad theory, and, more important, it provided a basic theoretical position from which the science could advance, often incrementally, but sometimes in giant ('revolutionary') steps, as occurred during the marginalist revolution.

But the classical economists not only did science, they proposed policy. They were able to deduce from their axioms, explicit and implicit, that if men acted in conformity to the psychological-egoistic assumption, then in the long run, in an unregulated market for goods and labour, the pleasures of all would be maximized, and in a regulated market some would be worse off. This theorem could then be used in Britain to support the policy of creating a free market, for that would be better for all in the long run – that is, the new science of economics could be mobilized in political debate to argue against monopolies and what remained of the old mercantile system. It would also be used in political argument against such regulations as the Corn Laws, which restricted trade in certain areas to the benefit of the wealthy landowners of the aristocracy: the landowners were short-sighted, and in the long run they too would benefit from the abolition of the laws that served only their short-run interest.

If the argument is to work, then certain constraints must be presupposed. In particular, men must conform to the principle of justice, that property rights be respected; to the principle of contract, that contracts (promises) be kept; and to the principle of allegiance, that one loyally support a government that enforces the principles of justice and contract. Men must not act contrary to these principles – that is, these principles must constrain our economic behaviour; if they do not, then that best distribution that can be effected by the market mechanism will not eventuate. Thus, if the political argument of the classical economists is to be sound, then the moral sentiments of men must be such as to secure conformity to these principles, that is, function psychologically as motives with the strength to so restrain the psychological-egoistic motives that the principles of justice, contract, and allegiance are conformed to. Among those who attempted in the first quarter of the nineteenth century to make the political argument derived from classical economics were a group of philosophic radicals or radical utilitarians associated with Jeremy Bentham.[1] This group aimed at not only economic reform, but also political and legal reform. Now, when these philosopher-politicians argued their case they tended to assume as a premiss that men always act in a self-interested way – that is, they tended to assume the general psychological-egoist thesis that *persons always seek only to maximize their own pleasure in all their voluntary acts*. On this thesis, if anything other than one's own pleasure is desired, then it is sought as a means to such pleasure. But among the means that one used – that is, used if one was enlightened – was the welfare of others. In fact, the best means, they argued, for securing one's own long-run maximum pleasure was by acting upon the utilitarian principle of the greatest happiness for the greatest number. The enlightened egoist was a utilitarian.

What these reformers then argued was that certain principles of morality and government could be justified on utilitarian grounds while others could not, and that the latter ought to be eliminated or at least replaced by some that could. Thus, they held that the principles of justice, contract, and allegiance could be justified on utilitarian grounds. They also argued that many specific features of the government and the legal system failed the utilitarian test, and on that basis they demanded reform of those institutions.

The philosophic radicals were reformers, not revolutionaries. But their critics on the right, the Whigs, including Macaulay and Adam Sedgwick (1834), and the Tories, including William Whewell (1845), were quick to charge that the doctrine had more revolutionary implications than its defenders recognized.

The argument of the radical reformers was this: it is in the long-run interest of each to act on the utilitarian principle. More specifically, as a means to that end it is in the long-run interest of each to conform to the principles of justice, contract, and allegiance. And still more specifically, given the theorems of the science of economics, it is in the long-run interest of each to operate in an unregulated market. This argument attacked the landed interest of the aristocracy while protecting the mercantile and industrial interests of the middle class. But what of the working class? In the first place, not everyone is enlightened. This fact alone means that they will be led to act contrary to what the utilitarian principle requires; for example, they will be led to steal, that is, violate the principle of justice about the preservation of property rights. In addition, in the long run, as Keynes said much later, we are all dead. A genuine enlightenment that recognizes the contingencies of life may lead one quite rationally to choose short-run interest over long-run consequences. For, given the contingencies, the long-run consequences will, with some probability, be of no interest. But finally, the interventions of Malthus made clear that the long run of the economic argument would have to include subsequent generations. If that is so, then the argument is undercut by the general psychological-egoist assumption of the radical utilitarians: psychological egoists will not be concerned with the fate of subsequent generations, only with themselves, and so in spite of long-run consequences the working class and the poor will, given their numerical superiority, expropriate the property of the aristocracy, and that of the middle class, and redistribute it. That may mean that industriousness and inventiveness will go unrewarded, and that, with no egoistic incentives to practise those virtues, economic development will, with long-run disastrous consequences, not only cease to improve, but actually be retrograde. But that's the distant future, and psychological egoists will not worry about it. In *their* interests, then, they will in the name of equality expropriate the property of all who, through natural inequalities of intellect or moral fibre, manage to make improvements that benefit all in the long run but only themselves in the short run.

Thus, the real problem facing the philosophic radicals was not to justify reform but to explain not only why the working class *ought not* to expropriate the more advantaged but, given the principle accepted by the reformers that men are psychological egoists, why the working class *does not* revolt. The response of the Whig and Tory critics of the radical utilitarians was to insist that psychological egoism was false and that our moral sentiments are not reducible to self-love. In fact, more strongly, they insisted upon the irreducibility of virtue to any other motive. There are two points: (1) we aim at virtuous behaviour for its own sake, and not merely as a means, whether to a utilitarian end or to an egoistic end – that is, our moral sentiments have virtuous behaviour as their *object*; (2) our moral sentiments have a power to move us towards their object that is irreducible to the motivating power of our other sentiments and passions – that is, our moral sentiments are motives that *differ specifically* from other motives, including other motives that might have the same object.

Psychological egoism denies both these points. The same act, for example, giving money to another, may be done either generously, for its own sake, or out of self-love. Psychological egoism denies that the former occurs. Thus, it denies point (1) when it insists that, if virtue is sought, it is sought only as a means to egoistic ends. But further, we often take pleasure in virtuous actions. Psychological egoism holds that there is no independent motive to such actions the satisfaction of which yields pleasure; rather, those actions are done out of self-love alone, for the pleasure they yield. Thus, psychological egoism denies point (2) when it insists that there are no motives beyond self-love.

When the opponents of the philosophic radicals asserted against the latter the falsity of psychological egoism and the irreducibility of virtue, they hoped to put morality on a sound foundation, where, as they saw it, the radicals undercut morality by denying points (1) and (2) and, consequently, that morality exists. They sought not only to justify such claims as those of justice or property, contract, and allegiance, but also, on the assumption that all persons, or almost all, have a sense of virtue, that is, are motivated by it, they proposed what the philosophic radicals seemed to lack, namely, an explanation of why we, in fact, find that people conform to these principles of justice, contract, and allegiance. There is thus both a *moral* and a *psychological* foundation for virtue.

The opponents of the utilitarians often argued that a firm moral foundation for virtue could be had only if one held that our moral sentiments had a cognitive component in which one came to know *objective moral truths*. In contrast, the utilitarians held that since nothing is good save that in which we take pleasure, *all value is relative*.

This contrast between judgments that are objective and those that are relative is important. A judgment that a is F is objective just in case that its truth or falsity depends only upon a and the properties that a has. Thus, the judgment that Socrates is snub-nosed is objective because its truth or falsity depends only upon Socrates and the shape of his nose. So, too, is the judgment that Socrates has an aquiline nose. In this sense, all judgments of fact are objective. In contrast, a judgment that a is F is relative just in case that its truth or falsity depends not only upon what it is about but also upon who utters it. Thus, the judgment that Socrates is virtuous is relative, upon the utilitarian position, since what it means is that the contemplation of Socrates and his actions gives pleasure to the speaker. In general, upon the utilitarian position, value judgments are relative. Many of the opponents of the utilitarian position, for example Adam Sedgwick and William Whewell, hold, in contrast, that value judgments are, like judgments of fact, objective.

Now, mental states are often said to be subjective, and are usually assumed to be private. The mental, the subjective, and the private are thus often held to coincide. It is important to recognize that judgments to the effect that a is in a certain mental state are objective judgments. Thus, for example, the judgment that Socrates is thinking of Phaedo is objective, since its truth or falsity depends only upon Socrates and his properties, and, more specifically, upon the mental states that presently characterize him. This means that judgments that a person has a certain subjective state are objective. So, too, the judgment that John Stuart takes pleasure in x, which attributes a subjective state to John Stuart, is an objective judgment. So, too, the judgment that John Stuart morally approves of Socrates is one which is objective, since it attributes a subjective state to John Stuart and is true or false depending only upon John Stuart and his subjective states.

The relative is often variable. Thus, those who defend utilitarianism often hold that value judgments are not only relative but variable. Such philosophers hold that the truth or falsity of these judgments depends upon the subjective states of those who make them, and that these subjective states vary from person to person. In fact, the term 'subjective' is often taken to be synonymous with the term 'relative.' So the utilitarian position has also been accused of making value judgments subjective.

There is yet another meaning of the term 'objective' that ought to be noted. Upon this meaning, a judgment is objective just in case that everyone agrees that it is so, that is, just in case that *inter*subjective agreement is achieved. Utilitarians tend to hold that value judgments are subjective in the sense of variable, and therefore that they are not objective in this sense of intersubjective. But such a combination of positions is not necessary, as the case of Hutcheson shows, as we shall see. That is, it is possible to hold that value judgments are relative while also holding that universal agreement can be achieved; or, what is the same, it is possible to hold that relativity does not imply variability. It is therefore possible to hold both that value judgments are relative and also that they are objective in the sense that intersubjective agreement holds. This position can be maintained if one argues that intersubjective agreement can be attained in the realm of moral judgments because such judgments are *instinctive* or *native*, rooted in the *innate mechanisms of human nature*.

At the same time, those who argue for the objectivity of value judgments and against the usual utilitarian position that such judgments are relative often also wish to give such judgments a firm psychological foundation. After all, the mere fact that judgments are objective, in the sense that their truth or falsity depends upon what they are about, does not guarantee that there will be intersubjective agreement on such judgments. Thus, while judgments of the colour of such perceptual objects as tables and chairs are normally assumed to be objective in the first sense, facts such as colour blindness and jaundice ensure that they are not fully objective in the sense of fully achieving intersubjective agreement. So anti-utilitarians such as William Whewell argued not only that value judgments are as objective as judgments of fact but that they also have a firm psychological foundation in the *innate mechanisms of human nature*. Value judgments are objective but, in addition, their status as *instinctive* or *native* principles guarantees that there will be no variability, only indisputable intersubjective agreement, on the facts of value.

In contrast, of course, utilitarians generally hold, and John Stuart Mill and the other radical utilitarians certainly held, that since moral behaviour is the result of education, self-culture, and enlightenment, virtue is not instinctive or native but acquired; they held, that is, that *virtue is learned*.

John Stuart Mill saw it as his task to defend the radical utilitarian position. Or rather, he recognized that the opponents' criticisms were substantial, and that the utilitarian position, if it were to be defended, had to acknowledge the irreducibility of virtue. However, if it were to be a utilitarian position that was defended, and one that could continue to defend the policy proposals of the philosophic radicals in law, government, and economics, then that irreducibility of virtue had somehow to be reconciled with the doctrine that what moves persons to action is pleasure and pain. Mill is claiming to have effected such a reconciliation when he claims in his essay 'Utilitarianism' (1861) that while men do seek ends other than pleasure or happiness – for example, for the good person, virtue, or for the miser, money – they seek them as *part of* their happiness' (1861, p. 235). More fully: 'What was once desired as an instrument for the attainment of happiness, has come to be desired for its own sake. In being desired for its own sake it is, however, desired as *part* of happiness. The person is made, or thinks he would be made, happy by its mere possession' (p. 236). In particular, virtue can in this way be desired for its own sake as part of happiness. In this way, Mill holds, the utilitarian can maintain 'not only that virtue is to be desired, but that it is to be desired disinterestedly, for itself.' The utilitarians 'not only place virtue at the very head of the things which are good as means to the ultimate end, but they also recognise as a psychological fact the possibility of its being, to the individual, a good in itself ... and hold, that the mind is not in a right state ... not in the state most conducive to the general happiness, unless it does love virtue in this manner' (p. 235). With this doctrine, then, of the parts of happiness the younger Mill attempts to reply to the critics of this father, of Bentham, and of the older generation of utilitarians.

How convincing is this defence of the utilitarian position?

Consider but one example. Dryer suggests that 'if Mill can succeed in showing that virtue, or fame, or money comes to be desired only as part of happiness, he can no longer hold that it is desired for its own sake' (1969, p. xciii). Thus, Dryer holds, Mill 'removes his ground for arguing that the "ingredients of happiness are very various, and each of them is desirable in itself"' (Dryer, ibid.; Mill 1861, p. 235). Dryer is not convinced.

Mill argues for the hedonist thesis that 'happiness is desirable, and the only thing desirable, as an end' (1861, p. 234). The seeking of other things as ends is supposed to be reconciled with this hedonism by the claim that the other things are sought as 'parts' of happiness. Dryer objects: if happiness alone is sought for its own sake, then what is sought as part of happiness is not sought for its own sake. Thus, suppose one wants, for its own sake, to possess a beautiful statue. Then, if a fragment of stone is part of that statue, one wants that fragment, for one wants the statue whole. But it does not follow that one wants the fragment for its own sake. It seems, then, that Dryer is correct: Mill has failed.

Or rather, Mill has failed if by 'part' he means 'spatial part.' But since the point is so obvious, it perhaps should be thought extremely unlikely that that is what Mill meant by 'part.' Another sense of 'part' should therefore be sought, one for which Mill's claim is at least plausible. Dryer does not develop an argument here but rather is flatly dogmatic: he makes his point about 'part' and simply fails to imagine that some sense of 'part' other than *his* might be relevant. In fact, however, there are other senses of 'part' that could be relevant.

Thus, meat, potatoes, and apple pie, as well as other things, are, as species, *logical parts* of the genus food. Suppose that food *as such* is desired for its own sake. That is to say, any thing that is food is desired for its own sake, that is, desired *qua* food. Thus, with respect to kiwi, carrots, roast beef, fish, potatoes, apple pie, and many other things, each and all *qua* food is desired for its own sake. And clearly one cannot eat food as such, only specific sorts of food. Thus, if food as such is desired for its own sake then it must be both that *a* specific sort of food is desired for its own sake and that *each* specific sort of food is desired for its own sake. Hence, if by 'part' Mill means 'logical part' in the sense in which each species is part of the genus, then it is legitimate for Mill to infer that if happiness, and happiness alone, is desired for its own sake, then any, and every, part of happiness is desired for its own sake.

The difficulty with proposing such a reading, however, is that *happiness* does not seem to be a nice neat genus in the way in which *animal* is. But then, it could not be. My happiness is not your happiness – that is, the parts of my happiness are not the same as the parts of your happiness – and moreover, the parts of my happiness change over time – what was originally desired as a means comes, after learning, to be desired for its own sake, that is, as a part of (my) happiness. The problem is not so much with happiness being a genus as with explaining the differences among persons and over time.

But even this problem can be solved by taking into account *learning*. The learning theory that Mill advances is that of *associationism*: through the mechanism of association, for what was originally desired as a means to pleasure there comes to be such an association or habitual connection between it and pleasure that it is desired as part of happiness. 'Will is the child of desire, and passes out of the dominion of its parent only to come under that of habit' (1861, p. 239). Roughly, the genus *happiness* has as its species *each thing that has come to have pleasure associated with it*.

The method by which this psychological law is established is that of 'practised self-consciousness and self-observation, assisted by observation of others' (1861, p. 237). This observation of consciousness by itself was later called *introspection*. Systematic self-observation yields an analysis (p. 231) of the conscious states observed. We may call this sort of analysis *introspective analysis*. Now, what an analysis yields has to be *parts*. This is yet another sense of 'part' that Dryer misses. In the case of happiness, introspection reveals two distinct analytical or introspective parts. What introspection observes in the case of happiness are conscious states of happiness; what introspective analysis reveals is that each state consists of two parts, namely, on the one hand, the something that is its object, and, on the other hand, feelings of pleasure that are associated with that object. A conscious state in which a certain object constitutes one's happiness is a specific case of the genus happiness because of the association, *which analysis reveals*, between the object and the feelings of pleasure. But this association is a *regular habit* that has been caused by a repeated experience in the past of a conjunction between that object and pleasure. Thus, in revealing that the conscious state consists of certain parts associated with each other, analysis uncovers the genetic antecedents of that state.

What we have just stated is the essence of the method of introspective analysis in psychology. We shall have more to say about this below. The point here is that the younger Mill appeals to it in order to justify his claim to have shown how the utilitarianism of the older generation of philosophic radicals is compatible with many of the claims of its critics, and, in particular, how it can provide a sound moral and psychological foundation for virtue without falling into either intuitionism or nativism.

Thus, in the first and most important place, virtue is sought for its own sake, and the motive is a specific kind of pleasure. Second, association can establish as firm a psychological foundation for these values as one needs. As Mill puts it, 'It is natural to man to speak, to reason, to build cities, to cultivate the ground, though these are acquired faculties,' and similarly the 'moral faculty, if not a part of our nature, is a natural outgrowth from it' (1861, p. 230). The firmness of the psychological foundation he mentions in his notes to his father's *Analysis of the Phenomena of the Human Mind*: 'those persons, things, and positions become in themselves pleasant to us by association; and, through the multitude and variety of the pleasurable ideas associated with them become pleasures of far greater constancy and even intensity, and altogether more valuable to us, than any of the primitive pleasures of our constitution' (1869, II: 233). And third, the utilitarian principle justifies morally the cultivation of the moral sentiments of virtue because of the felicitous consequences of people having such sentiments; 'the mind is not in a right state ... not in the state most conducive to the general happiness, unless it does love virtue in this manner' (1861, p. 238).

These responses suffice to accommodate the points the anti-utilitarians were trying to make. However, fourth, given Mill's argument that happiness and happiness alone is desirable, that is, *worthy* of desire,[2] it follows that what constitutes a moral good is relative; thus, the utilitarian can accept his critics' main points without conceding to their ethical objectivism or intuitionism. Moreover, fifth, on this account, that something is felt to be a moral good, or that certain actions are felt to be virtuous, is something that is, for the most part, learned; thus the utilitarians need make no concessions to their opponents' nativism.

Finally, sixth, the major thrust of the earlier utilitarian psychology, that people are moved by pleasures and pains, is preserved through the younger Mill's idea that *things can, through association, come to be pleasures*.

Clearly, what is crucial here is the associationist learning theory of introspective psychology.

Now, some have objected straight off to the psychological theory of associationism as inadequate to any genuinely human psychology since, if it were true, the mind would be something *merely passive*: if it is a correct account of human psychology, then the mind, as it were, simply receives sensations and, from these, ideas are generated according to regular laws that leave no room for the active mind. So, at least, its critics have construed it.[3] This view of association is, however, inaccurate:[4] there is no reason why associationists cannot introduce an active element into their psychology. John Stuart Mill was perfectly clear on this: the mind 'is active as well as passive,' and 'activity cannot possibly be generated from passive elements; a primitive active element must be found somewhere' (1859, p. 354). Activity is essential if the mind is to be more than merely receptive, if it is to be involved in the production of human acts – including acts of disciplining itself and guiding its own development. What the associationists argued on the basis of introspection was that the active part of the mind could be analysed into the influence of pleasures or pains. It is this claim, that all actions are produced (either immediately or ultimately) by pleasures and pains, that was central to the defence of the reforming policy proposals of the radical-utilitarian position. Bentham began his text on morals and legislation with this thesis. James Mill's 'Essay on Government' (1820) takes it as a basic axiom. Suitably restricted to economic phenomena, it was central to the Ricardian economics on which so many of the reformist proposals were based.

The point is that, since people are moved by concerns for pleasures and pains then, by suitably arranging these – for example, through a system of rewards and punishments – people, both subjects and governors, can be induced to act in ways that are to the advantage of all, that is, in ways that satisfy the reformers' moral test of utility. Thus, what links the various claims of the radical utilitarians together is the psychology that they all presuppose.

Specifically, what ties them together is the associationist psychological theory as summarized in James Mill's *Analysis of the Phenomena of the Human Mind*. It was argued there that every voluntary act is produced by a motive, and a motive is the idea of a pleasure contemplated as produced by our action (J.S. Mill 1869, II: 258). Moreover, desire turns out upon analysis to be the same as the idea of pleasure; hence, all voluntary acts are done from a desire for anticipated pleasures (II: 190–2). But both this general theory and also the specific arguments for the policy proposals left the radical-utilitarian reformers open to criticism.

In particular, such critics as Macaulay were quick to attribute to the utilitarians not only the thesis of psychological egoism – *persons always seek only to maximize their own pleasure or good in all their voluntary acts* – but also the thesis of psychological hedonism – *persons always act from a desire for pleasure (or to avoid pain); anything else is sought only as a means to pleasure.* The difference between the two theses is that psychological egoism precludes aiming at anything other than the maximization of pleasure, while psychological hedonism allows things other than pleasure to be aimed at provided they are aimed at, to use Mill's phrase, as parts of pleasure. Psychological egoism implies that all (voluntary) actions are only means, that is, means undertaken in order to produce pleasure. Psychological hedonism, in contrast, allows that certain sorts of (voluntary) actions can be done for their own sakes, provided that their performance is one of (has come to be one of) the parts of pleasure.

Of the two claims, the second, that of psychological hedonism, can indeed plausibly be attributed to Bentham and to James Mill. The first claim, that of psychological egoism, can be attributed to Bentham only if he is read carelessly. If one is not clear about what introspective analysis is – and, as we shall see, James Mill himself is not always entirely clear! – then there are passages in the *Analysis* that certainly suggest not only psychological hedonism but also psychological egoism. And in any case, the economics of Ricardo and James Mill, and the latter's views on government, definitely begin with the axiomatic assumption that what men seek exclusively is their own pleasure. So Macaulay had good grounds to attribute both of the theses cited above to the reformers, and to attack them accordingly.

What I have been suggesting is that much of John Stuart Mill's work can usefully be seen as developing a reply to Macaulay and other critics of the reformers' position. The younger Mill points out how Bentham 'distinguished two kinds of interests, the self-regarding and the social: in vulgar discourse, the name is restricted to the former kind alone' (1833, pp. 13–14). In one of the notes that he added to his father's *Analysis* he warned readers how his father's words misleadingly suggested both the thesis of psychological hedonism and that of psychological egoism:

> That the pleasures or pains of another person can only be pleasurable or painful to us through the association of our own pleasures or pains with them, is true in one sense, which is probably that intended by the author, but not true in another, against which he has not sufficiently guarded his mode of expression. It is evident, that the only pleasures or pains of which we have direct experience being those felt by ourselves, it is from them that our very notions of pleasure and pain are derived. It is also obvious that the pleasure or pain with which we contemplate the pleasure or pain felt by somebody else, is itself a pleasure or pain of our own. But if it be meant that in such cases the pleasure or pain is consciously referred to self, I take this to be a mistake. By the acts or other signs exhibited by another person, the idea of a pleasure (which is a pleasurable idea) or the idea of pain (which is a painful idea) are recalled, sometimes with considerable intensity, but in association with the other person as feeling them, not with one's self as feeling them. (1869, II: 217–18)

Our interest in the welfare of others is rooted in our faculty of sympathy, which is, he insists, 'as much an ultimate fact of our nature, as care for ourselves' (1869, II: 309), and in his essay on Sedgwick he wrote that 'the idea of the pain of another is naturally painful; the idea of the pleasure of another is naturally pleasurable' (1835, p. 60). James Mill argues that the idea of the pain (pleasure) of another and our feeling of pain (pleasure) is not unlearned or native, but arises through association (J.S. Mill 1869, II: 280ff), and his son is inclined to agree (II: 309). Indeed, in his essay on Whewell's moral philosophy, the younger Mill states quite definitely that the good of others is a pleasure to us only because we have 'learnt to find pleasure in it' (1852, p. 184n). But, as he in effect notes in his comments on his father's *Analysis*, this claim about learning is merely an hypothesis, and the contrary nativist hypothesis about feelings of sympathy may well turn out to be true (1869, II: 308–9). One can at least say this much, that the hypothesis that feelings of sympathy are learned is plausible; certainly, as Richard Brandt (1979, pp. 138–48) has argued, this claim fits in fairly easily with contemporary theories in psychology. For many purposes, however, whether our capacities to respond sympathetically are native or learned is largely irrelevant; for, as Mill also points out (1869, II: 321), even if the capacity to feel sympathetically with others is, as he suspects, learned, not much turns on that point since the learning occurs so early, and in contexts where the concepts of teaching and training make no sense, that for all practical purposes the result is largely indistinguishable from nativism (II: 322).[5]

We are not, then, psychological egoists. Are we psychological hedonists? That is, do we seek only pleasure, either our own or, non-selfishly, that of others? Again the younger Mill is clear: we *do* have *moral* feelings. Indeed, there are several varieties of moral feeling: 'The class of feeling called moral embraces several varieties, materially different in their character' (1869, II: 324). Such feelings are not native, however; they are acquired through a process of association. 'Young children have affections,' he tells us, 'but not moral feelings' (1835, p. 60). Such feelings are rooted in our capacity for sympathy – 'in this, the unselfish part of our nature, lies a foundation, even independently of inculcation from without, for the generation of moral feelings' (ibid.) – but associationist theory must, he also recognized, be able to account for the differences among the moral feelings themselves, as well as for the differences between the moral sentiments and other feelings (1869, II: 324). But, in any case, there is a difference between *moral* feelings and other feelings. We are therefore moved by the feeling that something is morally obligatory, as well as by the idea of pleasure. But it is also true that these moral feelings are 'generated,' that is, learned. Analysis reveals, we have seen, that such feelings can be analysed as objects that have come to be associated with pleasure. Our moral sentiments thus move us as *parts of* pleasure. In this sense, the younger Mill remains, like his father and Bentham, a psychological hedonist.

Moreover, to produce such moral feelings, one must establish the relevant associations. So, it remains as true for John Stuart Mill as for the earlier utilitarians that by adjusting the pleasures and pains people experience they can be brought to behave in ways that are to the advantage of all. The general reformist proposals thus emerge relatively unscathed by the claims of the Whig and Tory critics.

It is not the reformist proposals that disappear, but the simplicities of the psychology that lay behind them. In particular, learning is no longer a matter of being manipulated by externally produced rewards and punishments. The pleasures and pains that, by association, lead to adjustments in our behaviour also produce, in the feelings that result, new and higher kinds of pleasure. In particular, there is that higher kind of pleasure that is the moral feeling of duty or obligation, which in turn produces an internal regulation of our behaviour.

But here a criticism can be essayed. If such higher feelings as those of our sense of duty are indeed learned, then that is equivalent, as we have seen, to holding that these moral sentiments *can be analysed*. Thus, for example, the feeling of *duty* to perform an act or the feeling that an act *ought* to be done is described as arising from an animal desire to retaliate for a hurt suffered by ourselves or by others for whom we sympathetically care. But 'this impulse to self-defence by the retaliatory infliction of pain only becomes a moral sentiment when it is united with a conviction that the infliction of punishment in such a case is conformable to the general good, and when the impulse is not allowed to carry us beyond the point at which that conviction ends' (1869, II: 326). The punishment need not be that of the law; it may even be the 'displeasure and ill offices of his fellow creatures' (II: 325); it may even be 'the reproaches of his own conscience' (1861, p. 649). Be these details as they may, however, does it not follow that, if the moral sentiment of duty is analysable into a complex involving no motivating feelings apart from pleasure, as Mill seems to hold, then the moral sentiment, after all, is *reducible*? The critics' claim is that virtue is irreducible to self-love, the desire for pleasure. Does not the younger Mill's claim that the moral sentiments can be analysed into objects associated with feelings of pleasure show that, after all, those senti- ments, insofar as they are motivating, are *nothing but* pleasures and pains? Mill suggests that certain sentiments can indeed be 'analysed away' (p. 231). Does not the psychological theory that claims that our moral sentiments can be analysed *ipso facto* also claim that they are to be analysed away? Does not analysis mean elimination? If so, then that means that the younger Mill's defence of the utilitarian position has failed.

It thus seems to be that the psychology to which John Stuart Mill appeals in order to defend the utilitarian position entails that the defence will not succeed.

In fact, however, as I propose to argue, that is not so. John Stuart Mill can in fact reconcile his claims about psychological analysability while rejecting the thesis of psychological egoism. At least, that is a major thrust of the present essay. If such reconciliation can be done, then the younger Mill can also reconcile the associationist psychology of the reformers with the rejection of the psychological egoism that is necessary if the reformers are to be defended against Macaulay. Important to this reconciliation of associationism with the rejection of psychological egoism is, as we shall see, Mill's claim that the laws of psychology involve a chemical rather than mechanical mode of composition.[6] This point has been noted by others, for example Robson (1968, pp. 39–40), Berger (1984, p. 11), and Donner (1983, pp. 482–3). What Robson, Berger, and Donner do not recognize is that for Mill to be clear on this point he had antecedently to be clear on the nature of the research program of associationist psychology. It is another major thrust of the present essay to bring out how the younger Mill so rethought his father's *Analysis* that he moved psychology from the realm of philosophy to the realm of science.

Moreover, neither Berger nor Robson, nor even Donner, brings out clearly how the younger Mill's innovations involve a rejection of the inessential while retaining what was crucial for the utilitarian reformers; that is, they do not show how the clarifications Mill makes in the logic, if you wish, of psychology effect a cogent reply to Macaulay and the other critics of Bentham, Ricardo, and James Mill.

And finally, they do not show how this defence of utilitarianism ties in with the Ricardian economic doctrines that were also so central to the policy recommendations of the reformers.

In what follows, we begin in chapter 1 with background and context – some of the background in earlier British moral philosophy, epistemology, and psychology; and some of the context of the younger Mill's own intellectual, and also emotional, development.

Chapter 2 briefly discusses Mill's general philosophy of science. The notion of the chemical mode of composition is discussed in this context, but the chapter also attempts to show how Mill's general philosophy of science can be fitted into more recent developments in that discipline. On this basis it will be suggested in subsequent discussions that Mill's philosophy of psychology is not as dated as many might suppose; and that the replies to the critics of utilitarianism, which are based on this psychology, have a continuing relevance.

Chapter 3 presents a detailed account of the concept that is crucial for our whole subsequent discussion, namely, the concept of introspective analysis. This account attempts to lay out clearly, and in detail, what exactly is involved in this concept – a concept and method that were once central to the science of psychology but that are now almost wholly forgotten, even, or perhaps especially, by psychologists.

Chapter 4 shows how this notion of introspective analysis changed as psychology moved from James to John Stuart Mill. Specifically, it is argued that this change marks the transition in psychology from philosophy in James Mill to empirical science in John Stuart Mill. In addition, a particular example of analysis is discussed, namely, the example of spatial relations. This example was, in fact, a major point of disagreement in the history of psychology, between those who claimed that our capacity to identify relational wholes as such is acquired and learned and those who claimed that that capacity is innate or native. The claim that it was learned amounted to the claim that it could be introspectively analysed; those who defended nativism argued, therefore, that it could not be analysed. But with the younger Mill's clarification of the notion of psychological analysis, the issue turned out not to be so simple.

The detailed discussion has for us a further purpose, however, beyond its intrinsic interest. This purpose lies in the fact that, in both the economics and the moral philosophy of the utilitarians, *preference* plays a major role, and preference is a *relation*. What the Mills say about the introspective analysis of spatial relations will help us to understand their views on the analysis of preference. In particular, the issues of nativism and unanalysability are parallel in the two cases.

Chapter 5 continues the discussion of relations in introspective psychology to the case of perception, specifically the perception of ordinary objects with their component of spatial *depth*. The issues of nativism and unanalysability are continued, and the Millian account is defended against some recent criticisms, as well as against those of a nineteenth-century nativist, Samuel Bailey, who attacked the psychological analysis of the utilitarians at some length.

Chapter 6 takes up Bailey again, only this time some criticisms that he made of Ricardian economics. It is shown how Bailey's views on this issue tie in with his views on perception; and how the utilitarian discussion of Bailey's position in economics is more cogent, given his psychological theses, than is usually allowed. It is shown, moreover, how John Stuart Mill's notorious distinction between the quality and quantity of pleasures plays an important role. Some have suggested that Bailey's account of the relativity of value in economics points the way to more modern conceptions that supersede the discussion of such classical economists as Ricardo. This reading of Bailey, however, is, we argue, totally misguided, and in fact if there is anything that takes us beyond the position of the classicists towards more modern conceptions then it is Mill's position on the quality/quantity distinction.

Chapter 7 takes the discussion into ethical theory. It is shown how John Stuart Mill's psychology enables us to understand such notorious notions as that of the quality/quantity distinction; and more generally how it enables us to recognize the cogency of his replies to such critics as Macaulay of the older utilitarians. Indeed, it enables us to recognize that Mill has adequate replies to many subsequent critics whose points often repeat those of Macaulay and seem to have continuing relevance only because those critics have failed in their scholarly duty to read Mill carefully.

We all know, however, that introspective psychology has been replaced by objective or even behaviourist psychology. Perhaps this means that Mill's psychology is sufficiently dated and old fashioned as to render irrelevant the replies to criticisms that are based on that psychology. Chapter 8 sketches the history of psychology to argue that this is not so.

A brief conclusion summarizes our discussion of the role of introspective analysis in Mill's thought, and argues that the points that Mill made in terms of it against the critics are of continuing relevance to such contemporary discussions of ethical issues as those of Rawls (1971) and Nozick (1974).

ONE

Background and Context

British moral philosophy began with the *crise morale* that was provoked by Hobbes's philosophy.[1] Hobbes was a moral relativist and a psychological egoist. These doctrines provoked two sorts of responses, an objectivist one by such thinkers as Clarke and Shaftesbury, and a relativist one by such thinkers as Hutcheson and Hume. The relativist response led in turn to a restatement of the objectivist position by Price and Reid. In the first section, below, we discuss these three responses in turn.

Meanwhile, Berkeley and Hume criticized the traditional account of perception. Hutcheson's nativism in ethics was restated in objectivist terms in ethics by David Hume's relative Henry Home, Lord Kames, who then applied the same idea to reply to the Berkeley-Hume account of perception. Kames's nativist position in both ethics and perception was restated and defended by Reid. These themes are discussed in the second section of this chapter.

The third section presents the Benthamite position that the younger Mill proposed to defend. Or rather, it presents that position in the terms in which Mill himself saw it, through a discussion of Mill's various remarks on Bentham. It is clear that the moral realisms of Price and Reid challenge the utilitarianism that Mill describes; these were to develop into the challenges to utilitarianism by Sedgwick and Whewell that Mill was later to attempt to answer. Mill's own account of his development – both intellectual and emotional – from the Benthamite position of his youth to his mature position is also sketched and, in particular, how he came to recognize that to provide a psychological or introspective analysis of a feeling or value is not to eliminate that feeling or value, or to reduce it to parts that are something other than itself. This is the essence of the younger Mill's reply to the Whig and

Tory critics of utilitarianism, and the discussion here points the way towards the account of introspective analysis in chapter 4, where it is shown that Mill's point here about analysis not implying elimination or reduction is indeed sound.

1   Background: Moral Theory

Hobbes

Hobbes's general metaphysics is materialist: everything in the world, including human beings and their minds, is to be analysed in terms of corporeal atoms and their motions. Value is present in the world only as men have desires and aversions: 'good' and 'evil' are words that express only the relation of things to the speaker's desires. As Hobbes put it, 'Whatsoever is the object of any man's appetite or desire; that is which he for his part calleth *good*: and the object of his hate, and aversion, *evil*; and of his contempt, *vile* and *inconsiderable*. For these words of good, evil, and contemptible, are ever used with relation to the person that useth them: there being nothing simply and absolutely so; nor any common rule of good and evil, to be taken from the nature of the objects themselves' (1651, P 25). To say that a statement '*a* is *f*' is objectively true or false is to say that its truth or falsity depends only on the object, *a*, that it is about and its properties; in particular, its truth or falsity does not depend upon properties of the person who makes the statement. Conversely, a statement is relative if its truth or falsity depends upon who makes it. For Hobbes, to say that '*a* is good' is to say that '*a* is desired by me'; its truth or falsity depends not only upon *a*, but upon the speaker. We thus have in Hobbes a straight commitment to ethical relativism; in a world of fact there are no objective values.

But Hobbes defends a further thesis, namely, the thesis of psychological egoism, that all our desires are self-interested, that is, that persons always seek to maximize their own pleasure or good in all their voluntary acts (1651, P 54). He argues at some length, by considering a wide variety of examples, that all the desires that we think are altruistic and disinterested are in fact self-regarding.

Thus, for example, men act justly, respecting the property rights of others; men keep contracts; and men conform to the laws of their government. But, according to Hobbes, they do these things, not for their own sakes, but as means to further their own self-interest. His argument is well known. Men seek to acquire goods that will preserve them in existence. In conditions of scarcity and of rough equality among men, conflict ensues, with a state of nature in which there is a 'war of all against all' and where the life of man is therefore 'solitary, poor, nasty, brutish, and short.' But each person has sufficient intelligence to see that peace would better ensure his survival than war. This leads to the 'precept, or general rule of reason, *that every man, ought to endeavour peace, as far as he has hope of attaining it.*' But note that this is a rule of *prudence*; it specifies, not a moral duty to be sought for its own sake, but a pattern of behaviour to be conformed to only if it tends actually to ensure survival more than could be ensured through war in a state of nature. So Hobbes adds the rider, '*and when he cannot obtain it, that he may seek, and use, all helps, and advantages of war*' (1651, P 57). The first part Hobbes calls the first law of nature. From it he derives a second law: '*That a man be willing, when others are so too; as far-forth, as for peace, and defence of himself he shall think it necessary, to lay down this right to all things; and to be contented with so much liberty against other men as he would allow other men against himself.*' This second law recommends that men conform to a sort of non-aggression pact in which each respects the property rights of others. But conformity to the principle of justice is a means to peace, which is a means to our selfish ends; justice is aimed at, not for its own sake, but as a means. Hobbes next proceeds to a third law of nature. After explaining at length what an agreement is, he lays down the principle of contract, '*That man perform their covenants made.*' Once again, keeping our promises is not something done for its own sake, but as a means to selfish ends. In the end, and following this pattern, Hobbes formulates all told sixteen 'laws of nature' (PP 57–74).

These 'laws' prescribe behaviour, but only under certain conditions, namely, if they work; in particular, such behaviour as peace-seeking can be recommended to one person only if *others* will behave similarly towards him. My ends will not be achieved if I behave peacefully while others war on me. The problem is, if an agreement were made to seek peace, what assurance do I have, given the self-interest of others, that they will keep it? It seems, therefore, that if one starts from the war of all against all, everyone has the intelligence to recognize that it would be to the advantage of each to reach an agreement for the peaceful sharing the goods over which conflict arose, but also that no such agreement could ever come into existence because no one could trust any other one to keep it (1651, PP 77, 79). Hobbes's solution to this problem requires men to set up a 'common power' that would use force and the threat of punishment to ensure conformity to the peace-making agreement. Such a common power will be taken into account when one is tempted, for selfish reasons, to break the agreement, and, given the threat of punishment, one will, for selfish reasons, not succumb to the temptation. The common power will ensure that each will be able to trust every other. The only agreement that can be achieved in the state of nature, then, is one that provides for its own enforcement by establishing such a common power. The first and fundamental agreement must be one to set up and obey a political sovereign, that is, one man or group of men that has the primary function of punishing anyone who violates the peace-keeping agreement. This transforms the situation from one of mistrust, and therefore war, to one of peace-keeping where each subject, and the sovereign too, will now play his role in keeping peace, not because it is objectively right to do so, but because it is in his selfish interest to do so; and where, for each subject and for the sovereign, playing that role will be in his interest and be perceived to be in his interest because each knows that everyone else will be playing the same role for the same reason (PP 79–87). In this way, the state of nature is replaced by civil society. All sixteen laws of nature are now in force, in the sense that it is in everyone's selfish interest to obey them. It is in one's interest, first, because those laws are likely to be enforced against those who break them. And it is in one's interest, second, because conformity to them is, now with the common power established, the best means available for maintaining civil society and preventing a relapse into a state of war, and therefore, in turn, of providing the best opportunity for achieving one's selfish ends and of guaranteeing one's self-preservation. Moreover, with peace ensured, people now have the security that makes industry reasonable, and therefore the economic prosperity that industry produces (P 79).

It is not our purpose to discuss the soundness of Hobbes's derivation.[2] The point is that, once again, we have what is ordinarily taken to be a duty, namely, obedience to government, transformed into a maxim of prudence to which one is to conform only if such behaviour serves one's selfish interest. On Hobbes's account, there is no motive to virtue apart from self-interest, nor any justification for virtue apart from its capacity to serve our selfish interests. And many of his readers understood this to mean that, in this reduction of virtue to self-interest, virtue is in fact eliminated. Hobbes presented them with the challenge of, in effect, restoring virtue. But Hobbes's argument throughout presupposes the thesis of psychological egoism, that persons seek only their own good; given this premiss, then, however the details go, one can hardly expect anything other than some sort of reductive elimination of virtue as something sought for its own sake and from a felt sense of duty. The challenge, then, is that of refuting psychological egoism by establishing the irreducibility of virtue in respect of (1) persons having motivating moral sentiments that have virtuous behaviour as their *object*, and (2) these moral sentiments *differing specifically* from other motives. It can be turned around, however: proving points (1) and (2) is a challenge to Hobbes's opponents; but for them, it is equally a criticism of Hobbes that he fails to accept these two points. Precisely this same sort of criticism was made, as we have noted, by the Whig and Tory critics of the Benthamite utilitarianism of the philosophic radicals.

The Objectivist Response: Clarke and Shaftesbury

For Samuel Clarke, the response to the Hobbist challenge was to argue for the objectivity of value. He proposed to refute the Hobbist claim 'that there is no ... real Difference [between Good and Evil] originally, necessarily, and absolutely in the Nature of Things' (1705, p. 6). The grounds of objective duty are the *relations* things bear to one another:

> The ... necessary and eternal different Relations, that different Things bear one to another, and the ... consequent Fitness or Unfitness of the Application of different things or different Relations one to another ... ought ... constantly to determine the Wills of all ... rational Beings, to govern all Their Actions by the same Rules, for the Good of the Publick, in their respective Stations. That is, these eternal and necessary differences of things make it fit and reasonable for Creatures so to act; they cause it to be their Duty, or lay an Obligation upon them, so to do ... antecedent to any respect or regard, expectation or apprehension, of any particular private and personal Advantage or Disadvantage, Reward or Punishment, either present or future, annexed either by natural consequence, or by positive appointment, to the practising or neglecting of those rules. (p. 3)

There are objective duties and obligations. These arise directly from the nature of things, prior to and independent not only of God's will (Clarke is here agreeing with Cudworth)[3] and of any human authority, but also of self-interest. What are these relations that provide the standard of duty? They are relations of *moral fitness*. Thus, for example, one of the ends of man is to make himself easy in the world, but he lacks the capacity to achieve this by his own efforts; in this context what is *fitting* is that men relate to each other benevolently (p. 27). Such moral fitness is said to be 'as plain, as that there is any such thing as Proportion or Disproportion in Geometry and Arithmetick, or Uniformity or Difformity in comparing together the respective Figures of Bodies' (p. 4). Moral fitness is as self-evident as relations of proportion in arithmetic (for example, 12:8 :: 9:6) or the congruence of figures in geometry. Moral duty is self evident: ''Tis undeniably more Fit, absolutely and in the Nature of the thing itself, that all Men should endeavour to promote the universal good and welfare of All, than that all men should be continually contriving the ruin and destruction of All' (p. 5).

Clarke thinks that pretty well everyone will agree with him on these matters:

> These things are so notoriously plain and self-evident, that nothing but the extremest stupidity of Mind, corruption of Manners, or perverseness of Spirit can possibly make any man entertain the least doubt concerning them. For a Man endued with Reason, to deny the Truth of these Things, is the very same thing, as if a man that has the use of his Sight, should at the same time that he beholds the Sun, deny that there is any such thing as Light in the World; or as if a Man that understands Geometry or Arithmetick, should deny the most obvious and known Proportions of Lines of Numbers, and perversely contend that the Whole is not equal to all its parts, or that a Square is not double to a triangle of equal base and height. (1705, p. 6)

This is, of course, of a piece with the rhetoric of later intuitionists such as Sedgwick and Whewell with whom John Stuart Mill had to contend. But, in fact, the two cases Clarke discusses are just not comparable: geometry *is* (however one explicates the notion) self-evident and a demonstrative science whereas *there is no agreement* in morality: moral disputes are simply not resolved, nor resolvable, in the way that disputes in geometry are resolved.

The difficulty with Clarke's position, besides establishing its claim that there are self-evident moral truths, is that the reason that discerns the truth of arithmetic and geometry does not seem to be one that moves the will. If our knowledge of geometry or arithmetic moves us, it is only by providing a knowledge of means towards certain other ends, for example, when we use geometry in surveying to determine the limits of our property or use arithmetic when we calculate our accounts. But in these cases the motive comes from elsewhere; it is not provided by the reason that gives us knowledge of the geometric or arithmetic truths that we employ as means. It does not seem, therefore, that the reason to which Clarke appeals as yielding self-evident truths can provide any motive at all that moves the will, let alone a distinctively moral motive.[4]

Bishop Butler attempted to remedy this defect. He distinguishes two possible 'ways in which the subject of morals may be treated. One begins from inquiring into the abstract relations of things; the other from a matter of fact, namely, what the particular nature of man is ... from whence it proceeds to determine what course of life it is, which is correspondent to his whole nature. In the former method the conclusion is expressed thus, that vice is contrary to the nature and reason of things: in the latter, that it is a violation or breaking in upon our own nature' (1749, P 375). The first of these methods is Clarke's, and Butler gives it his general endorsement: this method 'seems the most direct formal proof, and in some respects the least liable to cavil and dispute.' However, Butler proposes to follow the other method, which, he says, 'is in a peculiar manner adapted to satisfy a fair mind, and is more easily applicable to the several particular relations and circumstances in life' (P 375).

The result is a descriptive psychology, in which various kinds of motives are described together with the ways in which they function in our mental and moral life. Specifically, Butler distinguishes four different sorts of motive, or parts of human nature: there is, first, the part that consists of the whole set of the various particular passions, for example, hunger, anger, and love of money (1749, PP 382–3); there is, second, benevolence, the disinterested desire to do good for others (PP 388–9); there is, third, self-love, a reflective passion that aims at maximizing the happiness of the individual, that is, at the satisfaction of a maximum number of desires, future as well as present (PP 382–3); and, fourth and finally, there is conscience, another reflective passion, one that morally approves or disapproves of our actions and motives (P 390). In this system, self-love functions with a natural superiority over the particular passions, controlling them so as to maximize one's long-run interest; and conscience functions with a natural superiority over all the other motives, controlling them so as to achieve ends of which it morally approves and avoiding things of which it morally disapproves.

With these distinctions Butler has no problems in disposing of Hobbes. Self-love is a long-range desire to maximize happiness; this is very different from the passion of hunger, or the desire for food, for example, or the passion of anger. Since they are distinct, there are, contrary to Hobbes, motives that are not selfish. Indeed, there must be these particular passions or self-love would have nothing to do: you cannot aim at happiness unless there are things that will give you the pleasures and satisfactions that make up happiness, and these must be the objects of other, particular, desires. The operation of self-love involves the operation of the particular passions, and so Hobbes must be wrong in holding that self-love is the whole of human nature (1749, PP 415–17). Once it is admitted that there are particular passions with objects other than the pleasure at which self-love aims, there is no reason not to admit that there are other motives – for example, benevolence and conscience – that have objects other than that of self-love. And further, once particular passions specifically different from self-love are admitted, there is no reason not to recognize that conscience, our moral sentiments, is also specifically different. Butler thus establishes that our moral sentiments, that is, the deliverances of our conscience, differ from self-love both *specifically* and in their *objects*.

In this psychology he attempts to accommodate Clarke's metaphysics of morals by making conscience not only motivating but also cognitive: it just is a species of reason that *also* can move us. Thus, he tells us of 'a moral faculty; whether called conscience, moral reason, moral sense, or divine reason; whether considered as a sentiment of the understanding, or as a perception of the heart, or, which seems the truth, as including both' (1749, P 429). This conscience recognizes the self-evident truth of such principles as those of justice, contract, and allegiance, and moves us to conform to these. Against Hobbes, Butler concludes that a survey of the parts of human nature reveals that man is *fit* for social life: 'it is as manifest, *that we were made for society, and to promote the happiness of it; as that we were intended to care for our own life, and health, and private good*' (1749, P 391).

But if Butler's account of conscience solves Clarke's problem of how reason moves us, it does so only to raise yet another problem. We cannot doubt the self-evident, but we often – too often, no doubt – act in a manner contrary to our conscience. If the deliverances of conscience simply *are* motivating apprehensions of self-evident moral truths, then, as the knowledge is infallible, why do they not infallibly move us? Conscience does, normally, function to control the other passions; why are there exceptions to this?

Now, it is *not right* that there are these exceptions; conscience *ought* to be obeyed. This is a *self-evident moral truth*; given human nature and the nature of conscience, it is *fit* that one conform to the deliverances of conscience. Thus, Butler speaks of conscience 'from its very nature manifestly claiming superiority over all others: insomuch as you cannot form a notion of this faculty, conscience, without taking into judgment, direction, superintendency' (1749, P 403). But this is only a *claim* to authority; is it a correct claim? This question still remains. To this Butler suggests that, as with a watch, we can discern in the functioning of the parts of the human system that it is a *goal-directed system* in the sense that the various parts function to maintain it in a certain state, which we may call the goal, or, if deviations occur, function to return it to that state. That is, Butler points out that, like the watch, the human system is a *teleological system*. In particular, the goal that the system *does, normally,* function to maintain is that which it self-evidently *ought* to maintain, namely, conformity to the deliverances of conscience. Deviations from the goal that the parts function to maintain simply show that such a system can get out of order; when the deviations occur the system is, if you wish, in an unhealthy state (PP 395–6). Note, however, that Butler's conclusion, that since conformity to conscience is the healthy state of the system, therefore it ought to be the state we maintain, presupposes a normative premiss of the sort Clarke defended, that the healthy is not only normal but also the *morally fit*. In the end, then, Butler's moral theory, based upon a psychological description of the functioning of the parts of the human mind, presupposes Clarke's account of moral truth in terms of *self-evident relations of moral fitness*, and has only the plausibility of this account.

Butler has another point to make, however. He accepts the argument from design, that is, the inference from the adaptation of organisms to ends, to the existence of a designer, commonly called God.[5] In particular, from the fact that man is a teleological system, adapted to survive in his environment, natural and social, ore can infer, Butler thinks, the existence of a God (1749, P 307). This entity which one has inferred then *explains* the existence of the teleological system; the various functions of the parts, all of which jointly serve to maintain the goal, are the result of the intelligent intentions of the deity. Nor is it only his wisdom; it is also his benevolence.

God's goodness is pure benevolence. From his point of view, the general happiness, that is, that *each* gains the maximum amount of happiness that is overall possible, is the ultimate object. But we, as finite creatures, are not competent to correctly or quickly enough discover what is in the long run general interest, nor, therefore, are we competent to aim explicitly and directly at that end; if we tried, we would be sure to miss. So God has provided us with a guide to those actions that will in fact bring about the general happiness, that is, the best happiness for our own selves as well as for others. This guide is conscience: 'as we are not competent judges, what is upon the whole for the good of the world; there may be other immediate ends appointed for us to pursue, besides that one of doing good, or producing happiness' (1749, P 427n). We should therefore follow our conscience, where it prescribes not only benevolence but other virtues as well. Since, as Clarke says, 'Tis ... Fit ... that all Men should endeavour to promote the universal good and welfare of All' (1705, p. 5),[6] we know, given our antecedent knowledge of God's wisdom and benevolence, that our conscience directs us, whether we can recognize it or not, to the means that best serve this end, an end that we therefore serve best, not by aiming at it directly, but by serving the ends of conscience. Thus, the psychological functioning of conscience as the controlling part of the mind is not only explained *by God but derives its* moral authority from him.

In Clarke's ethical system, it is the intellect that provides knowledge of virtue. In Butler the picture becomes blurred. The intellect itself moves, as it were, towards the passions in acquiring a motivating force. At the same time, for all that Butler acknowledges Clarke, moral insight for the bishop is to be derived from an empirical examination of the functioning of the human mind. It was Shaftesbury who had made this central to ethics. For him, knowledge of the good is never a mere intellectual process – it involves of necessity our affectional life, the 'trial or exercise of the heart' (1711, I: 252).

The problem with Hobbes, according to Shaftesbury, is that he adopted a metaphysical hypothesis that he put prior to the facts and then used it to interpret and, where required, explain away the latter (II: 286–7). But 'the most ingenious way of becoming foolish is by a system' (I: 189; cf. I: 88). The result is the absurd denial of the fact that virtue is 'really something in itself, and in the nature of things; not arbitrary ... not ... dependent upon custom, fancy, will' (II: 53). To eliminate such Hobbist absurdities, man must turn to a study of his own psychology. Man must 'proceed by the inward way,' and 'acquire a very peculiar and strong habit of turning [one's] eye inwards in order to explore the interior regions and recesses of the mind' (II: 286). For, 'we in reality can be assured of nothing till we are first assured of what we are ourselves' (II: 275). As he put it elsewhere: 'A plain homespun philosophy, of looking into ourselves, may do us wondrous service' (I: 31). This retrospective examination reveals that man does, contrary to

Hobbes, have a moral character, and that by his very nature he can discover and respond to moral distinctions. The mistake of the psychological egoists is, according to Shaftesbury, to make our ideas of order and virtue

> unnatural, and without foundation in our minds. Innate is a poor word he [Locke] poorly plays upon; the right word, though less used is connatural. For what has birth or progress of the foetus out of the womb to do in this case? The question is not about the time the ideas entered, or the moment that one body came out of the other, but whether the constitution of man be such that, being adult and grown up, at such or such a time, sooner or later (no matter when), the ideas and sense of order, administration, and a God, will not infallibly, inevitably, necessarily spring up in him. (1900, p. 403)

To counter the psychological egoists Shaftesbury points to the multitude of functions that animals perform in adapting themselves to their environment, all without example or instruction. They can find food and construct shelter, for example, and above all, know how to care for their offspring (1711, II: 76–7). But man, too, has need of food and shelter, and the period of his helpless infancy is particularly long.

Hence, if the 'natural habits and affection' of lesser animals are known, why not admit them in man (1711, II: 291–5)? And now, with the search for food and shelter and the care of offspring natural to men, society too follows naturally. If 'generation be natural, if natural affection and care and nurture of the offspring be natural, things standing as they do with man, and the creature being of the form and constitution he now is, "it follows that society must also be natural to him"' (II: 83). But if man is naturally to live in society, then he must also naturally have those 'notions and principles of fair, just and honest' that make this possible (II: 135) – that is, the principles of justice, contract, and allegiance. The regularity and universality with which these principles accompany life establish that they are from nature, that is, appear as a result of our innate constitutional development. They are instinctive moral principles (ibid.), which are, as Shaftesbury says, a part of man's 'natural moral sense' (I: 262) or natural 'sense of right and wrong' (I: 261). They are part of 'our constitution and make,' as 'natural to us as natural affection itself' (I: 260). Indeed, far from being the purely self-interested psychological egoist that Hobbes claimed he is, man is more correctly described the less selfish he is made to appear: the 'most truly natural' of man's principles are those 'which tend towards the public service and interest of society at large' (II: 294). The introspective descriptions of man that Shaftesbury has undertaken thus reveal that, as animals have natures with instinctive tendencies to fit themselves in an appropriate way into the world, so also there is a human nature with specific instinctual adaptive dispositions, including, more significantly, a disposition to act benevolently.

Shaftesbury agrees with Clarke in holding that we can discover the 'eternal measures and immutable independent nature or worth of virtue' (1711, I: 255). He moreover agrees with Clarke that this standard is constituted by the *relations* of things. But where, for Clarke, these relations are abstract connections among eternal natures, analogous to ideal geometrical and arithmetical relations, the relations for Shaftesbury are the concrete connections among the parts of a harmoniously functioning system. And so, for Shaftesbury, it is not our power of abstract reason that yields our knowledge or moral truth – indeed, it was just that abstract reason that led Hobbes astray. It is rather a faculty more analogous to *sense* that yields this knowledge. It is our 'moral sense.'

Shaftesbury views the world as a predominantly harmonious system; nature is a whole made up of parts, which in turn have parts of their own (1711, I: 239). Parts interact with each other in this complex structure; in particular, some parts contribute to the existence and even the well-being of other parts (I: 243). The relations and structures that contribute to the well-being of others constitute the objective basis of virtue or the good (I: 246). Creatures have, by nature, ends that they seek; these constitute their interest; and if men have passions that benefit not only themselves but also others then 'Virtue and Interest may be found at least to agree' (I: 244). Creatures are moved by various natural appetites, passions, or affections (ibid.), some of which are conducive to the good of the species, that is, the general good rather than the particular, selfish, good of the individual (I: 249). Moved by these appetites, creatures function harmoniously in the system of nature. Behaviour in accord with such affections will be good: 'to deserve the name of good or virtuous, a creature must have all his inclinations and affections, his dispositions of mind and temper, suitable, and agreeing with the good of his kind, or of that system in which he is included, and of which he constitutes a part' (I: 280). To be good, however, is not yet to be virtuous (I: 250). Man is a creature moved by affections conducive to the good of all; what distinguishes him from lower species is a 'reflective faculty' that enables him to

contemplate these affections and approve them. This is the moral
sense, which he insists, against Clarke, is not so much a faculty like
reason but one like perception. 'The case,' he says, 'is the same in the
mental and moral objectives as in the ordinary bodies or common
subjects of sense' (I: 251). When behaviour and action are perceived,
the natural senses observe their physical aspects, while their moral
worth is seen by the moral sense 'according to the regularity or
irregularity of the subjects' (ibid.). The mind has its own senses, and is
not without 'eye and ear, so as to discern proportion, distinguish
sound, and scan each sentiment or thought which comes before it. It
can let nothing escape its censure. It feels the soft and the harsh, the
agreeable and disagreeable in the affections; and finds a foul and a
fair, a harmonious and a dissonant, as really and truly here as in any
musical numbers or in the outward forms or representations of
sensible things' (ibid.). Thus, the relations of fitness or harmony that
are maintained by the functioning of our natural affections are the
objective standards of moral value; these are made conscious to us by
our moral sense, which is an equally natural faculty; the sentiments of
moral approval and disapproval that it produces function to strength-
en our natural affections, that is, strengthen our tendencies to do the
good; and one in whom the moral sense so functions is *virtuous*. 'In a
creature capable of forming general notions of things, not only the
outward beings which offer themselves to the sense, are the objects of
the affection; but the very actions themselves, and the affections of
pity, kindness, gratitude, and their contraries, being brought into the
mind by reflection, become objects. So that, by means of this reflected
sense, there arises another kind of affection towards those affections
themselves which have been already felt, and are now become the
subject of a new liking or dislike' (ibid.). The moral sense, in short, is
simply a self-conscious form of the social affections, and these both
have the function of constituting and maintaining the relations of
harmony that are the objective standards of right and wrong.

Like Butler, Shaftesbury places all this within a universe conceived
as designed and created by a benevolent deity. To be a theist is 'to
believe ... that everything is governed, ordered, or regulated for the
best, by a designing principle or mind, necessarily good and permanent' (1711, I: 240). As our nature leads us to a knowledge of morality,
so also it leads us to God! '[T]hese ideas of divinity and beauty ... [are] in
a manner innate, or such as men [are] really born to and could hardly
by any means avoid' (II: 178). God guarantees that 'virtue is the good,
and vice the ill of every one'; 'the wisdom of what rules, and is first and

chief in Nature, has made it to be according to the private interest and good of every one to work towards the general good ... So that virtue ... is that by which alone man can be happy, and without which he must be miserable' (1: 338).

Thus, one *explains* man's nature, the innate mechanisms that produce both his affections and the moral sentiments that judge them, by appeal to the wisdom and benevolence of God; and at the same time it is this same benevolence and wisdom of God that gives *moral authority* both to our natural or instinctual motives and affections and to the instinctual deliverances of our moral sense.

The Relativist Response: Hutcheson and Hume

The thesis of psychological egoism is just as the adjective describes: a thesis of psychology. Its truth, therefore, is a matter of fact. Its claim is that there are no motives or sentiments that differ, either specifically or in their objects, from self-love; in particular, there are no sentiments that are specifically moral and that have virtuous actions as their objects. Since this claim is a matter of fact, a turn to psychology can refute it if the turn succeeds in directing our attention to such sentiments. That is the significance of the turn to psychology in Shaftesbury and Butler. They, in fact, have little difficulty in establishing that psychological egoism is false; an accurate description of our conscious states, of the phenomena of the human mind, is sufficient. Hutcheson and Hume were to make much the same appeal to descriptive psychology.

Hutcheson holds that we have a genuine motive for benevolence; we desire it as an end, and not merely as a means (in any way) for our own happiness. He argues that 'without a moral Sense, we could receive no Prejudice against Actions, under any other View than as naturally disadvantageous to ourselves' (1726, P 143). If we look at how we evaluate our own actions and those of others we find we do so in a way that requires us to be acquainted with such a sentiment or motive. A gift of money or a bribe may be equally beneficial to us, but we evaluate them differently because the former is not, and the latter is, done from self-love. That is, we respond differently to an action that we take to have been done out of a generous motive, than we do to an action that may in itself be equally satisfying to our own self-love, but which we take to have been done from the agent's calculated self-interest (PP 73, 75, 78). But it is implausible indeed to suppose that apparent benevolence is always spurious. Parents *do* love their children, friends *do* care for their friends, we *do* feel unfeigned compassion for the sufferings of others, and so on (P 106). Mandeville (1723) had argued in defence of psychological egoism that, though this thesis is true, there is also apparently – though not really – benevolent behaviour; for, clever politicians have induced men to act as if they were public-spirited by convincing them through praise and flattery to believe that there really is such a motive, that it is good in itself, that it should be admired in others, and that it should be imitated in oneself. To this suggestion Hutcheson replies with the contempt it deserves: 'So easy a matter it seems to him, to quit judging of others by what we feel in our selves! – for a Person who is wholly selfish, to imagine others to be publick-spirited! ... Yet this it seems Statues and Panegyricks can accomplish!' (1726, P 84).

Furthermore, Hutcheson argues, we have moral feelings specifically different from self-love. This, too, we can recognize in our differential responses to actions, when we approve actions that harm us or disapprove actions that benefit us – for example, when we admire a gallant enemy, and dislike someone who, in war, betrays his own country to our own advantage (1726, P 78). Moreover, these moral sentiments have an object, namely, benevolence, and this object is other than that of self-love.

> It is true indeed, that the Actions we approve in others, are generally imagin'd to tend to the natural Good of Mankind, or some parts of it. From whence this secret Charm between each Person and Mankind? How is my interest connected with the most distant Parts of it? And yet I must admire Actions which are beneficial to them, and love the author [of these]. Whence this love, Compassion, Indignation and hatred toward even feign'd Characters, in the most distant Ages, and Nations, according as they appear Kind, Faithful, Compassionate, or of the opposite Dispositions, toward their imaginary Contemporaries? If there is no moral Sense, which makes rational Actions appear beautiful or Deform'd; if all Approbation be from the Interest of the Approver, *What's* HECUBA *to us, or we to* HECUBA? (P 77)

In fact Hutcheson goes farther than the claim that benevolence is *one* object of our moral sentiments; he also holds that benevolence *alone* is the object of moral approval; all other virtuous acts are such only to the extent that they are means to the end of benevolence. Thus, for example, courage, if it were mere contempt of danger, not connected with something like the defence of the innocent or the repairing of wrongs, would be madness, not a virtue (1726, p 89). Hutcheson offers a similar utilitarian defence of rights. 'Whenever it appears to us, that a Faculty of doing, demanding, or possessing any thing, universally allow'd in certain Circumstances, would in the whole tend to the general Good, we say that any Person in such Circumstances, has a Right to do, possess, or demand that Thing' (p 175). From this he derives the right to property, that is, the principle of justice, and the rights based on promises and contract. And the advantages of having 'unprejudiced arbitrators' and 'prudent directors' give men the right to 'constitute civil government, and to subject their alienable rights to the disposal of their governors under such limitations as their prudence suggests' (p 180).

Now, this latter may provide a moral justification for the principles of justice, contract, and allegiance, but it is surely bad descriptive psychology. Hutcheson's student Hume was to insist (1739; 1777) that we do have moral sentiments that are specifically different from those of self-love. As he puts it at one point, echoing Hutcheson's arguments: 'Those who have denied the reality of moral distinctions, may be ranked among the disingenuous disputants; nor is it conceivable, that any human creature could ever seriously believe, that all characters and actions were alike entitled to the affection and regard of everyone ... let a man's insensibility be ever so great, he must often be touched with the images of Right and Wrong; and let his prejudices be ever so obstinate, he must observe, that others are susceptible of like impressions' (1777, p. 170). But he was equally to insist, against Hutcheson, that the rights of property, the rights created by promises and contract, and the legitimate rights of civil government are *each* of them *objects* of our moral sentiments (1739, pp. 498ff, 523, 545). Hume's is, surely, the more realistic moral psychology. In this respect Hume sides with Butler and Shaftesbury against Hutcheson. But Hume and Hutcheson are agreed that the ethical objectivism of Clarke, Butler, and Shaftesbury is false.

Hume argues that, as a matter of descriptive psychology, one must distinguish acts of reason – that is, conscious states in which we grasp a priori relations or in which we grasp causal relations, and which are states that do not move the will – from those conscious states, the passions, motivate us – that is, do move the will (1739, Bk. II, Part iii, sec. 3, and Bk. III, Part i, secs. 1–2). Since reason is inert, it does not move the will; but moral judgments do move the will; hence Clarke's doctrine that reason is the source of our moral judgments is false (1739, pp. 415,

458).[7] But, moreover, the moral relations of fittingness and unfitting-
ness are sufficiently different from relations like those found in
arithmetic that it is implausible indeed that the former are species of
the latter (p. 464). Besides, the moral relations, as Shaftesbury insisted,
involve the causal interconnectedness of things in the universe, and,
Clarke notwithstanding, such causal relations are learned through
experience (p. 466). Moral distinctions are not, therefore, a priori.

However, contrary to Shaftesbury, neither do our moral sentiments
yield knowledge of matters of fact that are, somehow, objective moral
truths.

> Take any action allow'd to be vicious: Willful murder, for instance.
> Examine it in all lights, and see if you can find that matter of fact, or
> real evidence, which you call *vice*. In which-ever way you take it,
> you find only certain passions, motives, volitions and thoughts.
> There is no other matter of fact in the case. The vice entirely
> escapes you, as long as you consider the object. You can never find
> it, till you turn your reflexion into your own breast, and find a
> sentiment of disapprobation, which arises in you, towards this
> action. Here is a matter of fact; but 'tis the object of feeling, not of
> reason. It lies in yourself, not in the object. So that when you
> pronounce any action or character to be vicious, you mean
> nothing, but that from the constitution of your nature you have a
> feeling or sentiment of blame from the contemplation of it. Vice
> and virtue, therefore, may be compared to sounds, colours, heat
> and cold, which, according to modern philosophy, are not qualities
> in objects, but perceptions in the mind. (1739, pp. 468–9)

Hutcheson makes the same point. After distinguishing 'the idea of the
external motion ... and its tendency to the happiness or misery of some
sensitive nature' from the 'opinion of the affections in the agent,' he
goes on to declare that 'so far the idea of an action represents
something external to the observer, really existing, whether he had
perceived it or not, and having a real tendency to certain ends' (1742, P
371). To this he contrasts 'The perception of approbation or disapprobation arising in the observer, according as the affections of the agent
are apprehended kind in their just degree, or deficient, or malicious.
This approbation cannot be supposed an image of any thing external,
more than the pleasures of harmony, of taste, of smell' (ibid.). For
Hutcheson, the quality that evokes our feeling of approbation is
benevolence. For Hume there are other evoking qualities, for example,

justice. But, for both, such a quality being morally good consists not in some objective relation but rather simply in its being the object of a feeling or passion or sentiment of moral approbation. In short, Hutcheson and Hume are both *ethical relativists* (cf. Norton 1982, 1985; Winkler 1985).

Now, the important point here is that both Hutcheson and Hume insisted upon the reality of moral distinctions against the psychological egoism of Hobbes. Insisting thus upon the *irreducibility of virtue* consists in affirming that there are moral sentiments that differ from self-love both specifically and in their objects. It is now clear that one can insist upon the irreducibility of virtue while denying that value judgments are objective. That is, what the examples of Hutcheson and Hume demonstrate is that *one can consistently embrace both the irreducibility of value and ethical relativism.* John Stuart Mill was to insist upon this point against such critics of utilitarianism as Sedgwick and Whewell.

However, while it is true that Hutcheson rejects the ethical objectivism of Shaftesbury, he accepts the view of the latter that our moral judgments are innate. Our moral sentiments derive, he holds, with Shaftesbury, from a moral sense. Hutcheson characterizes a *sense* as 'a Determination of the Mind, to receive any Idea from the Presence of an Object which occurs to us, independent of our Will,' and the *moral sense* is 'a Determination of our Minds to receive amiable or disagreeable ideas of Actions, when they occur to Observation' (1726, PP 74, 88). Hutcheson notes the 'Principle of Gravitation, which perhaps extends to all Bodys in the Universe,' and suggests that the 'practical dispositions to Virtue implanted in our nature' are analogous to this 'Principle' (PP 144, 147). He argues not only for the 'Universality of this moral Sense,' but also for the claim that it is natural, or 'antecedent to instruction.' Both features are established, he holds, by 'observing the Sentiments of Children,' who, without the need of any teaching, are 'mov'd by ... moral Representations' (P 144). We thus see that ethical relativism is compatible with a nativist account of our moral sentiments.

It is true, as we have argued, that Hutcheson is a relativist. It is important to recognize, however, that there is also an objectivist component to his thought. It is the tendency of actions to produce pleasure and pain that evokes the attitudes of moral approbation and disapprobation. The former – that is, 'the idea of the external motion ... and its tendency to the happiness or misery of some sensitive nature' (1742, P 371) – is objective, but the moral feeling is not. Hutcheson distinguishes various kinds of sensation and pleasure. For example, there are 'the pleasant sensations arising from regular, harmonious, uniform objects; as also from grandeur and novelty' (P 356). These are the pleasures of the imagination. Distinct from these are the perceptions of the moral sense by which 'we perceive virtue or vice, in ourselves or others' (ibid.). These perceptions of the moral sense are judgments of approbation (or disapprobation) (P 358). The term 'approbation' 'denotes a simple idea known by consciousness' (ibid.). Feelings of approbation are pleasures. '*Approbation* of our own action denotes, or is attended with, a pleasure in the contemplation of it, and in reflection upon the affections which includes us to it. *Approbation* of the action of another has some little pleasure attending it in the observer, and raises love toward the agent in whom the quality is deemed to reside, and not in the observer, who has a satisfaction in the act of approving' (ibid.). This feeling of moral approbation does not have an objective correlate: 'This approbation cannot be supposed an image of anything external, more than the pleasures of harmony, of taste, of smell' (P 371). It is, of course, precisely this that makes Hutcheson an ethical relativist.

Now, Hutcheson also holds that the various kinds of pleasure are 'esteemed' to different degrees: 'the pleasures of sight, and hearing, are more esteemed than those of taste or touch: the pursuit of pleasures of the imagination, are more approved than those of simple external sensations' (1742, P 356). The point to be noticed is that this esteem is not merely a matter of liking some pleasures more than others; it is also a matter of 'approval,' that is, it is subject to judgment by our moral sense. But if the judgments of our moral sense about actions, to the effect that one action is morally better than another, have no objective correlate, then it is none the less also true that the judgments of our moral sense about pleasures, to the effect that one sort of pleasure is better than another, *do* have an objective correlate.

The pleasures we enjoy fall into qualitatively distinct classes, and these can be ranked into those that are higher and those that are lower. This ranking is not one that is based merely upon matter-of-fact preference; it is also one of *moral value*. Thus, 'We are conscious,' Hutcheson tells us, 'in our state of mature years, that the happiness of our friends, our families or our country are incomparably nobler objects of pursuit, and administer proportionately a nobler pleasure than the toys which once abundantly entertained us when we had experienced nothing better' (1755, P 478). This judgment that some pleasures are (morally) better, or nobler, is not merely a judgment evoked by their benevolent consequences. To the contrary, such judgments grasp an *intrinsic* feature of the pleasures, that is, an *intrinsic* moral feature of the pleasures: 'in comparing pleasures of different kinds ... we have an immediate sense of dignity, a perfection, or beatific quality in some kinds' (P 476).

Thus, when judging the worth of an action in terms of its benevolent consequences, one must take account not only of the quantity of a pleasure produced, but also of its moral dignity. Hutcheson proposed that we estimate the value of a pleasure by considering jointly its 'dignity and duration: dignity denoting the excellence of the kind where those of different kinds are compared; and the intenseness of the sensations, when we compare those of the same kind' (1755, P 477). Upon his view, any quantity of pleasure of a higher kind is superior to all quantities of every lower kind; no 'intense sensations of the lower kinds with sufficient duration may compleat our happiness' (P 477). Hutcheson even proposed that the 'superior orders of this world probably experience all the sensations of the lower orders, and can judge of them. But the inferior do not experience the enjoyment of superiors' (P 478). One finds something like this in J.S. Mill, of course, which is one reason why we are discussing it. But these connections are not the present point, which is the simple one that for Hutcheson the judgment that one pleasure is better than another is an *objective judgment* about an *intrinsic moral feature* of those pleasures.

In short, although Hutcheson is in one way a relativist, it is also true that there is an element of objectivism in his moral theory.

By way of contrast, we may consider Hume's comment on the same point. What we need, Hume suggests, is a 'just notion of the *happiness*, as well as of the *dignity* of virtue' (1739, p. 622). Virtue is a pleasure, and may be evaluated in terms of the amount of happiness it yields; but it may also be evaluated in terms of its dignity. In discussing this dignity what Hume does *not* appeal to is an *intrinsic feature* of the moral pleasures that renders them *morally better* than other pleasures. Rather, what Hume appeals to are, in the first place, the *consequences* of virtue, and, in the second place, as a specific sort of consequence, the greater *felt satisfaction* that virtue yields.

> Who indeed does not feel an accession of alacrity in his pursuits of knowledge and ability of every kind, when he considers, that besides the advantage, which immediately result from these acquisitions, they also give him a new lustre in the eyes of mankind, and are universally attended with esteem and approbation? And who can think any advantages of fortune a compensation for the least breach of *social* virtues, when he considers, that not only his

character with regard to others, but also his peace and inward
satisfaction entirely depend upon the strict observance of them;
and that a mind will never be able to bear its own survey, that has
been wanting in its part to mankind and society? (p. 620)

Thus for Hume there are two ways for ranking pleasures, once in
terms of felt satisfaction and once in terms of moral dignity. The moral
judgments that yield the latter ranking are not distinguished from the
moral judgments that rank actions. In *both* cases the moral judgment is
evoked by the quality of having benevolent consequences; and in both
cases the specifically *moral feature* lies in the judgment rather than in the
evoking quality. That is, the moral judgment is in *both* cases relative, not
objective.

Thus, although both Hutcheson and Hume offer a relativist
response to Hobbes, the former retains in his views on the moral
ranking of qualitatively different pleasures an objectivist feature that is
absent from the more thoroughgoing relativist position of Hume. As
we shall see, although J.S. Mill expresses himself in language that is
close to that of Hutcheson, his position is in fact of a piece with that of
Hume: like both Hutcheson and Hume, the younger Mill recognizes
qualitative differences among pleasures, but like Hume and unlike
Hutcheson this distinction is not an evaluative one. In other words,
contrary to what many hold, Mill's doctrine of a qualitative distinction
among pleasures is inconsistent neither with his further claim that the
maximization of utility is the sole criterion of moral evaluation, nor
with his other claim that judgments of preferability are purely
matter-of-fact judgments, that is, of simple experience.

If the relativist features of Hutcheson's moral philosophy tie his
position closely to Hume's, there are other features, besides the
objectivist one just noted, that tie the position to that of his predecessors Butler and Shaftesbury. And here too we have a contrast to the
position of Hume.

Like Butler and Shaftesbury, Hutcheson relates his account of
our moral sentiments to a divinely providential teleology. Our moral
sense, like the external senses, operates immediately, without any
process of conscious inference. Reason, Hutcheson suggests, is too slow
and full of doubt to decide what is most important to us. We have
instead faculties that operate immediately and instinctively. These
include our external senses, which assist in our preservation, and our
moral sense, which serves to direct our actions. 'Reason would recom-

mend for nourishment the meats that taste recommends as pleasant; but the sense of taste remains useful because it is quick and reliable where reason is slow. Similarly the moral sense prompts us to act morally where reason could be slow and hesitant' (1726, P 169). In this respect, as in others, the human system is well adapted for survival and for the social living that is essential both to survival and to happiness.

From such adaptation we can infer the existence of God. 'The obvious Frame of the World,' which 'seems plainly contriv'd for the Good of the Whole,' is such that it 'gives us Ideas of the boundless Wisdom and Power of its AUTHOR.' We hence conclude that 'the Deity [is] benevolent in the most universal impartial manner' (1726, P 187). Indeed, the moral sense itself is an instance of the wisdom of the design, as are its pleasures. With these we can serve the benevolent intentions of the Deity for the whole as we never could if we were moved by rational self-interest alone.

> Notwithstanding the mighty Reason we boast of above other Animals, its Processes are too slow, too full of doubt and hesitation, to serve us in every Exigency, either for our own Preservation, without the external Senses, or to direct our own Actions for the Good of the While, without this moral Sense. Nor could we be so strongly determin'd at all times to what is most conducive to either of these Ends, without these expeditious Monitors, and more importunate Solicitors; nor so nobly rewarded, when we act vigorously in pursuit of these Ends, by the calm dull Reflections of Self-Interest, as by those delightful Sensations. (P 169)

The inclusion of our moral sense among our faculties, because it thus serves our own well-being and that of the whole, thus provides one of the strongest evidences of design: 'this very moral Sense, implanted in rational Agents, to delight in, and admire whatever Actions flow from a Study of the Good of others, is one of the strongest Evidences of Goodness in the AUTHOR of Nature' (P 137). In turn, having inferred God, we can appeal to his wisdom, benevolence, and power to explain our native faculties.[8] We must, Hutcheson tells us, 'ascribe the present Constitution of our moral Sense to his [God's] goodness. For if the Deity be really benevolent, or delights in the Happiness of others, he could not rationally act otherwise, or give us a moral Sense upon another Foundation, without counteracting his own benevolent intentions' (1726, P 186). But then, if we have in our nature an innate faculty that moves us to approve of actions we perceive to be benevolent, then we can be assured that, on the whole at least, they *are* benevolent, that is, genuinely virtuous, and, of course, conversely for what is vicious. Once again, as in Butler and Shaftesbury, God not only *explains* but provides *moral authority* for our innate moral sense.

Hume would have none of this providential teleology. 'I cannot,' he wrote to Hutcheson, 'agree to your Sense of *Natural.* 'Tis founded on final Causes; which is a Consideration, that appears to me pretty uncertain and unphilosophical' (1932, I: 33). The uncertainty can be brought out by considering what Hutcheson says about restricted benevolence. The moral sense approves primarily universal or utilitarian benevolence. But there are more constrained sorts of altruistic motive that also count as benevolence, and in fact have greater motivating power than the concern for the general good. 'There are nearer and stronger degrees of benevolence, when the objects stand in some nearer relations to our selves, which have obtained distinct names; such as natural affection, and gratitude, or when benevolence is increased by greater love of esteem' (1726, P 145). According to Hutcheson our having these stronger but more restricted kinds of benevolence relative to those to whom we are closely related is proof of 'the wise order in which human nature is formed for universal love, and natural good offices' (P 146). To be motivated solely by universal benevolence would be inefficient, Hutcheson argues, since it would find itself dissipated when bestowed upon too many objects; the tendency, for example, to show gratitude to benefactors concentrates benevolence and makes it more effective. The strength of the motives of constrained benevolence functions to promote the general happiness that is the object of the general benevolence of which our moral sense approves but which that latter motive cannot promote effectively. Since gratitude, like parental affection, is innate, we have here another example of a device created by a wise God in order to promote the general happiness. But if it is indeed true that the constrained motives of benevolence are stronger than our concern for the general happiness, then these concerns with the happiness of a group smaller than the whole of humanity will lead, in conditions of scarcity, to conflicts with other groups. Constrained benevolence will, as Hume points out, lead to that conflict that is the contrary of all peace and happiness just as surely as would purely selfish motives. We indeed morally approve the motives of constrained benevolence, but 'tho' this generosity must be acknowledged to the honour of human nature, we may at the same time remark, that so noble an affection, instead of fitting men for large societies, is almost as contrary to them, as the most narrow selfishness' (1739, p. 487). So much for the certainty with which we can infer from such sentiments to the existence of a benevolent deity!

But if the inference is, as Hume said, uncertain, it is also, as he again said, unphilosophical to leap so rapidly to an explanation in terms of a providential designer outside the world we seek to understand: 'superstition is much more bold in its systems and hypotheses than philosophy; and while the latter contents itself with assigning new causes and principles to the phenomena, which appear in the visible world, the former opens a world of its own, and presents us with scenes, and beings, and objects, which are altogether new' (1739, p. 271).

Two points are to be made: (1) Butler describes the *functions* of the parts of the mind. That is to say, he describes the *effects* that these parts normally have. He then leaps directly to God. But it is more philosophical to seek *natural causes* for the mental phenomena in question. (2) To describe a capacity as 'natural' or 'instinctual' or 'innate' is *not* to explain it. For no one doubts that we are born with the capacity to come to make value judgments, and that this capacity develops over time. What one wants to know is *precisely how* it develops over time; that is, what are the factors, external and internal, that account for its vicissitudes and for when it changes and in what directions. Again, what one wants are the details of the *causal process* the system undergoes as the capacity develops towards maturity.

Now, as it was for Hutcheson, so it is for Hume: actions are virtuous to the extent that they tend to be productive of consequences that are good either for the agent himself or for others (1739, p. 587). Hume argues that acts of courage or prudence are in themselves productive of good consequences; he therefore refers to them as 'natural' virtues. In contrast, a single act of justice need not by itself be productive of good consequences, but only as an instance of a general pattern or convention conformity to which by all is productive of good consequences (p. 579). In the name of justice, judges will take from a poor man to give to a rich one, which, by itself, is hardly productive of the best consequences. But 'the whole scheme ... of law and justice is advantageous to the society; and 'twas with a view to this advantage, that men, by their voluntary conventions, establish'd it' (ibid.). Since a convention is involved for justice to be a virtue, it is an 'artificial' virtue rather than a 'natural' one (p. 537). In each case, it is the interest in the general advantage that leads men to institute the conventions, that is, to conform their behaviour as a matter of custom and habit to the convention (p. 486). Without the conventions, the advantages would be lost; indeed, the conflict Hobbes describes would obtain, since nothing would exist to so regulate self-interest or constrained benevolence that men could live together in peace. The remedy consists in instituting the conventions. Thus, 'the remedy ... is not deriv'd from nature, but from *artifice*; or more properly speaking, nature provides a remedy in the judgment and the understanding, for what is irregular and incommodious in the affections' (p. 489).

As for *why* we approve of the virtues, whether natural or artificial, this Hume attempts to explain, not by appeal to God's benevolence, but by reference to a causal mechanism. This mechanism is that of *sympathy*. When others feel pleasure, we tend to take pleasure in that, and when others feel pain, we tend to be uneasy about it. This is sympathy, and Hume attempts to describe, psychologically, how the process goes, by which we perceive the pleasure or pain of another and come to feel the corresponding passion ourselves (1739, p. 316ff). It is this mechanism by which the contemplation of the advantages to all, which the artificial virtues produce, *causes* us to have feelings of moral approval towards acts of justice (p. 499), promise-keeping, and allegiance. Similarly, the advantages produced by acts of natural virtue *cause*, by this mechanism, our moral approval of such acts (p. 576). The mechanism itself is part of human nature (p. 316), and in that sense natural. Thus, while not all virtues are natural, since some are artificial, our *sense* of their virtue derives from the natural mechanism of sympathy, and in that sense the artificial virtues are as natural as any other. Moreover, the principles of justice, contract, and allegiance serve such basic human needs that, while they are artificial, they are not arbitrary. 'Nor,' indeed, 'is the expression improper to call them *Laws of Nature*; if by natural we understand what is common to any species, or even if we confine it to mean what is inseparable from the species' (p. 484).

The point here is not to defend Hume's account of the virtues, either natural or artificial, or his account of sympathy as the causal process by which we come to feel the moral sentiments we have.[9] It is, rather, to suggest how a truly empirical account of the workings of the human mind, or, as Hume would say, a philosophical account, will proceed to search for natural causes and mechanisms to replace obscurantist appeals to divine teleology and innate principles. Whether Hume be right or wrong in his account, the point is that *his is the approach that natural science must take*. We shall find John Stuart Mill repeatedly insisting upon this against the critics of utilitarianism.

Objectivism Restated: Price and Reid

Not everyone was happy with the relativism of Hutcheson and Hume. One who was not was Richard Price. He clearly recognizes the relativism of Hutcheson's position:

> It is evident, he considered it as the effect of a *positive constitution* of our minds, or as an *implanted* and *arbitrary* principle by which a *relish* is given us for certain moral objects and forms and aversion to others ... our ideas of morality, if this account is right, have the same origin with our ideas of sensible qualities of bodies [i.e., the secondary qualities], the harmony of sounds, or the beauties of painting or sculpture; that is, the mere good pleasure of our Maker adapting the mind and its organs in a particular manner to certain objects. Virtue ... is an affair of taste. Moral right and wrong, signify nothing *in the objects themselves* to which they are applied, any more than agreeable and harsh; sweet and bitter; pleasant and painful; but only *certain effects in us*. (1787, P 657)

This is no doubt unfair to both Hutcheson and Hume, since both hold that there are intrinsic differences between the actions we morally approve of and those we disapprove of – for example, between courage and cowardice, or between honesty and theft. That is, moral distinctions do have *some* foundation in the natures of things. None the less, if we put this down to rhetorical excess, the basic point Price makes is correct: Hutcheson is a relativist. This Price takes as a challenge: 'The present inquiry therefore is; whether this [Hutcheson's] be a true account of virtue or not; whether it *has* or *has not* a foundation in the *nature* of its object; whether *right* or *wrong* are real characters of *actions*, or only qualities of our *minds*; whether, in short, they denote what actions *are*, or only sensations derived from the particular frame and structure of our natures' (1787, P 657).

In effect, Price's position is a return to that of Clarke, save that for Price the source of our knowledge of right and wrong is not the reason that we all use in doing geometry. Price shifted the focus from demonstrative reason to *intuition*, a 'power of immediate perception in the human mind' (1787, P 672). For Price, as for Clarke, morality is a matter of *relations*, that is, it is a matter of whether actions are apt or inapt, fit or unfit (PP 674, 707ff). These relations are not grasped by sense (P 674), but by the understanding (P 659). He simply rejects the claim of Hobbes, Locke, and Hume – and of the later utilitarians – that all ideas derive from sense (P 675) and that moral judgments could arise from sense through the work of associative mechanisms (P 685). In this respect, moral relations are grasped directly by the understanding in the same way that necessary *causal* relations are grasped (P 667). The result is certain knowledge of immutable and necessary moral truths (PP 684ff).

To defend his position, Price suggests that his opponents, whether Hobbes, Hutcheson, or Hume, attempt to *define* moral terms as synonymous with such terms as 'advantageous' or 'willed.' But such terms, he holds, refer not to 'what is the nature and true *account* of virtue, but, what is the *subject-matter* of it' (1787, P 658). It is one thing to ask what goodness itself is and another to ask what things are good.[10] If 'right' *means* 'advantageous' then the claim that the right is the advantageous would be trivial, a tautology; but it is not; so that is not the definition of 'right.' Price concludes that moral concepts are *indefinable*. On this point, however, Hutcheson and Hume are agreed: moral terms derive their meaning not from objective qualities but from our moral sentiments, but these sentiments are *specifically different* from all other sentiments; their quality as *moral* sentiments is indefinable. In other words, the claim that moral terms are, or that at least one of them is, indefinable is as compatible with relativism as it is with objectivism. John Stuart Mill was later to make this same point against the Whig and Tory critics of utilitarianism. He was to insist that, although our moral feelings are capable of introspective analysis, that does not imply that they are reducible to or definable in terms of the parts that such analysis yields. That is, introspective analysability is compatible with indefinability. It was Mill's clarification of the notion of introspective analysis that showed him how this could really be so.

However, objectivism is, according to Price, sheer common sense; it is the view that we all, in our unreflective moments, hold (1787, PP 676–9). This argument is hardly conclusive, however, especially since Price agrees with Hutcheson that secondary qualities are, contrary to an equally pervasive common sense, subjective (PP 680–1). None the less, Price's main argument consists in claiming that it is a *reductio ad absurdum* of relativism that it requires that people believe that what is subjective is objective, that is, that the subjective moral sentiment that defines the moral is objective; for, on the relativist position, one's making a moral judgment involves 'mistaking the *affections of his own mind* for *truth*' (P 683). But this sort of error happens all the time – as Hume says, 'there is a very remarkable inclination in human nature, to bestow on external objects the same emotions, which it observes in

itself; and to find everywhere those ideas, which are most present to it'
(1739, p. 224) – and since such an error is not surprising, it hardly
constitutes a *reductio* of relativism. Price, like so many objectivists, is
adept at finding ways to beg the question.

Price believes that the objections to Clarke do not apply to him.
What they establish is that morality is not demonstrable; but this is
compatible with morality being objective and known by intuition (1787,
PP 674–5). If one makes the empiricist reply that our ideas or concepts
must be derived from entities presented in sense experience, Price
replies that this is an unproved dogma (ibid.), and that the understanding is, in fact, contrary to empiricism, 'a spring of new ideas' (PP
659–68), that is, new simple or indefinable ideas, including not only
those of morality but also that of causation and many of those that
characterize objects of which we are aware in ordinary perceptual
experience, such as solidity, substantiality, and duration (ibid.). The
only reply to such claims is to show that the supposed underivable ideas
are in fact derived from ordinary experience. We thus find John Stuart
Mill showing how the supposed underivable moral concepts derive
from our felt moral sentiments (see chapter 7, below), how our idea of
causation derives from an awareness of constant conjunction (see
chapter 3, below), and how perception involves learned experience
that derives from sense experience (see chapter 5, below).

But there remains Hume's point against Clarke that reason is inert.
In order to meet this objection, and also out of a recognition that,
owing to the infancy of our intellectual faculties, the latter are not
always as capable of moving us as they ought to be, Price compromises
with Hutcheson. He holds that 'in men it is necessary that the *rational
principle*, or the *intellectual discernment* of *right* and *wrong*, should be
aided by *instinctive determination*' (1787, P 688). The Deity has therefore
created us with sensations and instincts to virtue tied to our intellectual
perceptions. Hence, echoing the same point Butler made in order to
save Clarke, Price holds that 'in contemplating the actions of moral
agents we have both a *perception of the understanding*, and a *feeling of the
heart*' and that the latter depends in part upon 'the positive constitution
of our natures' but also, and more important, upon 'the essential
congruity or incongruity between moral ideas and our intellectual
faculties' (ibid.). But how the instincts work, what the congruity and
incongruity consist in, or how either or both generate the feelings that
move us, is all left in remarkable obscurity – indeed, an indecent
obscurity from the viewpoint of what Hume called philosophy, that is,
empirical science, which attempts to discover the natural causes of

things; what one suspects, of course, is that, as empirical investigation, especially introspective analysis, proceeds and the obscurity disappears, so also will whatever plausibility is had by the objectivism that Price manufactures out of the obscurity.

Thomas Reid is perhaps more subtle in his psychology than is Price. Like Price, Reid abandons Clarke's claims to demonstration; moral claims, he holds, are self-evident. They are objective moral truths apprehended by 'an original power of the mind' (1788, p. 592). As with Price, Reid holds that duty is indefinable (p. 587), but he attempts more carefully than Price to specify its category and its location; as with other objectivists in this tradition, it is a *relation* (pp. 589, 677), one that obtains between an agent and an action; the action must be a voluntary action of the agent himself, the agent must be able to know his obligation, and the moral description of any action will depend upon 'the opinion of the agent in doing it' (p. 589).

On the central issue of *proving* his objectivism, Reid offers a psychology more sophisticated than that of Price, but in the end no more persuasive. Reid argues elsewhere that in perception we have a belief or judgment that is the immediate consequence of a sensation with which it is 'inseparably conjoined.' On this account, which we discuss in greater detail in the next section, 'when we perceive an external object by our senses, we have a sensation conjoined with a firm belief of the existence and sensible qualities of the external object' (1788, p. 672). Such beliefs, because they are innate, are, Reid holds, justified. Moral judgments, too, are a matter of intuition (cf. Stecker, 1987), which occurs innately and without inference: 'all moral reasonings rest upon one or more first principles of morals, whose truth is immediately perceived without reasoning, by all men come to years of understanding ... As we rely upon the clear and distinct testimony of our eyes, concerning the colours and figures of bodies about us, we have the same reason *to rely with security* upon the clear and unbiassed testimony of our conscience' (p. 591; italics added). In the case of moral judgments, belief and feeling are also inseparably combined, but here the feeling is a consequence of the judgment, which is partially a judgment about non-moral facts but also one about objective moral facts. Thus, I feel love towards a man who exerts himself for a public good, but the feeling changes if I come to believe that he was bribed or 'acted from some mercenary or bad motive' (p. 673). Reid's appeal is to how the phenomena of moral judgment appear in consciousness:

When I exercise my moral faculty about my own actions or those of other men, I am conscious that I judge as well as feel. I accuse and excuse, I acquit and condemn, I assent and dissent, I believe and disbelieve and doubt. These are acts of judgment, and not feelings. Every determination of the understanding, with regard to what is true or false, is judgment. That I ought not to steal, or to kill, or to bear false witness, are propositions, of the truth of which I am as well convinced as of any proposition in Euclid. I am conscious that I judge them to be true propositions; and my consciousness makes all other arguments unnecessary, with regard to the operations of my own mind. (ibid.)

This is the substance of Reid's argument. In both perception and value judgments there is a sensory content involved, a sensation in the former case, a feeling in the latter. But in both cases there is also a conscious *act* involved. In each case the act arises in me through the innate faculties of my human nature. No further parts are discernible in the conscious state besides the act and the sensory content. The *act*, therefore, is an *indefinable unity*. In the case of perception, the act is an act of believing (or disbelieving). This act has a certain object, namely, the ordinary thing that one is perceiving. The act is a believing that the object of the act exists. In the case of the value judgment, the act is one of moral assent (or dissent). This act has a certain object, namely, a voluntary action performed by an agent in a certain condition and context. The act is a moral assenting that the object of the act is right or fitting. *This is all there is to Reid's argument.*

There are two aspects to this: (1) the inference is that, since the act is an indefinable unity, there must be a corresponding indefinable unity in the object; this latter is the set of objective and indefinable moral properties; (2) since the act is innate it must therefore be a justified moral judgment.

However, concerning point (1): As John Stuart Mill will argue, from the fact that the act is a simple or indefinable unity it follows not at all that there must be a corresponding simplicity in the object. And concerning point (2): Innateness is no explanation; nor will it provide moral authority without added premises.

But here Reid does have other premises, namely, God's benevolence. We learn that 'the fabric of the human mind is curious and wonderful, as well as that of the human body. The faculties of the one are with no less wisdom adapted to their several ends than the organs of the other' (1785a, p. 97). These beliefs are guaranteed because they are based on powers or principles that are the 'gift of Heaven' (1785a, p.

97; 1785b, p. 425). It is the Supreme Being who has given us the power and faculties which he, in his benevolence and wisdom, saw would be necessary for our survival and progress, and it is he who has implanted in us innate principles and sources of knowledge that lead us both to think and to act in such ways as best adapt us to survival and happiness as part of his creation (1785b, pp. 422, 447). Hence, we find among the 'natural furniture' of the mind certain 'first principles' that are 'immediate dictates of our natural faculties' (1788, p. 591). These include the first principles of morals. But they also include, justifying on God's behalf, the remainder, namely, the principle that the natural faculties by which we distinguish truth from error are not fallacious (1785b, p. 447). Ultimately, then, Reid's appeal, like that of Butler, Shaftesbury, and Hutcheson, is to a providential teleology.

Once again, however, this is simply not good natural science. When the Mills pursue the natural science of psychology, the pretensions of this teleology will disappear, along with the obscurantism of the innatism.

Neither, moreover, is the appeal to innate mechanisms validated by God good moral philosophy. In effect it means only the appeals to 'intuition' and 'moral sense' are taken to be self-validating. Bentham was scathing in his attack on such positions, which he characterized as defending 'the principle of sympathy and antipathy,' by which he meant 'that principle which approves or disapproves of certain actions, not on account of their tending to augment the happiness, nor yet on account of their tendency to diminish the happiness of the party whose interest is in question, but merely because a man finds himself disposed to approve or disapprove of them; holding up that approbation or disapprobation as a sufficient reason for itself, and disclaiming the necessity of looking out for an extrinsic ground' (1789, Ch. II, sec. xi). As Bentham goes on to remark, 'this is rather a principle in name than in reality; it is not a positive principle of itself, so much as a term employed to signify the negation of all principle' (1789, Ch. II, sec. xii). One who defends this 'principle' holds: 'In looking over the catalogue of human actions ... in order to determine which of them are to be marked with the seal of disapprobation, you need but to take counsel of your own feelings; whatever you find in yourself a propensity to condemn, is wrong for that very reason' (1789, Ch. II, sec. xiii). As we shall see below, both Mills are concerned to criticize a certain metaphysics of relations. They are so concerned because the metaphysics has as much of its point the legitimation of this 'principle' of sympathy and antipathy. What this metaphysics does is (attempt to) provide a justification of the claim that these feelings of sympathy and antipathy are not merely subjective feelings but rather graspings – as intuitions or, perhaps, moral sensings – of necessary objective moral standards. Not surprisingly, the utilitarians were concerned to attack the metaphysics that thus attempts to sanctify subjective feelings as objectively valid moral judgments. In his notes to his father's *Analysis*, John Stuart Mill quotes a long passage from James Mill's *Fragment on Mackintosh* in which he argues against these views, concluding that, for example, 'Fitness is either the goodness of the consequences; or it is nothing at all' (1869, II: 317n).

2 Background: Perception

Berkeley and Hume

We perceive tables, chairs, trees, and so on. Call these *perceptual objects*. In perception we experience certain sensible qualities, but these are experienced as parts of a unified perceptual object that endures beyond the present. Prior to Berkeley and Hume, the account of perception went something like this.[11] A perceptual object consists of sensible qualities present in a substance. The substance is an entity that remains one and the same over time. Change occurs as sensible qualities come to be and cease to be present in it. The order in which the qualities come to be and pass away is a function of the *nature* of the substance. It is this nature that accounts for the *pattern* of sensible qualities as it changes over time; that is, the order and regularity in these changes is accounted for in terms of the nature of the substance.[12] In perception we experience sensible qualities but not all the qualities that a substance exemplifies; yet we perceive them as part of a pattern. For example, we experience green sensations and certain sensible shapes but these are perceived as the colours and shapes of a tree, that is, as parts of a patterned set that endures through time, and in particular beyond the moment of being perceived. Upon the account of perception that we are now considering, the sensible qualities are perceived as parts of an enduring object because the nature of the substance that they are present in is itself present in the mind. For this to work, a co-ordination of sensed qualities and the natures in the mind is required. How the co-ordination is effected has two accounts. For the Aristotelians, the nature is abstracted from the sensible appearances, and this process guarantees the co-ordination. For the Cartesians, sense experience is too variable for the mind ever to achieve an adequate co-ordination by abstraction; rather, the natures of things are innate ideas, and the co-ordination of natures and the sensible qualities to which they apparently apply is guaranteed by God. We do of course sometimes misperceive. When such error occurs, the sensible qualities that we experience either are in a substance that differs in nature from the nature present to us in our perceiving, or are not in any substance at all. For both Aristotelians and Cartesians it is assumed that error is abnormal and that we have the intellectual faculties to discover and correct error. It was often argued that the benevolence and wisdom of our creator guarantees that our faculties must therefore be adapted to our survival and happiness, and that, since knowledge of our environment is necessary to survival and happiness, those faculties must, on the whole at least, be reliable.

Berkeley (1734) and Hume (1739) challenged this tradition, by challenging the notion of substance. All our ideas or concepts must be derived from sense experience; all are agreed that substances are not given in sense experience; we therefore have no concept of such an entity; nor, therefore, can we ever have any reason for affirming their existence.[13] As a result, a perceptual object can be nothing over and above the collection of its sensible qualities (Berkeley 1734, PP 30–1, 37, 49). Or rather, it is not a *mere* collection, but a *patterned set* of sensible qualities. On the view of Berkeley and Hume, then, an ordinary thing is not, like a substance, a single entity that exists numerically one and the same through change, but is, rather, a *process*, that is, a sequence of sensibly qualified events that are connected together by a *pattern of spatio-temporal and lawful relations*. Moreover, since there is no substance, there is no nature. Upon both the substance account and the view of Berkeley and Hume, in perception the sensible qualities that we experience are identified as part of a pattern characteristic of the perceptual object in question. The substance account makes the nature the source of this pattern, but on the view of Berkeley and Hume, the pattern of regularities exemplified by the sensible qualities that constitute the perceptual object no longer derives from the nature of an underlying substance; there is *simply the pattern* and nothing else.

In perception, upon the substance account, one grasps the pattern – call it the 'perceptual object pattern' – by grasping the nature that lies behind it. Upon the account of Berkeley and Hume, there is no behind. In contrast, the whole set of sensible qualities that the perceptual object has endures beyond the present. Not all the entities, that is, the qualities, that are in this pattern are present to us at any given moment. In this respect, perception, in locating the experienced qualities in a pattern, points beyond the present to qualities that we are not experiencing (but could if we were differently situated) and to qualities that we will experience (when we come to be in certain situations). The question for the Berkeley-Hume account of perception is this: if we do not experience the whole set, how do we know what the pattern is? The old answer, that we know it by grasping the nature, is no longer available. Berkeley and Hume suggest, instead, that in perception we attribute to the unexperienced parts of the perceptual object those patterns that we have discovered in past experience to apply to collections similar to those that we are at present experiencing. Thus, take a very simple model. Suppose that we are experiencing a collection of sensible qualities of sort A, and that what we have experienced in the past is that As have been followed by Bs; on the basis of this past experience, we come in perception to locate As as part of a pattern in which As are followed by Bs; we even identify such patterns as characteristic of kinds of perceptual object – for example, the pattern of 'whenever A then B' is the perceptual pattern of, let us say, *trees*; hence, when we experience an A we *perceive it as a tree*. In other words, for Berkeley and Hume *perception is in effect a sort of inference* (cf. Berkeley 1734, P 108).

Hume describes the process in this way: 'There is scarce a moment of my life, wherein ... I have not occasion to suppose the continu'd existence of objects, in order to connect their past and present appearances, and given them such an union with each other, as I have found by experience to be suitable to their particular natures and circumstances. Here then I am naturally led to regard the world, as something real and durable, and as preserving its existence even when it is no longer present to my perception' (1739, p. 197).[14] It should be recognized that, on the view of Berkeley and Hume, in perception we in effect apply a generalization, 'whenever A then B' to a situation, A, on the basis of our past experience in which As have always been Bs. A perceiving is therefore a justified belief only to the extent that we are justified in asserting 'All A are B' on the basis of 'All observed A are B.' In this respect, so far as concerns our perceptual beliefs, the logic of their justification is identical to the logic of the justification of indicative inference. However, it is also important to note that, while in terms of the *logic of justification*, perception is the same as inference, it does not follow that perceiving and inferring are identical as kinds of states of consciousness. To be sure, Berkeley and Hume do both tend to construe perceiving as a kind of inferring. But it is one of John Stuart Mill's important points about perception that we can accept both of the claims of Berkeley and Hume – (1) that our capacity to identify objects perceptually as falling within a certain perceptual object pattern is learned through experience and (2) that the logic of the justification of our perceptual beliefs is the same as the logic of inductive inference – while we can also accept (3) that a conscious state of perceiving is different in kind from a conscious process of inferring.

We shall return to this third point shortly. Meanwhile, we must note that for the critics of the Berkeley-Hume analysis, the upshot is scepticism. There is, in the first place, the assimilation of perception to inductive inferences. This assimilation leaves the former open to the same infirmity as the latter. But, in the second place, there is the disappearance of substance. Since a sensible quality, on the substance account, is real only of it is present in an external substance, the disappearance of the latter will be understood as a claim that all sensible qualities are unreal. The position, by then standard, that the secondary qualities are not in external substances, and are therefore not real, raised problems about perception, but, since it retained substances, not everything was unreal. But on the Berkeley-Hume view, it seemed as if *all* perception was illusion: with substances gone, there was no reality there for perception to be *of*. The charge of scepticism was immediately forthcoming.

A complicating factor is Berkeley's idealism. Sensible qualities are not in material substances. But empiricism requires that there be no qualities apart from qualified objects. Berkeley takes this anti-Platonist principle to mean that there are no qualities apart from substances. He therefore infers that since sensible qualities cannot be in material substances, they must be in mental substances. Their *esse* is therefore *percipi*.[15] In spite of Berkeley's protests that he was aiming to defend a common-sense realism,[16] his attempt to draw a distinction between minds, which were substances, and perceptual objects, which were ideas, failed to convince because traditionally the distinction strong enough to secure independent existence was that between two substances; since qualities were, in this sense, not independent of substances – that, indeed, is the point of the anti-Platonist principle – Berkeley's perceptual objects construed as congeries of sensible qualities could not be seen to have the independence of our consciousness of them that common sense requires. The problems that arise here were resolved by later empiricists by denying the existence not only of material substance but also of mental substance. This move Hume made (1739, Bk. 1, Part iv, sec. 2, p. 206, and Part iv, sec. 6),[17] and in this he was followed by later empiricists, including John Stuart Mill (cf.

1872b, Ch. xii). This relieves the tension. As for Berkeley's anti-Platonist principle, what is required is that there be no qualities apart from the objects of which they are predicated.

On Berkeley's account of perceptual objects, the latter are collections of sensible qualities. Predication is thus a matter of attributing a part (a sensible quality) to a whole (a perceptual object). It is *this* that the anti-Platonism requires, and *not* inherence in a substance, as Berkeley wrongly claims. So, by rejecting this erroneous premiss, one can accept (1) Berkeley's denial of material substance, (2) his analysis of perceptual objects as patterned sets of sensible qualities, and (3) his anti-Platonism, all without falling into his idealism. In particular, in accepting these three points one can accept that *sensible qualities as parts of perceptual objects can exist unperceived*, as Hume insists (1739, p. 206), and accept, too, that perceptual objects exist when they are not being perceived, that is, that *perceptual objects have a continuing and independent existence*.

Moreover, the Berkeley-Hume account of perceptual objects can be defended against charges of scepticism. Neither of the charges that we mentioned above is fatal. The fallibility of inductive inference is simply a fact of our finitude; it is a fact to be accepted and lived with, not something to complain about and struggle against.[18] As for the charge that everything becomes illusion, the answer is that, while the disappearance of substances means that the reality/illusion distinction cannot be drawn by appeal to such entities, it does not follow that the distinction cannot be drawn. Indeed, the answer is simple: those qualities that we experience that cohere in perceptual object patterns are real; those that do not are unreal.[19]

This last point can be strengthened by noting that the substance ontology of the critics is itself not free of problems in respect of the possibility of charges of scepticism. A perceptual object cannot be more than one shape; it cannot be both, say, oval and circular. But when I look at a coin from one angle, the sensible shape I experience is circularity while if I look from another angle it is an oval. Only one is real; only one can be attributed to the substance. But there is no experienced difference between the two. So either both are real, which is impossible, or neither is. And this result is general: perspectival and similar considerations concerning sense variation will generate the same conclusion for any category of sensible quality.[20] We are forced to the conclusion that nothing we experience in perception is ever real: in this case scepticism really *does* result. On the Berkeley-Hume analysis, being in a substance does not entail scepticism, since presence in a substance can no longer be the criterion of reality. But their opponents, who retain substances, retain that criterion, and, as Berkeley correctly insists, the result is that they inevitably fall into scepticism (1734, PP 17–21; also Intro., P 4). In fact, once this is recognized, then it is also clear it is the Berkeley-Hume analysis that is the non-sceptical and realistic alternative, as Berkeley himself forcefully argued (PP 34–5).[21]

There is, of course, an important sense in which, on the Berkeley-Hume account, unlike the substance account, all sensible qualities are equally real in the sense that none differs from any other in ontological status. It is just that some cohere as parts of perceptual object patterns where others do not, and since perceptual objects *are* important to us in our lives and in our capacities to communicate with others, these objects (*not* substances) are singled out *by convention* as defining 'reality.' We adopt a certain standpoint in assessing the perceptible qualities we experience because this has a certain utility in communication. This is parallel, as Hume points out (1739, p. 582), to the artificial virtues. In each case we have a convention, explained by showing that it arises from self-interest in a context of constrained benevolence. In the case of justice it is an interest in establishing the property rights that are essential to peaceful living together. In the case of perception it is an interest in communication and action: we pick out from among all the patterns of sensible events that we experience those with respect to which we can most readily come to intersubjective agreement: 'corrections are common with regard to all the senses; and indeed 'twere impossible we cou'd ever make use of language, or communicate our sentiments to one another, did we not correct the momentary appearances of things, and overlook our present situation' (ibid.). Assessments both of the qualities of mind and of character, that is, recognition of virtues and vices, and also of the public qualities of perceptual objects are extremely important in action both in society and in the natural world. The convention therefore becomes instituted that these among all the qualities we experience are to count as real. The distinction among sensible qualities of the real and the unreal in terms of coherence is thus *artificial*, but it is *not arbitrary*. Then, once the conventions of reality have become instituted, and we talk about real colours, size, hardness, tasks, and so on, we come to morally approve of conformity to these conventions for the same reason that we morally approve of the artificial virtues, namely, their utility and our sense of sympathy.[22]

Berkeley took the analysis of perception to a deeper level than did Hume. As he points out in the *Principles* (1734), the sensible qualities[23] that we experience are all equally existent (P 42), but it is our sense of touch that we take as that which locates the *real* object (PP 43–4); that is the convention. The various visible qualities that we perceive, especially the visible shapes, are variable; they all exist, but only a few are counted as real, namely, those that coincide with the tangible shapes.[24] All of the visible appearances function as *signs*, however, of the real, that is, tangible, shape (1709, PP 52–6; 1734, P 43). Since the visible appearances vary systematically with distance, there is a regular connection – a pattern – between them and tangible sensations. These patterns are useful to us as we aim at, most generally, self-preservation: on the basis of the visible sensations that we have, we can infer that, for example, if we were to move in such-and-such a way, then we would have so-and-so tangible sensations. In other words, the patterns among the sensible qualities that we experience enable us to infer what is (by convention counted as) real.

Now, if we have the visible shape we experience and the distance, then we can infer the real shape; and knowing the distance and this shape we can further infer that if we were to move in such-and-such a way then we would have so-and-so tangible sensations. This is how the Cartesians construed it.[25] According to Malebranche (1674–5), when we view a man walking away from us, we experience an image that decreases in size (corresponding to the decreasing size of the retinal image) but none the less, by a 'natural judgment' (*jugement naturel*), we 'always see him as the same size.' Simultaneously with the image of decreasing size we receive an 'impression of distance.' This latter derives from the distance between our eyes and the 'change which occurs in the situation of our eyes' as the angle, formed by drawing straight lines from the eyes to the receding man upon whom they focus, decreases in size (1674–5, I: 97). Malebranche found this account in Descartes's *La Dioptique* (1637). Descartes assumes that the visual sensation that we experience is not a direct image of the object; we see objects not directly but 'only through the mediation of the brain' (1637, p. 141), which enables us to adjust the experienced sensation to reality. He holds that there is a kind of 'natural geometry' that enables us to make this adjustment. There are the data Malebranche mentioned, namely, the distance between our eyes and the angles they form when they focus on the object. The distance is determined on the basis of these geometrical data by a sort of automatic calculating process that occurs by means of 'an action of thought which, although it is only a simple act of the imagination, nevertheless in itself contains a reasoning quite like that employed by surveyors' (Descartes 1637, pp. 137–8).

Descartes seems to assume, as does Malebranche concerning the natural judgment, that on the whole the inference takes place 'in our eyes and in our brain' through a physiological process of which we are ordinarily not conscious (Malebranche 1674–5, I: 120). In any case, the geometry involved consists of a priori truths about the essence of the world external to me; this knowledge is innate, not derived from sense experience. The natural judgment based on sense experience leads to an immediate, non-inferential, awareness of intelligible distance, that is, the a priori cognition of an essential fact about the world. As Malebranche puts it in one place, 'there are outnesses (*des dehors*) and distances ... in the intelligible world which is the immediate object of our mind' (III: 61).

Berkeley was to take up the notion that we infer the *outness* of things, that is, their distance.[26] The nature of the inference is radically different, however. It is touch that gives us the real external object, and visual awareness of distance or outness is a matter of inference from our visual sensations. But distance is not 'judged of by lines and angles' (1734, P 43); our visual awareness of distance does not derive from an application of our innate knowledge of geometry. Our judgment of distance is, rather, the result of a process of learning by association (P 44), a notion that Berkeley had developed in his *Essay towards a New Theory of Vision* (1709, P 147). We experience visual sensations, followed by kinaesthetic sensations of bodily movement, followed by sensations of touch that get us to the object. There will be different sets of kinaesthetic sensations corresponding to the different distances we must move through to take us from the point at which we have the visual sensation to the point at which we come into tactual contact with the object. Different visual sensations come to be associated with different sets of kinaesthetic sensations. Once the association is established, a visual judgment of distance can be analysed on the pattern of inductive inference into an inference from a visual sensation to a certain set of kinaesthetic sensations, to wit, those appropriate to the distance of the object. Thus, where Descartes and Malebranche have it that we judge the distance of an object and then infer how we would have to move in order to reach the object, Berkeley reverses the inference and suggests that we judge how we would have to move in order to reach the object and then infer the distance. Or rather, he suggests, the judgment of how we would have to move *just is* the judgment of distance.

Now, just as the utilitarians objected to innate a priori intuitions in ethics, so they objected to them in the theory of knowledge. They therefore tended to locate themselves with respect to the perception of *distance* in the tradition of Berkeley, both in rejecting the innatist views of the Cartesians and in accepting Berkeley's theory of vision in which judgments of distance are the result of learning through association and, more generally, accepting the Berkeley-Hume account of perception of which Berkeley's theory of vision was but a special case.

It was not merely a case of adopting, however. The radical utilitarians not only adopted, but developed the theory, and modified it to meet objections. As we shall see, however, meeting some of the objections required not so much a modification of the theory in its empirical scientific structure but instead a rethinking of exactly what is involved in the notion of psychological analysis. This last was John Stuart Mill's major contribution. All this we shall discuss in chapter 5. First, though, we must turn to the earliest critics of the views of Berkeley and Hume.

Kames and Reid

Lord Kames (which Henry Home became in 1751) published his *Essays on the Principles of Morality and Natural Religion* in 1751 (second edition, 1758). [27] He takes himself to be answering the moral scepticism of such thinkers as Hobbes, and the epistemological scepticism of Berkeley and Hume. The latter has the effect of 'annihilating the whole universe' (1758, p. 207), while the former, which takes self-love to be the only motive, while obviously wrong, still needs an answer since errors in morality 'seldom fail to have a bad influence' (p. 23). Such errors arise from the indulgence of our tendencies to philosophical speculation and are to be corrected by using instead 'the slow and more painful method of facts and experiments; a method that has been applied to natural philosophy with great effect' (p. 24).

Kames applies this method of factual psychological description to the case of *belief*. Hume had proposed that beliefs can be *analysed* into images (ideas) that have a special force and vivacity. This won't do, Kames argues: poetry often produces forceful images, but no belief, while histories produce ideas that lack force but, equally, produce belief. Hume's analysis is therefore inadequate. Belief is indeed something mental, 'a certain peculiar manner of perceiving objects, and concerning propositions,' but upon examination shows itself to be a simple feeling, that is, a modification of the mind that cannot be defined, but only felt or experienced (1758, pp. 181–5).

In particular, contrary to Berkeley and Hume, in certain perceptions at least, namely, those of sight and touch, we have a perception 'of things as having an independent and continued or permanent existence' (1758, pp. 197–8). This perception is immediate and non-inferential or intuitive (p. 268n). In perceiving an object, say a tree, we perceive colour, extension, figure, and perhaps motion, but not as isolated entities bearing no connection to each other. We do indeed at times perceive such things as isolated, a colour here, a figure there, and so on, but such cases are totally different from the 'impression made by a tree, where the extension, motion, and other qualities, are introduced into the mind as intimately united and connected' (p. 198). To be sure, some senses, namely, smell and touch, make us aware only of themselves. Thus, if we smell a sweet fragrance, what we 'feel' is a smell and no more; it is only through additional experience obtained by sight or touch that we *learn* that a particular sort of fragrance is always to be found when a particular sort of perceptual object, say a rose, may be seen and touched (pp. 210–11). However, in taste and touch we are 'conscious not only of an impression made at the organ, but also of the body which makes the impression' (p. 211). The impression the object makes by sense causes us to perceive, or, what amounts to the same, have a perceptual belief in, the object that causes the impression. There is nothing to infer; we have a direct perception of the object sensed. Of all the senses, sight is the most complex, complicated by its involving action at a distance (p. 212). The perceptual object is at a distance from us, and is directly and non-inferentially perceived to be at a distance; its 'outness or distance' is 'discoverable by sight' and is 'not the effect of experience' (p. 214). But since the perceptual object is at a distance it cannot cause a perception unless there is a causal chain of events of 'intermediate means' by which the object affects the mind (p. 212). By these means the object causes an image to appear on the retina and this is transferred to the mind. Thus, like touch, sight involves an impression made at an organ, but unlike touch and all the other senses, this impression is not felt. Instead of being aware of the sensory image, with, for example, its figure very different from (though systematically related to) that of the perceptual object, we perceive that object at a distance and as it really is at that distance. Nature has 'carefully concealed [the] impression from us, in order to remove all ambiguity, and to give us a distinct perception of the object itself, and of that only'; in this way nature has eliminated all confusion as to where the object perceived is located since what we experience or perceive is that object as located at its distance from us and not the impression that the object makes upon the eye (pp.

212–15). Kames speaks of two impressions, one felt at the organ affected, and a second one that is the feeling or experiencing of the perceptual object, an independent and continuing existent. In smelling and hearing, we feel a first impression only; the connection to perceptual objects is learned by experience. In seeing, there is a second impression but we do not feel the first impression. In taste and touch, there is a second impression but we also feel the first impression. In sight, taste, and touch, we directly perceive the perceptual object. This direct perception is *caused by* the first impression, but the perceiving itself is non-inferential. Since it is non-inferential, Berkeley's theory of vision must be wrong (p. 214). But moreover, again since it is non-inferential, it is *not learned*; the causation of the second impression by the first is *natural*, part of our *innate* mental apparatus (pp. 194–5, 214–15).[28]

From the simplicity of the perceptual belief, in short, or, what is the same, from the fact that the conscious state of perceiving is not one of inference, Kames concludes that the perceiving is not the result of learning. It will be part of John Stuart Mill's argument that this conclusion does not follow: the simplicity of a state of consciousness is compatible with its being the product of a process of learning. If this is so, one can hold with Kames that perception is simple while agreeing with Berkeley that perceivings, that is, those of distance, are the result of learning through a process of association.

This may be put another way. If introspective analysis yields the causal antecedents of a conscious state, then what the younger Mill will argue is that the simplicity of a conscious state is compatible with its being capable of psychological analysis. Once again, to provide an introspective analysis is not to analyse away. Thus, it is perfectly possible to hold with Hume that belief can be given an introspective analysis (one need not accept the specific analysis that Hume proposes) while also holding, with Kames, that belief is a simple, undefinable state of consciousness.

There is a further inference that Kames makes, this one about the nature of the perceptual object. The perceptual object has a unity, and an enduring existence apart from being perceived. Now, to say that this is so is compatible with the Berkeley-Hume claim that such objects are patterned collections of sensible qualities. As Kames indicates, in an act of perceiving, perceptual objects are perceived as a unity, and, moreover, this perceiving is not an inference. Kames infers that since the perceiving is not an inference the unity of the object cannot be that of a pattern (1758, p. 198). The simplicity of the perceiving implies, according to Kames, the simplicity of the object. We often perceive a colour here and then perceive a figure there, but these perceivings are different from the 'impression made by a tree, where the extension, motion and other qualities, are introduced into the mind as intimately united and connected' (p. 198); the perceiving, in other words, is a unity and not a sequence of states of consciousness as it would be if it were an inference, as Berkeley and Hume claim. From this we can conclude that the qualities 'are perceived as inhering in or belonging to some *substance* or *thing*, of which they are *qualities* ... Thus it is that the perception of *substance*, as well as of *qualities*, is derived from sight' (pp. 198–9). Since the perceiving is a simple unity, so the object perceived must be a simple unity; it must be a substance, an entity that endures through change, and not simply a collection, even if it is a patterned collection, of sensible qualities.

Kames also makes the same sort of inference in the case of moral beliefs. Here the order of the perceiving and the feeling is reversed. We have a moral sense that enables us to grasp the moral qualities of actions. When we do, then we have 'without the intervention of any sort of reflection' (1758, p. 45) a particular feeling that moves us to perform the action. And because it is a matter of perception rather than inference it is innate: 'Thus we find the nature of man so constituted, as to approve certain actions, and to disapprove of others' (p. 36). In ordinary perception, the sense impression causes the perception; in the moral sense, the perception causes the feeling. Like Butler's conscience (pp. 43–4), the moral sense grasps objective moral facts and moves us to action. These objective moral facts are *relations of fittingness* (pp. 32, 34–5). From the simplicity of our moral judgments, Kames concludes that there must be a corresponding simplicity in the facts judged about, that is, a simple undefinable moral quality; 'fit, right and *meet* to be done' as well as '*unfit, unmeet* and *wrong* to be done' are 'simple perceptions, capable of no definition' (p. 34).

Kames makes this inference; but it is fallacious, as John Stuart Mill will argue: *From the fact that the perceiving is simple it does not follow that the perceptual object is simple.* If this is so, then though Berkeley and Hume held that perceiving is like inference, it would be consistent to hold that it is not, that is, rather, that it is a simple act of consciousness, and also to hold, as they do, that perceptual objects are patterns of sensible qualities. Similarly, from the simplicity of our moral sentiments or moral judgments, it does not follow that there must be a corresponding simple undefinable feature objectively there in the perceptual object. One can consistently maintain a relativism in which the value in the world derives wholly from our moral sentiments, with no objective non-natural moral qualities in things, while also holding that our moral sentiments are simple undefinable acts of consciousness.

The point goes the other way too. Berkeley at times suggests that perceptual objects are *not* external to us, not 'without the mind' (cf. 1734, PP 10, 18, 24). In part this is simply a way of stating his idealism. But, the implication sometimes is that distance does not exist at all. He is in part driven to this by the Cartesian claim that extension is the essence of material substance. In denying the existence of material substance, Berkeley was required to deny the reality of extension (PP 9–15). Extension does not exist. That is, *no* spatial relations exist. In particular, distance does not exist. The associations of sight, kinaesthesis, and touch that are the learned basis of capacities to perceive spatial extension and depth therefore provide a complex set of facts to *replace* the primitive facts of material extension. If Berkeley is correct, these judgments of spatial relatedness have as their *objective* content nothing extended but rather only *patterns of non-spatial sensory contents* (colours, kinaesthetic sensations, sensations of touch). What makes these judgments characteristically spatial is not their content but rather the associative patterns. All space, all extension, thus turns out not to exist objectively but to be rather something subjective. Berkeley's account of spatial relations thus turns out to be entirely parallel to Hume's account of causal relations, in that objectively causality is identical with regularity or pattern, and that what distinguishes causal judgments from others is not such an objective content but rather the mode of association (1739, p. 172).[29]

One need not be a Cartesian, however, in the analysis of space. It is possible to suggest an alternative ontology that is non-substantialist and in which ordinary perceptual objects are patterns of sensible qualities, but in which the spatio-temporal relations that in part constitute the pattern that defines the object, including relations of distance, are real unanalysable features of things. It was Russell who was to put such an ontology on a secure metaphysical footing.[30] The present point is that it is consistent to hold that relations of distance are simple and unanalysable while also accepting the Berkeley-Hume account of perceptual objects as patterns of sensible qualities. Moreover, from the fact that the perceiving of such a relation is the product of a process in which visual, kinaesthetic, and tactile sensations come to be associated, it does not follow, as Berkeley at times suggests, that therefore the relation perceived must be analysable into a corresponding pattern. It is consistent to hold both that spatial relations are indefinable features of reality and that the capacity to perceive such relations is learned on the basis of associations that involve no such relations. Berkeley's suggestion that learning implies a complex object derives from this notion that, since perception requires learning, perceiving is a matter of inference; and then from the further notion that since perceiving is complex, so is its object. But all this is as illegitimate as Kames's opposite inferences from the simplicity of the perceiving to its being unlearned, on the one hand, and to its having a simple object, on the other.

For Kames, just as we have from our moral sense an immediate feeling that makes us aware of the distinctions between right and wrong, so in perception we have an immediate feeling of belief that distinguishes reality from unreality. In an obvious way, Kames, as a student of Hutcheson, takes the latter's innatism in ethics and extends it to the realm of epistemology: just as the moral feelings that derive from the innate mechanism of our moral sense determine duty, so the perceptual beliefs or feelings that derive from the innate mechanism of our ordinary senses determine reality. What is meant by 'reality' is, of course, determined by Kames's substance ontology; upon this metaphysics, sensible qualities are real just in the case that they inhere in substances. In any case, however, belief will yield reality only to the extent that it is veridical. It is so, however, in the case of morality: our moral sense is, Kames declares, 'the voice of God within us' (1758, p. 45). And it is so in the case of perceptual objects. Thus, according to Kames, touch alone, the 'least intricate of our feelings,' suffices to overthrow Berkeley's entire philosophy: 'We have, from that sense, the fullest and clearest perception of external existences that can be conceived, subject to no doubt, ambiguity, nor even cavil' (p. 212). More generally, we believe what we have seen or heard because our nature is so constituted that we cannot, with rare exceptions, do otherwise. The innate structure of our human nature is such that, Kames says, our senses have an irresistible authority that commands and compels belief in their reports: 'There is nothing,' he tells us, 'to which all mankind are more necessarily determined, than to put confidence in their senses. We entertain no doubt of their authority, because we are so constituted, that it is not in our power to doubt' (pp. 194–5).

To be sure, perception is sometimes erroneous. Of error, there are two sorts, irregular and systematic. The secondary qualities are cases of the latter. The former come about through some temporary adversity – for example, distances, abnormalities in the sense organs – but in any case warn us of their erroneousness – for example, the impressions are confused rather than distinct and lively. As for the systematic sort, that is, 'deception established by the laws of nature' (1758, p. 193), we have the faculties by means of which we can discover such deceptions, and correct them. Thus, 'in the foregoing instance of secondary qualities,' for example, 'philosophy easily corrects the false appearances, and teacheth us, that they are to be considered as impressions made upon the mind, and not as qualities of object' (p. 194). The systematic deceptions in fact aid us in our survival; for example, sensations of warmth and colour facilitate our efforts to survive and adapt to a sometimes hostile world. As exceptions to the general veracity of our senses, they are sufficiently useful to our capacity to adapt that they in fact are a further proof that our senses are the best and truest guide for thought and conduct (pp. 193–4).

Kames puts the point this way: when 'any sense presents to our view an appearance that may be called deceitful, we plainly discover some useful purpose intended. The defect is not the effect of an imperfect or arbitrary constitution; but wisely contrived, to give us such notice of things as may best suit the purposes of life. From this very consideration, we are more confirmed in the veracity of nature' (p. 194). As this makes clear, the fact that we are adapted to survival, in this way, as in others, is evidence of our creation by a wise designer. This deity, then, not only *explains* the innate structure of our senses, but also guarantees their veracity and thus gives them *authority*.

In fact, the innate structures that the deity has given us are, according to Kames, elaborate indeed. Thus, while Kames agrees with Hume that our idea of power or necessary connection is not derived from reason or from sense impressions (1758, pp. 221–2), we none the less have an intuitive knowledge not only of the necessary tie between one's will and one's actions, but perceive as a quality of the acting substance the power that binds it to its effect in another (p. 227). We have, moreover, an intuitive self-evident knowledge that every event has a cause (p. 234). This tendency to infer that the future will resemble the past is an innate feature of our nature (pp. 239–40). We are, furthermore, so constituted that, with respect to an object apparently adapted or fitted to achieve certain goals, we cannot avoid drawing the conclusion that this must be explained by reference to a wise and benevolent designer (pp. 234–5); this inference is part of our nature. Our innate faculties thus lead us intuitively to an absolutely certain belief in God, and that same nature, which derives from him, prevents us from in any way accepting Hume's sceptical attack on the argument

from design (p. 269). In short, the nativist account of all our faculties
and knowledge and the providential teleology together provide a
blaze of obscurity in which Kames provides answers to everything but
really to nothing.

Thomas Reid was deeply influenced by Kames.[31] He adopts the
main points of Kames's position, while developing it in detail, and in
the psychological description of perception. Reid was undoubtedly a
better philosopher than Kames, but in the end, since he shares with
Kames the same basic position, his views are subject to the same
criticisms. We have seen already how Reid, in his moral philosophy,
shares with Kames the inferences that John Stuart Mill is later going to
challenge, from the simplicity of the act of consciousness to, on the one
hand, it innateness, and to, on the other hand, the simplicity of its
object. Precisely the same inferences are made by Reid in the area of
perception; precisely the same replies by Mill will be relevant.

Reid, in his *Inquiry into the Human Mind* (1785a, Ch. 1), traces the
history of philosophy from Descartes to Hume as one of a progressively
developing scepticism with respect to the existence of anything save
ephemeral and ever-changing sensible qualities. This scepticism was a
logical development from a premiss that Descartes adopted, and which
was accepted by his successors, that the only entities that we ever
experience are the sensible qualities ('ideas') given in sensation. As
Berkeley and Hume saw, this means that external substances must go.
Reid accepts the substantialist position that this means that, since
none of the qualities is in a substance, none of them is real. Reid simply
does not recognize the moves that Berkeley and Hume made to try to
reformulate the reality/unreality distinction in a way that fits their
account of perceptual objects as patterned collections of sensible
qualities. For Berkeley and Hume there is nothing about common
sense that commits one to construing perceptual objects as substances,
nor therefore anything that demands the substantialist account of the
reality/unreality distinction. But for Reid, in contrast, substances *are*
part of common sense, and thus, despite their disclaimers, Berkeley
and Hume are unable to give a sense to 'real' that will enable them
genuinely to escape the criticism that upon their account nothing we
experience is real. Why does Reid think common sense is committed to
substances?

According to Reid, to escape the scepticism that is implicit from the
beginning in the way of ideas that was initiated by Descartes and that
reached its logical conclusion in Hume was simply to deny the premiss

that the only entities that we ever experience are sensible qualities given in sensation (1785a, Ch. v, sec. viii). That is, what one must do is recognize that, besides sensations, there are also states of consciousness in which we experience perceptual objects. Reid thus distinguishes in perception a sensible impression and a perceptual judgment (pp. 126, 182). The latter is a distinct state of consciousness; its difference is a simple characteristic that can only be felt, not defined (p. 182). In the perceptual judgment we experience the perceptual object as an entity that endures and exists independently of being perceived. Upon Reid's view, recognition of the simplicity and distinctness of these perceptual judgments *suffices* to refute the scepticism of the way of ideas. Since that scepticism amounts to the denial of substances, the recognition of perceptual judgments can suffice to refute such scepticism only if such recognition itself implies the existence of substances, that is, only if the existence of perceptual judgments as simple undefinable states of consciousness implies the existence of a correspondingly simple entity as their object, a substance that endures through change and therefore independently of being perceived. 'I cannot explain how we know that [perceived qualities of perceptual objects] cannot exist without a subject, any more than I can explain how we know that they exist'; it is, Reid tells us, 'self-evident, and an immediate dictate of my nature,' and, he concludes, it is 'a judgment of nature, that the things immediately perceived are qualities, which must belong to a subject' (1785b, p. 322). Reid thus makes the same inference as does Kames, from a simple act of perceiving to a simple object, that John Stuart Mill will later criticize.

Reid attributes to the mind a host of innate faculties and principles similar to, but in a way more philosophically sensitive than, that of Kames (cf. Lehrer 1987, 1989; Pappas 1989). In all perception, there is a sensation. In the case of smell, the connection of the sensation with its cause is something learned, by association: one 'finds, by ... experience, that, when a rose is near, he has a certain sensation, when it is removed the sensation is gone, he finds a connection in nature betwixt the rose and this sensation. The rose is considered as a cause, occasion, or antecedent of the sensation; the sensation as an effect or consequence of the presence of the rose; they are associated in the mind, and constantly conjoined in the imagination' (1785a, p. 112). To be sure, 'the connection it [the sensation] hath with the rose is special and constant; by which means they become almost inseparable in the imagination, in like manner as thunder and lightning, freezing and cold' (ibid.). None the less, the connection is learned, and therefore inferential. So the Berkeleyan analysis of perception as inference correctly describes these sensory processes.

In the case of touch, we have a variety of sensations: heat, cold, softness, hardness, roughness, smoothness, figure, solidity, motion, and extension (1785a, p. 119). As for space, motion, and extension these are *not* derived from other sensations of secondary qualities, and so Berkeley's account of them must be wrong: 'These qualities do not at all tally with any system of the human faculties that hath been advanced. They have no resemblance to any sensation, or to any operation of our minds; and, therefore, they cannot be ideas either of sensation or of reflection. The very conception of them is irreconcilable to the principles of all our philosophical systems of the understanding. The belief in them is no less so' (p. 126). The judgments of extension that we make by touch are not inferences but simple perceptions, and, moreover, perceptions of those qualities as inhering in substances. This restores, as Reid thinks, the external world, the reality that Berkeley denied (p. 127). The perception itself is simple (p. 107), and is caused by the sensation, for example, a sensation of heat (p. 22). This causal process is not one that is learned but is an innate part of our human nature (pp. 122, 130). It is from this simplicity and therefore innateness that one can conclude from our sense of touch that substances exist (pp. 127, 130).

> That we have clear and distinct conceptions of extension, figure, motion, and other attributes of body, which are neither sensations, nor like any sensation, is a fact of which we may be as certain as we have sensations. And that all mankind have a fixed belief of an external material world – a belief which is neither got by reasoning nor education, and a belief which we cannot shake off, even when we seem to have strong arguments against it and no shadow of argument for it – is likewise a fact, for which we have all the evidence that the nature of the thing admits. These facts are phenomena of human nature, from which we may justly argue against any hypothesis, however generally received. (p. 132)

In the sense of touch, then, we have an innate capacity to recognize the extendedness of perceptual objects, that is, the volume they occupy. This means, of course, that we can recognize not only surface shape but also depth or distance, contrary to Berkeley who argued that all depth or distance perception is a matter of association. Since perceptual judgments are simple, they are not inferences. As a phenomenological description of our states of consciousness the correctness of this may be granted. However, what Reid concludes from this, that therefore our capacities to perceive are not learned but are innate, the younger Mill will later criticize. This will permit Mill to hold that our capacity to recognize depth is learned while accepting the phenomenological point that such perceptions are simple.

For Reid the case of sight is more complex. Here we have sensations that are coloured and have a certain shape, a certain length and breadth (1785a, p. 135). Visible figure and extension yield a geometry – non-Euclidean as it turns out – that can be treated mathematically (Ch. VI, sec. ix), and is related in certain geometrical ways to the geometrical properties of the external cause (p. 142). The visible figure is not a sensation, like those of smell or colour; it is, to the contrary, a property of the perceived object. It consists of *certain but not all* geometrical properties of the external object (pp. 145–6). By virtue of the visible geometrical properties, the mind can infer the full set of geometrical properties of the perceived object (p. 147). In particular, from its visible shape one can infer its *distance*. Distance or depth is, Reid insists, 'no immediate object of sight' (p. 136). The geometry of visibles is two-dimensional; but from these properties we can, and do, infer the third dimension (p. 149).

Berkeley is therefore wrong to hold that there is no similarity between what is given by sight and what is given by touch (1785a, p. 155). The inference to depth depends, however, upon an accurate focusing of the eyes, and our capacity to do this is a matter of custom; it is learned (p. 173). In this respect Berkeley is correct: 'we see only the visible appearance of objects by nature; but we learn by custom to interpret these appearances, and to understand their meaning. And when this visual language is learned, and becomes familiar, we attend only to the things signified; and cannot, without great difficulty attend to the signs by which they are presented. The mind passes from the one to the other so rapidly and so familiarly, that no trace of the sign is left in the memory, and we seem immediately, and without the intervention of any sign, to perceive the thing signified' (p. 182).

As this example makes clear, it is possible to hold that certain capacities to recognize spatial relations are in us 'by nature,' that is, are innate, while other such capacities are learned. One could thus hold, contrary to Berkeley, that some judgments of spatial relatedness are *not* associations while also holding that, so far as depth of distance is concerned, Berkeley's associationist account is correct.

The same point applies to other relations. Reid rejects Hume's analysis of causation into regularity.[32] Just as there are simple perceptions of perceptual objects, which implies the existence of substance, so there are simple judgments of causation (1785b, pp. 454ff). One could consistently hold that some relations are presented in simple perceptions, but that causation is not among them.

Throughout his discussions, however, Reid regularly obscures matters by the two invalid inferences, from the simplicity of the perception to the simplicity of the object, and from the simplicity of the perception to its innateness. It was the exhibition of these inferences as fallacies by John Stuart Mill that let in the breath of fresh air that could move the discussion from the level of metaphysics, where it did not belong, to the level of empirical fact, where it did.

Reid, though, is still involved in metaphysics, and so, like Kames, populates the human mind with a host of innate faculties. And also like Kames, Reid goes farther and populates the mind additionally with innate principles. These include the principle that every event has a cause (1785b, p. 455) and the principle that perceptions that we receive by sense are reliable (p. 330).

All this is put into the context of a providential teleology. The human system, physical and mental, has an innate constitution that so organizes it as to efficiently serve the ends of survival and life with our fellows. This constitution is evidence of the benevolence and wisdom of our Creator, and that benevolence and wisdom, in turn, gives authority to our perceptual mechanisms, to our moral sense, and to the other innate mechanisms of our human nature.[33]

But as Hume says, 'to have recourse to the veracity of the supreme Being, in order to prove the veracity of our senses, is surely making a very unexpected circuit. If his veracity were at all concerned in this matter, our senses would be entirely infallible; because it is not possible that he can ever deceive. Not to mention, that, if the external world be once called in question, we shall be at a loss to find arguments, by which we may prove the existence of that Being or any of his attributes' (1777, p. 153). In the end, however satisfying it might be psychologically, for one who wishes a natural scientific understanding of perception the appeal to a wise and benevolent designer is no answer at all. Reid and Kames simply leave the matter in obscurity. It was only when Thomas Brown (1820) reintroduced the notion of association (or, as he called it, 'suggestion') that the followers of Reid were to do more than appeal to the wise goodness of our Creator and attempt to gain insight into the mechanisms that he uses. But this takes us up to the work of James and John Stuart Mill.

3   Context: John Stuart Mill's Development

Mill's Bentham

The younger Mill came to view the context in which he was working in terms similar to those of Macaulay and the other critics of the philosophic radicals. Or rather, he saw the point of their criticism of Bentham. In contrast, he also saw, where they did not, the virtues of Bentham. And he was therefore able to reject their negative evaluations of Bentham as opposed to some of Bentham's doctrines. As he put in the essay on Bentham, 'to refuse an admiring recognition of what he was, on account of what he was not,' is an error, he suggests, that is 'no longer permitted to any cultivated and instructed mind' (1838, p. 82).

What was important in Bentham's work was not so much his substantive doctrines as his method. 'It was not his opinions ... but his method, that constituted the novelty and value of what he did; a value beyond all price, even though we should reject the whole, as we unquestionably must a large part, of the opinions themselves' (1838, p. 83). The method was similar to that of the natural sciences. Earlier thinkers, such as Bacon, Hobbes, and Locke, had begun to characterize this method, and in turn self-consciously to apply it. Bentham's novelty was the employing of this method in new areas, and employing it systematically; that is, the novelty consisted in 'the subjects he applied it to, and in the rigidity with which he adhered to it' (ibid.). What is important is not merely, as Robson (1968, pp. 267–8) has suggested, the simple fact of adopting a common method in ethics, politics, and sociology, but rather the adopting of a very specific method, that of natural science, and, still more significantly, that of applying it systematically so that it becomes a 'method of detail,' an 'exhaustive method.' It does indeed result in 'interminable classifications' and 'elaborate demonstrations of the most acknowledged truths' (ibid.), but that is its virtue and a sign of its strength. 'That murder, incendiarism, robbery are mischievous actions, he will not take for granted without proof' (ibid.). As a result, as Mill was later to put it in his essay on Whewell's moral philosophy, Bentham's 'great service' was for the first time to make possible 'a scientific doctrine of ethics on the foundation of utility' in which 'secondary or middle principles capable of serving as premises for a body of ethical doctrine not derived from existing opinions, but fitted to be their test' (1852, p. 173). Those who, as did Sedgwick (1834) and Whewell (1845), criticize utilitarianism in the name of an objectivist intuitionism in the tradition of Price and Reid simply proclaim the self-evident immorality of, say, theft; it requires no proof. And previous defenders of the utilitarian doctrine, while not making the immorality of theft a matter of intuition, tended to accept pretty well without proof that it was obvious that it was harmful, and therefore, contrary to the principle of utility, that is, immoral. But Bentham does not in either of these ways simply assume that existing opinion is correct; he seeks, rather, to justify it in detail, if it can be justified, and where it cannot, to reject. Only in this way can principles adopted in existing opinion become truly the *tests* of that opinion.

Thus, in his work on the law, Bentham is very successful. Anyone who has looked at, for example, Bentham's work on the principles of legal evidence (which the young John Stuart Mill edited) cannot but be impressed by its sheer reasonableness when it is compared to the then existing state of the common law and by its comprehensiveness and detail when it is compared to the work of his predecessors who similarly urged a reform of the system based on the empiricist epistemic principles of Locke and his successors.[34] As John Stuart Mill put it, in the area of legal thought, Bentham 'originated more new truths' than the world 'ever received, except in a few glorious instances, from any other individual' (1838, p. 100). Bentham is at his very best in his efforts to make of law a science, in his deductions of principles, and in his separating the historical, technical, and rational elements, in his exploding of 'fantastic and illogical maxims on which the various technical systems are founded' (1833, p. 10), and in his concepts of codification of the law.

But what works well here works less well in other areas. Thus, take a closely related one, the theory of government. Mill distinguishes three questions of government: 'to what authority is it for the good of the people that they should be subject,' 'how are they to be induced to obey that authority,' and 'how are abuses of this authority to be checked' (1838, p. 106). The first two, which must have different answers depending upon the 'degree and kind of civilization' already attained by a people, and their 'peculiar aptitude for receiving more' (ibid.), are largely ignored by Bentham. As for the third, Bentham's answer consists in making the authority responsible to 'the numerical majority' the interest of which is taken to be identical with that of the whole community. But this is entirely questionable since it means that not only actions but opinions and feelings should be 'under the despotism of Public Opinion,' and this can stifle those influences that tend 'to the further improvement of man's intellectual and moral nature' (p. 107). This point was, of course, to be elaborated in the essay *On Liberty* (1859b).

Bentham's failure here consists, in effect, of assuming an identity of 'partialities, passions, and prejudices,' that is, a 'human nature universal and perpetual,' which ignores 'the personality of the individual' and the 'superiority of cultivated intelligence,' precisely those factors, in other words, that could make the difference between status quo and moral improvement (1838, pp. 107–9). This view of human nature is one which allows Bentham to 'teach the means of organizing and regulating the merely *business* part of the social arrangements' (p. 99). To be sure, in this part of life, Bentham is 'indeed great' (p. 100). The narrow restrictions of his view of human nature are not, *in the business part of life*, restricting, and that part of life includes much of the legal system. Penal law, for example, 'enjoins or prohibits an action, with very little regard to the general moral excellence or turpitude which it implies'; the legislator's object 'is not to render people incapable of *desiring* a crime, but to deter them from actually committing it' (1833, p. 9). But the narrowness of the conception of human nature invalidates, not Bentham's method, but many of his substantive claims. Thus, Bentham's narrow view of human psychology leads him to ignore what Mill calls 'national character' – the feelings, opinions, sentiments, and values that men in a nation share in common, which vary from society to society, and which, as they are transmitted by educational processes from generation to generation, constitute the element of permanence in a society – that area, in other words, where such opponents of the utilitarians as Coleridge were, according to Mill, strongest (cf. 1840, p. 141). Bentham ignores, as Mill puts it elsewhere, what Burke calls 'prejudice' and which indicates an adaptation of institutions, 'associated with all the historical recollections of a people,' to their national character (1833, p. 17). It is this element of continuity or permanence 'which alone renders possible these innumerable compromises between adverse interests and expectation, without which no government could be carried on for a year, and with difficulty even for a week' (ibid.). The point is that, in the end, for whatever its other virtues, 'a philosophy of laws and institutions, not founded on a philosophy of national character, is an absurdity' (1838, p. 99). As a result, 'all that he [Bentham] can do is but to indicate means by which, in any given state of the national mind, the material interests can be protected,' leaving to others the important question whether the use of those means would injure or improve the national character (ibid.). Bentham's psychology in effect ignores inner states of character and feeling, which means it is incapable of dealing with the whole question of moral influences. And, in the end, for Mill, even the 'business part' of life cannot be dealt with apart from considerations of moral influence and national character.

The difficulty is that Bentham 'supposes mankind to be swayed by only a part of the inducements which really actuate them; but for that part he imagines them to be much cooler and more thoughtful calculators than they really are' (1833, p. 17). To be sure, in asserting that 'men's actions are always obedient to their interests,' Bentham did not intend in any way 'to impute universal selfishness to mankind, for he reckoned the motive of sympathy as an *interest* ... He distinguished two kinds of interests, the self-regarding and the social.' But the term 'interest' in its common use is restricted to the self-regarding, and in fact the 'tendency of Mr Bentham's own opinions' was to consider the self-regarding interest 'as exercising, by the very constitution of human nature, a far more exclusive and paramount control over human actions than it really does exercise.' Mill has no trouble in finding passages in Bentham's works that establish that, as soon as Bentham has shown the direction in which a man's self-interest would move him, he then 'lays it down without further parley that the man's interest lies that way' (1833, p. 14). This restriction of human motives is equivalent to having 'confounded the principle of Utility with the principle of specific consequences'; in ignoring states of mind as motives and causes of actions, Bentham is in fact ignoring some of the consequences, for 'any act ... has a tendency to fix and perpetuate the state or character of mind in which itself originated' (p. 8). Bentham, his intentions notwithstanding, has adopted the principle of psychological egoism, and by limiting his consideration of the morality of an action to its consequences taken in a very restricted way he has also provided some reason for the critics to charge that the principle of utility is merely a doctrine of expediency.

What is needed to combat the charge of expediency is 'a more enlarged understanding of the "greatest-happiness principle,"' which took into account more of the consequences than Bentham usually considers (1833, p. 7). But to do this it has to be allowed that human psychology is such that even though acts or habits may not be in themselves pernicious in being immediately productive of bad consequences, and may therefore be permitted by the expediency principle, they may none the less form part of a pernicious character, and ought therefore, upon the 'enlarged' principle, be reckoned as wrong. That is, the psychology implied by Bentham's calculus of consequences is that 'all our acts are determined by pains and pleasures *in prospect*' (p. 12), and this impoverished list of the 'springs of action' must be enlarged to include other motives, in particular 'the moral sense.' The morality of an act indeed lies in its consequences, but the virtuous man is deterred from an evil action, not by a view of the consequences, or future pain, but by the 'thought of committing the act,' a 'painful thought' that precedes the action; indeed, Mill says, 'Not only *may* this be so, but unless it be so, the man is not really virtuous' (ibid.). Mill is, of course, taking the term 'moral sense' in the relativist sense of Hutcheson and Hume, rather than the objectivist way of Shaftesbury. The 'painful thought' serves a motivational role, not a cognitive role. Mill's point is that having people so motivated is itself something that has useful consequences. 'We [that is, John Stuart Mill, in contrast to Bentham] think utility, or happiness, much too complex and indefinite and end to be sought except through the medium of various secondary ends' (1838, p. 110). For, to evaluate consequences we must deliberate, a process that is slow and uncertain: 'the attempt to make the bearings of actions upon the ultimate end more evident than they can be made by referring them to the intermediate ends, and to estimate their value by a direct reference to human happiness, generally terminates in attaching most importance, not to those effects which are really the greatest, but to those which can most easily be pointed to and individually identified' (p. 111). Hence, where an action is generally wrong, it is useful to have a motive that eliminates the need to deliberate. That such a motive occasionally leads to actions that are wrong in terms of their consequences is itself a consequence the evil of which is far less than the evil that would ensue if there were no such motive and we had always to take our risky chances with deliberation, for, as Mill says, he who deliberates 'is in imminent danger of being lost' (1833, p. 12). The 'painful thought' that motivates the virtuous man is a *pain*, and may therefore be placed in the calculus of pains and pleasures by which the reasonable person attempts to regulate his life for his long-run overall happiness. But it is a pain that is *not* reducible to self-interest; it is, on the one hand, characteristically *moral* – it derives from our '*moral* sense' – and, on the other hand, it has as its *object* something other than his own unhappiness (or happiness). It is *this* sort of pain – or pleasure – that Bentham's psychology excludes. Without such a motive, utilitarian ethics is totally useless for regulating 'the nicer shades of human behaviour, or for laying down even the greater moralities ... which tend to influence the depths of the character quite independently of any influence on worldly circumstances' (1838, p. 98).

Without such a motive as a 'moral sense,' utilitarian ethics can do nothing 'beyond prescribing some of the more obvious dictates of worldly prudence, and outward probity and beneficience' (ibid.). But even here, as a system of outward and basically prudential ethics, it will be inadequate, since self-education, 'the training, by the human being himself, of his affections and his will,' will remain 'a blank' and without it the regulation of our 'outward' behaviour 'must be altogether halting and imperfect' (ibid.). Thus, although Bentham, as we saw Mill point out, provided an ethics which showed how to justify 'secondary or middle principles' not derived from, but fit to test existing opinions (1852, p. 173), what his psychology prevented him from seeing was how these principles could themselves become existing opinion, and also from seeing the utility of this.

All this emerges fully in the essay 'Utilitarianism' (1861). The secondary principles that Mill mentions are the moral rules of the orthodox morality – 'do not steal' and so on, the rules that Bentham's method led him to seek to justify. These moral opinions on which we all generally act are, like national character, opinions transmitted by education from one generation to the next (1861, pp. 224–5). But they summarize effectively the inherited wisdom of mankind as to what is in its benefit. Existing opinion is not the test of morality but, on the whole, it survives the test. Mankind collectively, if unconsciously, has subjected it to the Benthamite test, and has found that these rules pass it. These principles become the object of conscience, 'a subjective feeling in our own minds' (p. 228). The aim of the utilitarian philosophy is to create, through education and the improvement of education, a 'feeling of unity with our fellow creatures,' and to root it deeply in our character (p. 227). This feeling of unity is in fact the conscious readiness to make a sacrifice of one's own pleasure; indeed, 'the conscious ability to do without happiness gives the best prospect of realizing such happiness as is attainable' (p. 218). The ability consciously to aim at goods other than one's own happiness is the 'highest virtue which can be found in man' (ibid.), and utilitarianism can only attain its end by the 'general cultivation of nobleness of character' (p. 214). In fact, when nobler parts of human nature are cultivated what we find is that we 'give a most marked preference to the manner of existence which employs [our] higher faculties' (p. 211). The cultivation of the higher faculties not only conforms to the utilitarian standard that requires not 'the agent's own greatest happiness, but the greatest amount altogether' (ibid.); it also in fact in the end yields the greatest pleasure to an individual because the pleasures of the higher faculties of the intellect, imagination, and moral sense are better than those of 'mere sensation,' where this superiority is not merely a matter of their 'greater permanency, safety, uncostliness &c.,' but also of the fact that they are '*kinds* of pleasure [which] are more desirable and valuable than others' (pp. 210–11).[35] The doctrine of utility is thus, upon the reformulation given it by John Stuart Mill, as connected as any other ethical system, for example, intuitionism or Christianity, with the 'beautiful or more exalted developments of human nature' and with the variety of 'springs of action' (p. 219). It achieves this by modifying Bentham's psychology to allow for, in particular, motives that are *specifically moral* in their quality and have as their *objects* non–self-regarding ends beyond oneself. But these motives are, though *qualitatively distinct*, none the less *pleasures*, and it thus does not escape the calculus of pleasures in which each individual seeks to determine, and act upon, what will be in his long-run and overall maximum happiness.[36] Nor does it escape the idea that behaviour is controlled by pleasures and pains. As Mill continues to insist, 'pleasure, and freedom from pain, are the only things desirable as ends' (p. 210). It only adds that besides the pleasures and pains of the 'business part' of life which Bentham supposed to be the 'only part of the inducements which really actuate [mankind],' there are also among the controlling pleasures and pains the internal factors that constitute man's capacity, in his higher faculties, for self-control, that is, his capacity not only to regulate and modify his own behaviour but also to regulate and modify his own controlling motives, that is, his own controlling pleasures and pains. Moreover, this moral sense of virtue by which we control our behaviour and improve our character itself grows and develops as it does under the impact of externally derived pleasures and pains that build upon, and modify, the natural social feelings of mankind (pp. 230–1). It follows that, however much it must be modified by considerations of the sort emphasized by Coleridge, the utilitarianism of the younger Mill retains the basic idea of the philosophic radicals that a better state of existence for mankind can be achieved through institutional, and especially educational, controls. The modification is that these controls usually work not directly, through the prospect of future pleasures and pains, but indirectly, through creating appropriate pleasures and pains, distinct in their species and object, as internal controls.

Thus, the younger Mill's defence of utilitarianism against the critics of Bentham consists in granting their points but also modifying the psychology so as to accommodate them. But, if Bentham's psychology is modified, it is not so modified that it forces the abandonment of the reforming program of the philosophic radicals. At least, that is the claim. It can be made good provided that Mill can justify inserting into the psychology of Bentham – and of his father – the notion that there are pleasures with distinctively moral objects that are not only specifically different in their quality from but are, by that quality itself, preferable to other pleasures.

Mill's Self-Analysis

Bentham's philosophical shortcomings lay in the deficiences of the psychology that he accepted. And these deficiences were the result of a limitation of his own capacities. This limitation, according to John Stuart Mill, was 'the incompleteness of his own mind as a representative of universal human nature. In many of the most natural and strongest feelings of human nature he had no sympathy; from many of its graver experiences he was wholly cut off; and the faculty by which one mind understands a mind different from itself, and throws itself into the feelings of that other mind, was denied him by his deficiency of Imagination' (1838, p. 91). Without this imaginative power of empathetic understanding, Mill continues, 'nobody knows even his own nature, further than circumstances have actually tried it and called it out' (p. 92). One discovers the laws of psychology through introspection, but the deficiency of Bentham's imagination meant that 'self-consciousness ... never was awakened in him' (ibid.). As a consequence, in spite of his advocating the analytical method, and using it elsewhere in elaborate detail, Bentham systematically fails to apply that method in psychology.

Thus, for example, 'man is never recognized by [Bentham] as a being capable of pursuing spiritual perfection as an end; of desiring for its own sake, the conformity of his own character to his standard of excellence, without hope of good or fear of evil from other source than his own consciousness' (1838, p. 95). Bentham to be sure does at times speak of the 'love of justice' as a motive present in almost all men, but what exactly he means by this is never clear since it is impossible to tell 'what sense is to be put upon casual expressions so inconsistent with the general tenor of his philosophy' (p. 95n). Neither the term 'self-respect' nor the idea that it connotes occurs even once in his writings. Neither this nor such other 'powerful constituents of human nature' as the sense of honour, the love of beauty, or the abstract love of power finds a place in his list of the 'Springs of Action.' Bentham does have a doctrine of sympathy, but even here his account is deficient, since it does not include 'the love of *loving*, the need of a sympathising support, or of objects of admiration and reverence' (p. 96). All these omissions arise, Mill suggests, not from the absence of these elements in Bentham's own nature, but from his having 'confounded all disinterested feelings which he found in himself, with the desire of general happiness' (ibid.). Where elsewhere Bentham would apply the method of analysis so as to result in 'interminable classifications' and 'exhaustive demonstrations of the most acknowledged truths' (p. 83), here in psychology there is a total failure to apply the method.

This lack of self-conscious reflection on the working of his own mind meant that Bentham's knowledge of psychology was 'wholly empirical' (1838, p. 92). Such knowledge is not useless, but it is of limited validity, and becomes knowledge of causes only when a broader theory is elaborated in which it can be embedded by being deduced from it, as Mill explains elsewhere (1872a, Bk. III, Ch. xvi). Thus, 'knowing so little of human feelings, he knew still less of the influences by which those feelings are formed' (1838, p. 93). However, a more adequate application of the analytical method in self-conscious intro-spection will lead one to this deeper and more adequate knowledge of the laws of human nature, which escaped Bentham. Mill undertook such an analysis in his own case, and discovered that knowledge of psychology that he needed if he was to defend utilitarianism against its critics.

As Mill looked back upon himself in his *Autobiography* (1873), he saw a young Benthamite. The 'description so often given of a Benthamite, as a mere reasoning machine,' he tells us, 'was during two or three years of my life not altogether untrue of me' (1873, p. 111). The whole system of Bentham and his followers such as James Mill for that regeneration of mankind which was to be the 'effect of educated intellect, enlightening the selfish feelings' (p. 113), was something to which the younger Mill fully subscribed. Bentham's principle of utility was the 'keystone' that 'gave unity' to his thought, and in fact more than mere unity since it was for him 'a creed, a doctrine, a philosophy ... a religion' (p. 69). Zeal 'for what I thought the good of mankind was my strongest sentiment ... But my zeal was as yet little else, at that period in my life, than zeal for speculative opinions. It had not its root in genuine benevolence, or sympathy with mankind; though these qualities held their due place in my ethical standard. Nor was it connected with any high enthusiasm for ideal nobleness' (p. 113). From the later perspec-tive John Stuart Mill could recognize in the Benthamite youth that he formerly was the potentialities the exercise of which would eventually distinguish him from Bentham. 'No youth,' he notes, 'of the age I then was, can be expected to be more than one thing, and this is the thing I happened to be,' but of the feeling of 'high enthusiasm for ideal nobleness' which he lacked he comments that, 'yet of this feeling I was imaginatively very susceptible; but there was at that time an intermission of its natural aliment, poetical culture, while there was a superabundance of the discipline antagonistic to it, that of mere logic and analysis' (ibid.). But whatever the potentiality was, it was none the less also true that the feelings that were absent from the Benthamite psychology that was part of the system to which he subscribed were equally absent from the lived experience of the younger Mill: '[my] father's teachings [like Bentham's] tended to the undervaluing of feeling' (ibid.).

Mill records how a reading of Pope's 'Essay on Man' powerfully affected his imagination, though its opinions were strongly at variance with his own. The 'inspiring effect' of poetry he connects with the equally 'inspiring effect' – that 'best sort of enthusiasm' – roused by biographies of wise and noble men. The significance of these was not then apparent, but in any case recorded only the as yet unrealized possibilities that distinguished him from Bentham; they did not affect the 'real inward sectarianism' that continued to grip the younger Mill (1873, p. 115). It was in fact the mental crisis of the fall of 1826 that broke the sectarianism and released his real potentialities.

In the psychology of Bentham and his father, the end for which he strove was pleasure or happiness but considered in an outward and external way in terms of essentially selfish feelings. What the crisis eventually led the younger Mill to recognize was the inadequacy of this concept of pleasure, and of the psychology of which it was a part. The crisis did this because its first manifestation consisted in Mill's coming to realize that his life as he was then leading it was in fact devoid of happiness. To the question 'Suppose that all your objects in life were realized; that all the changes in institutions and opinions which you are looking forward to, could be completely effected at this very instant: would this be a great joy and happiness to you?' his 'irrepressible self-consciousness distinctly answered, "No!"' (1873, p. 139). It became clear to him that 'my love of mankind, and of excellence for its own sake, had worn itself out' (ibid.). No end was capable of giving him pleasure; 'neither selfish nor unselfish pleasures were pleasures to me' (p. 143). Since pleasures and pains are the only motivators, there was thus for the young Benthamite nothing that could move him. Intellectually he was well equipped to find the means to secure desired ends, but there was nothing to point out the direction in which he should move. As he puts it, 'I was ... left stranded ... with a well-equipped ship and a rudder, but no sail; without any real desire for the ends which I had been so carefully fitted out to work for: no delight in virtue, or the general good' (ibid.). It was this crisis of apathy that brought home to the younger Mill the force of the often-stated criticism of utilitarianism and of the psychology of the philosophic radicals, that it provided no source for feelings of duty and moral obligation.

Why did it happen that Mill's 'love of mankind ... had worn itself out?' He attributed it to the education to which he had been subjected. This education on the one hand emphasized analysis. Now, this *method* of analysis is the source of our knowledge of the laws of nature: 'we owe to analysis our clearest knowledge of the permanent sequences in nature; the real connexions between Things, not dependent on our will and feelings; natural laws' (1873, p. 141). But to discover what connections hold in reality is to confront inherited prejudice, to test it, and, where it is wrong, to weaken and eventually suppress it in favour of the knowledge that analysis yields. 'The very excellence of analysis ... is that it tends to weaken and undermine whatever is the result of prejudice' (ibid.). The education, on the other hand, presupposed the simplistic psychology of Bentham. His teachers therefore 'seem to have trusted altogether to the old familiar instruments, praise and blame, reward and punishment.' These did indeed create a variety of associations, but analysis now revealed these to be artificial, that is, prejudices that the practice of analysis could only weaken. The education was based on an inadequate psychology. It did create the interests that the educators themselves desired, but only in a highly artificial way. The method of analysis was what led to the crisis of apathy by undermining the effects of the younger Mill's education, but in doing that it also revealed the inadequacies as a science of the psychology upon which the educators had attempted to base their art.

In the depressions of his mental crisis, Mill had come to believe that 'the habit of analysis had a tendency to wear away the feelings' (1873, p. 141). Since he had been taught by his education that the only proper exercise of the mind was the habit of analysis, but also that 'the pleasure of sympathy with human beings, and the feelings which made the good of others ... the object of existence, were the greatest source of happiness' (p. 143), Mill seemed to be faced with being forced to choose between analysis and having feelings that moved one. But of course one had to have feelings, and Mill searched his own nature to discover them. At one point he read through the whole of Byron, 'to try whether a poet, whose peculiar department was supposed to be that of the intenser feelings, could rouse any feeling in me' (p. 149). That Mill considered Byron the most violent stimulus he could find to evoke an emotional response within himself says much about both Mill and about the age. In any case, as is well known, it was from Wordsworth's poems that Mill derived 'a medicine for [his] state of mind' (p. 151). This medicine consisted in the discovery of 'a source of inward joy, of sympathetic and imaginative pleasure, which could be shared in by all human beings' (ibid.). The happiness no longer depended upon artificial connections, but had a real and permanent source within human nature. From Wordsworth's poems, Mill says, 'I seemed to learn what would be the perennial sources of happiness, when all the greater evils of life shall have been removed ... I needed to be made to feel that there was real, permanent happiness in tranquil contemplation' (p. 153). Mill thus discovered new motives, new sources of pleasure, which his educators, with their narrow psychology, had overlooked.[37] They are motives that moreover derive from real and permanent tendencies in his nature. Mill thus discovered dimensions of the psychology of motivation that earlier utilitarians had overlooked. Emerging from the crisis Mill can see clearly the limitations of his father's psychology and at the same time also the strength of the criticism levelled at it for being a mere psychological egoism. But, he also recognizes the core of truth 'which lay in my early opinions, and in no essential part of which I at any time wavered' (p. 175). In particular he discovered that he was not forced to choose between the habit of analysis, on the one hand, and, on the other, the new feelings that he had discovered could so motivate him that he once against felt inspired to action. For, since these feelings of happiness derive from a permanent source rather than from an artificial association, there is no fear that analysis will dissolve them: 'the delight which these poems gave me, proved that with culture of this sort, there was nothing to dread from the most confirmed habit of analysis' (p. 153).

It is out of this realization that emerges the doctrine of the moral sense that Mill uses to defend utilitarianism. This 'moral faculty,' he says in 'Utilitarianism,' 'if not a part of our nature, is a natural outgrowth from it' (1861, p. 230). The source of the feeling of moral obligation is conscience or the moral sense that is a development and also a cultivation of our natural social feelings. In fact, the utilitarian position, if it is to be defensible, must be based upon the naturalness, in this sense, of the social feelings of mankind. For, if those feelings were artificial associations, as implied by the earlier, inadequate psychology of Bentham and his father, then those social sentiments 'might be analysed away' (p. 231). Elsewhere Mill distinguishes three aspects of human action: the moral (its *rightness* or *wrongness*), the aesthetic (its *beauty*), and the sympathetic (its *lovableness*). 'The first addresses itself to our reason and conscience; the second to our imagination; and the third to our human fellow-feeling' (1838, p. 112). These are what in 'Utilitarianism' are called our 'higher faculties' (1861, p. 213), and are the sources of the qualitatively higher pleasure, 'kinds of pleasure [that] are more desirable and valuable than others' (pp. 210–11). It is all this that is implicit in the enlarged knowledge of human psychology that derives from the impact of Wordsworth and with which Mill emerged from his mental crisis.

In particular there emerges the recognition that, on the one hand, analysis is incapable of reducing the higher pleasures to do something else, and, also the recognition that, on the other hand, analysis remains the central method in psychology, the method by which we come to fit our merely empirical knowledge into a pattern of causes and effects. Since this more adequate understanding of the theory and method of psychology is central to the younger Mill's defence of utilitarianism and the reformist projects of the philosophic radicals, one could say in fact that this is the central truth that Mill discovered as he passed through his mental crisis.

TWO

John Stuart Mill's Philosophy of Science

An understanding of John Stuart Mill's theories in psychology and his views on the appropriate method to be used to develop such theories presupposes an understanding of his more general views on theories and on the nature of scientific research. A brief sketch of these general views is the aim of this chapter. The first section gives an account of Mill's views on explanation and on the nature of scientific theories, as well as an account of how the latter guide research. It will be seen that, though this is a standard empiricist account, much of it can be fit with little difficulty into more recent examinations of the scientific method by such thinkers as Kuhn and Lakatos. There is one aspect of Mill's views on explanation that is of especial relevance to psychology, however, and to the understanding of psychology that Mill achieved in his struggle to find a defence of the utilitarian philosophy of Bentham and his father. This aspect of Mill's views is briefly discussed in the second section.

1   Explanation, Theories, and Research

John Stuart Mill holds that the concept of scientific explanation can be explicated in terms of what has come to be called the 'covering law model' of explanation.[1] To explain an individual fact, say the fact that a is G, is to find some general law, say the law that all F are G, and some other individual fact, say the fact that a is F, called the 'initial conditions,' such that the initial conditions and the law deductively entail the fact to be explained. As Mill puts it: 'An individual fact is said to be explained by pointing out its cause, that is, by stating the law or laws of causation of which its production is an instance' (1872a, III, xiii, 1). He gives this example: 'a conflagration is explained when it is proved to have arisen from a spark falling into the midst of a heap of combustibles' (ibid.).

A similar deductive pattern obtains in the case of the explanation of laws. Mill mentions three cases. The first we shall discuss in the next section; the other two are relevant here.

The first of these obtains 'when, between what seemed the cause and what was supposed to be its effect, further observation detects an intermediate link' (1872a, III, xii, 3). Here we have a law that describes truly, but not completely, some causal process. It is, as J.L. Mackie (1965) described it, 'gappy,' or, as G. Bergmann (1957) did, 'imperfect.'[2] There is implied here an *explanatory ideal*, namely, a law that is 'gapless,' or not 'imperfect,' that is, 'perfect' – always remembering, however, that perfection of this sort does not require, for example, that one overcome the inductive uncertainty that we know, since Hume, attaches to any law, or overcome the natural limitations on accuracy in measurement. The imperfect or gappy law is explained when one fits it into, by deducing it from, a law in which the gaps are filled, the imperfections removed; or, if the ideal of a gapless or perfect explanation is not achieved, then at least by deducing it from a law in which some of the imperfections are removed, some of the gaps filled. An 'empirical law,' Mill later explains, is a confirmed regularity that, however, is not yet felt to be soundly grounded because one cannot yet see *why* such a law should exist (III, xvi, 1). It is thus a law that is recognizably imperfect and it ceases to be empirical once one understands *why* it obtains, that is, once one has fit it into a broader context, by deducing it from less imperfect laws.

Another example given by Mill of the explanation of the more by the less imperfect is this (1872a, III, xii, 2): when an external object is touched, a sensation is caused (A causes C). It is discovered that between the touch and the experiencing of the sensation, a change occurs in the thread-like entity called a nerve that extends from the outward organs to the brain. We now have the pattern: A causes B, which causes C. The original law is explained as part of this more detailed, less gappy, explanation of the process. Mill anticipates that there will be future discoveries that locate further details of the process by which the touch of the outward object effects the change in the nerve.

Still another example is this (1872a, III, ix, 1): metallic substances, such as arsenic, if introduced into an organism, cause death. This was a low-level empirical generalization. It was Leibig who discovered details of the process by which these metals, when dissolved and then brought into contact with animal products, combine with the latter in such a way as to prevent putrefaction, and therefore also the normal chemical reactions. In discovering the details of this process Leibig explained the empirical law about the effects of the introduction of metallic poisons into living organisms.

These sorts of example illustrate a general point that is relevant to our purposes. To talk of organs having a certain *function* is to talk of their effects.[3] Thus, the function of the heart is to circulate blood; that of the eyes is to enable us to see outward objects. Very often the function consists in the achieving or maintaining of a certain goal. Where we have a *goal-directed system*, there we have an explanatory interest in functions, that is, in discovering the organs and processes that function to move the system towards, or to maintain, the goal. But an explanatory interest does not end there. Descriptions of functions, since they give only effects, are imperfect laws. As such they ask to be explained. On the one hand, the details of the process by which the organ achieves the effect that is said to be its function must be filled in. And, on the other hand, the causal process by which there come to be organs having those functions must be ascertained. In psychology, the philosophers we have examined were often satisfied with functional descriptions. Thus, Butler, for example, described conscience as having the function of controlling our other impulses to action. But he leaves open the question of how it is that we come to have the conscience we do. Hume alone attempted to provide a causal explanation of conscience (in terms of the mechanism of sympathy). It was a task that the Mills, both elder and younger, took up. To *explain* our moral sense was part of the task of psychology; and it was in his mental crisis that the younger Mill discovered the inadequacy of his father's explanation, and how it could be improved. Other philosophers simply retreated to an appeal to innate faculties at the earliest opportunity, and from that inferred that no further explanation was needed. But in fact innateness is hard to establish; the arguments of such thinkers as Hutcheson, Kames, and Reid are notoriously weak. But, in any case, it is always allowed that there is a developmental factor; we are not born exercising immediately our innate faculties, but do so only after an appropriate period of maturation. Innateness cannot exclude the explanatory requirement to fill in the details of this process. Moreover, when a supposedly innate capacity reaches maturity, there still remains the details of the physiological and mental mechanisms through which it operates; innateness cannot exclude the explanatory requirement to fill in these details also. The Mills largely put aside the difficult issue of innateness and pursued the details of development. They limited themselves largely to the mental side. With Bain, and of course Wundt, came an increased emphasis upon physiology. The interest on the continent in physiology can be traced back to Descartes's speculations.[4] With Herbert Spencer, and later with the impact of Darwin, came a concern to offer explanations of a causal sort for the existence of innate mechanisms by referring to the evolutionary process by which the human species came to acquire organs so structured that they function as they do. The point is that our *explanatory interests* lead us away from the providential teleology of so many earlier thinkers towards genuinely causal explanations. In the Mills the concern is wholly causal; no obscurantist appeal to a deity and his innate mechanisms is allowed to hinder the drive towards the discovery of causes.

Let us now turn to the other sort of explanation of laws that younger Mill discusses. 'This ... mode is the *subsumption* (as it has been called) of one law under another, or (what comes to the same thing) the gathering up of several laws into one more general law which includes them all' (1872a, III, xii, 5). The example that Mill gives is the law of falling bodies, which asserts that each body near the surface of the earth, if unopposed, will fall freely towards the earth in a certain way, and the law of celestial bodies, which asserts of each planet in the neighbourhood of the sun that it moves towards the sun in a certain way. What Newton was able to show is that there is a *more generic* characterization of these systems, as involving *pairs* of objects, and an *abstract* characterization of their behaviour, according to which each member of the pair tends to move towards the other directly as the product of their masses and inversely as the square of the distance between them; then there is a *law* to the effect that *all* objects satisfying the *generic* characterization will exhibit behaviour of a sort that falls within the *abstract* description. It turns out that the terrestrial system and the celestial systems are both specific instances of the generic kind and their behaviour is in each case of a specific sort that falls within the · abstract characterization. By virtue of its generic and abstract nature the more generic law subsumes the two more specific laws within it.[5]

One of the important features of abstract generic laws is that, as Mill at one point puts it, they are laws about laws (1872a, III, vi, 1). They state that for any specific sort of system that falls within the generic characterization *there is* a law that the behaviour of the system will satisfy the abstract characterization. Such a generic abstract law is *a law that asserts that there are laws*.

Now, a law, being a generalization, applies to as-yet-unobserved systems. In the case of a generic law about laws what this means is that the law asserts about specific systems for which specific laws are not yet known that there are such laws and that these satisfy certain abstract conditions. *The generic law about laws thus predicts the existence of as-yet-unknown or unconfirmed laws.* The law about laws thus creates a research task to discover the law that the generic law – or 'theory,' as it is often called – asserts to be there. The theory delimits a certain range of hypotheses that can then be subjected to experimental tests. The set of hypotheses consists of those that satisfy the abstract characterization; and the theory, in asserting that such a law exists, guarantees (within the inductive limits) that experiment, if carried out systematically, will discover that one of the hypotheses of the set is in fact a law. Mill emphasizes this special role of theories in guiding research by generating a range of hypotheses from among which the true law will be discovered (1872a, III, xiv, 4–6). Lakatos (1970) has spoken of a theory that predicts the existence of unconfirmed laws as one that is 'theoretically progressive'; if it leads to the confirmation of a specific law then it is 'empirically progressive.' For John Stuart Mill, then, it is characteristic of an explanatory theory that it is theoretically progressive, and its confirmation as a theory consists in showing that it is empirically progressive.

The methods by which one eliminates from a range of hypotheses all contenders but one are the methods of elimination that we have come to know as 'Mill's Methods' (1872a, II, viii). These methods use observational data to eliminate or falsify all but one of a range of contenders. But process of falsifying hypotheses results in the confirmation of one as true only to the extent that one has available, as a guide to one's research, a confirmed generic abstract theory that asserts that there is, within the range, one hypothesis that is true, as Mill recognizes (III, xxi).[6] If two specific laws are independently (III, xiv, p. 4) confirmed, then that confirmation also supports a generic abstract law under which they are both subsumed (III, iii and xxi). Suppose that the generic abstract law about laws now predicts the existence of a new specific law in a hitherto unexamined area. The result is that it delimits a range of possible hypotheses. It says that one of the hypotheses of this range is true; that is, it is a confirmed law that makes this prediction, and so far as it is confirmed, it in turn confirms this prediction. Suppose now further that the observational data eliminate all but one hypothesis in the range. Since the generic abstract law confirms that one hypothesis in the range is true, and this is the only hypothesis in the range that could be true, it follows that the generic abstract law confirms that this hypothesis is true. Thus, the data that support the acceptance of the laws in the other areas, and therefore also the acceptance of the generic abstract law, come to support through the latter the acceptance of the specific law in the new area. At the same time, the observational data in the new area support the acceptance of the hypothesis as a law. And since this law is subsumed under the generic abstract law, those data support this theory also. But then in turn, via the generic abstract law, these data also strengthen the support for the specific laws in the original areas from which the theory was first generalized (III, iv, 3). The generic abstract theory thus provides a linkage among specific laws by which the data that support the acceptance of one law support the acceptance of each of the laws (III, iii, iv, xxi).[7]

We have seen that generic abstract theories are important in guiding research. We now see that they are also important in establishing a network of inductive support that transmits such support from one area to another.

Before looking at an example of such a theory, it is worth noting one other logical feature. A generic abstract theory asserts about each of a variety of areas that in it *there is* a law of a certain sort. Now, an existence claim, to the effect that *there is* something of such-and-such a sort, is *not* shown to be false – except under very special circumstances – by *a failure to observe* something of the sort that is said to exist. The special condition obtains when we have a complete enumeration of things that could possibly be of the relevant sort. A generic abstract theory *may* yield such an enumeration of possible cases. In that circumstance, Mill's Methods give an automatic result. And in fact, if the data eliminate *all* possibilities, when the theory asserts that one of those possibilities is true, then the theory has been *falsified* and must be rejected. But a generic abstract theory may not yield an enumeration of all possibilities; for example, it may delimit a range with an infinite number of possibilities. In the latter case, *failure to find the law* asserted to exist will *not* show that the generic abstract theory is *false*. Thus, in general a generic abstract theory is *not falsifiable*. Lakatos (1970) has pointed out that an empirically progressive theory has a 'hard core' that is immune to falsification; and Kuhn (1970) has also drawn our attention to the non-falsifiable theories – he calls them 'paradigms' – that guide research. We see that Mill's views on theories are in these respects very much of a piece with these more recent discussions of scientific method and research.[8]

As an example of a law about laws that subsumes other laws under it, Mill cites one of the *laws of learning* (1872a, III, xiii, 6): 'Ideas of a pleasurable or painful character form associations more easily and strongly than other ideas, that is, they become associated after fewer repetitions, and the association is more durable.' Falling under this law, and therefore explained by it, is the law that thoughts connected with our passions are more easily excited than others; another such derived regularity is the law that thoughts connected with our interests are more firmly held in our memory; and so on. Now, the associations that the law says will be formed will depend upon individual differences, 'being proportional to the sensibility of the individual mind, and to the consequent intensity of the pain or pleasure from which the association originated.' This suggests a research program: 'It has been *suggested* ... that the same elementary law of our mental constitution, suitably followed out, *would* explain a variety of mental phenomena previously inexplicable, and in particular some of the fundamental diversities of human character and genius' (ibid.; italics added). An association is itself a regularity, but a conditioned one; that is, that an association obtains is contingent upon certain causes. The law of learning asserts that *there are* causes of associations, it asserts the sorts of things these causes are (experienced repetitions), and it asserts that *there is* a functional relationship (in the mathematical sense of 'function') between certain features of the association (its quickness of formation and its durability) and certain features of the causes (their pleasurable or painful character). This function varies from individual to individual (the variation measures their different sensibilities). We now observe that there are different mental habits, that is, associations, in poets and painters on the one hand and in historians and scientists on the other – those whose mental habits are those of the 'imagination' with its richly elaborated imagery and those whose mental habits tend to reflect the order of the facts of the world. The learning theory asserts that *there are* causes for these different habits, and gives a generic and abstract characterization of them. The research task is to attempt to discover more specific laws, which the theory asserts to be there, that is, to discover more specific characterizations of the causes that the theory asserts to be there.

Upon John Stuart Mill's account, then, associationist learning theory is a generic abstract theory that has been confirmed by, and explains, a variety of specific laws and generates a research program for the discovery of specific laws in further areas.

2   The Composition of Causes

The final case of explanation of laws is important, and Mill is correct to stress it, but as it turns out, he misunderstands its logic. In this case, as he describes it, there is 'an intermixture of laws, producing a joint effect equal to the sum of the effects of the causes taken separately. The law of the complex effect is explained by being resolved into the separate laws of the causes which contribute to it' (1872a, III, xii, 2). The example that he gives, that of the deduction of the motions of the objects in the solar system, makes clear the sort of thing that he has in mind. For Mill, there were seven planets and the sun in the solar system, to make an eight-body system. To calculate the motions of a planet in such a system, one conceptually decomposes it into a set of two-body systems. One assumes for each two-body system that the force is gravitational. One computes, for each conceptually distinguished two-body system, the motions the objects would have were each such two-body system isolated. The actual motion of an object is the vector sum of the motions imputed to it in the calculations for all the conceptually distinguished two-body systems in which it occurs. The rule that enables one to deduce the law for the complex systems is the law of vector addition of accelerations. Such a law is, for obvious reasons, known as a *composition law*.[9]

In this situation we begin with a law for complex systems. Within the complex system one conceptually distinguishes *simple* systems. Note that the distinction is conceptual only; the simple systems do not exist as isolated entities. One then takes a law for such simple systems, and deduces what would happen under the contrary-to-fact assumption that the simple systems are isolated. From this information about what would happen in the simple systems if they were isolated, the composition law enables us to deduce the law for the complex system.

What must be noted is that the composition law is a *matter-of-fact generalization*. The composition law enables us to deduce what happens when objects are not in isolated simple systems from what happens when they are in isolated simple systems. For such a deduction one needs two additional pieces of information, besides the information (that is, laws) about how the system would behave if it were isolated. The first of these further pieces of information that is needed is a knowledge of additional initial conditions telling one the relational structure by which the objects are arranged in the complex system. The second further piece of information is knowledge of a law – the composition law – that enables one to deduce the law for the complex systems from this structural knowledge and from the laws for the simple systems. Thus, in the case of the planets, the series of simple systems is the two-body systems. In each of these, one takes into account the distance along the lines joining the two objects. But to know these distances is not to know how they are arranged in the eight-body system; one needs to know as well the angles between the lines joining them. Then, given this structure, the composition law permits the deduction of the law for the complex system. However, there is nothing self-contradictory in supposing that the law for the complex system is determined not by the angles but by the volume enclosed. That shows the empirical or matter-of-fact nature of the composition law.

It is this last which Mill does not understand. What he tells us is this, that in these cases 'if we happen to know what would be the effect of each cause when acting separately from the other, we are often able to arrive deductively, or *a priori*, at a correct prediction of what will arise from their conjunct agency' (1872a, III, vi, 1). What he leaves out is the composition law. It is *not* true that from a knowledge of the laws of the simple systems, that is, from this knowledge *alone*, one can arrive *deductively* at the law for the complex system. Nor is the omission of any mention of the composition law accidental, for Mill carefully explains elsewhere (III, xi, 1–2) there are *two* stages of deductive explanation, the first in which one discovers the laws of the simple systems, and the second that consists of 'ratiocination' alone and in which the law for the complex system is deduced (1872a, III, xi, 2). Thus, on Mill's account, we have as premisses the laws for the simple systems. As Mill makes clear with his reference to 'conjunct agency' in the passage quoted just above, these are *conjoined*. From this conjunctive premiss one then deduces, a priori and by pure ratiocination, the law for the complex system. To hold this is to ignore the relevance to the behaviour of the objects in the complex systems of the *relations* that structure the object in the simple systems into the complex system; it says, in effect, that the only relation that one needs for the deduction of the law for the complex system is the *non-relation* of *logical conjunction*. This failure to acknowledge the causal relevance of the structural relations also is evident when Mill characterizes this sort of case of explanation as one 'in which the joint effect of causes is the *sum* of their separate effects' (1872a, III, vi, 2). There is a blur here between the (very different) 'and' of logical conjunction and the 'and' of arithmetical addition; but in either case – and this is the point – the 'relation' is logical and formal, not real.

This failure to recognize the causal relevance of structural relations is relevant to the criticism that the Gestalt psychologists made of their predecessors in classical psychology.[10] One of the concerns of classical psychology was (as we shall see in more detail in chapters 4 and 5) whether *relations* can be introspectively analysed into sensory contents. Wundt, somewhat implausibly, insisted that they all were (cf. 1902, pp. 278ff). Stumpf (1873 and 1883, 1890), Mach (1886), Meinong's student von Ehrenfels (1890), and, following them, Wertheimer (1922, 1923), all argued to the contrary.[11] Mach put the point this way: 'According to the view which we have so far developed, an important fact, which we shall have to discuss, remains unexplained, even though explanation must be demanded from any complete theory. If we let two series of tones begin with different tones and progress according to the same ratio of vibrations, then we recognize in both the same melody as immediately through sensation as we recognize the same figure [*Gestalt*] in two geometrically similar and similarly placed configurations. Equal melodies in different keys can be called tone configurations of the same tone figure [*Gestalt*] or similar tone configurations' (1886, p. 128). There is something common to, say, several successions of tones – the melody. This melody is a *relation* that structures each set of tones in the same way. This common structuring feature is, it is clear, given in sensation. This relational structure could, like all relations according to Wundt, be analysed introspectively into non-relational elements (1902, pp. 110–11). But it is *not* a collection of elements, of sensory contents, as von Ehrenfels argued against Wundt. Considering 'spatial figures' and 'melodies,' von Ehrenfels asks what they are 'in themselves – a mere collection of elements, or something new, something which appears with that collection, but can be distinguished from it?' (1890, p. 250).

The proof for the existence of *Gestaltqualitaeten* in our sense of the term, at least in regard to visual and auditory presentations, is provided by the similarity of spatial figures and melodies with completely different tonal or spatial foundations (which is pointed out by Mach in the passages cited). This fact cannot be reconciled, as we shall show now, with the conception of spatial and tonal configurations as mere sums of tonal and spatial determinations.

For, it can be asserted at once that different complexes of elements, if they are nothing else but the sums of these, must be the more similar, the more similar their individual elements are to each other. However, that this condition is not fulfilled for melody and spatial configuration can be proven decisively by examples. (1890, pp. 258–9).

Von Ehrenfels then gives an example, and concludes: 'Thus there can be no doubt that the similarity of spatial and tonal configurations rests on something other than the similarity of the elements with whose collection in consciousness they appear. Those configurations must therefore be something other than the sum of the elements. – The stringency of this proof seems to us unavoidable' (p. 260). What remains constant is a relational structure, even though all the non-relational sensory contents, the notes that we hear, have changed when the melody is played in a different scale or key. Since the non-relational contents all change, but the tune remains constant, this relational structure cannot consist in non-relational contents. The point here is similar to the point Reid insisted upon when he held that visible geometry was an objective feature of complex situations involving one's body, the perceptual object – both objects having a three-dimensional spatial structure – and the relations between them. Within this complex, spatial relations that are presented visually are *not*, according to Reid, the three-dimensional structures we grasp by touch, but rather another set of relations, those of the geometry of visibles, determined by those other relations given in touch, and as objectively there as the latter. These relational judgments of visual perception, Reid insists, are, contrary to Berkeley, not associations of non-spatial elements such as colours of kinaesthetic sensations.

Wertheimer (1921–3) took up the thesis of Mach and von Ehrenfels. He put the relevant point this way:

> I stand at the window, and see a house, trees, sky.
>
> And I could, then, on theoretical grounds try to sum up: there are 327 brightnesses (and tones of colour).
>
> (Have I '327'? No: sky, house, trees: and no one can realize the having of the '327' as such.)
>
> Let there be, in this particular calculation, about 120 for the house, 90 for the trees, and 117 for the sky; in any case I have *this* togetherness and *this* distribution, not 127 and 100, or 150 and 177.
>
> I *see* it in specific togetherness and specific distribution; and the manner of unity and separation [togetherness and distribution] in which I see it is not determined simply by my whimsy. It is quite certain that I cannot actualize another desired kind of coherence according to the dictates of my whimsy. (1923, p. 202)

Or, as he later expressed the point: 'What is given to me by the melody does not arise (through the agency of any auxiliary factor) as a *secondary* process from the sum of the pieces as such. Instead, what takes place in each single part already depends upon what the whole is. The flesh and blood of a tone depends from the start upon its role in the melody: A *b* as leading tone to *c* is something radically different from the *b* as tonic. It belongs to the flesh and blood of the things given in experience, how, in what role, in what function they are in the whole' (1925, p. 5). The *b* that leads to *c* is different from the *b* that does not in that the former does, while the latter does not, stand in a *relation* to *c*. Parts of wholes, as parts, are different, that is, different in kind, from what they would be by themselves, since, as parts of wholes, they stand in relations to each other. The relations cannot be reduced to a mere association of non-relational contents. This is a plausible argument against Wundt. Certainly, it is conclusive on the phenomenological point: here one must agree, relations are indefinable. However, Wundt had other axes to grind. In particular, he wanted to insist, with Berkeley, that our capacities to recognize relations are not innate but learned. On this latter, Wertheimer's case against Wundt is not as strong as he thought: as we shall see, the phenomenological indefinability of relations, upon which Wertheimer insists, is not necessarily incompatible with their being capable of introspective analysis. This is one of the implications of John Stuart Mill's account of the nature of introspective analysis. But be this as it may, Wertheimer's insistence upon the importance of relational structures is surely correct.[12] Such relational structures Wertheimer, following von Ehrenfels, called 'Gestalten.' He called attention to the existence of these relations by means of the formula that 'the whole is greater than the sum of its parts.' In the context of these Gestalts (W-Gestalts), what this means is that a relational whole consists not merely of a *mere set* or sum of the non-relational contents, but of two or more sensory elements united into a whole by an entity that is intrinsically relational. An artificial enumeration of elements is a *sinnlose Und-Verbindung*, a meaningless conjunction; a whole is not a bundle, and its integration is more than an *Und*. On the traditional (Wundtian) point of view, 'Every "complex" consists of a sum of elementary contents or pieces (e.g., sensations)' (1923, p. 12) but in fact 'The given is itself in varying degrees "structured" ("gestaltet"), it consists of more or less definitely structured wholes and whole-processes with their whole-properties and laws, characteristic whole-tendencies, and whole-determinations of parts. "Pieces" almost always appear "as parts" in whole processes' (p. 14).

Another aspect of the program of classical psychology was to analyse the sensory nervous processes that an organism undergoes before (and after) conscious experience. Wolfgang Köhler (1920) wanted to emphasize what he thought earlier psychologists had neglected, that conscious processes reflected the overall process of the nervous system as a whole, and not merely the partial processes of the subsystems: 'one cannot treat the complex of physical processes which correspond to a given visual field as a mosaic of individual excitations in purely *geometrical* (as opposed to dynamic) interrelation' (1920, p. 23); that is, as he put it more abstractly, 'an attempt to derive the validity of [a] law [for a whole] additively from parts of a system would necessarily fail. The law of the system prescribes what must take place in the parts, not the reverse' (p. 27). The partial processes are not isolated but interact; there is in fact a *total interaction* among all the parts.[13] 'The facts of vision require that we treat them as properties of a *single* physical system in which the totality of the stimulus conditions both individually and collectively is determined by the whole which they comprise' (p. 20). Thus, to discover the conscious state that reflects a sensory process interacts with others. For, in a total system of total interaction the behaviour of the parts is *not* the behaviour that the parts exhibit when the latter are isolated. Köhler, like Wertheimer, used the formula that 'the whole is greater than the sum of the parts.' In the context of Köhler's discussion, the Gestalts (K-Gestalts) were complex systems of total interaction, and what the formula meant was that the behaviour of the entities in the system was different from, and not merely the sum of, the behaviours those parts would exhibit were they undergoing the various processes they would undergo were they to exist in isolated simple systems.

Both Wertheimer and Köhler meant to attack 'analytical' philosophies of science. They had in mind by this, philosophies of science of the empiricist sort defended by John Stuart Mill. (Their immediate background in psychology was Wundt.) These philosophies of science were, the Gestalters held, 'reductionist,' and, since 'a whole is greater than the sum of its parts,' reductionism must be false. It is clear, however, that empiricism can easily accept the points of Wertheimer and Köhler. Thus, first, with reference to W-Gestalts, there is nothing incompatible with empiricism to admit both that relations are among the ontologically fundamental entities of the world and that we are acquainted with these entities. Empiricism can therefore accept Wertheimer's point that a (relational) whole is greater than the sum (set) of its (non-relational) parts. And John Stuart Mill had already made clear, as we shall see, admitting this is compatible with holding that such relations are capable of introspective analysis. It was this last point in particular that Wertheimer, like Kames and Reid before him, never understood.

Second, with reference to K-Gestalts, it is compatible with empiricism to admit that the behaviour of objects in a system of total interaction is *not* the sum of the behaviours those objects would exhibit in isolated simpler systems. In admitting the need to introduce a *composition law* to deduce the behaviour of complex systems from that of simpler systems, empiricism accepts Köhler's point that a whole (a system of total interaction) is greater than the sum of its parts (because the law for the total system is not deducible from the conjunction of the laws for its simple part systems). However, to admit this is compatible with holding that the law for the complex system is reducible to that for simpler systems: it is reducible just in case that there exists a composition law that permits such a deduction.

It must be said, though, that both Wertheimer and Köhler had some reason for their mistaken views about empiricism and what it could admit. Many empiricist psychologists were not as careful as was John Stuart Mill in acknowledging that introspective analysability is compatible with phenomenological simplicity. And John Stuart Mill himself failed to recognize the role of the composition law, and held that the behaviour of objects in complex systems could be analysed as the sum of the behaviours of those objects in simple systems.

Even here, however, we must be careful. For John Stuart Mill specifically exempted psychology from the realms to which the rule of the composition of causes applies. Mill contrasts the composition of causes of the sort found in mechanics with what he calls the 'chemical' mode of composition. 'The chemical combination of two substances produces ... a third substance with properties different from those of either of the two substances separately, or of both of them taken together' (1872a, III, vi, 1). In the case of the mechanical composition of causes, 'the joint effect of causes is the sum of their separate effects,' while in the chemical mode the effect 'is heterogeneous to them' (ibid.).

In the chemical mode of combination, when certain simple systems are put into relation, a new property or entity comes into existence. This property cannot be defined in terms of the non-relational properties of the entities in the simpler system or in terms of the relations among those objects that structure them into the complex system. Now, a composition law permits one to deduce the law for the complex system from a knowledge of the laws for simple systems and a knowledge of the relations that structure the simple systems into the complex. It follows that if there is a property or entity that cannot be defined in terms of the non-relational properties the objects have in the simpler systems or the structuring relations, then a composition law is not possible, or, at least, if there is one, then it breaks down at the level of complexity at which the new property or entity appears, or, as one says, *emerges*. The important point for our purposes is that this chemical mode of combination occurs regularly in mental phenomena: 'the laws of the phenomena of mind are sometimes analogous to mechanical, but sometimes also to chemical laws. When many impressions or ideas are operating in the mind together, there sometimes takes place a process of a similar kind to chemical combination' (1872a, VI, iv, 3). There are, he argues, 'cases of mental chemistry, in which it is proper to say that the simple ideas generate, rather than that they compose, the complex ones' (ibid.). Mill does not deny that there are cases of mechanical composition in psychology. To the extent that Mill misunderstands the idea of a composition law, Köhler's criticism will apply. But Mill also, we see, holds that there are levels of complexity in which new mental phenomena emerge. To this extent Köhler's criticism does not apply.

The criticisms by the Gestalters of classical psychology that are based on an appeal to the formula that a whole is greater than the sum of its parts are thus, we see, entirely mistaken; the best that can be said is that the Gestalters were making the same mistakes as the classical psychologists whom they criticized. As for those criticisms that concern, not the philosophy of science, but the specific empirical theories of their predecessors, these we shall have occasion to look at, if only briefly, below (chapters 4 and 5).

For our immediate purposes, however, what is important is the distinction that Mill draws between a complex idea *consisting* of simpler ideas and a complex idea being *generated by* simpler ideas of which, however, it does *not consist*. If one goes back in the empiricist tradition to Locke, this is a distinction that does not exist: a complex idea consists of the simpler ideas from which it was generated. However, the distinction is clearly useful to John Stuart Mill in his efforts to defend utilitarianism by modifying the psychology of his father and of Bentham. For, what it permits Mill to hold is that certain simple mental states generate further states that are qualitatively distinct from those simpler ones. Thus, for example, a reply to Reid in perception becomes possible: a judgment may be simple, and *not consist* of simpler ideas, while yet being *generated by* simpler ideas. A reply to those who charge utilitarianism with eliminating specifically moral motives is also possible: value judgments can be qualitatively distinct with that quality being simpler and not definable in terms of quantitative differences, while yet emerging out of a quantitative accumulation of simple mental states.

It is this notion that we must explore. In particular, we must connect it to the notion of 'analysis.' If a 'complex idea' does *not consist in* simple ideas, can it be *analysed into* them? The answer is affirmative, but it depends upon the particular account of introspective analysis that John Stuart Mill proposes. It is this account that we discuss in chapter 3. In chapter 4 we look at the relation of this account of the younger Mill to the way 'analysis' works in the psychology of James Mill.

THREE

Introspective Analysis

John Stuart Mill holds that a complex idea may consist of elements that have so fused together, and coalesced into a unity, that those elements are no longer distinguishable as separate parts of the complex idea. In such cases, he says, the elements are not 'integrant' parts but rather 'metaphysical' parts (1872b, p. 259). It is our task to come to a clear understanding of this notion of a 'metaphysical' part, that is, to understand how a mental entity can be said to consist of parts that are not really, that is, not integrant, parts of that entity. It is perhaps not surprising that introspective analysis reveals these metaphysical parts that are not literal parts.

In going about this task, we begin historically, with a discussion of the notion of analysing an idea in Locke and in Hume. In the second section we see how John Stuart Mill can be understood as modifying this traditional notion of analysis so as to overcome certain difficulties raised by Berkeley and Horne Tooke.

1   Integrant Parts

Consider Locke's account of an idea of some particular sort of substance (1700, II, xxiii, 3, 14). Take the example of an apple. This complex idea consists of various simple ideas, those of colour, shape, taste, smell, texture, and so on. These simple ideas are all of a sensory character, and when they are combined into the complex idea the result is an image of the apple.

Three things should be noticed. First, upon Locke's account the complex idea has the simple ideas as genuine parts; in Mill's phrase, they are integrant parts. Second, we can describe the complex in two ways. We describe it once as an apple; in this case we use a term that refers to the complex as a whole. But we also describe it by naming and listing its (integrant) parts. Third, the several parts of the complex are derived from different sense organs; they are the products of different sensory processes in the organism. The external object, the apple, affects each of the organs (roughly) simultaneously; the sensory contents that these processes produce are experienced simultaneously; experienced thus, they are associated together in the mind to form the complex idea of an apple.

When we describe the complex as an *apple*, we are attending to the complex itself, as a whole, and as a unity, rather than to its parts. A description of an entity simply as it appears to consciousness and without any attempt to attend to parts that may be in it let us call the *phenomenological description*.[1]

The second description proceeds by listing the parts. Since the complex idea is analysed into these parts, let us call it the *analytical description*. The analytical description uses a more restricted vocabulary than does the phenomenological description. The vocabulary of the analytical description refers to simple sensory contents, colours, shapes, tastes, and so on; no terms in this vocabulary refer to the wholes that the simple parts constitute when associated together. The vocabulary of the phenomenological description is much richer; it contains terms that refer to the wholes as such.

However, the *model* for analysis is, for Locke, clearly that of *definition*. In fact, the parts into which the complex idea of an apple, or of any substance, is analysed are said by Locke to be the 'nominal definition' of the substance (1700, III, vi, 2, 7).[2] Now, in a nominal definition, the defining phrase is mere shorthand for the term that is defined.[3] It follows that from the *analytical description of a complex one can infer the phenomenological description*. For Locke, what justifies this inference is the definitional connection that links both the words in the two vocabularies of the phenomenological and the analytical descriptions, and also the complex with its simple, integrant parts.

As we shall see, the notion of introspective analysis, on the account of John Stuart Mill, will retain this feature of two descriptions, one phenomenological and one with a reduced, or analytical, vocabulary. Retained, too, is the idea that the phenomenological description can be inferred from the analytical description. What will change is that the analytical description will no longer refer to integrant parts; Mill gives up the notion that the analysis undertaken by the introspective psychologist is anything like the logical analysis of a concept. Thus, when Mill continues to hold that the phenomenological description can be inferred from the analytical description, he has abandoned the notion that the basis of this inference is a definition; the basis of the inference must therefore be found elsewhere.

Notice about Locke's account how the *logical structure* is supposed to reflect the *genetic history* in the sense that the logical analysis of the complex idea into the definitional parts at the same time reveals the products of sensory stimuli, which in turn produce by association the complex idea: *the logical parts of the complex idea are also the mental states that causally produce that idea*. Analysis thus reveals both the logical structure of a concept and the genetic antecedents of a complex mental state.

When John Stuart Mill gives his revised account of introspective analysis, he gives up, as we have said, the model of logical analysis that Locke used; the parts that analysis reveals are no longer integrant parts. But he retains the notion that introspective analysis of an idea or mental state reveals the genetic antecedents. Thus, the 'parts' of an idea or mental state that are revealed by introspective analysis are the genetic antecedents of that idea or mental state. Introspective analysis does not yield integrant parts; the parts that it yields Mill calls 'metaphysical parts.' Thus, the metaphysical parts of an idea or mental states are the genetic antecedents of that idea or state.

Before turning to Mill, however, another point about logical analysis must be made, since this point is relevant to the development of the notion of analysis.

For Locke 'the meaning of words' consists in 'the ideas they are made to stand for by him that has them' (1700, III, iv, 6), and 'the only sure way of making known the signification of the name of any simple idea is by presenting to his senses that subject, which may produce it in his mind, and make him actually have the idea, that word stands for' (III, xi, 14). The main function of language is the recording and communication of our ideas (III, x, 23). But, as the Swiss philosopher Crousaz was to point out, 'most words, used by Men, express their Sentiments and Passions rather than their ideas' (1724, I: 7–8). It was precisely this point that the moral relativists, whether moral sceptics such as Hobbes or moral realists such as Hutcheson and Hume, insisted upon when they rejected objectivist interpretations of our moral sense. But it also appears elsewhere in Hume's philosophy.

According to Hume, the judgment that As cause Bs involves the assertion that there is a *necessary connection* between something's being A and something's being B (1739, p. 77).[4] If however, we examine the objects of such judgments, namely, As and Bs, we discover no necessary connection, only As being followed by Bs (pp. 91–2). Objectively, then, there are no necessary connections, only regularities: objectively, causation *is* regularity. In this sense, we may define a cause to be 'an object precedent and contiguous to another, and where all the objects resembling the former are plac'd in a like relation of priority and contiguity to those objects, that resemble the latter' (p. 172). This omits, however, the idea of necessary connection that was in the original judgment of causation. What distinguishes the judgment that all As are Bs from the judgment that As cause Bs is not something objective – it has been established that there is no objective difference between the judgments that all As are Bs and that As cause Bs. Rather, the difference between the two judgments lies in the fact that in the case of the causal judgment the idea of a B is *as a matter of habit associated with* the idea of an A; that is, when an impression or an idea of A is before the mind then that, as a matter of habit, is regularly followed by the idea of a B (pp. 155–6). This means that we may also define a cause to be 'an object precedent and contiguous to another, and so united with it in the imagination, that the idea of the one determines the mind to form the idea of the other, and the impression of the one to form a more lively idea of the other' (p. 172). This habit works independently of our will – Hume rejects (pp. 623ff) the Cartesian doctrine that the will alone can determine our beliefs; the habit is therefore *felt* as a 'determination' (p. 166). The idea of necessity is not derived from the objects judged about; our impressions of such objects contain no impression of a necessary connection (pp. 164–5). Nor can a habit, as such, that is, a propensity, yield an impression from which our idea of necessity is derived. The impression from which the idea of necessity is derived is thus the *feeling* that the mind is *constrained by the habit* of inferring Bs from As: 'necessity is nothing but the determination of the thought to pass from causes to effects and from effects to causes' (p. 166). Thus, the complex mental state 'the judgment that As cause Bs' may be analysed into the components '(the judgment that whenever an A then a B)' and '(the feeling of being constrained to infer a B from an A).' The former is the objective content, the latter a subjective feeling. And the idea of causation has two ideas as parts, namely, the idea that 'one sort of thing regularly follows another' and the idea that 'the mind is determined habitually to infer one sort of thing from another.' In the causal judgment, however, the two components are *fused into a unity* in which the subjective feeling becomes inseparable from the objective content. This fusion is caused by the fact that 'the mind has a great propensity to spread itself on external objects, and to conjoin with them any internal impressions, which they occasion, and which always make their appearance at the same time that these objects discover themselves to the senses' (p. 163); that is, we have a *habitual association* not only of the idea of an *A* with the idea of a *B* but also with the feeling of determination that accompanies this inference, and this association unites not only the ideas but also the ideas with the subjective feeling. And the idea of causation creates the illusion that causation involves an objective necessary connection because it, too, is a *fusion* of two ideas, that of regularity and that of a felt subjective determination (cf. Wilson, 1989d).

A habit is a regularity, but it is a conditioned regularity. Hume proposes that habits of inference are acquired by association: if we experience regularly an *A* being followed by a *B* then this observed constant conjunction *causes* the habit to form of an impression or an idea of an *A* being followed by the idea of a *B*, and in turn the feeling that the mind is determined to infer a *B* from an *A*: 'after a frequent repetition, I find, that upon the appearance of one of the objects, the mind is *determin'd* by custom to consider its usual attendant, and to consider it in a stronger light upon account of its relation to the first object. 'Tis this impression, then, or *determination*, which affords one the idea of necessity' (1739, p. 156). The habit is thus an acquired pattern of thought; it is a pattern that is *learned*. The conditions of learning are thus the conditions under which the regularity holds.

Several points should be noted. First, the analysis of causal judgments and of the idea of causation yields not only objective contents, but also subjective elements or feelings. Thus, judgments about external objects may turn out upon analysis to have subjective elements as parts. Our objective judgments are, in other words, often the product of both objective contents and subjective contents too.

Second, Hume tends to think of analysis, upon the model of Locke, as logical analysis, so that the analysis of the idea of causation is an analysis into its logically distinct components. But at the same time he also tends to think of the parts as, to use his terms, 'spreading' one onto the other so as to form a unity that is more than a mere conjunction. When such a fusion occurs, it is evident that the parts that analysis yields cannot be integrant parts. Hume is thus moving away from an idea of analysis as yielding integrant parts to one that yields, in Mill's terms, metaphysical parts.

For, third, the judgment, that whenever an *A* then a *B*, is itself analysable into ideas of an *A* and a *B* conceived in a certain way (1739, p. 96), and these ideas are derived from the antecedent impressions that produced both the habit that associates them regularly in judgment and the feeling of determination that also comes to be associated with them in the causal judgment. Thus, as analysis proceeds we are led to metaphysical parts, which reveal the genetic antecedents of the judgment.[5]

Hume is thus moving away from Locke to a position that is closer to that which, as we shall see, John Stuart Mill develops.

Mill himself agrees with the substance, though not the details, of Hume's account of causation. He agrees with Hume that, objectively considered, causation, or, more generally, lawfulness, is the same as regularity (1872a, III, i, 2; III, iv). He also agrees with Hume that what distinguishes laws from regularities that are, as one says, accidental generalities is that there is in the former case a habit of inference that is absent in the latter case (1869, I: 350, 402ff). But Hume's account of the habit is in fact simplistic. On the one hand, Hume argues that we know there is no necessary connection between two things A and B, because we can conceive A apart from B, that is, we can separate the idea of the other (1739, pp. 79–80). On the other hand, when we judge that an A causes a B then there is a habit such that the mind is so determined that whenever the idea of an A enters the mind, then it is followed by the idea of a B; and, if that is so, it would seem that we cannot, after all, conceive an A apart from a B. John Stuart Mill takes up this point, and offers a more complex account of the habit forma-tion which allows that there are habits of association of ideas such that, in spite of the association, under certain conditions the associated ideas can be separated; the account remains, however, faithful to the basic assumptions of the generic abstract theory of learning that Hume proposes, and specifically to the theoretical assumption that learning consists in the formation of habits of thought on the basis of experi-enced patterns of objects (1869, I: 364n, 404–13).

This sort of modification illustrates quite nicely the point that there was in classical psychology a research program in which hypotheses are advanced, criticized in the light of data, and then revised, all within the context of a framework provided by a generic abstract theory.

In his development of the theory, Mill does allow, in contrast to Hume, that there are associations that become sufficiently strong that it is in fact impossible under any conditions to separate the associated ideas (1869, I: 97ff; 1872b, p. 257). One such inseparable association is, he suggests, that between the ideas of an event and that of a cause which constitutes judgment that every event has a cause (1872a, III, v, p. 1). This principle is a generic abstract hypothesis – it asserts about each member of the most generic class, namely, that of events, that *there is* a cause for that entity, where the notion of cause is itself abstractly characterized in terms of a gapless regularity – and in the logic of induction this principle functions as the supreme principle for the eliminative techniques of 'Mill's Methods' (1872a, III, viii).[6] Hume suggests that the idea of an event and that of a cause are separable (1739, I, iii, 3), but Mill concedes to opponents of Hume such as Kames and Reid the possibility that the contrary of the causal principle may be inconceivable (1872a, II, vi–vii). Besides arguing that Kames and Reid are in fact wrong because there are many people who believe that there are uncaused events, and because those practised in analysis *can* conceive the ideas, Mill makes three points.

First, even if the contrary is inconceivable, that does not make the contrary logically impossible (cf. 1872a, II, vi, 5). In Locke, separability by psychological analysis and logical separability are one; but in Mill these two have themselves been separated as the notion of psychological analysis has come to be elucidated. Mill's account of psychology thus leads to a break with a long tradition that goes back through Locke and Descartes to Aristotle, identifying psychological conceivability with logical possibility.[7] Second, even if the contrary of a proposition is inconceivable, it does not follow that knowledge of the proposition is instinctual, or that it is a priori (cf. 1872a, II, vi, 4). But recognizing that inconceivability does not imply innateness raised the problem that if introspective analysis separates a mental state into its genetic antecedents, then how does one conclude that a belief is not innate if one cannot rely upon inseparability as evidence? As we shall see below (chapter 5), Mill addresses this question, and proposes that we may discover that a belief is learned or acquired rather than innate through means other than introspective analysis.

Third, in any case, strong belief is not the same as evidence. The fact that a belief is firmly implanted does not imply its truth. One must distinguish the firmness of a belief from the strength of its evidential support. Evidence is only one of the sources, or causes, of firm beliefs. Like Hume, Mill points out that there are many sources of firm belief besides evidence, for example, education, national character, and prejudice. Indeed, even if the belief were instinctual, even that would not establish its truth (cf. 1872a, II, vii, p. 1): all that would follow is that all of mankind is under the permanent necessity of believing what may be false. Even for instinctual beliefs one can ask if there is evidence for their truth where the evidence is such that we *ought* to assent to it, quite independently of what we *do* assent to. Mill's point here is entirely correct, and it shows how ineffectual is the Kames-Reid appeal to instinct once that appeal is separated, as science *must* separate it, from the providential teleology in which Kames and Reid place it.

2   Metaphysical Parts

Berkeley attacked Locke's doctrine of abstract ideas. One of his points is important for our purposes. He asks us to consider the abstract idea of a triangle as such. On Locke's analysis of a complex idea, like that of an apple, a whole is analysed into its parts. Now, the idea of a triangle as such is a whole, for it is a genus that comprehends several mutually incompatible species under it – equilateral, scalene, and so on. But since one of these species excludes the others, they cannot all be part of the whole in the way in which the taste, colour, shape, and so on, are all part of the idea of an apple. So much the worse for Locke's doctrine of abstract ideas, Berkeley concludes (1734, Intro. PP 7–10, PP 13– 16). This argument is often dismissed as being singularly weak, but, given Locke's model of analysis as dividing a whole into its *integrant* parts, it is in fact a substantive criticism of Locke. In effect, Locke's model requires that a mental state be a *conjunction* of elements:

apple = taste *and* colour *and* shape *and* ...

But the idea of a triangle that Berkeley introduces requires a *disjunctive* account:

triangle = equilateral *or* isosceles *or* ...

One could suggest that since *and* and *or* are two different ways of compounding ideas one could analyse ideas of the sort

(α) $A = a_1$ & a_2 & a_3

into the parts a_1, a_2, and a_3 together with a feeling corresponding to conjunction, much as Hume analysed the idea of causation by reference to a feeling. Correspondingly, ideas of the sort

(β) $T = t_1$ or t_2 or t_3

will be analysable into the parts t_1, t_2, and t_3 together with a feeling corresponding to disjunction.[9] But then we have A analysed into the parts

(γ) a_1, a_2, a_3, *and*

while T is analysed into the parts

(δ) t_1, t_2, t_3, *or*

and so long as the parts are thought of as *integrant* parts we will still have the mutually exclusive t_i jointly present in a single idea. The suggestion is therefore no solution. In fact, it seems evident that the problem will remain so long as mutually exclusive species must be treated as integrant parts of complex ideas.

Whether he knew it or not, the solution to the problem was given by Horne Tooke. What we *define*, he proposed, is *words, not ideas* (1798, pp. 47–51). 'Indeed I do not,' he says, 'allow [the parts of speech] to be the *signs* of different sorts of *ideas*, or of different *operations* of the mind.' He continues: 'The business of the mind, as far as it concerns Language, appears to me to be very simple. It extends no farther than to receive impressions, that is, to have Sensations or Feelings. What are called its operations, are merely the operations of Languages.' And so abbreviation or definition is 'Abbreviation of Terms' and not as Locke (1700, III, vi, p. 2) would have it, the forming of a 'nominal essence' which is 'that complex idea the word ... stands for.' This move to separate the definition of terms from the analysis of ideas creates a context that permits one to accept (β) as a definition on an equal basis to (α), that is, *as definitions of words*, while at the same time rejecting the impossible (δ) as the *analysis of the idea* expressed by the word defined by (β). In Locke, the psychological analysis of ideas and the logical analysis of concepts coincided. We have seen that Hume, in a tentative way, moved away from this. Although the logical model was retained in principle, Hume also held that the ideas that we analyse are unities in which the parts into which it is analysed are fused together and are not themselves literally there in their own persons as integrant parts. What Horne Tooke does is break the tie between logical analysis and psychological or, as we have called it, introspective analysis. In fact, it is now possible that the idea (or, more generally, the mental state) that is introspectively analysed is different in kind from the metaphysical parts that appear only upon analysis; and that it may even have integrant parts that do not appear as metaphysical parts. But to suggest a solution to a problem is not to work it out; that task was left to John Stuart Mill.

The notion of learning by association is, very crudely, this. Several times we experience a conjunction:

an *A* and (at the same time/then) a *B*

The conjunction is simultaneous or successive. As a result of experiencing several of these conjunctions we acquire the habit:

> Whenever we experience an *A* we experience a whole
> consisting of *A* and (at the same time/followed by) *B*

If it is simultaneous, we have a synchronous association; if it is successive the association is diachronic. Which sort of association depends upon whether the experienced conjunctions were simultaneous or successive. In either case, however, on the simplistic model of the mental states that are analysed, the product of the associative process is a *whole* in which the *parts are together as integrant parts*, either simultaneously or successively. This is the *law of learning by association*.[10]

Introspective analysis consists of two tasks when it is carried out in a systematic way. The first task is to identify the whole with which we are concerned. This identification consists in applying to the whole the *phenomenological description*. Performing the task involves, first, forming the intention to apply such a description when the whole is experienced, and then, second, carrying out that intention when we experience the whole. When we form the intention to carry out the task, we are said to be *set* to perform the task. Specifically, the first task is performed under a *phenomenological set*.

The second task is to identify the parts of the whole with which we are concerned. This identification consists of attending to the parts in turn and applying to them terms from a reduced vocabulary; the task, when completed, yields the *analytical description*. Again, in performing the task, there are two parts; forming the intention, and carrying it out. In particular, the second task is performed under an *analytical set*.

(The vocabulary of 'task' and 'set' derives from a later stage of the history of introspective psychology, when the psychologists at Würzburg, led by Külpe, found it necessary to begin to label explicitly and formally what had been left informal by previous psychologists.[11] But, as Mill makes clear in a variety of places, analysis is something that, to be well done, requires practice, and is something which, when practised, is done so deliberately and intentionally [cf. 1871a, III, xxi, 1; 1873, p. 141]. So the later vocabulary simply makes explicit what really is implicit in Mill's own practice and in his own characterization of that practice.)

On the simple account of association given by Locke, Hume, and Hartley, the law of learning by association immediately establishes that the parts which the analysis yields are the genetic antecedents of the complex whole that is analysed. Note that there is no a priori reason why the parts obtained by analysis are genetic antecedents. As the parts of a chicken are not like the parts of an egg, so there is no a priori

reason why the product of a mental process should have as parts the
entities that are its genetic antecedents. Hence, if it *is* true that the parts
into which a mental whole is analysed are the genetic antecedents of the
whole, then that is something that is true only a posteriori. In fact, in
this case, that connection between the parts and the genetic antecedents is established by the a posteriori laws of the associationist theory of
learning.

John Stuart Mill modifies this simplistic model to eliminate the
requirement that the genetic antecedents be integrant parts of the
whole being analysed. The idea or mental state being analysed is, once
again, a *whole*, which is a *unity*. But now it is not assumed that the ideas
of the sensations that are the genetic antecedents of the whole are
actually present in the latter; it is not assumed that what one does under
the analytic set is to distinguish integrant parts of a whole. But from the
fact that the genetic antecedents are not actually present in the whole
being analysed, it does not follow that they are not *recoverable from* that
whole, that is, *potentially* present and ready to be realized by association
if the occasion permits. It is just this that John Stuart Mill suggests
actually happens. An association of elements produces, by fusing those
elements, a mental state different in kind from those elements that
cease to be distinguishable in it as real parts. But under analysis, that is,
as a consequence of being in the analytic set, the associations that
produced the whole are recovered by consciousness. Upon Mill's
account, then, the genetic antecedents of the mental state that is being
analysed are not actually, but only potentially, present in the whole
being analysed; and under the analytic set that disposition is actualized
and the associations that produced that mental state reappear before
consciousness. If the mental chemistry works so that the ingredients
out of which a mental state is produced are no longer parts of that state,
none the less those ingredients are always potentially there. Analysis, if
you wish, undoes the mental chemistry and uncovers the ingredients
that are always potentially recoverable from the mental state that they
produce.

John Stuart Mill presents these points in the *Logic* (1872a, VI, iv, 3),
where 'The principal investigations of Psychology [are] characterized'
(p. 851). The elementary laws of psychology, we are told, are of two
kinds, namely, first, the laws according to which every sensation
produces its corresponding idea (image), and, second, the laws of
association for ideas (pp. 852–3). These basic laws he holds to have
been established as any basic law must be, by the methods of eliminative
induction, that is, 'the ordinary methods of experimental inquiry'

(p. 853). Having obtained these laws, the investigator can go on to ask how far they can go towards explaining the whole of psychology.

> It is obvious that complex laws of thought and feeling not only may, but, must, be generated from these simple laws. And it is to be remarked, that the case is not always one of Composition of Causes: the effect of concurring causes is not always precisely the sum of the effects of those causes when separate, *nor even always an effect of the same kind with them* [italics added]. Reverting to the distinction which occupies so prominent a place in the theory of induction; the laws of the phenomena of mind are sometimes analogous to the mechanical, but sometimes also to chemical laws. When many impressions or ideas are operating in the mind together, there sometimes takes place a process of a similar kind to chemical combination. When impressions have been so often experienced in conjunction, that each of them calls up readily and instantaneously the ideas of the whole group, those ideas sometimes melt and coalesce into one another, and appear not several ideas, but one; in the same manner as, when the seven prismatic colours are presented to the eye in rapid succession, the sensation produced is that of white. But as in the last case it is correct to say that the seven colours when they rapidly follow one another *generated* white, but not that they actually *are* white; so it appears to me that the complex idea, formed by the blending together of several simpler ones, should, even when it really appears simple (that is, when the separate elements are not consciously distinguishable in it,) be said to *result from*, or *be generated by*, the simple ideas, not to *consist* of them ... These therefore are cases of mental chemistry; in which it is proper to say that the simple ideas generate, rather than that they compose, the complex ones. (pp. 853–4)

Analysis, that is, psychological or introspective analysis, yields *parts*. Yet these parts are not literally *in* the wholes of which they are said to be parts. As we have seen Mill put it elsewhere, they are not *integrant* parts (1872b, p. 259). Nor is the whole a *sum* of those parts. This point of the *Logic* is also made clearly in a note to the *Analysis*: 'When a complex feeling is generated out of elements very numerous and various, and in a corresponding degree indeterminate and vague, but so blended together by a close association, the effect of a long series of experiences, as to have become inseparable, the resulting feeling always seems not

only very unlike any one of the elements composing it, but very unlike
the sum of those elements' (1869a, II: 321). Analysis is thus of wholes
into parts that are, often at least, different in kind. But it is also evident
that if all this is to work, then several *empirical assumptions* must be
made, parallel to, but different from the empirical assumption that was
made even in the simple case and which guaranteed that the parts into
which a mental state was analysed were the genetic antecedents. Let us
look again at the notion of introspective analysis as John Stuart Mill
presents it in order to discover what these empirical assumptions are.

One experiences a certain phenomenon, for example, a house.
One is required to give two descriptions of it. One first gives a
description of it as a *whole*, for example, 'This is a house.' This we have
called the *phenomenological* description. This description is given under
a phenomenological set. One then gives a second description of it in
terms of what the younger Mill calls its *metaphysical parts* (1872b, p. 259),
for example, in the case of the house one describes it thus: 'This is a
composite composed of bricks, mortar, etc.,' or, more ultimately, 'This
is a composite composed of colour, shape, resistance, etc.' (ibid.). This
is an *analytical* description, given under the analytical set. The
phenomenological description D_p is given by means of the phenomenological vocabulary v_p; and the analytical description D_A is given by
means of the analytical vocabulary v_A. The research program of
introspective analysis consists in the attempt to discover, first, the
minimal vocabulary v_A, the terms of which are generally assumed (*this
is an empirical assumption*) to refer to the sensory qualities (both external
and internal); *second*, the laws associating each specific D_p with a specific
D_A where, *third*, with these laws and this v_A for any D_A one can infer a
unique corresponding D_p (*this too is an empirical assumption*). Then there
is one further crucial ingredient in the orienting theory of this research
program. This is the *genetic hypothesis* that the entities into which a
whole is analysed are also those from which, as we saw Mill say, the
whole *results* or is *generated*. The laws of this generation are, of course,
the laws of association and the laws by which ideas are caused by
impressions. That is, *the guiding assumption is that the introspective analysis
of a phenomenon uncovers the genetic antecedents of that phenomenon*. Thus,
what replaces the logical model of analysis is the *empirical assumption*
that *the sensory contents that generate a mental phenomenon continue to be
associated with that phenomenon; this association is dispositional and is made
actual under the analytical set*. Thus, something is a part – a metaphysical
part – of a mental state and a genetic antecedent of it only if it is in fact
recovered by association under the analytical set; that is, something is a

metaphysical part of a mental phenomenon only if association reveals it to be in fact such. The empirical assumption that thus replaces the logical model may be expressed as two laws. The first is:

(L₁) There is a minimal analytical vocabulary, and there are laws of association, such that for any phenomenon the laws yield from it under the analytical set a description in terms of the analytical vocabulary and such that for any such analytical description the laws ensure that it determines a unique phenomenon.

The second is:

(L₂) For any phenomenon, the description of it in terms of the analytical vocabulary is also a description of the causal antecedents from which the phenomenon was generated in accordance with the laws of association.

These two generic abstract laws guide the research program of introspective analytical psychology.

Several points are here in order. First, Mill clearly recognizes that genetic investigation is not the whole of psychology. The wholes described by the D_p's not only have causes but also effects, and these, too, must be investigated (1872a, VI, iv, 3). As we have seen, earlier thinkers like Butler were content to describe how various sorts of mental state, for example, the deliverances of conscience, function in our mental life, and ignored the search for (empirical) causes. What James Mill, in the *Analysis of the Phenomena of the Human Mind*, insisted upon was that such causes exist and must be investigated. The *Analysis* is therefore largely concerned with genetic questions. What John Stuart Mill comes to feel constrained to point out is that the search for causes is not the whole of psychology and should not exclude the equally important investigation of effects, that is, functions.

Second, the younger Mill also feels constrained (1872a, VI, iv, 3) to point out the weakness of some of his father's conclusions. Guided by the associationist theory of learning, the author of the *Analysis* often points out against his opponents that because an effect *C* is different from *A* and *B* that does not preclude that *A* and *B* are causes of *C*, and he then, too often, concludes that since *C* is regularly preceded by *A* and *B* the latter *are* the causes of *C*. But this sort of appeal to the Method of Agreement establishes only that *A* and *B* are necessary conditions for *C*, not that they are sufficient. The elder Mill's conclusion of causal sufficiency requires more experimental data than he often supplies.

Third, the younger Mill clearly recognizes the *empirical nature* of the claim that such-and-such constitutes the analytical vocabulary v_A, that is, that such-and-such are the elements into which all compound ideas can be analysed: 'nothing can positively prove that any particular one of the constituents of the mind is ultimate. We can only presume it to be such, from the ill success of every attempt to resolve into simpler elements' (1859a, p. 349).[12] It is not at all surprising, therefore, that one finds different psychologists making different claims about what is in the analytical vocabulary, that is, as they would put it, different claims about what the basic elementary contents are, and then claiming that there is empirical evidence one way or another. It should be noted, however, that the evidence can never be absolutely conclusive. Those who claim that such-and-such constitutes the set of elements, that is, the minimal vocabulary, are claiming that the negative existential 'it is not the case that there are other elements,' is true, and negative existentials, like their logically equivalent affirmative generalizations, cannot be proved conclusively on the basis of the limited data that alone can be provided by observation. Furthermore, if one wishes to deny that such-and-such phenomenon is an element, then what one is claiming is that, in the analytical vocabulary that one is proposing, 'there is an analytical description sufficient to determine that phenomenon.' This is an existential claim, and failure to find such a description does not necessarily falsify one's claim; depending upon the context, it may follow merely that one has not tried sufficiently hard to discover the correct analysis. So the debates over the number and nature of the elements in classical psychology were never simple.

Fourth, for Locke the analysis determined a unique idea being analysed, but also, conversely, the idea determined a unique analysis, since the model of analysis was definitional: the parts into which a complex was analysed *defined* the complex. But Mill relaxes this requirement somewhat. He points out that in fact the same antecedents may generate different phenomena (1872a, VI, iv, 4). Thus, for example, pleasure and pain have a role to play in learning, and people have different susceptibilities to pleasure and pain; learning will thus be different according to these different susceptibilities. Such differences may be due to (a) innate differences (for example, some people have more acute hearing than others; some people are colour-blind); or to (b) different previous histories (for example, the second reading of a poem is very different from the first, though the stimuli are the same); or to (c) a variety of physiological factors. Thus, the same causal factors operating in different contexts will produce different effects.

This means, for *one*, that (L_1) might hold while (L_2) does not. That is, it is possible that every analysis uniquely determines a phenomenon, but that not all the relevant causal antecedents appear among the things mentioned in the analysis.

It may also mean, for *two*, that the same sort of phenomenon may, in different contexts, yield different analyses; that is, even if every analysis determines exactly one sort of phenomenon, there may be several analyses that yield the same sort of phenomenon. In such a case (L_1) will hold at best *ceteris paribus*. In particular, which analysis will be given will depend upon whether factors (a), (b), and (c) that Mill mentions are held constant.

It may turn out, then, that different people give different analyses of the same phenomenon. This sort of concern became relevant when psychologists set about to actually try experimentally to determine the analytical vocabulary v_A, that is, the set of psychological elements, something that both Mills approached only programmatically, assuming such a set exists, without trying by experimental test to delimit it. Disputes between rival schools about what can be found in the set of elements may thus turn out to be matters of individual differences rather than fundamental disagreement. It was proposed by Titchener (1896) in this context, as a way of saving the Wundtian system, that psychology should concern itself with the 'average' or 'generalized mind,' and should, in effect, use statistical procedures so to average out the variations that (L_1) does hold (cf. Boring 1957, pp. 414, 507). This saves the research program of the psychology of introspective analysis in a sort of purity that keeps it as close as possible to the original Lockean model of logical analysis, but does so only by insisting that psychology restrict itself to imperfect knowledge of the statistical sort. The pull to explanatory power remained, however, to move scientists towards trying to eliminate the imperfections that Wundt insisted were essential to the research program of psychology; in other words, so much the worse for the research program, there are scientifically better things to do. This scientifically better task was to investigate the relevant causal factors (a), (b), and (c) that Wundt attempted to 'average away' but which had to be investigated if the explanatory gaps marked by the presence of statistical averaging were to be filled. These factors are, however, often not parts of the conscious process. Psychology was thus forced in the end, by the pull of the notion of explanatory power, to go beyond the idea that it was simply a science of the consciousness. In the end, the program of introspective analysis that required psychology to limit itself to the study of conscious states was seen as a sterile block to progress towards a more genuinely explanatory science (cf. Boring 1957, pp. 331, 506–7). In pointing out the relevance of factors (a), (b), and (c), Mill was not only allowing for the possibility that psychology, or at least that science which would include the science of mind as a part, would advance beyond the program of introspective analysis towards a broader concern with the whole person as a consciousness incarnate; but Mill, in indicating the relevance of these factors, was in a way pointing to the inevitability of the development of such a science broader than introspective psychology. His own emphasis remained, however, on the program of introspective analysis, and it would take much work before psychology would in fact break away from it – much work that, from the perspective of later developments, was the boring sort of detailed undertaking the only significant upshot of which is to show the sterility of the old program of psychology as the science concerned with the analysis of mental, that is, conscious, phenomena.

For our immediate concerns, however, with John Stuart Mill, the point that we require is simply that, of the two laws (L₁) and (L₂), which define the role of analysis in the research program of introspective psychology, *one might accept the first of these while rejecting the second.* The significance of this will become apparent in the next chapter.

In the passages from Mill that we examined just above, he makes explicit reference to the idea that, in psychology, the mode of composition is chemical, not mechanical, and that the effect may often in this mental chemistry be more than the sum of its effects. This point bears emphasis.

As we saw in the preceding chapter, John Stuart Mill distinguishes two sorts of case for the joint action of several causes (1872a, III, vi, 1). One is the mechanical, in which the effect of several causes is the *sum* of the effects those causes would have were they acting separately. The principle of the 'Composition of Causes' applies such cases. To the mechanical, Mill opposes the chemical: 'The chemical combination of two substances produces ... a third substance with properties different from those of either the two substances separately, or both of them taken together' (1872a, p. 317). Hence, mechanics is, while chemistry cannot be, a deductive science. We noted in the preceding chapter the weakness of Mill's account of mechanics and the deductive science. The point here is not to once again discuss this contrast in detail but to recall it, and to emphasize that, for John Stuart Mill, in mental science what we have is 'mental chemistry: in which it is proper to say that the simple ideas generate, rather than that they compose, the complex ones' (p. 854). The same point is made in the preface to his father's *Analysis* in much the same terms. He distinguishes Newtonian and chemical analysis: the former is purely deductive, the latter is not. 'The difference is, that the one [the chemical] analyses substances into simpler substances; the other, laws into simpler laws. The one is partly a physical operation; the other is wholly intellectual' (1869, 1: vii). In the case of mental phenomena, 'Not only is the order in which the more complex mental phenomena follow or accompany one another, reducible, by an analysis similar in kind to the Newtonian, to a comparatively small number of laws of succession among simpler facts, connected as cause and effect [that is the basic laws of association]; but the phenomena can mostly be shown, by an analysis resembling that of chemistry, to be made up of simpler phenomena' (1: viii). And he quotes Brown on the same point: 'as in chemistry, it often happens that the qualities of the separate ingredients of a compound body are not recognizable by us in the apparently different qualities of the compound itself, – so in this spontaneous chemistry of the mind' (1: ix). Bain, too, makes the same point in a note of his to the *Analysis* (1: 303): unlike the case of physical phenomena, *quantities* are not clear in mental phenomena; we therefore cannot use the deductive method that we use in physics – we 'cannot show, by casting a sum, that the assigned constituents of a compound exactly amount to the whole'; hence, instead of the deductive method we must use in psychology Mill's experimental canons.

Thus, because the chemical mode of composition applies in psychology, we can speak of wholes being analysed into parts of which they are the causal resultants, but where, however, the whole is *not* the sum of the parts, and can be *qualitatively different* from those parts. This is an important point in the transformation of James Mill's philosophical psychology into one that is observationally adequate, purged of those elements that could not but elude the experimentalist's grasp. In making this point, the younger Mill transformed his father's psychology into an empirical theory that could be handed over to the experimentalists for systematic development, a theory capable of guiding an ongoing research program.

But for ourselves it has a further importance: understanding it is indispensable if we are to understand the moral psychology Mill uses to criticize the intuitionists, whether the earlier ones such as Price and Reid or their successors and Mill's contemporaries Sedgwick and Whewell; and moreover we need it in particular if we are to understand the famous – or infamous – distinction between quantity and quality of pleasure. It is precisely this that Mill discovered, or so we have claimed, during his mental crisis. Of all this, more later. For, we have not yet dealt with some of the important points about Mill's psychological theorizing.

3   Mill's Analysis of Analysis: Successors and Precursors

The associationist theory of learning at its simplest is this: If events of sorts A and B are associated in experience, then that produces an association in thought of the ideas of A and B as the complex idea C; psychological analysis of C reveals the parts A and B, which are the (ideas of) the genetic antecedents of C. Thus, for any complex idea *there are* laws of a certain general form that relate it to causes in experience, and the nature of these causes can be discovered by means of psychological analysis of the idea in question. Locke and his successors up to, and including, James Mill assumed a model that construed psychological analysis upon the model of logical or definitional analysis. It was this model that John Stuart Mill challenged. But the theory of learning itself retained much the same form.

Upon the Lockean model of introspective analysis, in which the analysis provides a definition of the phenomenon analysed, there is a logical, and therefore necessary, equivalence between the phenomeno-logical description D_P and the analytical description D_A. For John Stuart Mill, there is an equivalence between the two descriptions. This equivalence is not universal; the relevant generalizations are imperfect. But, relative to the conditions, (a), (b), and (c) of the preceding section, it is an equivalence. That, at least, is the empirical theory that Mill proposes as the basic framework for psychology. And since this is an empirical theory, the equivalence is contingent rather than necessary. This is in fact the thrust of the law (L_1): subject to the mentioned *ceteris paribus* qualifications, (L_1) establishes the one-to-one connection between the phenomenological description and the analytical description, and this equivalence is contingent because (L_1) is contingent.

Given (L_1), then, the method of introspective analysis yields what Mill calls metaphysical parts, that is, parts that are not present actually but only potentially or dispositionally, to be recovered during analysis. These metaphysical parts are, by (L_2), also the genetic antecedents of the whole that is being analysed. (L_1) and (L_2) thus together capture the traditional associationist doctrine while ensuring, through the contingency of (L_1), that analysis proceeds empirically rather than a priori, as upon the Lockean or definitional model of psychological analysis. The younger Mill in this way eliminates the tension in the traditional theory between its claims to be an empirical theory of psychology and its a priori method: an empirical method that conforms to the theory is substituted for the a priori method of Locke.

Associationism came in this way to be able to function as a paradigm guiding research in psychology. The paradigm asserts that *there are* certain sorts of cause or laws, there to be discovered by the scientist. It also asserts that a certain method, that of introspective analysis, can be used to discover those causes. Then, when such causes are discovered by use of this method, that discovery tends to confirm the paradigm or abstractive theory that guided the research. This is similar to the way in which the paradigm of electromagnetic theory asserts the existence of certain laws without asserting specifically what those laws are, and at the same time both explains how a voltmeter works and justifies its use as a tool in discovering the laws that it asserts are there to be discovered. Then, when specific laws are discovered by means of the voltmeter, that discovery tends to confirm the paradigm, electromagnetic theory, that guided the research.

It was this theory of associationism – that is, (L_1) and (L_2) – and the method that it justified that John Stuart Mill passed on to his successors who made psychology, in practice, into an empirical, and, indeed, experimental science. This is the form in which it was taken up by Wundt.

For Wundt, the product of an association is an entity of the sort he calls a 'process' to distinguish the aims of empirical psychology from that of metaphysical psychology, which aims to find the 'permanent object' or substance that underlies all mental phenomena (1902, pp. 24, 101, 6–9). This terminology is, no doubt, not the best, since it blurs the distinction between a mental phenomenon as an event and a series of such events. A mental event is first described and then explained by subsuming it, together with other events, under a generalization or law. An event, as part of a process, is first described and is then explained by fitting it into the developing process. Wundt's terminology thus blurs the distinction between description and explanation. One of the consequences of this was the failure of the Gestalt psychologists to distinguish between W-Gestalts (description) and K-Gestalts (explanation). The formula 'the whole is greater than the sum of its parts' that they used to criticize the 'elementarists' was therefore a thoroughly confused doctrine, and the criticisms, as we have seen, largely missed their intended target.

Be that as it may, upon Wundt's view, the entities or processes that are the products of association are wholes the parts of which are to be discovered by introspective analysis. 'An elementary process,' he tells us, 'never appears in actual psychical processes except in a more or less complex form, so that the only way to find out the character of elementary association is to subject complex associated products to a psychological analysis' (1902, p. 247). The first stage of psychological research therefore consists of the 'analysis of composite processes' (p. 29). The next step is the 'demonstration of the combinations into which the elements discovered by analysis enter' (ibid.), that is, the establishment of the specific laws of cause and effect that govern the formation of complexes out of elements. These two stages correspond, of course, to what we have called the laws (L_1) and (L_2), respectively. To these Wundt adds a third step, what he calls the 'investigation of the laws that are operative in the formation of such combinations' (ibid.), by which he understands the investigation of the mind-body relation and its impact upon psychological development (pp. 370–2). Mill, too, recognizes the importance of this latter area of investigation, as something that had to be added to the sort of purely introspective research that his father undertook in the *Analysis of the Phenomena of the Human Mind*; thus, Mill, in his review (1859a) of Bain's psychology, praised the latter for introducing physiological concerns that had previously been absent from psychological texts. Wundt's psychology in this way takes off from where Mill leaves that science.

In particular, Wundt recognizes the important point that introspective analysis is not analysis of the definitional sort that Locke had used. Wundt argues that the Lockean model, what he calls the 'logical theory' of psychology, is 'intellectualistic' and assimilates all mental phenomena to 'processes of judgment and reasoning' (1902, pp. 14–15). At the same time, Wundt also rejects what he calls 'association theory,' which 'seeks to reduce [the] totality [of psychical processes] to lower and, it is assumed, simpler forms of intellectual activity' (ibid.). Psychical processes are *not* nothing but the simple parts into which they are analysed. Both these theories in effect assume a model of analysis in which the whole that is analysed can have no properties that are not properties of the parts or at least entailed by the properties of the parts. On both these views, the whole that is analysed cannot be anything more than the sum of its parts. But precisely because the connection between the entity analysed and the elements into which it is analysed is contingent, as Mill insisted, the whole which is analysed can have properties that are not properties of the parts. As Wundt puts it, complex ideas are 'fusions' of simpler elements (pp. 247, 248), and these fusions can have properties over and above those that are entailed by the parts; 'the attributes of psychical compounds,' Wundt insists, 'are never limited to those of the elements that enter into them' (p. 101). However, while psychological wholes can have properties that cannot be reduced to the properties of the analytical, or, in Mill's phrase, the metaphysical parts, these properties do not somehow elude the web of science. The laws of psychology can causally explain the origin of the attributes of the whole; as Wundt also insists, 'new attributes, peculiar to the compounds themselves, always arise as a result of the combination of these elements' (ibid.). Wundt refers to the basic feature of psychological processes as the 'law of psychical resultants' (p. 364) or the 'principle of creative synthesis' (p. 365). This law 'finds its expression in the fact that every psychical compound shows attributes which may indeed be understood from the attributes of its elements after these elements have once been presented, but which are by no means to be looked upon as the mere sum of the attributes of these elements' (p. 364).

This latter shows that Wundt has clearly assimilated John Stuart Mill's notion of 'mental chemistry' (cf. Boring 1957, pp. 335–6), which is to say, the core of Mill's account of psychological analysis. This shows that the common criticisms of Wundt's 'elementarism' of the Gestalt psychologists, e.g., Lewin (1926, pp. 283, 288), were in general quite far from the mark. It is simply not true to say of the psychology of Mill and Wundt that it held, as Wertheimer (1922, p. 12) put it, that 'Every "complex" consists of a sum of elementary contents or pieces (e.g., sensations),' or, as Köhler (1920, p. 20) put it, that 'the real assumption [of this psychology] ... was that to be scientific one had to treat wholes as bare aggregates.' Moreover, when the classical psychology is attacked as being a form of 'mechanism' or of 'mental chemistry' (cf. Köhler, 1922), the objector is thinking of a simplistic atomic-molecular chemistry characteristic of James Mill rather than the more reasonable mental chemistry of John Stuart Mill and Wilhelm Wundt. As Boring (1957, p. 336) has put it, 'Such an argument is always confusing, for it was John Stuart Mill who used the term *mental chemistry* in opposition to the very doctrine that is now often intended by the phrase.' To be sure, Wundt held that all relations can be analysed (1902, pp. 278ff), and we have to put the criticisms of the Gestalters in this context (Wertheimer 1922, p. 14). But it is one thing to criticize particular claims and quite another to criticize the whole framework and method. The Gestalters moved quite illegitimately from the former to the latter.

The views on 'mental chemistry' and on the nature of introspective analysis that were developed by John Stuart Mill and passed on by him to later psychologists were foreshadowed by earlier thinkers. Howard C. Warren, in his study *History of the Association Psychology from Hartley to Lewes* (1921), draws attention to two predecessors of Mill whose accounts of psychology also allowed that the products of a psychological process may have properties different in kind from those of their genetic antecedents. These were Thomas Brown and Abraham Tucker. Brown's use of the notion of 'mental chemistry' was noted by Mill himself in his Preface to his father's *Analysis* (1869, pp. viii–ix). But in spite of Mill's remark, it turns out that Brown's notion of chemistry is akin to that of James Mill, based like the latter on the crude atomic-molecular model that is so often wrongly foisted upon Wundt. Brown's view is that 'in the mind of man, all is in a state of constant and ever-varying complexity,' and 'the complex, or seemingly complex, phenomena of thought, which result from the constant operation of this principle of the mind, it is the labour of the intellectual inquirer to analyze, as it is the labour of the chymist to reduce the compound bodies, on which he operates, however close and intimate their combination may be, to their constituent elements' (1820, Ch. x, p. 60). Now, this sort of analysis yields a set of parts that are equivalent to the whole that is analysed. 'In cases of this kind ... it is the very nature of the resulting feeling to seem to us thus complex; and we are led, by the very constitution of our mind itself, to consider what we term a complex idea, as equivalent to the separate ideas from which it results' (p. 61). But the whole itself is also a *simple* whole.

> It is this feeling of the relation of certain states of mind to certain other states of mind which solves the whole mystery of mental analysis, that seemed at first so inexplicable – the virtual decomposition, in our thought, of what is, by its very nature, indivisible. The mind, indeed, it must be allowed, is absolutely simple in all its states; every separate state of affection of it must, therefore, be absolutely simple; but in certain cases, in which a feeling is the result of other feelings preceding it, it is its very nature to appear to involve the union of those preceding feelings; and to distinguish the separate sensations, or thoughts, or emotions, of which, on reflection, it thus seems to be comprehensive, is to perform an intellectual process, which, though not a real analysis, is an analysis at least relatively to our conception. (ibid.)

Moreover, this simple whole that is analysed can apparently have properties that are not had by the parts: 'in this spontaneous mental chymistry of the mind, the compound sentiment that results from the association of former feelings, has, in many cases, on first consideration, so little resemblance to the constituents of it, as formerly existing in the elementary state, that it requires the most attentive reflection to separate and evolve distinctly to others, the assemblages which even a few years have produced' (p. 62).

Thus far, Brown's view is indeed close to that of John Stuart Mill. None the less, it is also clear that he thinks of the equivalence between the simple whole that is analysed and the parts of that whole as a *logical* relation, after the model of Locke. Thus, one of his examples of a complex idea is that of the 'golden mountain.' This, he holds, is a unity, but one that can be analysed into two parts, namely, the conception of gold and the conception of a mountain (1820, pp. 60–1). Equivalence, he holds, is the basic relation in the demonstrative science of geometry and algebra (p. 61); and is in fact the central relation in all reasoning (pp. 312–13). Brown's psychology, then, is clearly intellectualistic in Wundt's sense. Moreover, if the whole is a simple, it is also true that the parts are integrant parts, in Mill's sense, rather than metaphysical parts. They are *actual* parts, not elements that are only potentially present, to be recovered only upon the process of analysis.

This construal of analytical parts as integrant parts is required by the Lockean logical model of analysis that Brown adopts; it is also what Brown clearly holds. The slow progress of mental science is due to the 'very feebleness of our discriminating powers': 'If we could distinguish instantly and clearly, in our complex phenomena of thought, their constituent elements ... we should then feel as little interest in our [psychological theories], as ... we should have done in our theories of combustion, if the most minute changes that take place in combustion had been at all times distinctly visible' (p. 64). Chemistry would not be a science in which progress was possible 'if our senses were so quick and delicate, as to distinguish immediately all the elements of every compound,' and similarly 'if ... our perspicacity were so acute that we could distinguish immediately all the relations of our thoughts and passions' there would be no discovery in psychology. 'It is,' Brown holds, 'to the imperfection of our faculties ... as forcing us to guess and explore what is half concealed from us, that we owe our laborious experiments and reasonings' in mental science as in physical science (p. 65). It is evident that it is Brown's view that the parts of mental wholes are there, present in the parts, at all times; the reason that we do not discern them is due to the weakness of our faculties. The parts are, in other words, integrant parts. For John Stuart Mill, by way of contrast, when we are presented with a mental phenomenon, the analytical parts of this whole are not noticed because they are not actually present, there to be noticed but for the feebleness of our faculties; rather, they are not noticed because they are there only potentially.

Brown's account of mental chemistry, while superficially similar to that of the younger Mill, is in fact quite different, and is to be located as part of the older tradition. Brown's psychology is rightly to be seen as more akin to that of James Mill than that of John Stuart Mill.

Abraham Tucker, in his voluminous *The Light of Nature Pursued* (1768), sought to derive the principles of morality from experimental data. Tucker develops an associationist account of mind. He distinguishes ideas that derive from sensation (pp. 78ff) and those that derive from reflection (pp. 83ff). Association occurs with both classes of ideas: 'From ideas thus received by sensation and reflection, there grows up a new stock, framed up of these as so many materials, by their uniting together in various assemblages and connexions' (p. 87). There is an 'attraction' between ideas (p. 96), so that the earlier idea generally determines which associated idea shall appear (p. 97). The association of ideas, once it is formed, ties the ideas together, and 'practice joins them more firmly' (ibid.). Ideas that have become associated tend to appear in regular succession; ideas tend to 'introduce their several associates successively to the thought' (p. 95), and such a pattern of successive ideas, provided that they all bear 'a reference to some one purpose retained in view,' Tucker calls a 'train' (ibid.). 'Our trains once well formed, wherever suggests the first link, the rest follow readily of their own accord' (p. 97). As collections of ideas form trains, so trains become connected into 'courses of thinking' (p. 100). Reasoning is not a separate psychological faculty; it is, rather, simply the 'discerning [of] the agreement of two ideas between themselves by their agreement with some third' (p. 110). For the doctrine, traditional then in logic, epistemology, and psychology, that there are separate faculties of apprehension, judgment, and ratiocination, Tucker 'can see no foundation' (p. 124); all the processes usually described as the operations of these separate faculties can all be described in terms of perception (pp. 124–5). Indeed, various supposed faculties such as remembering, thinking, and studying, are all 'but modes or species of perception' (p. 128). We do, however, divide perception into two kinds, namely, imagination and understanding. Tucker characterizes 'the latter [as] growing out of the former' (ibid.), so it is the imagination which is more basic. But 'neither [is] born with us'; both are 'acquired by use and practice' (ibid.). Besides the faculty of perception, we need to suppose only one other faculty, 'the active' (p. 127), that is, the 'faculty by which we perform whatever we do' and which has 'usually been styled the Will' (p. 12).

Tucker's doctrine is thus of a piece with others in the mainstream of associationism. But, unlike others in the tradition, Tucker describes the 'junction' of ideas in association as *combination*, and this he then divides into two modes, *association* and *composition*. By composition Tucker understands a mode of combination of ideas in which 'they so mix, and as I may say melt together as to form one single complex idea'; while by association he means a combination of ideas in which the ideas 'appear in couples strongly adhering to each other, but not blended into the same mass' (1768, p. 87). Composition thus involves what Wundt called a fusion of ideas. Tucker clearly recognizes the important feature of such processes, that the wholes that result can have properties not implied by the parts: 'a compound,' he tells us, 'may have properties resulting from the composition which do not belong singly to the parts whereof it consists' (p. 127). Composition is thus a case of what John Stuart Mill called mental chemistry and what Wundt called mental synthesis. Indeed, it is likely the first such statement of the position (cf. Warren 1921, p. 22).

This is certainly an anticipation of the younger Mill's account of psychological processes. But Tucker does not use the idea of mental chemistry to attempt to understand the nature of the introspective method in psychological research. Thus, although Tucker speaks of ideas as forming by composition new wholes with properties distinct from their genetic antecedents, and although he speaks of these antecedents as parts of the wholes so formed, he does not at the same time think of these parts, these genetic antecedents, being discovered through a process of analysis. The notion of fusion is there, but no notion that the fused ideas remain present only dispositionally, nor any notion that there is available in analysis a method for recovering those metaphysical parts. In fact, there is in Tucker very little sense of the notion of research. All we get from him is a lengthy process of description of psychological processes with very little sense of how one would go about confirming these results, or extending them. The notion of psychological analysis as a *method of research* is more or less absent from Tucker, as much as, by way of contrast, it is present in Thomas Brown and John Stuart Mill. Thus, while Tucker certainly anticipates Mill, he does not anticipate him in giving to psychology an empirically sound method of introspective analysis. The latter contribution to the science of psychology was Mill's alone. To recognize the impact that Mill's rethinking of the method of psychology had upon the science, we must turn to the history of that subject from the elder to the younger Mill. This is the topic of the next chapter.

FOUR

Psychology from Mill to Mill

John Stuart Mill's psychology, so far as specific content is concerned, is largely that of his father's *Analysis of the Phenomena of the Human Mind* (1825), which the younger Mill edited in 1869, adding a series of notes that qualify or explain or defend his father's position, but not modifying it in any substantial way. (Added at the same time was another series of notes by Alexander Bain, which also corrected and extended James Mill's doctrines.) It was in these notes that the younger Mill made his real contribution to the history of psychology. This science was not an experimental science in his father's hands; it became an experimental science only when Wundt founded his laboratory in Leipzig in 1879. But there is no experimental science, no research program, without a theory – or, as Kuhn puts it, a paradigm – to guide the research: the emergence of an empirical theory capable of guiding research is a necessary condition for the emergence of an experimental science. For James Mill, psychology is part empirical theory and part a priori principle incapable of test, and, indeed, capable of running roughshod over observational data that are contrary to it. What John Stuart Mill did, in his 'Notes,' and elsewhere, in the *System of Logic* (1872a), the *Examination of Sir William Hamilton's Philosophy* (1872b), and several essays, was not add substantially to the empirical theory, or introduce significantly new experimental data, but rather think through his father's positions from the viewpoint of the logic of science, and rescue the theory of associationism from his father's philosophical dogmatism, thereby transforming it into an empirical theory that could be turned over to the others who would be the first experimentalists.

The aim of this chapter is to examine how John Stuart Mill transformed the psychology that he inherited from his father. The content, as we shall see, remained largely the same. It was the program that changed: rethinking the nature of analysis, he replaced the analysis as Lockean logical analysis that he found in his father's work by analysis as introspective analysis that recovers by association the causal antecedents of the states analysed. But in changing the program, the content also changed at certain crucial places. Where, on the basis of a priori considerations, his father insisted upon certain analyses, the younger Mill, bound by the requirement of restricting himself to what is empirically possible, was required to reject certain of his father's analyses: a priori metaphysical dogmatism was replaced by empirical science.

In the first section the basic distinction of classical psychology, between sensation and idea, is presented, together with James Mill's account of association and the younger Mill's comments on the latter. The second section deals with the transition from the psychology of the older Mill to the younger Mill. The third section looks at the impact of this transformation on the discussion of the basic elements that introspective analysis is supposed to uncover. The final section turns to a discussion of the crucial case of spatial relations, and whether introspective analysis uncovers as their genetic antecedents only non-relational contents. Since preference is also a relation, Mill's account of spatial relations will help us later on to understand the discussion of preference in economics and in moral philosophy.

1   Sensations, Ideas, and Association

There are two basic distinctions in James Mill's *Analysis*. The first is between *sensation* and *idea*. The second is between *sensation* and *perception*. (The second distinction we discuss in the next chapter.)

Sensations are 'the feelings which we have by the five senses – smell, taste, hearing, touch, and sight' – it is from these that 'we derive our notions of what we denominate the external world' – as well as those feelings 'which accompany the action of the several muscles of the body: and ... those which have their place in the alimentary canal' (1825, I: 3). Sensations are feelings that exist when the object of sense is present. But there is another class of feelings that exist after the object of sense has ceased to be present (I: 52). For example, after looking at the sun, one shuts one's eyes, yet there remains in one's consciousness a sensory impression or image of the sun. 'I have still a feeling, the consequence of the sensation, which, though I can distinguish it from the sensation, and treat it as not the sensation, but something different from the sensation, is yet more like the sensation, than anything else can be; so like, that I call it a copy, an image, of the sensation, sometimes, a representation, or trace, of the sensation' (ibid.). These copies of sensations are *ideas*. Ideas, let us note, are, like sensations, sensory; they are images, copies of sensations. As it was later to be put, ideas and sensations are both sensory contents.

The order in which sensations are experienced is determined by the objects that cause them. But there is also a pattern among ideas. 'Thought succeeds thought; idea follows idea, incessantly. If our senses are awake, we are continually receiving sensations, of the eye, the ear, the touch, and so forth; but not sensations alone. After sensations, ideas are perpetually excited of sensation formerly received; after those ideas, other ideas: and during the whole of our lives, a series of those two states of consciousness, called sensations, and ideas, is constantly going on' (1825, 1: 70). What are the laws that describe the train of ideas?

Sensations occur in the order of the objects that cause them. Two sorts of such order are distinguished, the synchronous or simultaneous and the successive (1825, 1: 71). The various sensations of resistance and taste that occur when I bite an apple are synchronous; but the sight of the flash of a gun and the hearing of its discharge occur successively. Many synchronous sensations are frequently experienced synchronically; and many successive sensations have been frequently experienced successively. James Mill proposes that this can account for the order of our ideas:

> As ideas are not derived from objects, we should not expect their order to be derived from the order of objects; but as they are derived from sensations, we might by analogy expect, that they would derive their order from that of sensations; and this to a great extent is the case.
>
> Our ideas spring up, or exist, in the order in which the sensations existed, of which they are the copies. (1: 78)

'This,' he tells us, 'is the general law of the "Association of Ideas."' The younger Mill does not challenge or modify this characterization of the law of association of ideas.

An 'association' is, clearly, a regularity, a habitual connection. Yet it is not an *unconditioned* regularity. It is only under certain conditions that such a habit is acquired: the order of ideas is caused by an order in the sensations. Moreover, while ideas may be associated, there may be variations in just how they are associated: different orders among sensations can cause different orders among ideas. To say this with Mill is to assert a generic abstract hypothesis, specifically, the hypothesis that, for ideational events, *there are* orders among them, and *there are* causes among our sensations for these orders among ideas, and that an order among ideas is of *the same general form* as the order among sensations that causes it. This generic abstract hypothesis can then be used to guide research into the specific details of the associations and their causes. As for this generic abstract hypothesis itself, its acceptance as a law can be justified by appeal to the principle that every event has a cause and to the recognition that the only possible proximate causes for ideas are sensations. The latter claim, that *these* are the only factors that *could* be relevant, is an assumption of limited variety, and is an empirical and lawful claim — as is the principle of determinism that every event has a cause. But an initial examination of the phenomena certainly renders it reasonable to assert as a law the assumption of limited variety. And, if further research succeeds in discovering among sensations the appropriate causes of associations of various sorts, then that will further confirm the assumption that it is among sensations that the causes of associations are to be found — and also, of course, tend to confirm the principle that every event has a cause.[1]

Associations, orders among ideas, are distinguished in form, in the first place, as are orders among sensations, into synchronous and successive. Moreover, the data available argue that associations of ideas synchronously are caused by synchronously occurring sensations, and that associations of ideas successively are caused by successively occurring sensations (1825, 1: 78–81).

Next, associations are distinguished in form according to their degree of *strength* (1825, 1: 82). Three criteria of strength are provided. Each of these is obviously intended to suggest a rank order. Somehow these rank orders are combined to give a rank order of strength. Needless to say, the distinction of rank as opposed to cardinal order, and the problem of combining scales, nowhere occurs to Mill. It would be sheer anachronism to suppose that such issues ought to have been discussed. Rather, we should recognize that we now are aware of such issues only because psychologists become aware of the fact that associations vary in strength and that there are several criteria for the strength of associations. Only after one has come explicitly to recognize that there are several criteria for the strength of associations can one raise the *detailed* questions that we now ask. It is the virtue of James Mill's *Analysis* that, for the first time, it is recognized that there are degrees of strength of association, and that there are criteria for such strength. How these combine to form a *significant* measure, that is, one that is useful in stating the laws of association,[2] is a research task that is left for later researchers – as, indeed, is the issue whether the list of criteria is exhaustive.

The first criterion of strength is 'permanence' (1825, I: 82): associations may endure for greater or shorter periods of time, and those that last longer are of greater strength. The second criterion is 'certainty' (I: 82–3): statements of association are statements of tendency, and an association will proceed only if possible counteracting factors are absent; an association is the more certain the less likely it is that counteracting factors will prevent it. The third criterion of strength is 'facility' (I: 83): an association is the more facile the more spontaneous it is, the more it proceeds independently of the will and attention. Since the associations that proceed spontaneously proceed more quickly than those that proceed only when the subject attends to the process – cf. searching for one word that is associated with another – this last criterion is the ancestor of the technique that later experimentalists were to develop of measuring reaction times as a criterion of strength of association.

Two conditions for forming associations are discussed. The first is *frequency* (1825, I: 83). Ideas are associated (either synchronously or successively) if the sensations of which they are copies are presented together (either synchronously or successively), and the greater the frequency with which the sensations are presented then the greater the strength of the association they cause (I: 87–8). The second condition is *vividness* (I: 84): where the cause of the association is more vivid then the association is stronger. Three sorts of vividness are distinguished: sensations are more vivid than ideas, pleasures and pains are more vivid than sensations and ideas that are hedonically indifferent, and recent sensations are more vivid than the more remote (I: 85). Vividness can cause a strong association of ideas even where the relevant sensations have occurred but once. 'The most remarkable cases' of this sort, James Mill suggests, 'are probably those of pain and pleasure' (I: 86).

James Mill later on characterizes certain complex ideas as more obscure than others (1825, I: 105). This leads Bain to distinguish, what the elder Mills runs together, the distinctness and indistinctness of sensations, on the one hand, and on the other, their emotional tone, or feeling in the narrower sense in which it is opposed to intellect or thought (1869, I: 116n); only the latter is appropriately referred to as 'vividness.' Or rather, 'the associating stimulus expressed by "vividness" is better expressed by "strength of the feelings"' (1: 117n). John Stuart Mill agrees with Bain on the subject (1: 86n). But the point of his father's presentation remains valid, John Stuart goes on to remark: 'the property of producing a strong and durable association without the aid of repetition, belongs principally to our pains and pleasures. The more intense the pain or pleasure, the more promptly and powerfully does it associate itself with the accompanying circumstances, even with those which are only accidentally present' (ibid.).

2   Psychology: From Metaphysics to Science

There is thus substantial agreement by John Stuart that his father's psychology got things right. Let us now turn to where the younger Mill distinguishes his views from those of his father.

We can begin by considering what it is that James Mill holds to be associated together to form complex ideas. If the elder Mill is correct, then it is imagistic copies of sensations, that is, entities that themselves have the various sensory properties – colours, tastes, sounds, etc. – had by the sensations they copy. Ideas ought to be sensory contents, or else complexes composed of (synchronously) associated sensory contents. This is how it ought to be, but it is not quite what we are told, however, at least if we take the examples seriously.

Consider this example: 'The idea of Professor Dugald Stewart delivering a lecture, recalls the idea of the delight with which I heard him; that, the ideas of the studies in which it engaged me' (1825, 1: 87). These are not so much ideas in the sense of sensory images, but rather Lockean ideas – that which is before the mind – which are not in any obvious ways simply sensory copies of what they are supposed to be about. However, the explicit account of ideas as copies requires them to be the latter. Thus, James Mill takes to be sensory images things that are at least not obviously images.

The point is, of course, that if they are sensory images, and therefore complexes of sensory parts, then when such an idea is before the mind we are not aware of the parts. The elder Mill is not entirely insensitive to this point:

The idea expressed by the term weight, appears so perfectly simple, *that he is a good metaphysician, who can trace its composition.* Yet it involves, of course, the idea of resistance, which we have shown above to be compounded, and to involve the feeling attendant upon the contraction of muscles; and the feeling or feelings, denominated will; it involves the idea, not of resistance simply, but of resistance in a particular direction; the idea of direction, therefore, is included in it, and in that are involved the ideas of extension, and of place and motion, some of the most complicated phenomena of the human mind. (1825, 1: 91; italics added)

The suggestion here made is that the idea is indeed a complex of parts – sensory parts – but he who has the idea normally does not attend to those parts. 'We say, our idea of iron, our idea of gold; and it is only with an effort that reflecting men perform the decomposition' (ibid.). Nor is this the only point at which James Mill appeals to attention to account for a lack of awareness of parts of certain associated wholes. The ideas of weight, iron, and gold are the result of synchronous associations. There are also successive associations. Often in these, too, the sensation or idea that introduces an idea is not noticed.

It not infrequently happens in our associated feelings, that the antecedent is of no importance farther than as it introduces the consequent. In these cases, the consequent absorbs all the attention, and the antecedent is instantly forgotten. Of this a very intelligible illustration is afforded by what happens in ordinary discourse ... The sound of the voice, the articulation of every word, makes its sensation in my ear; but it is to the ideas that my attention flies ... The words which have introduced the ideas ... have been as little heeded, as the respiration which has been accelerated, while the ideas were received. (1825, 1: 98–100)

There is in all this the crying out for a research program. First of all, an account of *attention* itself is needed. As Bain suggests, in his notes to the *Analysis* (1869, 1: 228), attention involves a cognitive effort, and, as the younger Mill goes on to point out, also in a note to the *Analysis* (1: 231), what evokes that effort is the pleasure and pain associated with the idea attended to: 'It frequently happens ... that certain of our sensations, or certain parts of the series of our thoughts, not being sufficiently pleasurable or painful to compel attention, and there being no motive for attending to them voluntarily, pass off without having been attended to; and, not having received that artificial intensification, they are too slight and too fugitive to be remembered.' But even with the notes of Bain and the younger Mill, the whole thing is very sketchy. And second, one also needs experimental work to describe the *specific* conditions for evoking the cognitive effort that constitutes attention, for example, the specific amount of pleasure or pain required for a specific amount and duration of cognitive effort. To say this is not, of course, to *criticize* Mill. Attention remained a problem for psychology through Wundt and Titchener, and, suitably transformed, the problem passed into behaviouristic psychology (cf. Boring 1957, pp. 338–9, 415, 537, 644–5). To make the points just made is simply to say that as scientific psychology, Mill's *Analysis* proposes, together with some plausible but essentially anecdotal evidence, a set of gappy or imperfect laws or, perhaps, plausible hypotheses that, given a cognitive interest in removing gaps, demand further research rather than constitute a definitive statement.

The point to be made is that, even if such a program were carried out in greater detail than it is taken in the *Analysis*, it is still highly unlikely that it could succeed in producing an account of attention that was capable of doing what James Mill required of it. Consider the following account of ideas:

> Brick is one complex idea, mortar is another complex idea; these ideas, with ideas of position and quantity, compose my idea of a wall. My idea of a plank is a complex idea, my idea of a rafter is a complex idea, my idea of a nail is a complex idea. These, united with the same ideas of position and quantity, compose my duplex idea of a floor [a duplex idea is a union of two complex ideas]. In the same manner my complex idea of glass, and wood, and others, compose my duplex idea of a window; and these duplex ideas, united together, compose my idea of a house, which is made up of various duplex ideas. How many complex, or duplex ideas, are all united in the idea of furniture? How many more in the idea of merchandize? How many more in the idea called Every Thing? (1825, I: 115–16)

Boring (1957, p. 226) has reasonably commented on this passage: 'in this *reductio ad absurdum* we see the persistent danger of philosophical psychology, unchecked by scientific control. A rational principle is captured by the empirical method and may then be turned loose to carry us even to the brink of absurdity. There is no logical reason to suppose that the idea of *everything* might not be an association of every idea of a thing, but there is not the least observational ground for maintaining, even with maximal telescoping, that a consciousness can contain a literally unlimited number of ideas at once. What meaning can one give to the conception that ideas [that is, sensory images] coexist when indistinguishable?' The rational principle to which Boring refers is that of 'fusion' in synchronously associated ideas: 'in admitting fusion in synchronous association, Mill has admitted to systematic psychology a rational principle capable of devouring observational fact' (ibid.).

James Mill introduces the notion of fusion, or coalescence, as follows:

> Where two or more ideas have been often repeated together, they sometimes spring up in such close combination as not to be distinguishable. Some cases of sensation are analogous. For example, when a wheel on the seven parts of which the seven prismatic colours are respectively painted, is made to revolve rapidly, it appears not of seven colours, but of one uniform colour, white. By the rapidity of the succession, the several sensations cease to be distinguishable; they run, as it were, together, and a new sensation, compounded of all the seven, but apparently a simple one, is the result. Ideas also, which have been so often conjoined, that whenever one exists in the mind, the others immediately exist along with it, seem to run into one another, to coalesce, as it were, and out of many to form one idea; which idea, however in reality complex, appears to be no less simple, than any one of those of which it is compounded. (1825, 1: 90–1)

He goes on to give examples:

> The word gold, for example, or the word iron, appears to express as simple an idea, as the word sound. Yet it is immediately seen, that the idea of each of those metals is made up of the separate ideas of several sensations; colour, hardness, extension, weight. Those ideas, however, present themselves in such intimate union, that they are constantly spoken of as one, not many. We say, our idea of iron, our idea of gold; and it is only with an effort that reflecting men perform the decomposition. (1: p. 91)

Or again:

> Particular sensations of sight, of touch, of the muscles, are the sensations, to the ideas of which, colour, extension, roughness, hardness, smoothness, taste, smell, so coalescing as to appear one idea, I give the name, idea of a tree. (1: p. 93)

The elder Mill is clearly trying to have it both ways. The ideas have sensory parts. These sensory parts often occur together. When they do, they coalesce – forming one idea out of many, an idea that is *apparently* simple, apparently as simple as the parts that are in it. So, the sensory parts *are* there, but the idea of which they are the parts is *apparently* – *that is, so far as observation can tell* – as simple as those parts into which it is analysed. If this is so, then clearly we can say *anything* is part of an idea; for, even if we can't discriminate it as a part, we can always maintain that it really is there except we can't notice it because of the fusion that has occurred. As Boring says, something has clearly gone wrong.

What is required is a rethinking of what is meant by 'analysis' in psychology. The elder Mill tends to think of analysis on the model of a spatial whole being analysed into parts, or on the model of a concept being logically analysed by its definition. Neither squares with what he is trying to do. The spatial model won't do, because it does not account for the *observational fact* that the ideas being analysed are *not complex* in that sense. The logical model won't do, because there is no reason to suppose that *logical parts* are also *genetic antecedents*, as the elder Mill also, quite clearly, requires.

It was the younger Mill who effected the rethinking of what is involved in the notion of *introspective analysis*. In doing so, John Stuart Mill, though not himself an experimentalist, thought the matter through clearly enough in the logic of science to rescue the doctrine of association and mental combination from the philosophical prejudices of his father and turned it over to others who would be the first experimentalists in psychology.

This rethought notion of analysis is the one that we examined in the preceding chapter. Upon it, the idea being 'analysed' is indeed simple, as James Mill implies, when his metaphysics is not running away with him; it is a *whole*, which is a *unity*. The ideas of the sensations that are the genetic antecedents of that idea cannot be shown to be actually present in the latter; they are not immediately distinguishable in the idea when it is before the mind. But it does not follow that they are not *recoverable from* the idea, that is, *potentially* present, ready to be realized by association if the occasion permits. It is this non-presence but recoverability that John Stuart Mill emphasizes as the core idea of analysis. But what is it that links this notion of analysis with the model of logical analysis that James Mill derived from Locke and that conflicted with the notion that mental chemistry fused several ideas into a new unity unlike those ideas that were its genetic antecedents? What replaces the logical model is, as we saw, the empirical assumption that the sensory contents that generate an idea or any mental phenomenon continue to be associated with it; this association is dispositional, and is made actual under the analytical set. This empirical assumption that replaces the logical model we expressed as the two generic abstract laws that we labelled (L_1):

There is a minimal analytical vocabulary (v_A), and there are laws of association, such that for any phenomenon (given a description D_P from the phenomenological vocabulary v_P) the laws yield from it under the analytical set a description (D_A) in terms of the analytical vocabulary and such that for any such analytical description the laws ensure that it determines a unique phenomenon (D_P).

and (L_2):

For any phenomenon, the description (D_A) of it in terms of the analytical vocabulary (v_A) is also a description of the causal antecedents from which the phenomenon was generated in accordance with the laws of association.

What introspective analysis reveals, upon this account, is not integrant parts, but, as the younger Mill calls them, metaphysical parts, that is, the sensory contents that one actually discovers, under the analytical set, to be connected by association to the phenomenon with which one is concerned. *One can no longer call a part of an idea whatever one a priori determines must be a part; one can now call something a part only if association reveals it to be in fact such.* In this way a priori metaphysics is replaced by an empirical research program, one guided by the generic abstract laws (L_1) and (L_2).

Moreover, since the parts of a mental state are no longer literally *in* it, that is, are no longer integrant parts, but are parts only in being *recoverable from the state* by association, there is no requirement that the parts be *like* the state analysed; that is, the state can be qualitatively different from its parts as it can from its genetic antecedents – which, of course, it is assumed those parts are. Motivational states can thus come to be acquired through a process of learning by association, but can themselves be a form of pleasure qualitatively distinct from its genetic antecedents. Introspective analysis can, moreover, uncover those metaphysical parts without the state being analysed losing its own unique and distinctive character. It was the discovery of this, made during his mental crisis, that was essential to John Stuart Mill's defence of utilitarianism against its Whig and Tory critics. We now see that what this discovery consists in is in effect so rethinking the notion of introspective analysis that these facts can be admitted or acknowledged within the utilitarian psychology.

3 Introspective Elements and Causal Antecedents

Introspective analysis uncovers the *elements* from which mental chemistry has produced the state being analysed. These elements are described by the minimal analytical vocabulary v_A mentioned in the law (L_1). Exactly what are the elements here in mental chemistry, as in physical chemistry, is a matter of fact. Moreover, as we saw in the preceding chapter, the law (L_1) about the elements is independent of the law (L_2), which asserts that the elements uncovered by introspective analysis are the genetic antecedents of the state analysed. Thus, in principle at least, the question of what are the details of the minimal analytical vocabulary mentioned in (L_1) is independent of the genetic hypothesis (L_2). Yet in fact, for the Mills, they are not independent. For, on the one hand, the minimal analytical vocabulary is assumed to refer to sensory contents while, on the other hand, such contents are, in the *Analysis, classified according to their genetic causes.*

The initial eight sections of the *Analysis* take up, in turn, Aristotle's five senses (smell, hearing, sight, taste, touch), the sensations of disorganization (mainly pain but including itching and tickling), muscular sensations (the book was written just after Charles Bell had 'discovered' the muscular sense in 1826, though Reid, Hartley, and Brown, as Mill notes, had preceded Bell in including these among the data of psychology), and sensations of the alimentary canal.

In starting this way with the sensory elements and their causes, Mill contributed to a custom for textbooks, which Wundt, when he created the experimentalist program, was later to fix upon psychology for many years (cf. Boring 1942, p. 8). The fact that Mill was thus able to establish a textbook tradition for the science shows how the *Analysis* marks the transition from, to use Kuhn's terms, pre-paradigm to paradigm science. In fact, if one pursues the remaining chapters of the *Analysis*, we find the third discussing association, and the remaining twenty-two, consciousness, conception, imagination, classification, abstraction, memory, belief, ratiocination, evidence, reflection, pleasure, pain, motives, interaction with others, will, intention, and related topics. The list shows how Mill more or less succeeded in establishing the convention about what is the scope of psychology. Long after the experimentalists and the physiologists took over the research program of psychology, and long after the earlier traditions had become absorbed into objective, behaviourist psychology, the textbook writers dealt with the topics on this list, or at least dealt with them in some way or other since their experimental techniques were usually unable to deal in any serious way with the 'higher mental faculties.' Nor have we yet lost that convention. Since James Mill at least, everyone knows what psychology is about, even if they don't know exactly what it is (cf. Boring 1957, p. 221).

There is nothing wrong in principle with this starting-point. That is, there is nothing wrong with classifying entities in terms of their causes. Thus, for example, we distinguish viral infections from other sorts of infections; this is to distinguish them in terms of their causes. Technically, a description of something by means of its cause is given in terms of what Russell called a definite description:[3] the logic of it is not problematic.[4] But one must also recognize that effects have intrinsic descriptions, which are logically prior to their being described in terms of causes; and recognize further that no causal account can be complete, or gapless, until those logically prior descriptions are provided. Suppose 'visual sensations' are defined to be 'those sensations caused by changes on the retina.' Supposing that there are such sensations,[5] then it is true that visual sensations are caused by retinal changes. Moreover, that is a factual, not an analytic or tautological truth, since it is true only if retinal changes do have effects. But the prediction it makes is no more than that such changes have effects. That may be true, but it would be better, cognitively, to be more specific in one's predictions: one wants to know what, specifically, are the effects.[6] In the case of visual sensations, it was assumed by Mill that these were colours (1825, 1: 23). But what about the other categories that the classification yields? Here, we are told, there is 'more vagueness' (1: 28). When one separates the dubious (for Mill) cases of resistance, and of hot and cold, all that one is left with is 'the feeling which we have when something, without being seen, comes gently in contact with our skin, in such a way, that we cannot say whether it is hard or soft, rough or smooth, of what figure it is, or of what size' (1: 31). Notice that this is still only a definite description in terms of causes, not a specific description of the sensations in question. There are therefore many gaps in the *Analysis* in the description of sensations, that is, the effects of sensory processes, and these gaps are, in fact, not merely gaps in descriptions but gaps in the lawful explanations proposed.

Moreover, as the work of Charles Bell in discovering the 'muscular sense' showed, perhaps there were sensory processes not yet discovered. In such a case, there would be sensations not caused by the sense organs so far enumerated, which would therefore inevitably escape categorization in the system that classified in terms of causes.

Relying upon the vocabulary derived from causal antecedents to constrain v_A and describe the elements may lead one to misdescribe the latter class. In fact, Titchener not unreasonably was later to come to refer to this lapsing from the psychologist's point of view into some other – for example, that of the physiologist or physicist – as 'stimulus-error' (1909–10, pp. 202f). The point he wishes to make can be clear by an example (cf. Boring 1957, p. 418). In the determination of the two-point limen upon the skin, it is quite a serious matter whether the subject describes the sensations from the psychologist's point of view, that is, in terms of their intrinsic properties, or from the physicist's point of view, in terms of what the subject takes to be their causes. In the former case, the subject is given the analytical, or introspective, set; and if he feels only one sensory pattern he reports *One*. The subject can, however, take the other point of view, and try to say on the basis of the tactual sensations whether one or two points are in contact with the skin. Now, there are certain 'stretched-out' patterns of 'oneness' that mean to him unequivocally stimulation by two points. In that case he would report *Two*, meaning one pattern that is caused by two points. The second description is not erroneous – to that extent the phrase 'stimulus error' is wrong. But *not* to distinguish the two different descriptions *is* an error, and by using the language of their causes to classify sensations one may be led to describe them in very misleading terms. Thus, the *Two* may be taken to mean that two elementary sensations are present, where in fact there is only one.

There are, therefore, real problems with using the language of causal antecedents to classify sensations. That language had to be replaced by a vocabulary that describes sensations in terms of their intrinsic properties. It was Helmholtz (1878) who solved this problem, and provided a method of systematically characterizing sensations in terms of their intrinsic properties. His proposal was to classify sensations according to their *modality*, where a modality is a class of sensations connected in a qualitative continuum (cf. Boring 1942, p. 10). Colours lie in a single modality because they can be placed on a single three-dimensional continuum, that is, the colour is solid. Tones also form a modality. But touch does not, since there are at least three unconnected but distinguishable classes, namely, as Mill says (1825, I: 29–30), pressure or resistance, temperature, and pain.

Once this classificatory scheme is laid down, it is possible to advance the hypothesis that *for each sensory modality there is a distinct sensory process.*

The point is that such an hypothesis allows the possibility that there are sensations to be enumerated that are not caused by known sense organs and sensory processes. That is, it separates in a clear way the language used to describe sensations from the sensory processes that are supposed to be their causes. So long as sensations can be described only by means of definite descriptions in terms of the sensory processes that cause them, then those sensory processes impose constraints upon what can appear in the minimal analytical vocabulary v_A. Conversely, once the vocabulary used to describe sensations is made independent of that for sensory processes, it allows that there may be analytically indecomposable elements that yet are the effects of several different but jointly acting sensory processes. But what this last means is that *there may be minimal parts such that introspective analysis* cannot *recover their several causal antecedents.* Thus, as we put it before, one may accept (L_1) while rejecting (L_2).

Mill assumes that indecomposable elements that do arise from several different sensory processes will be the result of association of the sensations that are the separate consequences of those processes. However, since these elements are indecomposable, the association is indissoluble (1869, I: 97ff). Elsewhere Mill speaks of the Laws of Obliviscence as among the basic laws of learning: 'It is one of the principal Laws of Obliviscence, that when a number of ideas suggest one another by association with such certainty and rapidity as to coalesce together in a group, all those members of the group which remain long without being attended to, have a tendency to drop out of consciousness' (1872b, p. 257). How many of the genetic predecessors drop out of consciousness, and thereby become irrecoverable, is a function of attention. But however that may be – and it clearly demands research as to specific details and mechanisms – the point is that where there has been such an association, and the genetic antecedents cannot be recovered by introspective analysis, then the fact such elements arise as a result of association, that is, learning, is something that must be inferred from sources of information other than introspective analysis. Mill distinguished the 'introspective method' and the 'psychological method' (pp. 138ff). The former takes as *unlearned* what *analysis cannot decompose.*[7] The latter makes no such assumption. Only the psychological approach is justified, since it imposes no a priori assumption on the facts: 'Introspection can show us a present belief or conviction, attended with a greater or less difficulty in accommodating the thoughts to a different view of the subject: but that this belief, or conviction, or knowledge, if we can call it so, is intuitive [that is, unlearned], no mere introspection can ever show; unless we are at liberty to assume that every mental process which is now as unhesitating and as rapid as intuition, was intuitive at its outset' (p. 138). Not surprisingly Mill links those who practise the 'introspective method' with those who argue similarly in ethics, that is, the intuitionists (pp. 143ff).

Mill argues that inferences from what we have discovered about learning can establish that various indissoluble elements are a result of learning.

> Being unable to examine the actual contents of our consciousness until our earliest, which are necessarily our most firmly knit associations, those which are most intimately interwoven with the original data of consciousness, are fully formed, we cannot study the original elements of mind in the facts of our present consciousness. Those original elements can only come to light as residual phenomena, by a previous study of the modes of generation of the mental facts which are confessedly not original; a study sufficiently thorough to enable us to apply its results to the convictions, beliefs, or supposed intuitions which seem to be original, and to determine whether some of them may not have been generated in the same modes, so early as to have become inseparable from our consciousness before the time to which memory goes back. (1872b, p. 141)

This is what Mill calls the 'psychological method' (ibid.).

All this is fair enough, but Mill does also make certain *empirical assumptions* about the relation of sensory processes to the primitive elements upon which the associative processes can work. In particular, he assumes, as we have suggested, that

(A) Different kinds of sensory processes cause different sorts of elementary sensations; and different sorts of elementary sensation are caused by different kinds of sensory processes.

Indeed, the second clause is, we have suggested, more or less forced upon him by the requirement, which still binds him, to classify sensations into sorts in terms of the sensory processes that are their causes.

Mill uses (A) to infer that apparently indissoluble elements *must* have arisen by association. Since the parts of these elements are fused together, coalesced into a unity, they are not 'integrant' parts, but rather 'metaphysical' parts.

> our idea of an object, whether it be of the man, or of his head, or of his feet, is compounded by association from our ideas of the colour, the shape, the resistance, &c., which belong to those objects. These are ... the metaphysical parts, not the integrant parts, of the total impression. Now I have never heard of any philosopher who maintained that *these* parts were not known until after the objects which they characterize; that we perceive the body first, and its colour, shape, form, &c., only afterwards. Our senses, which on all theories are at least the avenues through which our knowledge of bodies comes to us, are not adapted by nature to let in the perception of the whole object at once. They only open to let pass single attributes at a time. (1872b, p. 259)

This account of the sensory processes is used as a premiss from which Mill infers that certain ideas of *structured wholes* must have arisen by association from certain elements. *If* this is so, then Mill is in a position to explain, or, rather, sketch an (imperfect) explanation of, why the metaphysical parts disappear from consciousness and are not recoverable by analysis. The explanation is in terms of attention: we are interested in the whole, and not its parts, so we do not attend to the latter which, as a consequence, not only drop out of consciousness but become irrecoverable to it (p. 258).

The interesting question, however, is whether the assumption (A) is true. This we look at in the next section.

4   Spatial Relations

We can discuss the question of the truth of Mill's empirical assumption (A) by means of one of the cases that Mill discusses in detail (1842–3; 1872b, ch. XIII). This is the case of *spatial wholes*.

The issue is complex. Spatial wholes are such by virtue of *relations* that structure non-relational entities into these wholes. Relations are described by *two-place predicates* rather than, as qualities, by *one-place predicates*. In one sense the issue is whether relations must be included among the elements, that is, whether the minimal analytical vocabulary v_A contains only one-place predicates or also includes two-place, or relational, predicates. Whether or not it is true, it is at least compatible with the existence among mental phenomena of relational wholes that there be no relations among the elements. It is to this issue that (A) is relevant. But the problem is complicated because it becomes involved with a prior, ontological issue, whether there are any relations at all, even among the phenomena to be analysed, or, to put it another way, whether the phenomenological vocabulary v_P contains any irreducibly relational predicates. These different concerns must be disentangled.

All this is relevant to understanding Mill's psychology. It is also relevant, as we have said, to understanding what Mill has to say about the *relation* of *preference* in economics and moral philosophy.

Let us turn, then, to what the *Analysis* says about *extension*.

In this work, James Mill adopts the position of Berkeley, that all judgments of extension are produced by processes of association. He holds that visual sensory processes yield coloured sensations (1825, I: 22–3), and that tactile sensory processes yield those sensations consequent upon an object gently touching the skin (I: 31). Extension, however, is *not* a product of processes of this sort (ibid.). Sensations of extension are, rather, *learned*, that is, a product of association. Crucial to these associations are *muscular sensations*, changes of feeling that occur when muscles change, for example, when I move my arm (I: 41–2): 'The idea of extension is derived from the muscular feelings in what we call the motion of parts of our own bodies; as for example, the hands. I move my hand along a line; I have certain sensations; on account of these sensations, I call the line long, or extended' (I: 92).

Let the *phenomenological description* of a spatial whole be something like

(d_P) Red spot next to a green spot

Besides the (implicit) reference to two individuals, there are three terms here: the two colour terms, *red* and *green*, and the relation *next to*. The colours are the product of visual sensory processes. But the *spatial relation* is *not* a product of these processes. *The analytical description*

(d_A) Red spot and such and such muscular feelings and green spot

mentions *muscular feelings* rather than the relation. The analysis of the whole yields *separable parts*. In the analysis there is no real unity, only conjunction. The unity of what is described by (d_P) is a matter of the parts mentioned by (d_A) having become *inseparably associated* and having *coalesced* through mental chemistry into a *compound idea* of which the *metaphysical parts* are the real (i.e., integrant) parts given in the description (d_A). Note that from the fact that the metaphysical parts of the whole described by (d_P) are the real parts of (d_A), it does *not* follow that the whole (d_P) is somehow a *conjunction* of non-relational facts *rather than* a *relational structure*. The sort of analysis John Stuart Mill describes is not something that 'analyses away.' *What happens when the separable parts given by the analytical description coalesce into the structured whole given by the phenomenological description is that the mental chemistry of the associative processes reconstitutes these parts as a relational or structured unity.* Of course, upon James Mill's account, in which the parts of the analytical description are the real or integrant parts of the whole that is analysed, if no relation appears in the analysis then that whole is itself but a conjunction of non-relational facts rather than a relational structure. But upon the younger Mill's account, there is no reason why a non-relational analysis should entail that it is an unstructured, or merely conjunctive, whole that is being analysed.

Now, there is no a priori reason why relational terms should not appear in the analytic vocabulary v_A. Yet the *Analysis* excludes them from that vocabulary. This is clear for facts concerning space, as we have just said, but the *Analysis* asserts it more generally for *every* relational whole. In the section devoted to 'Relative Terms' we discover: 'If it is asked, why we give names in pairs? The general answer immediately suggests itself; it is because the things named present themselves in pairs; *that is, are joined by association*' (1825, II: 7 [italics added]; see also I: 185). What reasons are given for this exclusion, for this *empirical claim* that relational facts can always be introspectively decomposed into non-relational facts?

Three points are to be noted.

In the first place, the metaphysical account of relational facts that was then current was that one finds in, for example, Coleridge, for whom relational wholes not only are connections of two individuals, but are substantial wholes in their own right and ones in which the two ordinary individuals are but dependent aspects. Thus, in the essay 'On Method' we are told by Coleridge that

> in whatever science the *relation of the parts to each other and to the whole* is predetermined by a truth originating in the mind, and not abstracted or generalized from observation of the parts, there we affirm the presence of a law, if we are speaking of the physical science, as of astronomy for instance; or the presence of funda-mental ideas, if our discourse be upon those sciences, the truths of which, as truths absolute, not merely have an independent origin in the mind, but continue to exist in and for the mind alone. Such, for instance, is geometry. (1818, p. 350; italics added)

And again:

> In all aggregates of construction ... which we contemplate as
> wholes, whether as integral parts or as a system, we assume an
> intention, as the intiative, of which the end is the correlative.
> (p. 365)

Relational wholes derive their unity from laws or ideas that cannot be
known if one relies on only the sort of observation used by empirical
science. Certainly, it cannot be obtained by 'mere' analysis. Moreover,
wherever one has a whole rather than a mechanical or merely
conjunctive aggregate, there one also has a teleological unity. The ideas
that constitute genuine relational wholes are *active* ideas. Note, by the
way, how close this is to Whewell's thought, though the latter is, of
course, much more sophisticated.[8] In any case, the empiricists could
not but react against this, and emphasize that relations in *this* sense do
not exist. J.S. Mill remarks in his notes to his father's *Analysis* that 'No
part of the Analysis is more valuable than the simple explanation here
given of a subject which has seemed so mysterious to some of the most
enlightened philosophers, down even to the present time. The only
difference between relative names and any others consists in their
being given in pairs; and the reason of their being given in pairs is not
the existence between two things, of a mystical bond called a Relation,
and supposed to have a kind of shadowy and abstract reality' (1869, II:
7–8). But from the fact that there are not relations in this mystical
sense, it does not follow that there are no relational wholes. One can,
however, understand how one anxious to deny the metaphysical
speculations of Coleridge could slide from the former to the latter.

In the second place, Mill tends to adopt the traditional empiricist,
or, more precisely, nominalist, *ontology* of relations in which a relational
statement that

   a R b

is analysed as (1) a statement *about the objective non-relational facts*

   a is r_1
   a is r_2

where r_1 and r_2 are said to be the *foundations* of the relation; and (2) a
statement *expressing a judgment of comparison*. This account is, for
example, Locke's (cf. *Essay* 1700, II, xxv, 1) and in fact has a long
tradition (cf. Weinberg 1965). This nominalist account is not tenable,

nor need one abandon empiricism in order to reject it – for, as Russell showed, to admit ontologically irreducible relations is quite compatible with empiricism.[9] None the less, the Mills followed this tradition. Thus, J.S. Mill draws our attention in his notes to the *Analysis* to the 'set of facts, which is connoted by both the correlative terms' that constitute the *fundamentum relationis*; and goes on to remark that 'objects are said to be related, when there is any fact, simple or complex, either apprehended by the senses or otherwise, in which they both figure. Any objects, whether physical or mental, are related, or are in relation, to one another, *in virtue of any complex state of consciousness into which they both enter*; even if it be a no more complex state of consciousness than that of merely thinking them together' (1869, II: 9–10).

For present purposes, however, it is the third point that is most relevant. This is the *empirical claim* about 'our senses,' that, as the younger Mill puts it, 'they only open to let pass single attributes at a time' (1872b, p. 259). The traditional view goes back to Heraclitus, Democritus, and Epicurus (cf. Boring 1942, pp. 4–5). The notion is that the senses are passages capable of carrying certain data from the object to the mind, but not others. Specifically, each sense responds to a different attribute, that is, *non-relational* quality of an object. It is this which is carried to the mind and appears as a sensation. This – rather crude – theory about sensory processes entails that no relational data are ever given directly in sensation; all sensation consists of non-relational facts. It follows that all relational wholes are not a direct consequence of sensory processes, but arise only through a further process of association.

The claim here is that

(E) Sensory processes produce only non-relational sensations.

This *empirical claim* about how the senses operate is what, for the Mills, constrains the analytical vocabulary v_A, restricting it to non-relational predicates. Further, it is this theory that justifies the claim that all consciousness of relations is learned. Both these last two points deserve further comment.

The first point that must be emphasized is that, even if (E) is true, it does *not* follow that the analytical vocabulary v_A contains no relational terms. To say that v_A contains certain relational terms is to say that the data described by such terms cannot be introspectively decomposed. As we put it before (L_1) does *not* entail (L_2). Thus, v_A containing indecomposable relations is compatible with such data being the result of association. All that follows, as John Stuart Mill says, is that, if they are the result of association, then the association is indissoluble. *Even on John Stuart Mill's own account, relational data can be indecomposable while not being primitive, that is, not the result of learning.*

In terms of the logical structure of the theory, what is in the analytical vocabulary v_A is a matter to be discovered empirically by reference to responses under certain psychological sets. In particular, what is in v_A can (in principle, at least) be determined independently of any genetic hypothesis about the (physiological) sensory processes that cause sensations.

Thus, in terms of the logic of psychological analysis as clearly articulated by John Stuart Mill, the empirical claim (E) *cannot* be used to argue that relational wholes *must* be decomposable into non-relational facts. The *most* that (E) entails is that the discrimination of relations is learned, that is, is a result of associative processes working on non-relational elements. But as John Stuart Mill saw clearly, what is learned may none the less be incapable of analysis. The most one can say is that if one knows something is learned, then that makes it a *plausible hypothesis* that that thing can be analysed. The point is that knowing that something is learned does not establish the truth of the hypothesis that it can be analysed; only analytical research itself can establish the latter.

It is, I think, safe to say that both Mills overemphasize the support that (E) lends to the claim that relational facts are all capable of analytic decomposition. The difference between father and son lies in this fact, that analytic research would never lead James Mill to reject his claim – for him, principle can swallow observational fact – whereas for John Stuart, who thought through the logic of analytical research, it could. Through John Stuart's work, the theory had been rendered thoroughly empirical. As a consequence, while a crude theory or philosophical preference could prejudice the younger Mill to favour a certain hypothesis, empirical research could very well lead to the rejection of that hypothesis.

In John Stuart Mill's case, empirical research did not, of course, do that. He himself did not undertake the serious experimental research that was needed, or, therefore, the work that could lead him to reject the claim that all relational wholes are analysable. The point is that his thinking through the idea of psychological analysis from the perspective of empirical philosophy of science made it possible for such research to determine the issue. *That* was his significant contribution. Even if he could not free himself from his father's prejudices, he put psychology in a position where others could so free themselves.

It was in fact the next great textbook after Mill's *Analysis* that took the step of granting that (some) spatial relations could not be analysed. I refer to Herbert Spencer's *Principles of Psychology* (1902, II: 195; also pp. 183ff, 363; cf. Boring 1957, p. 241). The debate did go on through the remainder of the nineteenth century (cf. Bergmann 1952), until the unanalysability of relations was settled once and for all by Mach, von Ehrenfels, Stumpf, and the Gestalt psychologists (cf. Boring 1957, pp. 441ff). The point is, it had become an empirical debate, to be settled by experimental research.

It is still open to the psychologists to infer from such empirical claims as (E) and the weaker (A) that the indecomposable relations are none the less discriminated only as a consequence of learning. Once again, however, it must be emphasized that whether or not something is learned is a *matter of fact*. Throughout the nineteenth century the nativists argued that the capacity to discriminate (some) relations was unlearned, while the (so-called) empiricists argued that that capacity was acquired through association (cf. Boring 1942, pp. 28ff). It must be emphasized that 'empiricism' in this sense refers to a *psychological theory*, and not to a *philosophical* position, e.g., John Stuart Mill's. For, the latter is compatible with the claim of psychological theory that capacities to discriminate relations are innate.[10]

The question addressed by both nativists and empiricists was: How do sensory processes cause the awareness of structure? For the empiricists, the answer involved a *mental* process as well as a *physiological* process. That is, besides the processes in the sense organs and nervous system, there is also a process of association. For the nativists, the answer was that no mental process is involved. Helmholtz therefore insisted, not without reason, that nativism was no theory at all, since it says nothing about space and structure except that it is *not* generated in experience – that is, by a *mental* process of association – and must therefore, *faute de mieux*, be native. It was certainly not a psychological theory, though there is a physical-physiological process involved leading from the distal stimulus through the proximate stimulus to the response. Moreover, once the theory of evolution was on the scene, there would be the question of how these sensory information-processing mechanisms evolved. Herbert Spencer argued that structures not only cannot be analysed but also that our capacity to discriminate them is innate, native; it is a result, however, of an evolutionary process (1902, II, p. 195). The capacity is innate to the individual, but learned, as it were, by the species; the association works, if you wish, phylogenetically. In any case, however, the science of psychology which John Stuart Mill had made out of his father's *Analysis* could safely accommodate this version of nativism – that is, could accommodate it provided that experimental facts tended to support it.

Now clearly, if the capacity to discriminate structure is unlearned, then that calls into question any empirical theory that, like (A) or the even stronger (E), entails that such capacities must be learned.

John Stuart Mill himself, elsewhere than in the *Analysis*, tends to question (E). In the *Examination of Sir William Hamilton's Philosophy* we are told:

> A *rudimentary* conception [of extension, that is, of structure] must be allowed, for it is evident that even without moving the eye we are capable of having two successive sensations of colour at once, and that the boundary which separates the colours must give some specific affection of sight, otherwise we should have no discrimina- tive impressions capable of afterwards becoming, by association, representative of the cognitions of lines and figures which we owe to the factual and muscular sense. (1872b, p. 230; italics added)

Mill continues:

> But to confer on these discriminative impressions the name which denotes our matured and perfected cognition of Extension, or even to assume that they have anything in common with it, seems to be going beyond the evidence. (ibid.)

This is no doubt true: awareness of, that is, the capacity to discriminate, complex spatial structures is no doubt learned; but at the same time, and as Mill here very tentatively admits, *some* capacity to discriminate structure is unlearned, built into the sensory apparatus itself rather than derived from the effects of the latter by association. And to thus admit that there are unlearned capacities to discriminate relations is to reject as false the factual claim (E). Mill is here allowing that there was something to be said in favour of Reid's claim that there is an unlearned two-dimensional (and non-Euclidean) geometry of visibles; and is admitting the justice of Spencer's move to include relations among the basic building-blocks or elements upon which association can work. In order to account for the complexity of our mental life, the association- ist needs as much in the way of elements as he can, as it were, lay his hands on. James Mill simply tried to generate too much out of too little. He was able to convince himself of success only by virtue of letting his a priori convictions run roughshod over observational fact. His son, adapting psychology to transform it into an empirical science, was in that act constrained to add relations and awareness of structure that empiricists such as Berkeley and his father had themselves, on metaphysical grounds, felt constrained to reject. Once the metaphysics goes there is no 'problem' of relations for psychology, only the empirical questions whether they or, rather, some are analysable and, if not, whether the capacity to discriminate them is purely sensory (unlearned) or a consequence of mental associations (learned).

FIVE

Perception

While John Stuart Mill was prepared, as we saw in the last chapter, to allow that *some* relations are unanalysable and our capacity to discriminate them innate, it was, as we also saw, only a small part of our capacities to discriminate spatial structures that he allowed to be innate. In particular, he insists that our ability to recognize *distance* is learned: 'the notion of length in space, not being in our consciousness originally, is constructed by the mind's laws out of our notion of length in time' (1872b, p. 220).

There are two points here. The first concerns how Mill concludes that distance is not 'in consciousness originally.' The second concerns the associative process that yields the idea of distance. On the second issue Mill in effect adopts Berkeley's account of how we learn to perceive distance. He adopts, too, the Berkeley-Hume account of perceptual objects as patterns of sensible qualities. As for the first issue, Mill's argument here turns upon what he believes he knows about the physiology of perception. We shall look at these two issues in reverse order in the first section below. In considering Mill's views on these topics we look in particular at one of the critics of the Berkeleyan account of the perception of distance – Samuel Bailey. Bailey is hardly original – he makes many of the points made earlier by Kames and Reid – but he is interesting in the present discussion not only because Mill devoted an essay to refuting his views but also because Bailey, as we shall see in the next chapter, was also a critic of another aspect of the position of the philosophic radicals, that of Ricardian economics, and his judgments in both areas are of a piece. In the area of perception Bailey's criticisms depend upon assuming, as had Kames and Reid before him, that because a judgment is, phenomenologically, an intuition, that is, non-inferential, therefore it is innate. Bailey makes this inference in the case of causation, using it to argue against the Humean account of causation that the Mills accept. And he makes the same inference in the area of perception, to attack the Berkeleyan account of perception. We look at the first inference in the case of causation in the second section, and look at it in the case of perception in the third. The general point is that the inference is simply invalid: it confuses the phenomenological description with the analytical description, and it wrongly assumes that what cannot be introspectively analysed cannot be learned. In the final section we turn to look at some of the assumptions concerning the physiology of perception that Mill used in his argument against Bailey, and argue that developments going on even in Mill's own day were to show that those assumptions were invalid. Even so, we are able to conclude that in his main points against Bailey, Mill's position remains sound.

Before turning to the discussion of perception, that is, the perception of distance, a remark is in order on a comment of Sparshott (1978) that attempts to establish that the whole enterprise of the Mills, to attempt to show that depth perception is learned, is a priori misguided.

Mill, like Reid, allows that there is a spatial order among visibles, but this order lacks depth. In that sense, it is two-dimensional. This two-dimensional order is assumed as given in the account of perception. But we locate visible events in a three-dimensional space, that is, in a spatial order that includes depth. This localization of visibles in three-dimensional space is, according to Berkeley and to the Mills, a consequence of a process of learning by association. Sparshott wants to establish that this position is untenable. The capacity, he holds, to discriminate three-dimensional structures cannot be acquired or learned subsequent to our capacity to discriminate two-dimensional structures. For, he argues, the capacity to distinguish two-dimensional structures *presupposes* the capacity to discriminate three-dimensional structures. 'Our visual data can be neither two-dimensional nor three-dimensional, since those terms derive their meaning from reference to a space within which both solid and flat objects can be distinguished' (1978, p. liii). But the premiss is false. Whether or not a set of spatial relations constitutes a two-dimensional structure depends on *only* the *structural properties* of those relations. To discover whether structural properties (e.g., transitivity) hold of a relation one needs to know only the relation, its relata, and the facts about how it actually relates those relata. In particular, no comparison need be made to any other spatial structure. Sparshott's argument is thus unsound, and the Berkeley-Mill enterprise of attempting to show that the

perception of distance is a learned capacity has not been shown to be
a priori impossible.

1   Sensation and Perception

Let us begin by looking at Mill's claims about the associative process
that yields our idea of distance (cf. 1869, 1: 250ff).

According to the account Mill offers (1872b, pp. 220–1), we acquire
our notion of Extension, i.e., the fully developed notion that includes
the notion of distance, by moving our hand, or some other organ of
touch, along the line from A to B, or by walking over it if the parts are
far apart (1872b, p. 223). This yields a consciousness of a series of
muscular sensations. To say a space separates A from B is to say some
amount of these sensations do, or would, intervene; and to say it is a
greater or a lesser distance is to say that the series of sensations (amount
of muscular effort being given) is longer or shorter. An extended body
is a variety of resisting points (the feeling of resistance is a sensation of
our muscular frame [p. 214]), which exist simultaneously, but which
can be perceived by our tactile sense only successively, at the end of a
series of muscular sensations that constitute the distance. The sensation of muscular motion unimpeded is the idea of empty space; that of
motion impeded is that of filled space. The idea of an object at
such-and-such a distance is the idea of a series of simultaneously
existing resisting-points associated with a determinate temporal series
of muscular sensations of motion. (This idea, of course, given the
chemical mode of combination appropriate to mental phenomena, is
not the sum of the ideas of resistance and muscular sensations. Nor are
the latter literal, that is, integrant, parts of the idea of being at a certain
distance: in no sense are the ideas of muscular sensation literal parts of
the idea of a certain distance.) The idea of distance in general is the idea
of a (determinable) series of muscular sensations. The idea of a body
with depth (a three-dimensional object) is the idea of a (determinable)
series of muscular sensations.

Finally, sensations of touch or contact invariably accompany the
sensation of resistance. Thus, the former become representative of the
latter, that is, a mark or sign of the 'permanent possibility' of the latter
(1872b, p. 215). Similarly, simultaneous visual sensations are *symbols* of
tactual and muscular ones (p. 227). This accounts for the notion we
have of space as given visually with depth – an 'eye picture,' as Mill puts
it at one point (p. 222). For, it enables one to account, in terms of association, for how the visual awareness of points simultaneously existing

at a distance from one another can be 'generated by the mind out of its consciousness of succession – the succession of muscular feelings' (ibid.). A mass of visual sensations do not, as such, introduce a depth or distance structure – though, as we saw, they will not come without *some* spatial structure. But, by association, when such a mass of visual sensations enters consciousness it introduces the ideas of all the successive tactual and muscular feelings that accompany the passage of the hand over the whole coloured surface; the latter are made present to the mind all at once, and impressions that were successive in sensation become simultaneous in thought (pp. 224–5). Moreover, in this process we must recognize the role not merely of the visual sensations proper, the colours, but also of the muscular sensations present when the eyes focus on an object. Two objects at different distances may generate the same colour sensations but different eye motions will be required for focusing upon them. In this way, different muscular sensations from the eye serve as the *cues* for different distances; and it is these muscular sensations from the eye that introduce the ideas of touch and muscular change that constitute the idea of depth (pp. 226–7).

Such, then, is the associative process that Mill proposes will account for our capacity to discriminate depth visually. Although there is some evidence in its favour (cf. 1872b, p. 223ff; 1842–3, pp. 250, 255ff), the details, and even the general structure of the explanation, must be considered an *hypothesis* or plausible conjecture, rather than as inductively supported. Moreover, how much of the content can be recovered in analysis would also be an open question. In contrast, the general notion, that much of our capacity for depth perception is learned, *is undoubtedly sound.*

The only real question is, how much? To this Mill gave an unequivocal answer: all. Spatial structures not involving depth or distance may be unanalysable, and the capacity to discriminate them unlearned, as we saw in the preceding chapter (cf. 1872b, p. 230) – though even here, much is learned, since when the eye regards a figure and its boundary that organ travels, as it were, along the boundary, and the required muscular sensations in the eyeball can account for our capacity to discriminate the relevant structures (p. 229), and they rather than unanalysed relations can appear in the analysis. But in the case of depth or distance, *all* is learned: as Mill says, distance, or the notion of length in space, is not 'in consciousness originally' (p. 220). The question we have not answered is why Mill holds this opinion.

He is most explicit on this matter in his discussion (1842–3) of Bailey (1842), who had criticized the Berkeleyan theory of vision, that is, that theory of vision shared by both James and John Stuart Mill. The powers of vision, Mill tells us, are two: the original and the acquired (1842–3, p. 249). Depth vision is one of the latter. It is based on cues, including diminution of apparent magnitude (linear perspective), dimness or faintness of colour, and outline (aerial perspective). We know that depth vision is based on cues because

> those coloured appearances which are called visual or apparent position, figure, and magnitude, have existence only in two dimensions; or, to speak more properly, in as many directions as are capable of being traced on a plane surface. A line drawn from an object to the eye, or, in other words, the distance of an object from us, is not a visible thing. (ibid.)

Or, as he restates the argument later:

> We cannot see anything which is not painted on our retina; and we see things alike or unlike, according as they are painted on our retina alike or unlike. The distance between an object to our right and an object to our left is a line presented sideways, and is there-fore painted on our retina as a line; the distance of an object from us is a line presented endways, and is represented on the retina by a point. It seems obvious, therefore, that we must be able, by the eye alone, to discriminate between unequal distances of the former kind, but not of the latter. Unequal lines drawn across our sphere of vision, we can see to be unequal, because the lines which image them in the eye are also unequal. But the distances of objects from us are represented on our retina in all cases by single points; and all points being equal, all such distances must appear equal, or rather, we are unable to see them in the character of distances at all. (pp. 253–4)

Sensations are caused by the state of the sense organ, the proximate stimulus, which is in turn caused by some state of affairs in the environment, the distal stimulus. Depth, as well as distance, are features of the distal stimulus. Mill argues from what he knows of the physiology of the eye that these features could not casually affect that organ. This is, of course, an *empirical claim*; but, clearly, it is one with some plausibility. In any case, given that distance cannot affect the retina, it follows that there is nothing in the proximate stimulus to cause its effects, the sensations, to exemplify some feature correspond-ing to the distance.

To this argument Bailey replied (1842, p. 29): 'When an object is printed on the retina, the object is *seen* to be external as directly and immediately as the object is *felt* to be external.' No matter what are the facts concerning the proximate stimulus, Bailey asserts, we *do* recognize distance visually, and it is a fact, so far as we can tell, that tactual sensations are not ingredient in that awareness. In response to Mill's review (1842–3), Bailey continued to insist (1843, pp. 29–30) that, if 'distance is in reality a mere tactual conception,' it seems impossible that this could be 'mistaken for a visual perception.' To all this the appropriate reply consists of two points. First, to have the capacity to discriminate distance visually does not imply that it is not learned, or that tactual processes are not among the conditions of learning. Second, the tactual sensations that are among the conditions of association need not all be recoverable under the analytic set. As for the first point, Mill remarks that 'what experience does is to *superadd* to the impression of sense an instantaneous act of judgment' (1843, p. 257; italics added); it is not merely a matter of addition, but, in keeping with the chemical nature of mental phenomena, a matter of 'superadding.' As for the second point, 'the indistinctness ... of our ideas of tactual extension and magnitude, and the fact of our carrying on most of our mental processes by means of their visual signs, without distinctly recalling the tactual impressions upon which our ideas of extension and magnitude were originally grounded, is no argument against Berkeley's theory, but is exactly what, from the laws of association [including the law of obliviscence], we should expect supposing the theory to be true [and which therefore confirm that theory]' (p. 260).

The problem is that Bailey practises what we earlier saw Mill refer to, in his *Examination of Sir William Hamilton's Philosophy*, as the 'introspective' method, which assumes that if a notion *appears* intuitive, that is, is not consciously an inference or association, then it is *not* an association, or inference, *or* the result of learning (1872b, pp. 59, 216). The 'introspective' method is simply inadequate; the *known facts* of mental life concerning learning and analysis *conclusively establish* that, if one follows the method, one will *often* be led to infer *conclusions that are contrary to fact*. Mill's 'psychological' method, since it leads less often to contrary-to-fact conclusions, is a method it is much more reasonable to adopt. Bailey, like James Mill, adopts a principle on philosophical grounds and refuses to let the facts run counter to it. What John Stuart Mill does with respect to Bailey, as with respect to his father, is insist that the conjectures be so construed that experimental data could test their truth. Thus, where Bailey merely *insists* that, since depth is given, therefore it is intuitive and original, John Stuart Mill introduces *empirical considerations*. It may well be that his empirical claims concerning the proximate causes of sensations are false. That is a minor point compared with the far more important one of so transforming psychology as to establish that empirical tests are indeed relevant.

Some recent critics have been less than fair to John Stuart Mill in this matter. Thus, Pastore (1971, p. 158) argues that on Mill's view only one *minimum visible* would originally be perceived at a given moment, for, 'if two *minimum visiblia* were simultaneously perceived when two luminous sources stimulated the retina, the perceived interval would represent an original perception of extension.' But, as we saw, Mill admitted this much. And that is hardly the same as admitting an innate, or original, capacity to discriminate complex three-dimensional spatial structures.

Similarly, Sparshott (1978, p. liv) remarks, by way of criticism of Mill: 'Seeing is a complex activity, not a passive reception of stimuli.' This is true, but it is exactly the point Mill insists upon when he argues that our capacities to discriminate depth are *learned*: such capacities are not mere sensory responses but are, and are consequences of, ongoing *mental processes*. Interestingly enough, Bailey saw this point (1843, p. 44; 1855–63, I: 157, 174–7), and insisted that his view, which made perception of space 'original' rather than a consequence of association, is one in which the 'mind is passive in perception.' The states of consciousness that result from a stimulation of the nerves depend only on the 'respective constitution of the nerves' and the mind does not 'determine or even modify the result.' Stimulation of the retina will directly 'produce in us states of consciousness termed the perception of objects and their qualities,' and any activity of the mind, for example, association or inference, is denied. Conversely, of course, when Mill insists that acts of perception are a consequence of an associative process, he is insisting that the mind is active in perception. When Sparshott asserts that for Mill perception is passive, he shows that, unlike Bailey, he has just missed the point of what Mill was up to.

Again, Sparshott (1978, p. lvii) comments on Mill's point that we often forget elementary parts of mental processes to which we do not attend. For Mill (cf. 1842–3, p. 259) the meaning of a word (sound) is an idea associated with it, and therefore with the parts of that idea that are recoverable from it by analysis. Now, on most occasions of the use of a word, the word recalls to consciousness only a few of those parts – to be recoverable is not to be recovered! As Mill put it: 'words, as used on common occasions, suggest no more of the ideas habitually associated with them, than the smallest portion that will enable the mind to do what those common occasions require; and it is only to persons of more than ordinary vividness of imagination, that the names of things ever recall more than the meagrest outline of even their own conception of the things' (ibid.). All this not only seems true, but is readily comprehended, in principle, once we grasp the idea of introspective analysis as described by John Stuart Mill. After making this point about words as signs of ideas, Mill proceeds to argue that this, which is true of conventional signs, is true of natural signs also. Visual sensations suggest, after long experience and through association, ideas that have ideas of tactile sensations, muscular sensations, and ideas of motion as their metaphysical (*not* integrant) parts, most of which are, on any given occasion, not recovered in consciousness when the visual sign appears; rather, only so much appears as is needed to get on with ordinary tasks (pp. 259–60). Sparshott remarks (p. lvii) that 'we *can* distinctly recall the meaning of any familiar word, if we choose to attend to it, but we cannot by any analogous feat of attention recover the alleged tactile content of our visual impressions of distance.' But there is an ambiguity here that indicates a failure to understand Mill, or what introspective analysis attempts to do. For, what we attend to when we attend to the distinct meaning of the word (sound) is the idea under its *phenomenological description*; but to attend to this is *not* to *recover* by analysis all the genetic antecedents. And it is the recovery by analysis of the genetic antecedents of the idea of depth that Sparshott says is impossible. With the latter Mill would not, and does not, disagree. However, the idea of depth itself, as opposed to its metaphysical parts, is as distinct as any idea that forms the meaning of a word. Sparshott accuses Mill of using an improper analogy, but the appearance of disanalogy is generated only because Sparshott focuses upon the phenomenological rather than upon the analytical description in the case of words, and upon the analytical rather than the phenomenological description in the case of the (natural) visual signs. Once one notes that both descriptions apply to both cases, Sparshott's supposed disanalogy disappears. What this illustrates is Sparshott's failure to understand the notion of introspective analysis, the systematic account of which is John Stuart Mill's major contribution to psychology.

What Sparshott misses, in effect, is John Stuart's correction of James Mill. The idea of Everything does *not* have in it the idea of every thing. The whole is both less than, as well as more than, the sum of its parts. In the synthesis of ideas, the parts combine through the mental chemistry in which the parts are lost in the compound and in which the compound has properties not contained in the parts. In analysis the parts of the idea, which are not literally there, are *recovered. The parts are there dispositionally, not actually*: they can become present to consciousness *if* the mind is in the analytic set, but otherwise are not actually, only potentially present. The phenomenological description gives what is actually present; the analytical description recovers what are only potentially present in the data previously described phenomenologically.

Mill adopts the *context* account of meaning, as it was later called (cf. Boring 1942, p. 27). On this account, it takes at least two sensations or images to make a meaning. Or, at least, that is so at first. Later, when learning has occurred, one sensation or image may be enough; the other need be there only dispositionally. The two examples continually used are visual perception and language. The unfamiliar words of a new language may need the conscious contexts of their equivalents in the mother tongue, but this is not so for the words of the mother tongue itself: the accomplished reader reads rapidly, getting the meaning of every word. Originally the word (sound) causes the (compound) idea that is its meaning only if other sensations and ideas were actually present. Later the word causes the (compound) idea directly, without the other ideas being present. Or rather, they are present dispositionally – and if, as seems reasonable, such dispositions do as a matter of fact[1] have a physiological basis, then one can say with Titchener (1909) that they are carried in purely physiological terms. Originally, the other sensations and ideas had to be consciously realized; subsequently it suffices if they are 'there' in the sense that they will arise if given opportunity. A reader all along knows the meanings of the words he passes over so rapidly, simply because he can state each meaning *if* asked, if given the appropriate set.

Similarly, a visual sensation may need additional conscious sensation and imagery – may need a conscious *context* – before Voltaire's face is recognized; but the familiar face of one's mother is recognized instantly before any context can accrue to the sensory core. Originally, the visual sign causes the idea that is its meaning only if other sensations and other ideas are present, but later, after habituation, the other ideas need not be present; it suffices that there is only the tendency for them to be there if given the opportunity.

With these remarks about ideas, we can introduce what has been hovering in the background: the second crucial distinction of associationist psychology, that between *sensation* and *perception*.[2] The basic

distinction between sensation and perception was clearly made by
Locke (1700, I: 185–6) when he remarked 'concerning perception, that
the ideas we receive by sensation are often, in grown people, altered by
judgment, without our taking notice of it.' He continues:

> When we set before our eyes a round globe of any uniform colour,
> e.g. gold, alabaster, or jet, it is certain that the idea thereby
> imprinted on our mind is of a flat circle, variously shadowed, with
> several degrees of light and brightness coming to our eyes. But we
> having, by use, been accustomed to perceive what kind of
> appearance convex bodies are wont to make in us; what alterations
> are made in the reflections of light by the difference of the sensible
> figures of bodies; – the judgment presently, by an habitual custom,
> alters the appearances into their causes. So that from which is truly
> variety of shadow or colour, collecting the figure, it makes it pass
> for a mark of figure, and frames to itself the perception of a convex
> figure and a uniform colour; when the idea we receive from thence
> is only a plane variously coloured, as is evident in painting. (ibid.)

J.F.M. Hunter has recently, in his essay 'Seeing Dimensionally'
(1987), challenged this distinction between sensation and perception.
He suggests that what Locke might mean is 'either that on apprehend-
ing the flat, variously shadowed circle, we *think* "That will have been
produced by a sphere" – or that something happens and an alabaster
sphere replaces the variously coloured circle in the mind' (p. 559).
Naturally enough, Hunter finds difficulties in both these views. The
first requires that when we perceive a sphere we are always thinking
that something three-dimensional is producing our idea and also that
when we judge it to represent a sphere we continue to experience it as a
disc. The second supposition raises questions about the sort of medium
in which the sphere exists. These absurdities all derive, Hunter
suggests, 'from the supposition that what we apprehend is not the
sphere itself, but a representation of it' (p. 560). Since the consequences
of the supposition are absurd, we should give up the supposition and
simply 'say we see the sphere, rather than a representation of it' (ibid.).
   Berkeley mounted a similar attack on representationalism in his
Principles of Human Knowledge (1734; cf. Luce 1945). But Berkeley also
accepted Locke's distinction between sensation and perception and, in
fact, as we have seen, he offered, in his *New Theory of Vision* (1709), an
account of the habits that lead the mind to move from sensation to
perception that was far more detailed than Locke's. This suggests that

the coupling of Locke's distinction to the representationalist account of perception is not nearly so close as Hunter suggests.

Now, it is true that if Hunter's two readings were the only ones that could be given, then in all likelihood it would be reasonable to abandon Locke's distinction between sensation and perception. But neither of those two readings is necessary. Nor, in fact, is there anything in Locke's presentation of the distinction that presupposes the representational premise to which Hunter attributes all the philosophical problems that arise.

Consider a sphere in which one side is coloured green and the other side is coloured red. Suppose that this sphere is situated at eye level and that we are looking at it from straight on. Suppose further that the red side is turned directly towards us and the green side is turned away from us. It is certainly true that when we look at this sphere what we *perceive* is a sphere. Hunter is right to insist upon this. But, then, neither Locke nor Berkeley disagrees. What we see, Locke insists, is 'a round globe.' Indeed, we must also insist that what we perceive is a sphere, half of which is coloured red and half of which is coloured green. What we must also insist upon, however, is that, in the situation that we have supposed, we have *no sensory experience* of the green side that is turned away from us. There is a sensory experience of the red side that is turned towards us, but, while we perceive a sphere that is half red and half green, the green colour on the side of the sphere turned away from us is simply *not part of the sensory content* of our experience. This is a perfectly sensible point, and it is hard to understand why Hunter does not recognize it, why he does not recognize that there are many parts of the objects that we perceive which are not given in sense experience. But once that is recognized, then we have all that Locke was driving at with his distinction between sensation and perception.

It is, of course, true that Locke, and Berkeley after him, defends the further thesis that the sensory contents of which we are aware are all 'in the mind' in the sense of being properties of a *substantial* mind. But this, contrary to what Hunter (1987, pp. 561, 565) suggests, is a *further* thesis. Drawing the distinction between the sensory contents that we experience and the objects that we perceive in no way by itself entails that we construe the former as 'in the mind,' or, even more strongly, that they are in the mind construed ontologically as a substance. One could argue, as Hume did (cf. Wilson, 1989a), that this doctrine of a substantial mind is the thesis that leads to the sort of absurdity which Hunter quite rightly wishes to exorcise from philosophy. But then

Hunter should be going after the real culprit that generates the absurdities, namely the substantialist account of mind, rather than the innocuous, and, indeed, commonsensical distinction that Locke drew between sensation and perception.

We should in this context note also that many aspects of the dimensionality of objects are not given in sensation. We have considered a sphere, one half of which is red and the other half green. But now consider a hollow hemisphere, the convex surface of which is coloured red and the concave surface green. If we place them both at the same height, with the red surface facing us directly, then it is the red surfaces that are given in experience. In particular, we have no sensory experience of the spatial relations among the parts of the surface that are not given to us in sensory experience. It is no doubt true that in the one case what we perceive is a sphere and that in the other case what we perceive is a hollow hemisphere. But the spatial relations that constitute the one as a sphere and the other as a hollow hemisphere are *not* among the contents of our *sense* experience. This is not to say that no spatial relations are given in sense experience. As Locke indicates, we certainly would in each case experience a circular shape. To what extent we might perceive some sort of depth is a further issue. Locke suggests that *no* depth relations are given in sensation; the circle that is given in our *sense* experience is, upon his view, one that exhibits no depth; that is, when we perceive the globe, its circularity is given in sense experience but not the relations that constitute it as having depth. This view, that relations of depth and distance are not given in sense experience, was subsequently developed in detail by Berkeley, as we have already seen, and, as we shall see in this chapter, was also defended by John Stuart Mill. Hunter in fact states the relevant problem for those who hold that depth is not given in sense experience. 'What would show,' he asks, 'that it [the contents of sensory experience] had no thickness [depth]? Might we look at it from the side, and see how thin it was?' (1987, p. 554). We have sense experience of what is directly in front of us, and depth *ex hypothesi*, as we have seen Mill point out, is not directly in front of us. None the less, it is perfectly possible to argue, as Reid did, that certain depth relations are, in fact, given in sense experience. The point is that this is a dispute that is, as it were, within the ring: it takes for granted the commonsensical distinction that Locke draws between sensation and perception.

And once this distinction is granted, then, contrary to what Hunter asserts, there *is* a problem of 'seeing dimensionally.' We should certainly agree with Hunter that 'there is no need to *argue*' that 'we see

... trees, houses, globes and so on, ... and see in what spatial relations they stand' (1987, p. 566); there is no doubt that this phenomenological claim is true. Now, the dimensionality of things, and, more specifically, their depth and distance, is given in perception. But, as we have just noted, many of these spatial relations that are given in perception are not given in sensation. On this point, Locke, Berkeley, and, as we shall see, the Mills are undoubtedly as correct as is Hunter on the phenomenology of perception. The problem of 'seeing dimensionally' is in effect nothing other than the problem of explaining the connection between sensation and perception.

Once the distinction between sensation and perception is granted, then that poses the question that is implicit in Locke's discussion. There is, it is clear, some connection between sensing and perceiving; somehow that latter is the product of the former. But what, precisely, is the causal connection between the two? Hunter disparages the asking of this question; to raise it is to betray philosophical naïvety, it is to imply that one has not read Wittgenstein (Hunter 1987, p. 560). Hunter refers to the discussion of David Marr in his *Vision* (1982). Marr states the problem in terms of 'images' rather than 'sense experience,' but the point is the same. How is it, asks Marr, that starting from images we discover 'what is present in the world, and where it is' (p. 3); and how is it that we 'reliably derive properties of the world from images of it' (p. 23). These are, quite clearly, the very same questions that were asked by Berkeley and later by John Stuart Mill. Where Marr differs from these earlier thinkers is not so much in the questions asked as in the answers given. Marr plausibly supposes that the process that leads from sense experience (images) to veridical, or at least reliable, perceptions is mediated by certain brain processes that are analogous to the processes in a computer; and he takes it as his research task to discover what sort of computations are made in the mediating brain processes. This answer to the questions raised is very different from the sorts of answer given by Berkeley and John Stuart Mill. It is necessary to note, however, that the two sorts of answer are, in principle at least, compatible. Mill at least, if not Berkeley, allowed that there are physical processes that underlie mental processes, and that these occur in the central nervous system (that is, the brain). It is entirely possible to hold that the brain processes that underlie complex associational processes are analogous to the computational processes that take place in a computer. Mill, for historical reasons, could never have thought of the issue in these terms, but that is not the point. What must be emphasized, rather, is that Marr is quite appropriately addressing the same issues that Berkeley and Mill addressed, and that his approach to these problems does not invalidate theirs.

Hunter complains that Marr 'does not ... make it a question for investigation whether we start with images' (1987, p. 566n). In this way Hunter calls into question the intelligibility of the set of problems that Marr's research aims to answer – and also the problems that the research of Berkeley and John Stuart Mill aimed to answer. But, as we have just seen, the distinction that Locke drew between sensation and perception is a real distinction, and once this distinction is recognized, then it is legitimate to try to discover the processes that link the two. Perhaps Hunter is misled by Marr's use of the term 'image' to describe the contents of sensory experience. It does suggest that these contents are somehow 'in the mind'; and this in turn suggests a representational-ism akin to that of Locke. Since Hunter, like Berkeley and Hume, finds this latter doctrine the source of scepticism in philosophy, it may be that Marr's unfortunate terminology misleads him into thinking that the question that Marr is trying to answer is that of how the representation-alist is able to infer from ideas that are ontologically dependent upon his own mind, and with which alone he is acquainted, to the public objects that cause those ideas. This is, indeed, a problem that likely admits of no solution that does not generate the sorts of absurdity to which Hunter draws our attention (cf. Wilson 1970). None the less, however poorly Marr states the questions he is attempting to answer, it is clear that they concern not the *philosophical* problems of representa-tional realism but the *scientific* problem of the connections between sensation and perception.

So, Hunter notwithstanding, Locke's distinction between sensation and perception is perfectly legitimate. And this raises the question, as Locke also recognizes, of the relation between sensation and percep-tion. The transition from sense to perception is the transition, as Locke speaks, from an idea of sensation to the idea of a perceptual object. Locke describes this transition as one of 'habitual custom'; it is a habit established through 'frequent experience'; and as a result of this frequent experience the habitual transition is 'performed so constantly and quick' that only the 'idea formed by our judgment' is noticed (Locke 1700, pp. 185–6). But Locke proceeds no farther with any deeper account of the connection between sensation and perception. The use of 'habit' and 'custom' by Locke certainly suggests a deeper account in terms of associative processes, and Berkeley, as we know, was to pursue this theme. But it was also possible to argue that, in fact, no deeper explanation could be given, that the connection between sensation and perception is primitive, and that Locke had taken the matter as far as it could be taken.

The position that one cannot proceed farther than Locke had done and cannot develop an associationist account of the connection between sensation and perception was defended most vigorously by Reid (1785a, 1785b). There is sensation on the one hand and perception on the other. Sensations, that is, the contents given in sense experience, are not referred to objects. That is to say, a sensation is not *qua* sensation taken to be in an object that is external, is at a distance, has size and solidity, and has constancy and shape. Perception is caused by sensation, but is much more than the latter: it includes both a conception of an *object* perceived – what we may call a 'percept,' that is, an *idea* of the object perceived – and also an immediate and irresistible conviction of the object's present existence. As sensation, the smell of a rose is caused by, but not referred to, the rose; however, as perception, the smell of the rose is referred to, and actually in, the rose itself. If the rose that causes the sensation is to be perceived, then both the conception or idea of it and the instantaneous conviction of its objective existence must be added to the sensation. But how does this expansion of sensation into perception and objective reference take place? Reid goes no farther than Locke in providing an explanation. In the end all he does is insist that God, in his wisdom, causes the necessary additional aspects to transform sensation into man's knowledge of the external world.[3]

Thomas Brown later argued (1820) that science could do better than this retreat into theology, or, what is the same, this proclamation of ignorance. Brown brought to bear the principles of association, or, as he called it, 'suggestion' (in order to avoid the bad associations that had by then accrued to 'association' [p. 258]). Using these notions, he added a positive hypothesis about how reference to an external object is added to sensation in perception. An object, he held, is something that has extension and depth, and that furnishes resistance; and knowledge of extension and resistance is gained through the sense of touch and (in the case of resistance) the sense of muscular exertion. It is these latter that give us belief in a real external object. The smell of the rose is at first pure sensation, but it comes to be referred to the extended and resistant object, which is the perceived rose; this reference occurs because the sensation 'suggests' (by association) the tactual and muscular feelings of extension and resistance (pp. 157ff).[4] This is an early version of the context theory of meaning, as applied specifically to perception. As Boring remarks (1942, p. 14), 'this insight into the Creator's methods was scientifically an advance over Reid.'

Reid took the pure sensation to be mental. Since it was a quality, and since it was not in the external (material) substance, and since all qualities must be in substances, he concluded it must be in a mental substance, that is, the mind of the perceiver. This presupposes an ontology of substances.[5] But (Reid notwithstanding) Berkeley had exorcised material substance, and Hume, mental substance, on grounds of an empiricist principle of acquaintance.[6] Mill accepted both these points (1872b, Chs. x–xii). In particular, Mill accepts the Berkeley-Hume account of perceptual objects as patterns of sensible qualities. And the rejection of mental substance leads Mill to a correction of Reid's (and Berkeley's) account of pure sensation: the latter is neither mental nor material: 'Berkeley alleged that to a person born blind, and suddenly enabled to see, all objects would seem to be in his eye, or rather in his mind. It would be a more correct version, however, of the theory, to say that such a person would at first have no conception of *in* or *out*, and would only be conscious of colours, but not of objects' (1842–3, p. 251). Rather, a sensation may be *either*, that is, either mental or material, depending upon the *context* it is in. The colour sensation, when taken as the effect of a certain sensory (physiological) process, and apart from any further associative context, is taken as a feeling. Learning causes this feeling to suggest tactual and muscular sensations. When this context is provided, the sensation is given external reference. The result is a perception (i.e., a perceiving) that is of an external object, and by which the colour is perceived as residing in that object. This object that the perception is of, and the quality residing in this object, together constitute (in the veridical case) the cause of the sensory process that has the quality *qua* felt sensation as its effect (pp. 251–2).

The sensation *causes* a perception (perceiving). As Mill puts it in the *Logic*: 'Besides the affection of our bodily organs from without, and the sensation thereby produced in our minds, many writers admit a third link in the chain of phenomena, and which consists in the recognition of an external object as the exciting cause of the sensation' (1872a, p. 53). Nor does Mill disagree with these writers: 'These acts of what is termed perception, whatever be the conclusion ultimately come to respecting their nature, must, I conceive, take their place among the varieties of feelings or states of mind' (ibid.). These perceptions are not inferences, but appear as intuitions. Whether they are unlearned, and the conditions under which they are veridical, are not the concern of logic but of the science of psychology: 'In these so-called perceptions, or direct recognitions by the mind, of objects, whether physical or spiritual, which are external to itself, I can see only cases of belief; but of belief which claims to be intuitive, or independent of external evidence. When a stone lies before me, I am conscious of certain sensations which I receive from it; but if I say that these sensations come to me from an external object which I *perceive*, the meaning of these words is, that receiving the sensations, I intuitively *believe* that an external cause of those sensations exists. The laws of intuitive belief, and the conditions under which it is legitimate, are a subject which ... belongs not to logic, but to the science of the ultimate laws of the human mind' (pp. 53–4). The perception caused by the sensation is an affirmed *idea*. This affirmation makes the idea a case of *belief*, rather than, say, imagination. Being a belief or believing is a quality or property of the act of perception that contains the idea. This quality is itself unanalysable, as is the quality that makes the having of an idea a case of imagination. As John Stuart Mill puts it in the notes to his father's *Analysis*: 'What ... is the difference *to our minds* between thinking of a reality, and representing to ourselves an imaginary picture? I confess that I can perceive no escape from the opinion that the distinction is ultimate and primordial' (1869, 1: 412).[7] The idea that is affirmed in the perception is *of* an external object, or, to use the language of Brentano (1874), intends it, and this object is (normally) the cause of the sensation. This idea has as metaphysical (*not*: integrant) parts sensations of touch and muscular assertion. Originally, these latter sensations would have actually to be present, but after habituation they are only potentially present, ready to be realized by association if the opportunity permits, but not immediately distinguishable in detail in the perceptual instant. The idea which is the percept is the compound, formed by mental chemistry, of the sensations of colour, touch, and muscular exertion.

Mill describes this compound idea in the *Logic* as follows:

It is certain ... that a part of our notion of body consists of the notion of a number of sensations of our own, or of other sentient beings, habitually occurring simultaneously. My conception of the table at which I am writing is compounded of its visible form and size, which are complex sensations of sight; its tangible form and size, which are complex sensations of our organs of touch and of our muscles; its colour, which is a sensation of sight; its hardness, which is a sensation of the muscles; its composition, which is another word for all the varieties of sensation which we receive under various circumstances from the wood of which it is made, and so forth. All or most of those sensations frequently are, and, as we learn by experience, always might be, experienced simultaneously, or in many different orders of succession at our own choice: and hence the thought of any one of them makes us think of the others, and the whole become mentally amalgamated into one mixed state of consciousness, which, in the language of the school of Locke and Hartley, is termed a Complex idea. (1872a, p. 57)

This passage makes clear several things. First, the Berkeley–Hume account of perceptual objects is taken by Mill to be correct: the perceived external object is a complex of *qualities*. These qualities are *structured*, both by *relations* and by *laws*. The complexity occurs both simultaneously and successively.

Second, ingredient in the act of perception is a conception, or compound idea, of the table perceived. The compound idea is compounded of the qualities of the table perceived. These qualities 'frequently are' and 'always might be' experienced. *Taken as experienced, these qualities are sensations. And when not experienced, these qualities that 'might be' experienced are possibilities of sensation.* 'A body ... is not anything intrinsically different from the sensations which the body is said to produce in us; it is, in short, a set of sensations, or rather, of possibilities of sensation, joined together according to a fixed law' (1872a, p. 58).

The qualities that are possible sensations often are not, and may never be, perceived; they exist even if the person who could sense them is annihilated. This is what it means to say that the objects constituted by these qualities exist externally to, and independently of, the perceiver (1872b, pp. 178–9). (Boring [1942, p. 15] suggests that objects are subjective; nothing in Mill supports this Berkeleyan or idealistic reading.) Some sensations appear only in certain circumstances, for example, a special state of the environment of the object (lighting affects colour) or a special state of the sense organs (e.g., jaundice) (cf. p. 181); the possibilities for such sensations change with changing circumstances, they are not permanent. But other qualities are there independently of changing circumstances; these are 'certified or guaranteed possibilities of sensation' (p. 180). Actual sensations are seldom common to two perceivers, but the permanent possibilities are (p. 182). It is therefore these 'permanent possibilities' that we identify as matter or external nature (ibid.).[8]

Third, the above passage also makes clear that the idea constituting the perception contains, that is, *contains as metaphysical parts*, both the felt sensations and also the ideas of the unfelt or possible sensations that constitute the perceived object. These sensations and ideas are 'amalgamated' into the compound idea constituting the perception. Such 'amalgamation' is, of course, a result of the compounding of mental chemistry. Thus, the parts so 'amalgamated' are metaphysical, rather than integrant, parts. They are not literally in the compound idea, not actually present to the mind, but they are potentially present, ready to be realized by association if the opportunity permits. If they are not actually present to the mind, their *possibility* is actually present as the idea of which they are the metaphysical parts.

Fourth, in a perception, the idea is of an object. The object is a unity, where the unity is a matter of its being a relational or structured whole, including the relations of depth and distance in three-dimensional space. In the analysis of the idea, there are among the metaphysical parts therein recovered no relations, at least no relations of depth or distance. Correlated with the latter (via the laws connecting analytical and phenomenological descriptions) are non-relational muscular sensations. It does not follow from this that the perceived relations do not exist. What has happened is an associative process. This process begins – or so the theory holds – from non-relational elements, that is, muscular sensations, tactual sensations, and bi-dimensional visual sensations. These elements are reconstituted in the associative processes as an idea of a relational whole. The process does not merely conjoin the parts mechanically, but reconstitutes them into a new unity in a process of mental chemistry. This new unity is an idea, and, more specifically, an idea of a certain structured object. The fact that this idea is generated out of non-relational sensations entails neither that the idea cannot have as its object a structured whole, nor that the entity that is the object must be unstructured. *Mill's proposals or hypotheses concerning the analysis of acts of perception into non-relational elements are quite compatible with one maintaining with respect to the objects perceived an ontology of relations.*

Fifth, in a perception, the idea is a phenomenologically simple entity, compounded chemically out of metaphysical parts but without integrant parts. The object of this phenomenologically simple idea is also a unity, but its unity is not that of a simple but rather that of a *patterned* or structured set of events; the object is, as Berkeley and Hume argued, not a simple entity, that is, not a substance. Kames and Reid, as we saw, argued from phenomenological simplicity of the perceptual judgment to the simplicity of the object; that is, from the simplicity of the perceptual judgment they inferred a substantialist account of perceptual objects. Mill's discussion makes clear the invalidity of this inference.

But if one accepts that this inference is invalid, there does arise the further issue of how a simple entity can be *of*, or *intend*, a complex entity. This question is indeed a difficult one in the ontology of mind, and one that we cannot go into here.[9] But one need not solve it to accept Mill's point against Kames and Reid: for all that it raises further difficulties, Mill's point remains sound.

2   Intuition and Causation

As we saw in the preceding section, Mill's hypotheses about how acts of perception are introspectively analysable into non-relational elements are quite compatible with maintaining an ontology of relations with respect to the objects perceived. It does not, however, follow from this that one must accept an ontology of relations. And, in fact, as we saw, John Stuart Mill is hesitant about relations, although that is not here the issue. The important point is one we have already made, and that Mill emphasizes, namely, that what he calls the 'introspective method' is no safe method in metaphysics. Thus, a judgment or perception being apparently intuitive or non-inferential does not entail that it is unlearned, native, or original. Nor, therefore, does it entail that what is discriminated in a perception must be taken as an ontologically unanalysable whole.

Bailey and Hamilton make just this inference. Nor do they do it only in the case of space. Thus, for example, Bailey makes the same inference in the case of causation.

The Mills, of course, accept the Humean account of causation as, objectively speaking, regularity and as, subjectively, a habit of inference.[10] For James Mill causal belief is a matter of simple association (1825, 1: 362–74, 389–91). John Stuart adds required qualifications. Belief is a sort of association, but it is not so rigid a habit that the mind cannot imagine the contrary – something for which neither Hume nor James Mill makes allowance. The difference between an act of believing or accepting as true, and an act of imagining, that is, the difference between propositional attitudes,[11] is a primitive qualitative difference, according to the younger Mill (1869a, 1: 412). A causal belief is a compound idea that is accepted as true, that is, an idea qualified as a believing, and this compound idea is an association of the ideas of the cause and of the effect. Originally, felt succession of sensations causes both the association of the ideas and also the qualifying of the compound of ideas as a belief. But, as a result of learning, the process by which a compound idea becomes a believing rather than, say, a fantasizing, becomes more complicated. We need to distinguish, John Stuart Mill correctly argues in his notes to the *Analysis*, association as causing mechanical belief from belief that is regulated by evidence and conforms to successions in reality, that is, is true (1: 407).[12] When people are young, mere association causes belief or expectation, but mere association, or what amounts to the same, induction by simple enumeration, is unreliable and the frustration of expectation causes us to come to rely upon evidence (1: 437–8). Even here, one must distinguish with respect to evidence what it does cause and what it ought to cause (1: 435). Evidence for general truths rests ultimately upon the evidence for the uniformity of nature (1: 436), but it relies not only upon fulfilments of expectations but also upon their disappointments (1: 438), that is, it is the logic of eliminative induction.[13] Experience leads to the conclusion that, relative to the goal of arriving at general truths (1: 434), these methods are the ones we ought (so far as we can tell) to adopt (1: 438). When the mind discovers these things, it disciplines itself in the interest of truth, disciplines its generalizing tendency (1:437), so that not every observed succession generates an association of ideas that is believed or accepted as true.

It was Berkeley's achievement, as we have said, to break out of the substance philosophy that had gripped men's minds to that time. It was he who first proposed that ordinary things were not substances, that is, continuants that endured through change and had sensible properties but were not themselves given in sense. Rather, Berkeley proposed, an ordinary thing has no component that endures through change, and is to be analysed as a process, that is, as a sequence of events. These events are the sensible properties of the substantialists without the underlying substance. These events form a sequence that is ordered – spatially, temporally, and causally. The Mills accept this analysis. For James Mill the idea of a thing is a cluster of ideas (1825, 1: 348), and, most important, this includes ideas of causal relations: 'In my belief ... of the existence of an object, there is included the belief, that, in such and such circumstances, I should have such and such sensations' (1: 349). The younger Mill also accepts this Berkeleyan account: 'The Object is thus to be understood as a complex idea, compounded of the idea of various sensations which we have, and of a far greater number of sensations which we would expect to have if certain contingencies were realized' (1869, 1: 414). It is this account that is developed in detail in the *Examination of Sir William Hamilton's Philosophy* (1872b). Now, in an act of perception we have an idea that is accepted as true. It follows that this act involves *expectation* (1869, 1: 414; 1872b, pp. 177–9). Thus, *among the parts of any act of perception are causal beliefs.*

However, if causal beliefs are involved in any act of perception, such beliefs are to be analysed into associations, that is, as compound ideas that arise through associative processes. And to say that they arise through associative processes is to say that they are acquired as a result of learning. However, such acts of perception are themselves *simple unified wholes*. Causal beliefs are, objectively, about regularities; they are true if and only if certain regularities obtain in nature. Thus, from the fact that such beliefs are parts of acts of perception, and acts of perception are simple unified wholes, the Mills are, quite correctly, not prepared to conclude that therefore causation is a primitive unanalysable notion. Once again, simplicity on the side of the act does not entail simplicity on the side of the object.

In contrast, Bailey makes just such an inference in the case of spatial relations. We would not be surprised, then, if he were to do the same with respect to causation, inferring a non-Humean view that objectively causation is a simple unanalysable relation from the fact that we often recognize through a simple unitary act of perception that one event causes another event.

Bailey argues that causation cannot be the same as regular sequence. In the first place, he argues, there are regular sequences that are not those of cause and effect, for example, the notes of a tune follow one another and the flash of a piece of artillery is followed by the report, cases of sequence that are not causation (1855–63, III: 45). These examples are, of course, inconclusive: one must bring to bear, as Mill did in the *Logic* (1872a, pp. 338ff) in response to like examples from Reid, the distinction between an invariable antecedent and an unconditioned invariable antecedent. Once this is done Bailey's examples are easily enough disposed of.[14]

Second, Bailey argues, there are 'instances of causation which we directly discern as such' (1855–63, III: 43), and: 'It is obviously impossible for us to perceive this invariableness in a single instance, or in other words to perceive it from a cause once producing an effect; for the simple reason that it is a relation which can have place only amongst a number of instances. We may perceive a cause producing an effect without reference to any similar event, but to perceive it *invariably* produce an effect, we must witness a number of similar events' (ibid.; his italics). In response to this, two things must be said. One, given background knowledge, then perceiving a single event or, at least, a single experiment *can* legitimately justify the conclusion that a certain invariable sequence holds. This can be illustrated by an example adapted from Ducasse (1951, pp. 91–100):[15] 'I bring into the room and place on the desk a paper-covered parcel tied with string in the ordinary way and ask the students to observe closely what occurs. Then, proceeding slowly so that observation may be easy, I put my hand on the parcel. The end of the parcel the students face at once glows. I then ask them what caused it to glow at that moment, and they naturally answer that the glowing was caused by what I did to the parcel immediately before' (p. 95). He concludes: In this case it is clear that what the spectators observed, and what they based their judgment of causation upon, was not repetition of a certain act of mine followed each time by the glow, but *one single case* of sequence of the latter upon the former. This case, Ducasse argues, as Bailey argues, does not conform to Hume's definition of causation as constant conjunction but is nevertheless judged by unprejudiced observers to be a case of causation. So much the worse for Hume, and regularity views of causation, is the conclusion Ducasse draws.

But is it legitimate?

Ducasse describes a situation. In the situation a causal assertion is made. From his description Ducasse draws certain conclusions that have the anti-Humean import that the causal assertion in the situation does not involve the assertion of a generality. But Ducasse's description is by no means complete. By filling in certain details that may quite reasonably be assumed to be part of the situation, it is possible for the Humean to deny that Ducasse's conclusions may be inferred from the situation he describes. The reasonable filling out of Ducasse's description enables the Humean consistently to maintain that the causal assertion made in the situation does, after all, involve the assertion of a generality.

Hume described the Ducasse-type situation in this way: 'Tis certain, that not only in philosophy, but even in common life, we may attain the knowledge of a particular cause merely by one experiment, provided it be made with judgment, and after a careful removal of all foreign and superfluous circumstance' (1739, p. 104). And if we look carefully at Ducasse's example, then we find that there is precisely this 'careful removal of all foreign and superfluous circumstances' at work.

Think in terms that Mackie (1965) has made familiar. Let H = hand on box, G = box glowing. The field F is objects of this boxy sort, which are able to glow, and so on. Let this particular box be a. Then we have *two* events: a at t_1 when H and G are absent and a at t_2 when both are present. Ducasse describes it as one experiment: it is that, but there are two events in the one experiment. This last is the clue. For the existence of the *two* events enables one to begin to employ the methods of eliminative induction – that is, provided one has available those crucial

major premisses that permit these methods to work. It is such
premisses that Hume had in mind when he spoke of the 'connexion
being comprehended under another principle, that is already habitual.' More fully: 'the connexion of the ideas is not habitual after one
experiment; but this connexion is comprehended under another
principle that is habitual; which brings us back to our hypothesis. In all
cases we transfer our experience to instances, of which we have no
experience, either *expressly* or *tacitly*, either *directly* or *indirectly*' (1739,
p. 105; his italics). But let us see in detail how the eliminative mechanisms work, and see if it is reasonable to suppose that Ducasse's students
have the necessary principle or principles available in the situation
described.

On the basis of background knowledge we can list a set of conditions the
presence or absence of which could be relevant to the presence of G in a
in field F. Thus we have wires (W), antenna (A), internal structure (I)
(which we know is there though we may not know its details). On this
basis we can use Mill's Method of Difference, which is also the sixth of
Hume's 'Rules by which to judge of causes.' We apply this method
according to data such as these (a = absent, p = present):

$$G\ H\ W\ A\ I$$
$$a \text{ at } t_1 \quad a\ a\ a\ a\ p$$
$$a \text{ at } t_2 \quad p\ p\ a\ a\ p$$

and infer that in this context being H is sufficient for being G, that,
relative to the field F, all H are G, or, in symbols, that $(x)\ (Hx \supset Gx)$
obtains. Here, the context is defined by the field F *and the background
knowledge* that implies *there is* a sufficient condition for G and that it is
one of H, W, A, and I (or perhaps a complex, e.g., disjunctive or
conjunctive, property built out of these but, for the sake of simplicity,
let us ignore this complication). This background knowledge is
knowledge that regularity obtains, though, to be sure, it is of a more
complex form than the simple '$(x)\ (Hx \supset Gx)$' that is ultimately
concluded. Rather, it involves mixed quantification: 'there is property f
which is one of H, W, A, or I, and which is such that for all x, if x is f then
x is G.' By virtue of this complex quantificational form, this regularity is
able (to speak with Hume) to 'comprehend other principles under it.'
And certainly, there is no reason why Hume or a Humean such as Mill
might not hold that the students, through prior experience, had
confirmed this regularity, made it already 'habitual.'

On the basis of this lawful knowledge, then, and the observations,
as they are recorded in the table, one can deduce that being H at t is

sufficient for being G at t (relative to F). In other words, one does know a causal relation in this context. However – and this is the point – this knowledge involves knowing a generality that has been discovered in the context. The events (a, t_1) and (a, t_2) are used to arrive at the law. This law is then used in asserting a causal relation between $G(a, t_2)$ and $H(a, t_2)$. The events are used to infer the law, and then the law is used to explain the events.[16]

This reply to Ducasse – and Bailey – depends upon the perfectly reasonable assumption that the students enter the situation with a certain amount of *background knowledge of regularities*. This knowledge permits a number of hypotheses to be formulated about the circumstance that confronts them. They then reason from observational data that they *come to acquire* in the circumstance to the conclusion that, of the possible hypotheses, one alone is consistent with those data. The uneliminated hypothesis is, of course, a generality and as such asserts *more than* what is in the observational data available at the end of the situation. The point is not that we here overcome the logical gap between sample and total population, but simply that, of the possible hypotheses, this one alone is justified by the one present experiment and another principle that already, on the basis of previous experience, is (in Hume's terms) 'habitual.'

I conclude, then, that Ducasse and Bailey have not refuted the Hume-Mill 'regularity' theory of causation and therefore that Mill can consistently hold this 'regularity' theory and agree with Bailey that some causes are known on the basis of a single experiment.

And in response to Bailey's second point one must say, two, that when one perceives a pair of events, the idea in that act, which is of, or intends, those two events, may be a fusion of not only ideas of those two events but also of the belief that events of the one sort are a consequence of events of the other sort. Mill, we saw, holds just this position. Thus, he can agree with Bailey, concerning a fire that consumes a piece of paper and a stream that turns the wheels of a mill, that 'these are events which are perceived through the organs of sense. No one doubts that he sees the fire consume that paper thrown into it, or that he sees the stream turn the wheel on which it impinges' (1855–63, III: 29). The point is that involved in the act of perception in which a cause produces a (singular) effect may very well be the idea of invariable sequence. Thus, perceiving a pair of singular events and perceiving an invariable sequence are not, as Bailey suggests, incompatible.

However, the idea of invariable sequence will be fused into the idea in the act of perception only if association has antecedently produced that idea of invariable sequence. But Bailey has produced no grounds at all to suppose that our capacity to perceptually recognize instances of causal connection is unlearned.

His case against the Mills and Humeans in general is thus unsound.

Bailey's own view is that the idea of causation is derived from direct perception: 'Every case of *inferred* causal connexion must be analogous to cases which we *directly perceive*' (1855–63, III: 46; his italics). Causation is a primitive relation that admits of no more analysis than the sensation of *red*:

> We doubtless apply the common epithet *red* to the poppy and the geranium because they resemble each other in a certain visible attribute or property.
>
> But if you ask me to assign the particular property or circumstance or attribute in which they resemble each other I will not say they are alike in colour, for that would be an evasion; I can answer only that they are alike in being 'red,' in having a red colour. It is an ultimate fact that I perceive them to be similar in a certain visible respect which I designate by the epithet 'red,' and the inquiry is at an end.
>
> Precisely in the same way I call the fire when scorching a piece of paper and the water when melting a lump of sugar or turning a wheel, by the common name cause, on account of their resembling each other in the circumstances of producing results. I call them causes for doing what I cannot better express than by the word causing. (III: 35)

Bailey draws this conclusion from the premiss that in perceiving we discern or recognize causal connections. The argument here parallels that for other relations.

> We have reached the extreme length of our speculative and of our expository tether.
>
> We are in this case [A resembles B] at one of those primary facts beyond which it is, in the nature of the case, impossible to go.
>
> All that can be said is that we are so constituted as to perceive that things resemble one another.
>
> So we perceive objects to be equal or near or opposite to each other, as well as a multitude of other relational facts – facts in which the two objects at least must bear a part, and which, if we wish to

express in language, we must resort for that purpose to definite phrases not resolvable into others more significant.

It is just the same with 'causing' as with 'resembling': they are both general terms expressive of primary facts or circumstances of a relational character which we directly perceive. (III: 37–8)

But once again, the argument is invalid. From the fact that we 'directly perceive' something, from the fact that the judgment is apparently intuitive and non-inferential, it simply does not follow that the connection it is about is unanalysable. Nor does it follow from that premiss that the capacity so to discern such a connection is unlearned, that is, that it is a fact beyond further explanation that 'we are so constituted as to perceive' such connections.

Once again we may conclude that the phenomenological method, what Mill calls the 'introspective' method, is not a sound method in philosophy. We do 'directly perceive' certain spatial relations. We do 'directly perceive' certain causal connections. We may consistently hold this and agree with Russell and against Mill that those spatial relations are basic ontological building-blocks, while agreeing with Hume, the Mills, and Russell that the causal connections are not primitive and can be analysed into invariable sequence. Bailey and those who argue with him from what we 'directly perceive' – for example, more recently Gibson in the case of perception[17] – simply do not come to grips with the issue.

3   Intuition, Innateness, and Perception

Bailey appealed elsewhere in his discussion to the 'direct perception' that we have of relations to attack views of the Mills.

Recall from chapter 4, sections 3 and 4, that Mill, in his discussion of our perception of spatial relations, assumes both

(A) Different kinds of sensory processes cause different sorts of elementary sensations; and different sorts of elementary sensation are caused by different kinds of sensory process

and the even stronger

(E) Sensory processes produce only non-relational sensations.

What Bailey attempts to argue is that *all* such appeals are out of place in the psychology of our perception of spatial relations. The premiss to which Bailey appeals is the 'direct perception' or intuition that we have of spatial facts. This 'direct perception' guarantees innateness, he holds, and therefore simply renders irrelevant appeal to facts, or rather, tentative hypotheses, such as (A) and (E), to establish that our capacity to discriminate spatial wholes is learned.

To discuss these issues, let us again consider the perception of spatial structures.

Bailey argued by way of criticism that in perception the colour sensation itself had to be considered external or, at least, converted into the perception of the coloured external object (1842, p. 21). Since these alternatives are absurd, he rejects the theory. Mill argues, however, that his theory (and Berkeley's) is committed to neither alternative. In the first place, the sensation *qua* sensation could, of course, not be external, that is, taken to have external reference, since the latter, as Mill points out, is not a matter of the sensation itself but also of its context (1842–3, p. 252). As for the sensation being 'converted' into something else, the theory in no way entails that 'experience or association alters the nature of our perceptions of sense'; the theory holds, to the contrary, that 'all that belongs to sense ... remains the same; what experience does is superadd to the impression of sense an instantaneous act of judgment' (p. 257). It is not addition, but 'superaddition'; that is, mental chemistry is at work. The idea that the process of mental chemistry generates does not alter the sensations that are its metaphysical parts, that is, those parts that generate it. For, those parts, if recovered through association, turn out to be unchanged in their nature. Bailey's problem arises only because he does not accurately understand the nature of introspective analysis, or, what is much the same, the chemical nature of the laws of mental composition. Once these notions are clarified, as they were by J.S. Mill, then Bailey's criticisms become clearly irrelevant. Oddly, Pastore (1971, p. 216) holds that Mill does not use his notion of 'mental chemistry' to support his case against Bailey. To be sure, Mill does not use the term 'chemistry,' but the term 'superaddition' is an equivalent, as, for example, Mill's use of this latter notion in the *Analysis* (1869, p. 255) makes clear.

Bailey argues that a percept is a 'simple' or 'indivisible whole' and not a 'compound.' In looking at a cube, the 'three dimensions of space' along with its colour are perceived as a unity. From this Bailey infers that its colour and spatial dimensions are not separable entities brought together by a process of association; and that the percept is not analysable or decomposable into sensation and idea or inference (1842, pp. 92f, 105f; 1843, pp. 44, 48). With Bailey's premiss, that, phenomenologically, percepts are simple unities or wholes, Mill need not, and does not disagree. He acknowledges the point when he insists that acts of perception are 'among the varieties of feelings or states of mind' (1872a, p. 53). However, he goes on, 'in so classing them, I have not the smallest intention of declaring or insinuating any theory as to the law of mind in which these mental processes may be supposed to originate, or the conditions under which they may be legitimate or the reverse' (ibid.). They may in fact be indecomposable, and original rather than learned. But the point is that this does not follow from Bailey's premiss: from the fact that *in the phenomenological description* perceptions are a unity, it does not follow that they do not result from learning, an associative process. Nor does it follow that the percept is not analysable, in the relevant sense of 'analyse,' that is, that its metaphysical parts can be recovered by association if the opportunity arises; all that follows from the fact that percepts are phenomenologically simple unities is that whatever parts they have are not integrant parts. Bailey perhaps has a case against James Mill, but not against the psychology that the latter's son made safe from such criticism already in the 1843 edition of the *Logic* with its crucial distinction between 'metaphysical' and 'integrant' parts. When Pastore (1971, p. 211) supports Bailey against the associationists on this point, he simply indicates how thoroughly he has failed to understand the scientific psychology into which John Stuart Mill had transformed his father's *Analysis*.

Bailey holds that, for the associationists, only sensation affords direct knowledge of an object; the rest is inference. For Bailey, in contrast, perception also affords direct knowledge, and, like sensation, it is original rather than acquired (1855–63, II: letter i). However, if by 'direct' is meant 'not an inference' then for Mill the percept is a unity, not an inferential process, or, as he puts it, 'intuitive, or independent of external evidence' (1872a, pp. 53–4); while, if by 'direct' is meant 'without an intermediary,' that is, an intermediary of the sort proposed by representationalists,[18] then again Mill will agree that perception is directly of the object, since the sensation is a causal antecedent of the act of perception but *not* an entity that comes between the act and its object, a point that Mill emphasizes in his *Examination of Sir William Hamilton's Philosophy* (1872b, p. 156). As for whether or not the perception is knowledge, that is, veridical, or, as Mill puts it, legitimate (1872a, p. 54), that is not established by its originality, since there is no a priori reason why unlearned beliefs must all be true. A perception is a belief to the effect that what is perceived does, in the first place, exist, and is, in the second place, the cause of the perception. Whether what is perceived exists, or is the cause of the perception, is an empirical fact.

Thus, whether, and under what conditions, a perception is legitimate is a matter for empirical investigation; it is a matter that 'belongs not to logic, but to the science of the ultimate laws of the human mind' (ibid.). Pastore (1971, p. 212) again fails to see that Bailey fails to touch the associationist position.

According to Bailey, a percept is a primary fact of consciousness. Knowledge of material operations or physical causes does not affect its status as a fact of consciousness. Its entire content, if you wish, is given in the very consciousness of it. As he puts it: 'Perceiving must be considered as a primary state of consciousness in the same way as pain or hunger or fear or joy, the causes of which you ascertain, but the nature of which no knowledge can alter and no knowledge can elucidate' (1855–63, I: 177; cf. p. 148). Mill, again, would not disagree: the act of perception is the fact it is, and no amount of physiological research will change it. However, Bailey perhaps has a point. Mill often classifies sensations and ideas in terms of the sensory processes that are their causes. That means that an impoverished, or mistaken, physiology may lead to biased and mistaken phenomenological descriptions. Bailey, however, makes a stronger point: The only way we can secure information concerning mental states is from a percipient, or through self-observation. Thus, to know what the mental effect is when a retina is accidentally touched with a needle, as sometimes happens in operations for cataracts, the patient's report is essential; it is from this alone that we can learn that he is conscious of light and colour only and not pain (II: 194–6). From this Bailey concludes that physiological investigation is irrelevant to understanding and predicting the 'phenomena of consciousness' (I: letter xviii; II: letter xvi). This is true no matter how well the physiological processes are understood. For these reasons he holds: 'You may trace the course of light from the object to the organ, you may follow its refractions by the lens of the eye, you may detect the picture of the retina, you may explore the connection of the optic nerves with the brain; but you do not by all these discoveries, valuable as they are, alter in the slightest degree the resulting state of consciousness denominated seeing the object (I: 155–6). And so he rejects the argument that since distance can make no impression on the retina, therefore recognition of distance must be learned. Now, it is true that physiological discoveries cannot alter the 'feelings or states of mind' into anything other than what they are phenomenologically. But it does not, to repeat, follow from this that those mental states are original or unlearned. Nor, therefore, does it follow that physiological discoveries are irrelevant to the question whether acts of perception are the result of learning (association) and, if so, the question of what are the elements from which the associative process commences. Bailey once again draws an invalid inference from phenomenology.

Bailey practises what Mill in the *Examination of Sir William Hamilton's Philosophy* calls the 'introspective method of psychological inquiry' (1872b, pp. 147–8), that is, the method of phenomenological description. But as Mill points out, no matter what this reveals about a mental state, it says nothing about the genetic origins of that state (p. 139).

It is to precisely this issue that Mill's turn to physiology is designed to illuminate. He is perfectly clear that there is a distinction between the physiological sensory process, on the one hand, and the sensation, on the other (1872a, p. 52), and that the connection between them is contingent, a matter of law (p. 859). And, of course, the *hypotheses* that Mill brings to bear are (A) and (E), the former the *empirical assumption* that different kinds of sensory processes cause different sorts of elementary sensations, and different sorts of elementary sensations are caused by different kinds of sensory processes, and the latter the *empirical assumption* that sensory processes produce only non-relational sensations.

Now, we saw that John Stuart Mill, in contrast to his father, tended to reject (E), and admit that some relations are incapable of analytic decomposition. These were relations among visual phenomena, or among tactual phenomena. But John Stuart Mill insists that our capacity to recognize *distance* is learned. The ideas of distance and depth, 'extension' in the most fully developed sense of the term, relate visual, tactual, and muscular sensations, that is, *sensations from several different sensory processes*: the depth of the perceived cube relates visual sensations but it is at once the distance it takes to move one's hand a certain amount; the idea of extension, in its most fully developed sense, is inseparable from the idea of motion, and the latter idea includes the idea of our moving, which is inseparable from ideas of tactual and muscular sensations. Given this point, then it follows by (A) that relations of distance cannot be among the sensations, that is, among the immediate, or original, products of sensory (physiological) processes. Thus, it follows from (A) that the capacity to discriminate distance, or any co-ordination between visible, tactual, and muscular sensations, must be learned.

Two points must be made. One: against Bailey, Mill recognizes the continuity of physical and mental processes, and that any adequate theory of learning that deals with mental processes cannot, in the end, fail to proceed to physiological causes and invoke, at that point, laws, or at least hypotheses, connecting the mental and the physical. Two: Mill's hypothesis (A) is in fact false.

Thus, Mill's argument against Bailey, based on the hypothesis (A), had support that at its best was weak and, in the end, turns out to be false. But Mill at least had the methodological sophistication to recognize, as Bailey did not, that the issue is one that can be settled by causal arguments and inference, and not merely by phenomenological inspection of one's mental states!

4 Perception and Central Processes

Mill accepted the hypothesis (A) that different kinds of sensory processes cause different sorts of elementary sensations, and different sorts of elementary sensations are caused by different kinds of sensory processes. This hypothesis entails that what appears in consciousness is the direct product of non-interacting sensory processes. But is this assumption of non-interaction really acceptable? What of the role of the central nervous system? Does not (A) assume in effect that there are no relevant central processes, or, conversely, that perception involves only peripheral processes, that is, peripheral processes plus learning?

In adopting (A), Mill was following a tradition that goes back to (at least) Galileo, when the latter, studying tones, correlated pitch with frequency. That established the tradition of looking for one-to-one relations, or, rather, correlations, between the dimensions of the sensation and the dimensions of the stimulus. Thus, pitch is supposed to correlate with stimulus-frequency, and loudness with stimulus-intensity (energy or amplitude – it was never clear which). But since the 1930s it has been clear that pitch is a function of both frequency and intensity, and that loudness is a different function of the two. Then there is the attribute of volume: tones can be large or small, and the judgments made of their size are reliable and precise. Low tones tend to be large, high tones small; loud tones tend to be large, faint tones small. But, as Stevens (1934a) showed, a faint low tone can be the same volume as a loud high tone. So this attribute also depends on frequency and intensity. The same is true for a fourth attribute of tones, density (Stevens 1934b). Thus, we have four attributes of sensations of tone – pitch, loudness, volume, and density – each depending on both the stimulus attributes frequency and intensity. The case of colour is similar: hue, brightness, and saturation, all vary as joint functions of wavelength and intensity (Boring 1939). As it was traditional to see one-to-one correlations of attributes of sensations and attributes of stimuli, so it was traditional to seek in the sense organ explanations of the attributes of sensations. Thus, for example, it was hypothesized that pitch depended upon the place of stimulation in the ear, and that loudness depended upon the amplitude (or later total amount) of excitation. But such hypotheses have no empirical support: there is at present no known way in which one can localize the causal conditions for attributes of sensations at some place in the sense organs. The attributes of sensations are the capacities of organisms to discriminate certain relationships among stimuli. There is in fact no a priori reason why the attributes may not be learned. Thus, it is possible that low and loud tones are called 'large' because they usually come from large instruments. This is not so, but it is possible. The only reason to believe that attributes of sensations are original or native and not learned is the close agreement of many persons with respect to their measurements, and the ease and immediacy with which they are judged. All that can be said is that the attributes depend upon properties of the nervous system, either congenital properties or, possibly, properties acquired in experience. The genetic background to sensations is a state of the central nervous system, and the old treatment of the senses as non-interacting that is embodied in Mill's hypothesis (A) is now recognized to be a gross over-simplification.[19]

The most famous rejection of (A) was by the Gestalters. They emphasized that what happened in perception was not a set of non-interacting simple sensory processes; there was rather a system of total interaction.[20] They rejected the 'atomism' implied by (A) as much as they rejected the 'atomism' they felt was implied by the claim that relations could, by introspective analysis, be analysed into non-relational contents. They failed to see that the latter did not imply the elimination of the relations that, phenomenologically, *are there*, presented to us in experience. And they failed to recognize that a system of total interaction could be explained in terms of, and even, if you wish, be reduced to, (the laws for) simple systems, provided that a composition law is available. Much confusion was generated by uncritical uses of the term 'sum' and the formula 'the whole is greater than the sum of the parts.' In some of this, they were aided by similar confusions in some of their opponents – John Stuart Mill included, as we saw in chapter 3. None the less, they are surely correct on the particular point that perception involves not merely a set of non-interacting sensory processes, but to the contrary is a process that involves interaction in the central nervous system. Even if their specific description of this process of interaction turns out to be incorrect (as indeed it does), they are still correct in their general point that perception *is* a process of interacting.

What the Gestalters proposed specifically was that a perceived spatial pattern is not a consequence of compartmentalized and non-interacting sensory processes the products of which are associated to form the perception of the pattern: the perceived spatial pattern is, rather, caused by the *spatial pattern of the underlying states of excitation in the brain* that are the termini in the central nervous system of the sensory processes leading from the stimulated organs. In fact, it was suggested that the spatial pattern as perceived is *isomorphic* with the spatial pattern of excited brain states. 'Isomorphic' means topological, not topographical correspondence: shapes need not be preserved, but order, such as *betweenness*, is.[21] We need not here discuss this notion in detail.[22] It suffices to say, first, that, like (A), the hypothesis of isomorphism is an empirical hypothesis; and second, that even if it is false, there could be some other systematic correlation between perceived spatial structures and sorts of complex states in the brain – isomorphism is but one way for decompartmentalizing sensory processes. What is crucial to the challenge of (A) is not isomorphism but the more general notion that the states of consciousness that are the direct effects of physiological processes are not the result of non-interacting sensory processes but rather are the effects of processes in the central nervous system that can perform an integrating or, if you wish, reconstituting function.

John Stuart Mill did in fact recognize the role of the central nervous system. But little changed with respect to his actual position concerning his views on the acquisition of the capacity to discriminate depth, distance, and extension. The views in his notes to his father's *Analysis* (1869) are little different from his views in his criticism (1842–3) of Bailey. We may well wonder, with Sparshott (1978, p. lxiii), whether Mill was aware that 'the ground rules for such discussions had changed' when the role of the central nervous system was admitted. But be that as it may, Mill, drawing on Bain's work in introducing a solid account of neural activity into the physiological underpinning of psychology, did come to acknowledge that the integrating role of the central nervous system is inescapable: 'That the central organ of the nervous system, the brain, must in some way or other co-operate in all sensation, and in all muscular motion except that which is actually automatic and mechanical, is also certain' (1859, p. 353). Once this is admitted, or, what is the same, once (A) is rejected, then the argument that depth and distance *must* be learned is deprived of its premiss. It becomes possible to argue that some capacities to recognize depth and distance are innate, original, native, unlearned. Which ones are, if any, is, of course, a matter of fact. But that was just how Mill himself saw it, since he emphasizes that the precise role of physiology in perception is a factual matter to be discovered and established by empirical research (1872a, pp. 859–60). (A), for him, was an empirical hypothesis, and its rejection on the basis of further data would not have bothered him one bit. Moreover, Mill's *main point* against Bailey and Sir William Hamilton remains unscathed: it continues to be incontrovertibly supported by a mass of data. This main point, which is denied both Bailey and Hamilton, among others, is that *many of our capacities to perceive are learned, including our capacities to discriminate most depth and distance relations.* The relevance of learning to perception has more recently been put this way by Ittelson (1960, p. 31):

> Any present perceptual experience consists of a total complex of significances ... Through the course of experiencing, certain significances are found by the perceiver to have high probabilities of being related to each other and other aspects of the situation ... These probabilities, high or low, are in turn weighted in terms of the relevance of the unique situation in which they have occurred ... All this is accomplished through a largely unconscious process and results in a set of assumptions or weighted averages of previous experiences, which are brought to the present occasion, and they play a principal role in determining how the occasion is experienced ... The assumptive world of any particular individual at any particular time determines his perceptions, that is, provides him with predictions of probable significances.

For visual shape and distance, the point has been put by Epstein (1967, p. 23) in this way:

> apparent size and apparent distance are psychological variables the values of which may or may not correspond with the values of their corresponding physical variables, i.e., physical size and physical distance. For example, a playing card may have a larger apparent size than a calling card even though the playing card has been especially designed so that it is the same physical size as the calling card. In this example, apparent size is determined by the assumptions which the perceiver has learned regarding the relative physical sizes of the cards.

Sparshott (1978, p. lxiii) notes that the program of locating genetic antecedents to perceivings changed once the role of the central nervous system in organizing information was recognized. He goes on to remark: 'From now on one had a choice. Either one took account of the central nervous system, in which case the old-fashioned compartmentalization of the senses is irrelevant, or one confined oneself to epistemology and phenomenology, in which case Mill's style of generic [genetic?] analysis became inappropriate.' It is certainly true that once the role of the brain is recognized, genetic analysis relying upon the compartmentalization hypothesis (A) is no longer justified. But it is certainly false that the only alternative is phenomenology, and even more certainly false that the only alternative is the nativism of the phenomenologists, Bailey and Hamilton, or the earlier Kames and Reid, against whom Mill was arguing. In the first place, phenomenology, as Mill emphasized, is *not* an alternative to genetic explanation. To the contrary, accurate phenomenology is necessary prior to the explanatory enterprise in order to know precisely what it is that is to be explained. Second, the alternative to genetic accounts based on (A) is better, more accurate genetic accounts. Perhaps Mill's 'style' of analysis must be rejected, but his *project*, that of genetically explaining perception, or, what is the same, that of explaining perceptual learning in terms of more general and basic principles of learning, for example, the laws of association – this *project* remains a living enterprise.

Titchener, in effect, followed Mill in all these matters. Spatial localization of sensations is handled in terms of the context theory of meaning applied specifically to perception. For a sensation, it is a conscious context of imagery or kinaesthetic feelings that provides the localization. Titchener followed Mill and earlier thinkers in arguing that localization in the third visual dimension is contextual, consisting of the addition to the visual core of a kinaesthetic context derived from the muscular sensations generated by accommodation or convergence. This context could, however, when it is habituated, be 'carried' physiologically. The meanings are then not actually, only potentially present. Unlike Mill, Titchener denied that an act of perception was also present, i.e., that the meanings were carried not only physiologically but by this act.[22] Külpe and the Würzburgers sided with Mill – and Brentano – on this point, and were able to develop experimental data that rendered Titchener's position clearly untenable.[23] But, because he denied such acts existed, and because the physiological carrier was unknown, Titchener had to develop tests for the potentialities being *really* there. These tests were indirect. If a reader, having forgotten the exact words, can still state in all detail the meaning of the paragraph, then he must have known the meanings of all the words as he read them: his subsequent performance shows it. The evidence that he had the meanings lies in his performance. Bain pointed out, in his notes to Mill's *Analysis* (1869, 1, 394), that an action can constitute the context of an idea – 'The practical test applied to a man's belief in a certain matter, is his acting upon it' – but it was Tolman who first recognized the fact that adequate behaviour thus carries meaning, and may be the effective context in a perception. The person or animal who responds in a specific fashion to a particular stimulus shows what meaning he attaches to the stimulus – or to the sensation, if one is talking about consciousness. The stimulus-object that the animal eats is food – that is, that object means food to the animal. Response is the context that gives the stimulus its meaning for the responding organism. The context theory of perception of John Stuart Mill thus became absorbed into the mainstream of behaviouristic psychology; and his project of studying perceptual learning has become part of that broad stream.[24]

Sparshott has accused both Mill and his opponents of dogmatizing (1978, p. lix). 'They ... dogmatize,' we are told, 'in different directions. The apriorists, instead of acknowledging a pragmatic limit to analysis, announce the discovery of an ultimate and forever irreducible intuition or instinct; the aposteriorists [i.e., Mill] invent a spurious analysis in terms of whatever entities their method postulates.' This is no doubt fair enough with respect to the 'apriorists' such as Kames and Reid and Bailey and Hamilton. It may even be fair with respect to James Mill. It is, however, certainly unfair to the younger Mill. The latter clarified the methodology of introspective psychology, and made it scientifically sound. That was his significant achievement in psychology. This method commits one *in no way* to any particular claim about the set of elements, or, what is the same, about what constitutes the minimal analytical vocabulary. As we saw, Mill correctly recognizes that what is in this set is an empirical matter to be determined by empirical research. So, contrary to Sparshott, the method Mill defends in no way requires him to 'postulate' a set of entities into which everything *must, facts notwithstanding*, be analysed. To be sure, John Stuart Mill does claim certain perceptions must be analysable into certain elements. This, however, is a consequence of a specific hypothesis Mill takes over from the tradition, the hypothesis (A) concerning the compartmental-ization of the senses. Mill's methodology correctly characterizes this hypothesis as empirical, and demands that it be subjected to empirical test. This was fully recognized by Mill. When Mill transformed psychology into an empirical science and turned it over to the experimentalists, the latter did put Mill's hypothesis to the tests demanded by Mill's method, and found the hypothesis wanting. With the excellent vision of hindsight we can now see that Mill's hypothesis is false and therefore that the analysis it tended to support is 'spurious.' But this can be transformed into a criticism of Mill only if one can show that it was methodologically unsound, upon the data *then* available, for Mill to tentatively accept the hypothesis he did. This has not been shown.

A further point must be made. It is fair to say that Bailey and Hamilton practised what has come to be called the 'phenomenological method' (cf. Boring 1957, pp. 601ff). It is the method since proclaimed by the Gestalters (cf. ibid.; Pastore 1971, pp. 271ff). Bailey and Hamilton inferred that whatever was phenomenologically a whole was original, native, unlearned. So do their modern successors (cf. Pastore 1971, p. 312; Boring 1942, pp. 32–3). Mill, too, insisted, as we saw, on the phenomenological method. Indeed, it is central to his account of analysis in psychology: for Mill, there can be no analysis without a prior phenomenology. However, phenomenology yields description, not explanation, and it is the aim of science to explain. Mill's general methodology lays it down that the aim of science is explanation, and the method of introspective analysis, as clarified by Mill, has as its aim the discovery of such explanatory laws in psychology, and, specifically, the discovery of a genetic explanation of our capacities to perceive the structured objects of everyday experience. When Mill introduces the hypothesis (A), he reminds us that there is nothing incompatible between something being phenomenologically a whole or a unity and its being analysable, in Mill's sense, and that there is nothing incompatible between something being such a whole and its being learned or having a genetic explanation. It is precisely these latter points that Bailey and Hamilton denied. Mill's demonstration that Bailey and Hamilton were wrong is equally a demonstration of the wrongness of their successors, the Gestalters and phenomenologists, who insist, as their predecessors did, that wholes cannot be analysed and must be native. In fact, it is to recognize that nativism of this sort is *not* a scientific theory but rather an anti-scientific and dogmatic assertion that in this area *theory must be impossible*. As Boring has put it (1942, p. 33), upon the position of Bailey, Hamilton, the Gestalters, and the phenomenologists, 'the givens are not to be explained. That is nativism, and, as Lotze implied, it is a faith and not a theory.' Mill's analysis, based on his hypothesis (A), of our perception of 'extension' may, in the light of hindsight, have turned out to be spurious. But, as a guess, there was nothing a priori wrong with it: it was a *possible* hypothesis. Bailey et al. deny its *possibility*. What Mill succeeded in doing was defend the thesis that it was possible. No doubt he thought he had done more. In the latter he did not succeed, but in establishing the *possibility* of the hypothesis he succeeded in showing the inadequacy of the position of Bailey and Hamilton. And *that*, as the Gestalters and the phenomenologists make clear, is a lesson that still bears repeating.

To conclude: We have argued that John Stuart Mill had an intelligible and adequate philosophy of psychology, and, indeed, that it was he who transformed psychology from a more or less a priori armchair discipline into a subject that could be turned over to experimenters for detailed empirical investigation. And in a detailed discussion of the account of the example of the perception of spatial structures, we have argued that Mill was on safer methodological ground than most of his critics, whether of his own day, such as Hamilton or Bailey, or more recent, such as Pastore and Sparshott. With this appreciation of Mill's position in psychology and its methodology we can now attempt to come to grips with a second example, one crucial to a correct under-standing of his views in ethics, namely, the quality/quantity distinction among pleasures. We shall again find that, given his account of the methodology of psychology, Mill is often on considerably stronger ground than his critics will allow.

SIX

Relations and Preferences in Economics

The distinction between the quantity and quality of pleasures is absent from the utilitarianism of the older generation of radical reformers: one looks in vain for it in Bentham's *Principles of Morals and Legislation* or James Mill's *Analysis of the Phenomena of the Human Mind*. It does appear in the younger Mill's essay 'Utilitarianism,' however, there to defend the doctrines of the reformers against such critics as Macaulay, Sedgwick, and Whewell. The distinction is intended, first, to render the ethical doctrines more plausible; second, to make the psychological theories acceptable, that is, to transform them from speculation to empirically adequate hypotheses; and, third, to provide an adequate account of the framework within which economic behaviour occurs, that is, an adequate account of the conditions that both limit the laws of economics and render them applicable, that is, useful for explanation and prediction. The first two of these intentions we shall look at in the next chapter; the third is the concern of the present chapter.

The laws that the classical economists developed presuppose that certain institutional constraints obtain. In particular, they presuppose that people respect property, or, as we put it earlier, conform to the principle of justice; they presuppose that people keep their promises, that is, conform to the principle of contract; and they presuppose that people respect the decisions of their government, that is, conform to the principle of allegiance.[1] Within these constraints, it was assumed that people are psychological egoists, striving to maximize their material pleasures. From this axiom, and others, certain theorems were deduced that then formed the basis for various policy recommendations of the reformers. These recommendations therefore require conformity to the principles of morality that we have mentioned. But as Macaulay (1829) and other critics pointed out, when one turns to the more general psychology defended by the philosophic radicals, then it becomes questionable whether men will in fact conform to these moral principles of justice, contract, and allegiance. The psychology of motivation of Bentham and James Mill puts these norms into the same sort of egoistic calculus that is presumed to hold in the economic sphere. That seems to imply that people will violate these norms whenever it is in their interest, narrowly conceived, to do so. To avoid this problem and thereby to save the policy recommendations of the reformers, it was necessary to modify the psychology of motivation in such a way that moral values could dominate, and control, self-interest. It was the contention of Butler, of course, that conscience did just this; that was, as a matter of fact, just how the mind functioned. What was required was a way of admitting this fact in the psychology of the utilitarians. It was this that John Stuart Mill was able to do once he had introduced the distinction between quality and quantity of pleasure, and argued that the moral sentiments, which move us to conform to the principles of justice, contract, and allegiance, are of a quality that leads us, often at least, to prefer that sort of behaviour to any quantity of economic benefit.

In the first section, below, we discuss value *in* economic theory and the values that provide the constraints on the laws of economics.

In the next section, we discuss some criticisms that Samuel Bailey made of the classical economics of Ricardo and in particular his criticism of Ricardo's notion (which we shall have looked at in the first section) that there is an absolute measure of value and that it is given by the quantity of labour required for something to be produced. Bailey has been praised for criticizing this notion and taking value in economics to be relative, thus anticipating more modern developments. We show that, to the contrary, such praise is misguided. Bailey's criticisms of Ricardo are unsound, and his own position, rather than pointing towards a more modern point of view, looks to the older tradition of ethical objectivism. The disagreement between Bailey and the utilitarians thus concerns the psychology of relations rather than problems of economic theory. This has been missed by economic historians who have unreasonably praised Bailey, but, given what we know about Bailey's views on the perception of spatial relations of depth or distance, it is hardly surprising.

In fact, if anyone points beyond the classicists to more modern conceptions of value, it is not Bailey but John Stuart Mill. In the third and final section we argue that, when he solves the problem of the moral constraints on economic behaviour by introducing the quality/

quantity distinction, John Stuart Mill moves away from the assumption of the classical economists, and of Bentham and James Mill, that a full cardinalization of our preference scale is possible, to the weaker and psychologically more plausible thesis that the best that we can do is attain an ordinal scale of preferences.

1   Value in the Economics of Ricardo and J.S. Mill

Economics, according to Adam Smith, investigates 'the nature and causes of wealth' (1776). The source of wealth is labour, and labour becomes more efficient with its division. The division of labour in turn implies, as Adam Smith puts it, that 'every man ... becomes in some measure a merchant' (1776, p. 23). At this point emerges the notion of 'relative or exchangeable value of goods' (p. 28). Smith notes the so-called paradox of value, citing the instances of water and diamonds to show that a high utility may be combined with little or no value when it comes to exchange, and conversely. This paradox introduces his distinction between 'value-in-use' and 'value-in-exchange' (ibid.). What economics, that is, the science, must do is *explain* exchangeable value. To do this it must provide a *theory* of value, that is, a set of laws that relate exchangeable value to other variables (cf. Schumpeter 1954, p. 588). For this reason Ricardo prefers to define economics differently: 'to determine the laws which regulate this distribution [of the produce of industry] is the principal problem of Political Economy' (1821, p. 5).

John Stuart Mill's *Principles* institutionalized what had come to be prevailing practice when he emphasized that the term 'value,' when used in economic theory, was essentially relative and meant nothing but the exchange ratio between any two commodities or services (1871, pp. 458–9).

Now, one of the variables that determine exchangeable value is, of course, utility. But that variable is necessary, not sufficient. Ricardo argued (1821, p. 12) that, 'possessing utility, commodities derive their exchangeable value from two sources: from their scarcity, and from the quantity of labour required to obtain them.' Thus there are, for Ricardo, two variables besides utility that are relevant to determining the exchangeable value of goods: (1) their scarcity and (2) the quantity of labour required to obtain them. The task then becomes that of, as it is sometimes put (e.g., Gray 1931, p. 173), 'apportioning the influence of these operative causes.' So to express it, however, is misleading, insofar as it suggests that exchangeable value is simply a sum of the values created by these two independently operating factors. It would be more accurate to note that the claim is that *there is* a function f such that

(*)   exchangeable value $= f$ (utility, scarcity, required labour)

and that the research problem is to determine what, specifically, this function is.

Ricardo approaches this task by examining two special, and extreme cases. If successful, this research would yield two pieces of imperfect knowledge, two conditioned generalities. The hope would be that one could move on from these to consider more complicated, less imperfect cases, to achieve finally after a series of such approximating steps the function f that satisfies (*). Ricardo considers, first, the case where no labour can increase the quantity; in this case, assuming a value or utility of the object (e.g., rare pictures, great auk's eggs) is given, exchangeable value is determined by scarcity alone. He considers, second, those commodities that can be multiplied 'almost without any assignable limit' by the exertion of human labour; in this case, the foundation of 'exchangeable value' is 'the comparative quantity of labour expended on each' (1821, p. 12). It is not to be assumed, however, nor does Ricardo assume, that when *both* scarcity and required labour are relevant their joint effect is an exchangeable value that is the sum of the exchangeable values they determine when they operate alone, as they are supposed by Ricardo to do in the extreme cases he discusses. Besides, neither of these extreme cases is real; they are idealizations, rather like the frictionless pulleys of physicists; but none the less, if sound, they can be useful as first approximations, pieces of imperfect knowledge from which further research can start and begin to improve the knowledge.

Ricardo then states his major proposition that, given utility, increasable commodities exchange in accordance with the quantity of labour expended on each (1821, p. 13). He gives no explicit proof of this proposition. The closest he comes occurs when he suggests that one can convince oneself of its truth if one were to 'suppose any improvement to be made in the means of abridging labour' (p. 25); the result, he tells us, will be a fall in the value of the final product – a proof of the proposition that rests on the truth of what is to be proved. Implicit, however, is the assumption that, as John Stuart Mill puts it, for people 'a greater gain is preferred to a smaller' (1872a, VI, ix, p. 3) and also the further assumption that Adam Smith (1776, p. 30) and James Mill (1824, pp. 56–7) make, that labour is, to use Smith's phrase, 'toil and trouble.' The first of these assumptions is that of *economic rationality* (cf. Ricardo [1821, p. 91]), and the second is that the *cost* to an individual of securing goods is the *pain* (or loss of pleasure, or both) involved in the labour of production. There is, moreover, a third assumption, that conditions of perfect competition obtain (Ricardo assumes this throughout the *Principles*). Under these assumptions, Ricardo's proposition 'that this [labour] is really the foundation of the exchangeable value of all things' (p. 13) is, on the one hand, a proposition concerning exchangeable values in conditions of perfect equilibrium under certain specific institutional constraints, and, on the other hand, a theorem derived from certain very general assumptions of economic rationality.

Ricardo clearly recognizes that the law he proposes is a piece of imperfect knowledge, a first approximation. For he introduces it in his first chapter, in the first section, and then spends the remainder of the chapter (secs. 2–7) attempting to show that his equilibrium law, while not generally true, does constitute a fairly close approximation throughout the range of perfect competition. Here he introduces, besides quantity of labour, such factors as length of time before a product can be brought to market, or the amount of labour that is invested in tools, machinery, and so on (i.e., capital goods). Moreover, once he introduces it as a law in the first chapter relating utility and labour in the absence of other variables relevant to exchangeable value, he then proceeds in subsequent chapters to complicate the model, that is, reduce its imperfection, by taking into account such further relevant variables as the scarcity of natural factors of production. (The latter leads into Ricardo's theory of rent.)

Ricardo does not explicitly use the concept of equilibrium, but he does have the idea (cf. Schumpeter 1954, p. 293), which he expresses by saying that this labour-quantity law of exchangeable value applies to 'natural prices' (1821, p. 88), that is, the prices that will obtain when fluctuations caused by temporary disturbances have ended. The fluctuations in the actual market price about the natural price are attributed to changes in supply and/or demand (pp. 90–1). This latter, however, he describes (Ch. 30) as a subsidiary mechanism. In fact, he contrasts his theory of exchangeable value with supply-and-demand theories. Ricardo lays it down that the quantity of labour is 'really the foundation of the exchangeable value of all things.' This position, which is a substantive proposition about exchangeable value, that is, a law-like assertion, is his basic assumption, given without any explicit proof. In later chapters (4 to 30) Ricardo compares this claim to Adam Smith's account of market price, which made the latter a function of supply and demand. For Ricardo, the 'natural price' is that of equilibrium. But there may be fluctuations around this 'natural price,' that is, disturbances away from equilibrium, occasioned by the fact that no quantity is supplied for any length of time in precisely the required degree of abundance. There will be a more or less constant oscillation of market price about the natural price, and this is explained by the supply-and-demand mechanism. Thus, the labour-quantity account applies to the long run, supply and demand to the short run. Thus, Ricardo does not see clearly that his own theorem on equilibrium values can be defended only by reference to the mechanisms of supply and demand (cf. Schumpeter 1954, p. 601). Unfortunately, Ricardo does not make his argument fully explicit: explicitly he merely states his law rather than asking *why* exchangeable values of goods should be proportional to the quantities of labour required to produce and put them on the market, and expecting an answer to be given by a deduction from a theory or set of laws concerning the principles of rational economic decision making to which agents can plausibly be assumed to conform. In answering the question of why exchangeable values are proportional to costs of production, Ricardo would have been driven to using the supply-and-demand mechanism by which alone – given appropriate assumptions, for example, perfect competition – his law of value can be established.

John Stuart Mill proceeds in a way that pays its respects to Ricardo, the chief economist of the radical utilitarian party of reform. There are three cases. Initially supply and demand are introduced by Mill as determinants of exchangeable value in the case of goods that are strictly scarce (1871, Bk. III, Ch. 2). Second, the exchangeable value of goods, quantities of which can be increased without additional cost, is determined by this cost (Bk. III, Ch. 3). Third, the exchangeable value of goods, quantities of which can be increased but only with increasing costs, that is, ultimately, labour, is determined by the costs of production in the most unfavourable circumstances (Bk. III, Ch. 5). Thus, in the first case, demand is relatively more important; in the second case, supply and the cost of production are relatively more important; and finally, since the supply of commodities in the third case can be augmented only under conditions of increasing cost, their (exchangeable) value is governed by the cost of producing them under the least favourable circumstances. While Mill does not draw supply-and-demand curves, his discussion makes it evident that he conceives of supply and demand in the schedule sense, that is, as a function of price. It is clear, therefore, that he recognized that the equilibrium price is the price that equates supply and demand, and he wrote out, though in words, not mathematics, this equation of supply and demand (pp. 467–8): 'The proper mathematical analogy is that of an equation. Demand and supply, the quantity demanded and the quantity supplied, will be made equal. If unequal at any moment, competition equalizes them, and the manner in which this is done is by an adjustment of the value. If the demand increases, the value rises; if the demand diminishes, the value falls: again, if the supply falls off, the value rises; and falls if the supply is increased.' Final equilibrium is reached when quantity demanded is equal to quantity supplied. But, while Mill was aware of the law of supply and demand, he did officially follow Ricardo in holding that it applied to short-run prices, while the long-run prices were determined by costs of production. The labour theory of value is, however, quickly qualified by Mill. In particular, he does so in the case of joint costs (pp. 582ff), which, as Stigler has argued (1955, pp. 296–9), is one of the original contributions that Mill made to economic theory. In this case of joint costs, a given production process is taken to yield two or more products in fixed proportions and in such a way that it is impossible to allocate quantities of labour, that is, costs, save on a purely arbitrary basis. The greater the demand for a joint product, the larger the proportion of the total cost of production that will be covered by the price of the product. Supply-and-demand conditions for each of the products will establish the price at which the market will be cleared of both, and the sum of the prices established will equal their joint costs of production. This makes clear that for Mill it is the law of supply and demand that is more basic, and the law to which appeal is made when the cost of production account is inapplicable. That this is the basic thrust of Mill's position is even more obvious in a passage in the chapter on international values: whenever, he tells us, the 'law of cost of production is not applicable' (i.e., Ricardo's proposition), then one must 'fall back upon an *antecedent law*, that of supply and demand' (Bk. III, Ch. 18, sec. 1, p. 596; italics added). In fact, Mill developed the supply-and-demand account in a way such that it required only loose ends to be tidied up and some rigour to be added for one to reach a position not far distant from Marshall's analysis (cf. 1961, II: 12).

This theory has as its central axiom the principle that, *ceteris paribus*, men prefer a greater gain to a less (Mill 1872a, VI, ix, p. 3). As for what men prefer, or, equally, what to them constitutes the greater gain, that is left unexplained by economics. Economics as a science takes preferences as given; it simply does not say anything about the nature of the wants or desires from which it starts (cf. Schumpeter 1954, p. 105–7). The latter are, to be sure, learned or acquired. But that fact is irrelevant to what economics, the science, is about. As Schumpeter puts it, 'A housewife's behaviour on the market may be analyzed without going into the factors that formed it' (1954, p. 889). Economics can, therefore, proceed independently of the hedonistic psychology that the radical utilitarians also accepted: economics is not hedonics. As Schumpeter argues, 'it is not difficult to show that the utility theory of value is entirely independent of any hedonist postulates or philosophies. For it does not state or imply anything about the nature of the values or desires from which it starts' (p. 1057). Marshall no less than Mill and Ricardo took utility as the source of (exchange) value, but at the same time deplored and renounced the old alliance with utilitarianism (1961, I: 17n). Even philosophers renounced the connection between wants or values and hedonistic psychologies; Frank Ramsey, for example, while developing his ideas on values and decision making, wrote: 'It may be observed that this theory is not to be identified with the psychology of the Utilitarians, in which pleasure had a dominating position. The theory I propose to adopt is that we seek things which we want, which may be our own or other people's pleasure, or anything else whatever, and our actions are such as we think most likely to reach these goals' (1931, p. 173). On the basis of Mill's discussions in economic theory and in the philosophy of economics, it is safe to say that Mill reckoned that economics, as a science, could be developed with such a concept of utility, that is, one unrelated to hedonics and hedonistic psychology. Nevertheless, once it is recognized that wants are simply givens so far as concerns economics, one who is moved by the ideal of scientific explanation will notice that this means that the laws with which the science of economics deals are imperfect and will therefore naturally be led to wonder what are the relations between, on the one hand, the utility account of value taken for granted by economics and, on the other hand, psychology. There is here a research problem the solution of which will eliminate the imperfection inevitably infecting economics by explaining what the latter simply takes for granted as givens, that is, unexplained facts. In fact, I would suggest, it is precisely this link that moved the radical utilitarians to connect their economic theories with their hedonistic psychology. In this they are followed by the younger Mill.

John Stuart Mill, in his essay 'On the Definition of Political Economy' (1844), and later in the *Logic* (1872a, VI, ix), argued for the autonomy of the science of economics. The defence is made by reference to the broad areas of life where decisions are made in terms of the principle that men prefer a greater gain to a less (VI, ix, 3). In order to understand the action of the householder as she shops in the market it is hardly necessary for one to search out the causes of how she came to acquire the wants that motivate her exchange behaviour. Because so many of our wants can be satisfied by exchange, and because such exchange takes place under the principle of seeking the greatest gain at the least cost, Mill can defend the notion that science can go forward under these assumptions, exploring their consequences, safe in the knowledge that limiting factors will not disturb the usefulness of these inferences for purposes of explanation and prediction; Mill, that is, can defend the notion of the autonomy of the science of economics. None the less, this autonomy remains relative or conditional: in truth, economics is only partially autonomous. In the end, the understanding that economics achieves is only partial, based on imperfect laws.[2] And the imperfection of those laws consists precisely in the fact that the patterns of behaviour they describe are *learned*. *Better* understanding can be attained once those imperfections are removed, that is, once the *givens* of economics are explained by locating them as pieces of imperfect knowledge within the context of less imperfect knowledge provided by psychology. However, having said this, one can hold that economics is indeed, as Schumpeter, Marshall, and Mill argue, a – relatively – autonomous science.

However, John Stuart Mill was, unlike say Marshall, not merely an economist. Unlike Marshall, Mill was concerned to place economics in the context of a full science of man. As a consequence he was quite prepared to address the questions of how housewives, and, more broadly, consumers in general, come to have the wants they have, and come to behave as they do. Mill both recognized that, from the standpoint of the ideal of explanation – if not of economics – such questions must be answered; and, as a defender of scientific psychology, proposed, in outline at least, answers to such questions. Those answers were, naturally, in terms of the associationist psychology at which we have been looking. In particular, those answers turned on the associationist account of motivation as grounded in the idea of pleasure. Of this, more in the next chapter. The present point is that these reasons for turning to psychology derive from Mill the philosopher of the human sciences rather than from Mill the economist. It is important to notice, however, that even the latter had a reason for turning to psychology. Most important, Mill the economist was concerned to establish, on the one hand, that the prevailing impression that the motives that economics dealt with were all egoistic was false, and, on the other hand, that non-economic and, more specifically, moral motives constituted a framework that constrained the operation of the economic motives. For Macaulay (1829) and the other opponents of the utilitarians, what needed explanation was not the fact that the hungry man stole from the rich but the fact that the majority of those who are hungry don't steal. It was the view of these critics that the utilitarians could not explain this fact: the psychological egoism which the utilitarians took for granted precluded such an explanation. Mill argued that, given associationist psychology, the moral ties that constrained people to recognize property rights could be explained in terms of a fundamental hedonism plus learning (association). But at the same time he was able to defend the case for reform. The distribution of the economic product is determined, Mill argues, by the rules for ownership of property (1871, Bk. II, Ch. 1, pp. 199f). These rules derive their sanction from our moral sentiments. Hence, if these moral sentiments or feelings are innate to human nature and therefore unchangeable, then any attempt to reform the norms of property in order to achieve a better distribution of goods would be pointless. For, if they are innate, as Hutcheson, Price, and Reid held, or, later and contemporary with Mill, as Sedgwick and Whewell held, then it would be impossible to change these sentiments, and it would be pointless to suggest that the existing order is wrong or to reckon that it ought to be changed: what must be can't be wrong.[3] But, Mill argued, our moral feelings *are learned*; they are not innate. And since the present rules are learned, so can alternatives be learned. It therefore *is* possible to achieve moral reform, or, what is part of that, reform of the property relations that determine the economic laws of distribution. 'The entire history of social improvement has been a series of transitions, by which one custom or institution after another, from being a supposed primary necessity of social existence, has passed into the rank of an universally stigmatized injustice and tyranny. So it has been with the distinction of slaves and freemen, nobles and serfs, patricians and plebians; and so it will be, and in part already is, with the aristocracies of colour, race, and sex' (1861, p. 259). The moral feelings that determine conformity to property relations constrain economic behaviour, deter-mining in fact the laws of economic distribution; but those feelings are not absolutes, they can be modified, and with them also the laws of distribution. A correct understanding of these moral feelings is thus essential according to Mill if one is to have an adequate account of how the economic system functions, and its laws of distribution in particu-lar, and also essential for an adequate understanding of how the system might be reformed.

If Mill's defence of the possibility of reform is to be successful, he must presuppose three things. First, he must presuppose, if economics is to be even a conditionally autonomous science, that men are moved to seek the commodities that appear in the market-place. If economics is to be separable from hedonics, then these goods must be sought, at least in part, for their own sake, and not *merely* as means for securing pleasure. Second, he must presuppose that men are moved to act in accordance with the institutional constraints on economic behaviour. Again, this requires that the relevant desires or motives have not merely pleasures narrowly conceived as their objects but certain forms of social behaviour that are pursued for their own sakes and not merely as means. And third, he must presuppose that the desires that move one to conform to the institutional norms have a non-economic force, a moral force that, almost always at least, enables these desires to constrain and override any economic ('lower') impulses that are at variance with those institutional norms.

In order to reconcile these three things with the hedonism that was an essential premiss of the utilitarian party, what John Stuart Mill had to show is, one, that desires having objects other than pleasure, that is, that things other than pleasures can be desired as ends, is compatible with that hedonism; and two, that having both moral and non-moral motives is compatible with hedonism. Of course, the philosophical psychology of his father would enable one to, as it were, ram these theses through without feeling the need for fidelity to phenomenological data. But the younger Mill rejected this philosophical approach to psychology, and proposed to transform psychology into a truly empirical science. That required that he provide, in terms of his learning theory – that is, the learning theory of associationist psychology – a sketch at least of how the mechanisms of association working on pleasure in various contexts can generate desires aiming at objects other than pleasure, and how the working of mental chemistry can produce moral pleasures that are both qualitatively distinct from and capable of controlling non-moral pleasures. It is the aim of the next chapter to see how the younger Mill goes about this.

There is an antecedent issue, however: one must recognize that there is indeed a problem, something that *does* require explanation. The suggestion that our preferences do *not* require explanation arose in fact in Mill's youth with respect to Ricardo's economics. The critic who made this point was the Samuel Bailey whose later criticism of the psychology of the utilitarians we examined above. It is to this antecedent issue that we turn in the next section.

2   Bailey: A Critic Criticized

Bailey made his criticism of Ricardo in a suitably thin work (1825). The utilitarians rose to the defence of their champion in an article in their official journal, the *Westminster Review*. This article (Anon. 1826) was apparently by James Mill.[4] Since the exchange has been much misunderstood, with Bailey receiving undue praise, and the real and legitimate concerns of the utilitarians being ignored, it will pay to examine it in detail. Certainly, if Bailey were correct, then the concerns of John Stuart Mill with respect to the analysis of desires and motives simply would not arise. For, argues Bailey, exchange values are relative, and therefore, like spatial relations, they are *simply given* and *therefore are objective and need no explanation.* This objectivist account of exchangeable value is quite incompatible with the utilitarian account, and the utilitarian response was adequate to its removal. For the younger Mill to get on with the task of adequately locating economics within the context of psychology, it remained only for him to transform his father's philosophical psychology into a truly empirical science.

Behind the utilitarian position are the same foundations that Bentham provided for the principles of morals and legislation.[5] The basic point is that, as a matter of lawful fact, men are moved by pleasure and pain, and only pleasure and pain: 'Nature has placed mankind under the governance of two sovereign masters, *pain* and *pleasure*' (1789, Ch. I, sec. 1). These are sensations (Ch. VI, sec. 3), and it is these sensations that constitute the *ends* that move men (Ch. I, sec. 1). But a person will *prefer* some pleasures (pains) to others: 'to a person considered by himself, the value of a pleasure or pain ... will be greater or less' (Ch. IV, sec. 2) according to various criteria. A pleasure will be valued more than another if it is more productive of further pleasures, less productive of further pains (Ch. IV, sec. 3). These are reasons *extrinsic* to a pleasure for preferring it to another. But there are also *intrinsic* differences: the value of 'a pleasure or pain considered *by itself*' (Ch. IV, sec. 2) will be greater if it is (1) more intense, (2) of longer duration, (3) more certain, and (4) less remote (ibid.). Pleasures and pains may be categorized in terms of their causes (Ch. v), but we must recognize that the same exciting cause may give different amounts of pleasure to different persons (Ch. VI, sec. 1) according to different 'circumstances influencing sensibility' (Ch. VI, sec. 5). James Mill's *Analysis* (1825, Ch. XXIII) was to attempt to sketch how learning (association) could account for the relevance of these circumstances and for the amount of pleasure produced in a person by an exciting cause in a given circumstance.

Bailey takes value to be a mental act: 'Value, in its ultimate sense, appears to mean the *esteem* in which any object is held' (1825, p. 1). The object valued is, in respect of some material quality of it, the exciting cause of this feeling (ibid.). It is only when objects are *compared* that one can speak of *value*, which Bailey *contrasts to pleasure* (p. 2). Value is a matter of 'relative esteem'; it is 'the relation in which [two objects] stand to each other in our estimate' (p. 3). As a relation it is analogous to distance, which is also a relation: 'A thing cannot be valuable in itself without reference to another thing, any more than a thing can be distant in itself without reference to another thing' (p. 5).

We note three things. First, Bailey treats preference as a *relation*. Second, for Bailey preference is contrasted to, and therefore not analysable in terms of, pleasure. And third, for Bailey the relation of preference is analogous to the relation of distance. Now, as we saw in the preceding chapter, Bailey treats spatial relations as phenomenologically given, and therefore unanalysable. Given the analogy between preference and distance, we are not surprised to find that Bailey holds that preference is not analysable in terms of pleasure. Here we can contrast Bailey to Bentham. For both, the relation of *preference* is what is crucial. Bentham takes preference judgments among objects to be analysable in terms of the pleasures of which those things are the exciting causes. In contrast, for Bailey, while objects are exciting causes of our judgments of preference, the latter are not further analysable into the pleasures those objects (also) excite. It follows that, for Bailey, preference is unanalysable, since there is no other plausible candidate for analysands. But 'analysis' has a specific meaning in this context. The reference is to learning theory, and, in particular to the learning theory – associationism – of the utilitarians: one can analyse that, and only that, which has arise by association. It follows that, for Bailey, *judgments of preference are innate, unlearned, and our making them requires no explanation.* Thus, from the point of view of the utilitarian party, *Bailey's judgments of preference are none other than the innate value judgments of the moral intuitionists.*

Bailey applies his account specifically to exchangeable value (1825, p. 2). This notion is a purely relative one (p. 3). With this claim, no one would disagree, not even Ricardo. But Ricardo also introduces a *second* concept of value, the 'real' or 'absolute' value of an object. Bailey argues from the definition of 'value' as exchangeable value that Ricardo's second concept is illegitimate (pp. 9ff). Now, on the face of it this is an odd argument indeed. The author of the anonymous *Westminster Review* response to Bailey (who was very likely James Mill) pointed out (Anon. 1826, p. 157) that there is nothing wrong with using one term with two meanings, so long as the meanings are made clear from the context, as in Ricardo they are (cf. Dobb 1973, p. 102). Rauner (1961, p. 12) has suggested that Bailey made a great contribution here, showing that Ricardo's 'logic [is] at fault.' But this is simply not so; there is no fault to be demonstrated. Nor, again contrary to Rauner (p. 16), is there any 'contradiction' in Ricardo by virtue of his using the term 'value' in two ways. However, as Rauner also remarks, 'beyond this there was an issue of equal importance: whether or not there was any significance or merit in Ricardo's *conception*' (p. 21). Rauner elsewhere (p. 97) suggests some criteria for the utility of concepts. A concept is more useful than another if it has 'greater consistency and generality to the theory of value.' One is hard put indeed to comprehend what is actually meant when these two criteria are laid down. Are there *degrees of consistency*, as 'greater consistency' suggests? Surely there is only consistency and inconsistency with nothing in between. And what is it for one concept to be more general than another? One sense would be that of a genus, as contrasted to a species, but that hardly seems to be relevant. What then is meant? Be that as it may, there in fact is (besides internal consistency) *but one* criterion for when a concept is useful to science: a concept is useful to science just in case that it is significant, that is, appears in statements of law. Thus, the issue with respect to the concept of 'real value' is indeed whether it is a *useful* concept in science, but what this amounts to is the question whether this concept is one that has *significance* in the sense of *appearing in statements of laws*.[6] This Bailey denies:

> What information is conveyed, or what advance in argument is effected by telling us, that value estimated in one way is real, but in another nominal? The value of any commodity denoting its relation in exchange to some other commodity, we may speak of it as money-value, corn-value, cloth-value, according to the commodity with which it is compared; and hence there are a thousand different kinds of value, as many kinds of value as there are commodities in existence, and all are equally real and equally nominal. We gain nothing in perspicuity or precision by the use of these latter terms, but, on the contrary, they entail upon us a heavy encumbrance of vagueness and ambiguity and unproductive discussion. (1825, pp. 38–9)

Bailey is here maintaining that there are no theoretical claims that would (if true) render Ricardo's non-relative concept of value significant. But, more strongly, he is proposing a view of economics in which a problem Ricardo was attempting to answer simply *does not arise.* Specifically, note that Bailey restricts economics to the discussion of the laws that explain why, say, two deer exchange for one beaver at a point in time. That is, he restricts economics to a discussion of short- and long-run equilibrium conditions. *Bailey is arguing that the concept of absolute value is not needed to state these laws, and further that, since this is all there is to economics, there can be no other use for this concept, that is, no other laws that could render the concept significant.* What we shall now argue is that Ricardo in fact has *two* uses for the concept of absolute value. One use Bailey does discuss, and criticize. This is the use Ricardo made of the concept to state the laws of economics in the subject-matter to which Bailey restricts the science of economics. But Ricardo has a *second* use for the concept of absolute value. That is, he uses it to state a *further* set of theoretical propositions or laws not encompassed by Bailey's restrictive definition of economics. This further set of laws Bailey does not discuss but rather simply dismisses by his restriction on the subject-matter of economics. And this dismissal, we shall also argue, amounts to the claim that *relational judgments of preference need no explanation, and are, therefore, innate and intuitive,* as are relational judgments of distance.

For Ricardo, real value is given by the *quantity of labour* required to produce a commodity. Thus, we are told in the *Principles* that 'Wages are to be estimated by their real value, viz., by the quantity of labour and capital used in producing them, and not by their nominal value either in coats, hats, money or corn' (1821, p. 65; quoted in Bailey 1825, p. 38). Capital goods, for example, tools, necessary for production, are, of course, accumulated labour; that is, the value they have is a consequence of the labour expended upon producing them (1821, pp. 23ff). This concept of real value is used to state the laws describing how distribution proceeds. Thus, for example, we are told that 'Profits, it cannot be too often repeated, depend on wages; not on nominal, but real wages; not on the number of pounds that may be annually paid to the labourer, but on the number of days' work, necessary to obtain these pounds' (p. 143). More generally, the quantity of labour necessary to produce commodities '*regulates* their relative value' (p. 30; italics added). All this derives, of course, from Ricardo's fundamental thesis: 'The value of a commodity, or the quantity of any other commodity for which it will exchange, depends on the relative quantity of labour which is necessary for its production, and not on the greater or less compensation which is paid for the labour' (p. 11). The idea of 'regulation' is that the quantity of labour determines the 'natural' or long-run relative or exchangeable value (p. 30) – while, of course, there are temporary short-run fluctuations accounted for by means of the mechanism of supply and demand. This much of Ricardo's theory we have already examined. Bailey is denying that the notion of 'real value' is of use in the laws needed to explain relative value. He insists that the only concept of value that we need for labour is that of exchangeable value: 'Unless we change the meaning of value in the case of labour from that which it bears when applied to anything else, the value of labour must signify the power of commanding other things in exchange' (1825, p. 46). Thus, labour has no absolute value, but is a commodity that, like all other commodities, possesses a relative value. The idea is, though Bailey does not work it out in detail, that Ricardo's theory that long-run exchangeable value depends upon 'quantity of labour' turns out to be substantially correct if this quantity is understood not in an absolute sense but relatively, in the sense of 'exchangeable value.' The younger Mill was to work out this idea of Bailey. He, like Bailey, insisted upon the relative nature of value: 'the value of a commodity is not a name for an inherent and substantive quality of a thing itself, but means the quantity of other things which can be obtained in exchange for it. The value of one thing must always be understood relatively to some other thing or to things in general' (1871, p. 479). Ricardo's theory of profits is translated into the proposition that profits depend on the 'cost of production or wages' (pp. 410f). Mill then goes on to argue that things on the average exchange for one another in the ratio of their cost of production (p. 472), where he defines cost of production explicitly to mean *wages* plus profit on the amount of necessary capital at a rate the expectation of which is the minimum necessary to persuade capitalists to continue producing (pp. 481ff, 498). Schumpeter has pointed out that this conception of value is entirely in line with Bailey's criticism of Ricardo and leaves no room for anything in the nature of 'absolute value.' 'The energy with which [Mill] insisted on the relative character of [value] completely annihilated Ricardo's Real Value and reduced other Ricardianisms to insipid innocuousness' (1954, p. 603).

So far, then, Bailey is correct. In order to state the theory of the long-run normal and short-run fluctuations in exchangeable value, it is not necessary to introduce any concept of 'absolute value.' But there is a *second use* for the concept of 'absolute value' in Ricardo's theory. That is, it is employed to state a theoretical proposition or law other than those that determine long- and short-run exchangeable value in a given social and technological context. The laws with which Bailey is concerned account for why two deer, say, exchange for one beaver *at a point in time*. Ricardo is interested in this ratio, and his theory uses the concept of 'absolute value' – though, as the younger Mill showed, the latter can be replaced without loss of explanatory power by the relative concept of value. Now, these laws are, in the younger Mill's terms, those of the *statics* of the subject,' the theory of equilibrium (1871, p. 705). But Ricardo is interested in a *further problem* (1821, pp. 24ff): what forces cause changes in this ratio over time?[7] That is, for example, what forces would cause the price of beaver to increase so that $3D = 1B$? These questions ask, in Mill's terms, for the laws of *motion* of a system, the laws of dynamics, as opposed to statics, describing how one set of equilibrium or static conditions is transformed into another set of static relationships (1871, p. 705). If the change in exchange ratios does happen, is it correct to say that the price of beaver increased, or the price of deer decreased? On the relative notion of value, *both* these conclusions are correct (cf. Bailey 1825, p. 5). However, as Ricardo points out (1821, p. 43), neither tells us as much as an invariable or absolute measure of value would. If we had an absolute measure of value, it would be possible to determine whether the price of beaver had increased because beaver had become more costly to produce or because deer had become less costly to produce. Quantity of labour is such an absolute standard – this is Ricardo's fundamental proposition – and other commodities can only approximate to such a measure, since all other commodities (for example, gold) are such that their value is exposed to the same variations or fluctuations as any commodity in general is exposed (pp. 43–4). Once this absolute standard is determined, one could go on to attempt to identify the additional causal factors that, operating differentially, cause the change in relative values. For example, such other factors as the invention of machinery, improved skills, or improved division of labour could be identified as relevant (p. 273). John Stuart Mill develops the same themes in some detail (1871, pp. 710ff). For Ricardo, quantity of labour is the *cause* and more specifically the *regulator* of exchangeable value – with reference to how it determines in the static state the long-run value about which short-run changes fluctuate. But it is also the *standard* of value – in the sense that, with respect to dynamics, it provides a common standard against which change in prices can be measured over time. This standard is also a cause, and how this cause regulates value at different levels in different static states is a matter of the changing social and/or technological context that effects the change from one static state to the next. Nor, in spite of Schumpeter's suggestion to the contrary, does John Stuart Mill eliminate *this* non-relative notion of value when he comes to discuss the dynamics of economic change (1871, Bk. IV, ch. ii). While Mill eliminates the notion of absolute value in favour of relative value in one of Ricardo's uses, he does not do so in the other. Ricardo was interested in the variations in value because they affected the distribution of the national income among landlords, capitalists, and labourers. His concern, as he says in his preface, is with the laws of distribution (1821, p. 5). Given his earlier essays on the Corn Laws, what was uppermost in his mind was no doubt the effect of the latter on the relative prosperity of landlords and capitalists. He recognized, as of course did many others of his class, that the protective duties so beneficial to the rent-receiving landlords were distinctly disadvantageous to those whose income came from profits on capital. If Ricardo had a political point in writing the *Principles*, then it was to establish this point beyond doubt (cf. 1821, Ch. xxii). The foundation for arguing this was the law of diminishing returns but the central point of the argument rests on the close relationship between, on the one hand, changes in the quantity of labour required to produce commodities and, on the other hand, the variations that take place in their relative values (cf. Cassels 1935, p. 87). John Stuart Mill also had a practical or, if you wish, applied economic, interest in dynamical changes, but this interest had a much more general focus than Ricardo's; Mill was concerned of course with the Corn Laws, at least until they were repealed, but he was also concerned with the much broader issue of increases in the general welfare, progressiveness, and material prosperity of society (1871, pp. 705–6), and, if there is a specific focus, then it is on 'the probable futurity of the labouring classes' (Bk. IV, ch. vii).

Given this interest of Ricardo in the laws of economic development we are now in a position to locate the central failure of Bailey's discussion of Ricardo's economics.

For Ricardo, the concept of absolute value, and, specifically, the notion of quantity of labour, functions, first, to state the laws of the static state, and, second, to state the laws of dynamical change. Bailey argues that the former laws can be stated using the concept of exchangeable or relative value. But the other use of the concept is ignored, or, rather, by omission, dismissed as without the possibility of being reconstructed in a significant way, one that captures a lawful connection. That is, in dismissing it, Bailey is proposing a conception of economics in which the possibility of a dynamical explanation of a given static state is excluded, and in which explanation restricts itself to (the limited purpose of) attempting to grasp the laws describing behaviour within the given static state. Thus, for Bailey, relational judgments of preference are simply given; they need no explanation. But, of course, we are not surprised at this conclusion, since we have seen, on the one hand, that Bailey takes judgments of preference to be analogous to judgments of distance, and, on the other hand, that the latter are innate and intuitive. Bailey's failure to acknowledge that exchangeable value ratios need any explanation amounts to the claim that such value judgments are innate, and intuitive. Thus, needing no explanation, such value judgments also need no justification.[8]

Such at least was how the author of the *Westminster Review* reply not implausibly read Bailey. Those who, as did Rauner (1961), uncritically praise Bailey for insisting upon the relative notion of value, thus, as Rauner (p. 137) sees it, paving the way for the economics of the younger Mill, completely miss this aspect of the issue. Rauner does not even bother to recognize, when he mentions (p. 97) the criticism of Bailey on this point, the real thrust of the remarks of the *Westminster Review* critic. Perhaps, because the point is philosophical rather than simply economic, Rauner does not understand it. But Rauner is at least in the company of Bailey himself, who answered (1826) the *Westminster Review* article but did not take up this point, as if he did not see that here was the central issue.

The crucial concept is that of 'relation' (Anon. 1826, p. 161): 'He [Bailey] makes vast use of the word "relation." But it is very evident to us, that he does not know what it means. Is he acquainted with Hobbes' profound remark, that there is nothing relative, but terms? With all his metaphysics, we will give him a month to explain what is meant by relation. He will find, if he likes, some excellent information in Hobbes' Logic, which may, perhaps, abate a little of his admiration of Dr Brown, who makes use of the word "relative" as an occult cause, to explain whatever he did not understand.' This is of a piece with the criticism that John Stuart Mill made of relations in his notes to his father's *Analysis* (1869, II: 7–8): 'The only difference between relative names and any others consist in their being given in pairs; and the reason of their being given in pairs is not the existence between two things, of a mystical bond called a Relation, and supposed to have a kind of shadowy and abstract reality, but a very simple peculiarity in the concrete fact that two names are intended to mark.' The objection in both cases is that relational judgments are assumed to be unanalysable and are therefore further taken to be about an objective and independent tie. In Bailey's case, the objective relation would be that of preference, and to hold this to be objective would be to adopt an intuitionist, non-utilitarian account of value. It is just this that the *Westminster Review* critic (Anon. 1826, p. 161) points out: 'The author's attempt reminds one of the mistake of Diderot, who wrote an eloquent and a much more plausible book than this, to show, what he too thought a great discovery, that Taste is a perception of relations; aye, and Moral Sense the same thing. It was not difficult to see, that this was a solution in words merely; not, however, more vain than that of the writers who resolve the principle of value into a relation; and then imagine that they have enlightened the world.'

It is not clear what work of Diderot is being referred to, but in any case Diderot does clearly hold the position attributed to him, with respect not only to morals but also to aesthetics. Thus, in an essay on the mathematics of music, we are told that 'Le plaisir, en général, consiste dans la perception des rapports: ce principe a lieu en poesis, en peinture, en architecture, en morale, dans tous les sciences' (1748, p. 39). We know these relations by perception, though they can also affect our emotions: 'ces rapports peuvent affecter notre âme de deux manières, par sentiment ou par perception' (p. 42). The point is repeated in the article 'Beau' of *l'Encyclopédie*, which was later republished alone in 1772 and then in 1798 as 'Recherches philosophiques sur l'origine et la nature du beau': to recognize beauty is to perceive relations (1752a, p. 501); in the case of beauty these relations establish a uniformity in variety (p. 480), and they are perceived by means of their 'sens propre' (p. 478). The theme recurs in the article 'Juste' of *l'Encyclopédie*: 'le bon ou le mauvais, en morale comme partout ailleurs, se fonde sur le rapport essentiel, ou la dissonance essentielle d'une chose avec une autre' (1752b, pp. 401–2). The relations are those of men to each other, more specifically, the social relations of mutual dependence as we attempt to survive and prosper. Insofar as our actions relate to others in furtherance of these goals, they are – *objectively* – right, and otherwise wrong. 'Car si on suppose des êtres créés, de façon qu'ils ne puissent subsister qu'en se soutenant les uns les autres, il est clair que leurs actions sont convenables ou ne le sont pas, a proportion qu'elles s'approchent ou qu'elles s'éloignent de ce but; et que ce rapport avec notre conservation fonde les qualités de bon et de droit, de mauvais et de pervers, que ne dependent par conséquent d'aucune disposition arbitraire, et existent non-seulement avant la loi, mais même quand la loi n'existerait point' (p. 402).

The *Westminster Review* critic of Bailey clearly locates Bailey within the context of this treatment of relations that construes them as providing an *objective standard of value*, and as recognized by a mysterious and special *moral sense*.

The anonymous critic would no doubt have been familiar with the British tradition from which Diderot's views derive. This is the tradition that we examined above, in chapter 1. It includes Samuel Clarke, but most especially Shaftesbury. These moral philosophers sought to reply to Hobbes and to defend an ethical-objectivist position – and any defence of the latter would apply equally as a criticism of the utilitarian position. The point is that, as we saw, these ethical objectivists, including the moral-sense theorists such as Shaftesbury from whose views Diderot derived his own, all hold that it is a *set of relations* that describes the *moral fitness* of actions and dispositions and which constitutes the *objective values of things*. For present purposes the point is that Bailey could quite reasonably be construed as adhering to this *metaphysics of objective value*. For the *Westminster Review* critic this was the central issue. Bailey was seen as fitting into a long tradition of moral philosophy that extended back through Diderot to British moralists all-too-familiar to the utilitarians as those who provided the intellectual underpinnings of the social and political and economic dogmas that the radical reformers were concerned to attack.

The anonymous critic (1826, p. 163) adopts the position of Mill's *Analysis* (1825) that relations are mental associations based on non-relational qualities of the things related. These qualities are the foundation of the relation. The suggestion is that Bailey, and others who take exchangeable value to be a relation, confuse the relation, a mental connection, with its foundation, thereby confusedly supposing the former to be as objective as the latter. In contrast, it is argued that what Ricardo and others seek is the foundation of the relation of exchangeable value. 'We ask them [Bailey et al.], if value be the *relatio*, to tell us what is the *fundamentum*. Let them do so, and they will probably discover, that they have less ground, than they thought, of complaint against Ricardo and his followers' (1826, p. 163).

What Ricardo is proposing, then, is to discover the properties of things by virtue of which they are the exciting causes of a judgment of preference, that is, the properties that cause, as Bailey would say, the mind to esteem them. This is the accurate way of saying that Ricardo proposes to discover what it is that causes things to have exchangeable value. The properties, whatever they are, excite a judgment of preference. In the terms of the utilitarian psychology, this means that the properties are associated in the mind when such a judgment occurs. The research method is, therefore, again in terms of that psychology, the method of *analysis*. The younger Mill was, of course, to sharpen this notion, eliminating the part of it that was speculative philosophy, thereby rendering it scientifically adequate. Even so, in the present context, what is going on is clear enough, and is clearly enough reasonable science: there is no reason why one cannot seek the properties of objects that are the stimuli that evoke certain responses.[9] Now, these properties need not be intrinsic; they may, for example, be causal properties, either causes or effects. Ricardo, of course, argues that the relevant properties are causes, and, specifically, the costs of production. As the anonymous *Westminster* reviewer puts it, 'Mr Ricardo says, the ordinary and natural causes of an alteration in the value of a commodity, as compared with other commodities, is an alteration in its cost of production, meaning the last elements, whatever they are, into which cost of production can be resolved' (1826, p. 160). The foundations for preference judgments, then, are non-intrinsic causal properties. Specifically, of course, the dominating causes are, Ricardo argues, labour costs. Thus, the greater the amount of labour required to produce an object, the more it is esteemed. It is misleading, by the way, to speak of labour as bestowing on an object an 'intrinsic quality' called value, as, for example, Bladen (1974, pp. 191–2) does. Quantity of labour provides an *absolute* standard of value, but it is an *extrinsic* property of the thing valued. It endows the object produced with no intrinsic property. What it does do is evoke the esteem in which the object is held. And to seek such an evoking cause is legitimate science. One may argue that Ricardo is *in fact* wrong, for example, that there are several evoking causes for such judgments, or that there are no such properties, that is, that the causes of such judgments have nothing to do with the objects the judgments are about. But what one *cannot* do is argue that what Ricardo is up to is *simple scientific nonsense*. The latter is, of course, what Bailey does, and the *Westminster* reviewer is *quite correct* in defending Ricardo's program. Rauner (1961), apparently not understanding the issues concerning relations and analysis – at least, he doesn't mention them – in his haste to rescue Bailey from largely deserved oblivion completely misses both this central disagreement between Bailey and Ricardo and the basic correctness of the *Westminster* reviewer's attack on Bailey.

3   Quantity and Quality of Pleasure in Mill's Economics

Ricardo's use of the notion of a real or absolute value of a thing that is measured by the quantity of labour required to produce that thing can, we have argued, withstand the criticisms of Bailey. But what, precisely, *is* this 'quantity of labour'? Marxist thinkers, following Marx himself, often root their discussions of economics in Ricardo's work, and often also wed Ricardo's notion of a 'quantity of labour' with strands of Hegelian philosophy to give this notion a metaphysical content. Such a content is foreign, however, to Ricardo himself, who, as we shall see in the present section, rooted his notion firmly in the psychological theories, such as that of James Mill, that were accepted by the philosophic radicals. John Stuart Mill was to modify that psychology and economics, and was to go on to emphasize the (*relative*) autonomy of economics from such considerations. None the less, we shall suggest, Ricardo's notion has a continuing significance for economics. As for the modifications in the psychology that were made by John Stuart Mill, the point of these for economic theory was to provide an explanation of how moral sentiments aimed at securing conformity to the principles of justice, contract, and allegiance can constrain economic behaviour and provide the institutional framework within which alone the laws proposed by the classical economists have any validity for explanation and prediction. In making these changes in the utilitarian psychology, we suggest, it is John Stuart Mill, rather than Bailey, who points the way towards more modern treatments of value in economics. For, in emphasizing that the moral sentiments are qualitatively distinct from, and, by virtue of that quality, preferable to quantities of 'lower' pleasures, what Mill is in effect pointing to is that one can have an *ordinal* ranking of preferences that does *not* involve a *cardinal* ranking, where by a 'cardinal ranking' is meant one for which the notion of a 'quantity' or measure of difference is defined, as it is not in a merely ordinal ranking of more or less. But this point is relevant not merely for economics but also, as we shall see in the next chapter, for Mill's moral theory, since there has been a variety of philosophical critics of Mill's quality/quantity distinction who simply fail to recognize the difference between an ordinal, or a merely ordinal, ranking and a cardinal scale of values.

Let us, therefore, return to Ricardo.

It has been suggested, for example by Cassels (1935, p. 93), that for Ricardo the notion of quantity of labour plays no role, that it is idle, since when it comes to *calculations* Ricardo everywhere works in terms of money. Now, the latter is no doubt true. But it does not follow that the notion of quantity of labour is irrelevant. Value is determined by quantity of labour. The latter is a causal property of objects; more important, it is a historical property in the sense that in order to decide

what quantity of labour attaches to a commodity one must trace the
history of production of that commodity, and the history of the
production of the implements used in its production, in the production
of the clothing worn by those who produce it, and so on (Ricardo 1821,
pp. 21ff). The exchangeable value is determined by 'the aggregate sum
of these various kinds of labour' (p. 25). As a consequence, it would be
nice (p. 44) to have a commodity that always, for its production, required
the same quantity of labour. Then that object could be used, via its
exchange value with respect to other objects, to measure the (absolute)
value of those other objects, that is, the aggregate quantity of labour
required to produce them. There is, however, no such commodity (pp.
44–5). But to make his presentation easier, Ricardo proposes to proceed *as if* gold or money were a commodity that could provide an
invariable measure of value (p. 46). He explicitly refers to his arguments based upon the supposition of such a commodity as proceeding
'hypothetically' and proceeding 'as if we had' knowledge of such a
commodity (p. 275). To the extent that Ricardo proceeds in this way,
then Cassels is correct when he asserts that Ricardo's calculations all
refer to money, not quantity of labour. But to say that therefore the
notion of quantity of labour plays no role in Ricardo's *theory* is to mistake a piece of technical shorthand for a concept central to that theory.

In fact, the theoretical concept and the propositions it is used to
express are to be linked to deeper theoretical principles. These deeper
principles tie Ricardo's economics firmly to the Benthamite utilitarian
tradition, and, specifically, to the psychological theorizing of these
thinkers, Bentham and the Mills. Moreover, it is in *this* context, that of
the utilitarian psychology, that the notion of a quantity of labour as an
absolute standard finds the assumptions that make it plausible.

Economic theory proceeds in terms of the assumption of economic
rationality for those who participate in the economy, that is, the
assumption that, in the younger Mill's terms, they prefer the greater
gain to the less. Ricardo explicitly ties his theorizing in with this
assumption of economic rationality (1821, pp. 90–1). The notion of
quantity of labour links up with this theoretical principle. Ricardo
approvingly quotes (pp. 12–13) Adam Smith's point that the real price
of anything, 'what everything costs to the man who wants to acquire it,
is the toil and trouble of acquiring it. What everything is really worth to
the man who has acquired it, and who wants to dispose of it, or
exchange it for something else, is the toil and trouble which it can save
for himself, and which it can impose upon other people' (Smith 1776,
p. 30). Elsewhere Ricardo points out that the hypothetical commodity

that is the invariable measure of all value is that which 'at all times requires the same sacrifice of toil and labour to produce it' (1821, p. 275). Contrary to what Rauner (1961, p. 16) asserts, in the last analysis it is not 'quantities of objective labour' that Ricardo compares and aggregates, but rather subjective pains and sacrifices. John Stuart Mill also locates himself in this tradition: for him the idea of labour includes not only the exertion itself 'but all feelings of a disagreeable kind, all bodily inconvenience or mental annoyance, connected with the employment of one's thoughts, or muscles, or both, in a particular occupation' (1871, p. 25). In fact, in dealing with 'the Definition of Political Economy' Mill includes among the costs not only the *pain of labour* but also the *pain of abstinence* that the capitalist must endure if he saves in order to invest:

> [Political Economy] predicts only such of the phenomena of the social state as take place in consequence of the pursuit of wealth. It makes entire abstraction of every other human passion or motive; except those which may be regarded as *perpetually antagonizing principles to the desire of wealth, namely aversion to labour, and desire of the present enjoyment of costly indulgences.* These it takes, to a certain extent, into its calculations, because these do not, like other desires, occasionally conflict with the pursuit of wealth, but accompany it always as a drag or impediment, and are therefore inseparably mixed up in the consideration of it. (1844, pp. 321–2; italics added)

The idea is clear enough: what is at issue is for Ricardo the *disutility of labour*, the pain of exertion and sacrifice. Mill adds the pain of abstinence, but for the moment let us, as does Ricardo, ignore this. *One commodity will exchange for another at that point at which the disutility required to produce the one is equal to the disutility required to produce the other.* Conversely, demand is a matter of the commodity being desired, that is, giving pleasure or *having positive utility.* Thus, under the assumption of economic rationality, *a person will exchange one commodity for another just in case that the positive utility it has for that person exceeds the real price, that is, the quantity of labour or disutility required to produce it.* As Mill puts it, 'the exchange value of a thing may fall short, to any amount, of its value in use [utility]; but that it can exceed the value in use, implies a contradiction [that is, it implies a contradiction *assuming* economic rationality]; it supposes that persons will give, to possess a thing, more than the utmost value which they themselves put upon it as a means of gratifying their inclinations' (1871, p. 457).

If labour were the sole cost of production, then, assuming perfect competition, the supply-and-demand mechanism will ensure that, in the long run, the desire for something will not only be no less than, but also no more than, the disutility required to produce it. That is, in such circumstances a commodity will exchange at that point at which a person is indifferent to the pain it costs to produce and the pleasure it will give. But Mill argues against Ricardo that labour is not the sole cost of production.

Mill locates profit within the same context as Smith and Ricardo had located labour: he relates it to disutilities, and specifically the disutilities of the capitalist. 'As the wages of the labourer are the remuneration of labour, so,' Mill proposes, 'the profits of the capitalist are properly the remuneration of abstinence' (1871, p. 400). That is, profit corresponds to the pain of waiting for utilities to which we just above saw him refer in his 1844 essay on the definition of political economy. Since most commodities can be produced only by labour and capital, cost of production is in general, contrary to Ricardo, not just quantity of labour, but also profit (pp. 471ff). *This* quantity – labour plus profit – which, in conditions of perfect competition, is 'the minimum with which the producers will be content, is also ... the maximum which they can expect' (pp. 471–2).

We can now see where the scale for measuring 'quantity of labour' in fact is to be located: in the Benthamite scale of utilities. To obtain the utility of an act, says Bentham, one should 'sum up all the values of all the pleasures on the one side, and those of all the pains on the other' (1789, Ch. IV, sec. 5). *It is the unit of the cardinal scale of utilities that is, at the same time, the unit for the scale of absolute values in Ricardo's economic theory, that is, the absolute standard by means of which dynamical economic growth is measured.*

Now, there are clearly a number of assumptions at work here. Two of them stand out as most significant. The first is that, for each person, *there is a unit* for the scale of pleasures and pains, or what is the same, that, for each person, there is a cardinal scale of utilities. The second assumption is that this unit or scale is the *same for all* persons, that is, that there are interpersonal comparisons of utility. It is no doubt true that today we are fully prepared to reject these assumptions. We know, on the one hand, that the science of psychology provides no grounds for supposing that either of these *factual* assumptions is true; we know, on the other hand, that the science of economics needs neither of them. None the less, as Schumpeter points out, neither assumption is 'simply nonsense' (1954, p. 1060).

Marshall is prepared to defend vigorously the idea of a scale of pleasure/pain. At the same time, he recognized the above two problems and proposed a solution to them.

> When we speak of ratio between effort and abstinence we assume, *ipso facto*, an artificial mode of measuring them in terms of some common unit, and refer to the ratio between their measures. The pure science of Ethics halts for lack of a system of measurement of efforts, sacrifices, desires, etc., for wide purposes. But the pure science of Political Economy has found a system that will serve her narrower ends. This discovery, rather than any particular proposition, is the great fact of the pure science ...
>
> A point of view was conquered for us by Adam Smith, from which a commodity is regarded as the embodiment of measurable efforts and sacrifices ... Proceeding from its new point of view, Political Economy has analysed the efforts and sacrifices that are required for the production of a commodity for a given market at a given time; she has found a measure for them in their *cost to the person who will purchase them*, and then enunciated her central truth. (1925, p. 126)

In his *Principles* (1961, Bk. I, Ch. v, secs. 2–9) Marshall affirmed that utility is indeed a measurable quantity but argued in detail that economics can proceed on the weaker assumption that, though we cannot measure utility *directly*, that is, cannot measure directly the pleasantness and unpleasantness of sensations, we can measure these *indirectly*, by their observable effects – a pleasure, for example – by the sum of money a man is prepared to give up in order to obtain it rather than go without it. If this proposal works – and, as we know, it is not unproblematic – then it solves both the problem of a unit and the problem of interpersonal comparison.

But Wicksteed had already pointed out (1933, I: 215–16) that, for economics, interpersonal comparisons are not always necessary:

> If A is said to have something in relative excess which B has in relative defect, this does not mean that A has more of it or is less keenly desirous of it *relatively to B*. That may or may not be the case. What the phrase means is that the marginal significance of this thing to A *relatively to the other exchangeable things he possesses* is lower than in the case of B. 'Relative' means relatively to the other possessions or alternatives in the estimate of the same man, not

relatively to the same possessions or alternatives in the estimate of another man.

In the British tradition, W.E. Johnson (1913) was similarly to argue that economics did not need the strong assumption of a cardinal scale of utility but could proceed on a much weaker assumption that persons could order their satisfactions in a unique ordinal 'scale of preferences.' Pareto (of whose work Johnson apparently had no knowledge) had, of course, preceded Johnson in stating the fundamentals of the modern theory of value in terms of the idea of ordinal utility (cf. Schumpeter 1954, pp. 106ff).

It was W.S. Jevons who first saw the possibility of redoing economics on a mathematical basis using the notion of 'marginal utility' – though, as he was also quick to acknowledge, much of what he proposed was already in the works of political economists such as Mill in their discussions of supply and demand. In a letter to his brother of June 1860, written when he was first developing his version of the theory, he locates it relative to previous work in just this way:

> During the last session I have worked a great deal at Pol. Economy; in the last few months I have fortunately struck out what I have no doubt *is the true theory of Economy* so thorough-going and consistent, that I cannot now read other books on the subject without indignation. While the theory is entirely mathematical in principle, I show at the same time how the data of calculation are so complicated as to be for the present hopeless. Nevertheless I obtain from the mathematical principles all the chief laws at which Pol. Economists have previously arrived only arranged in a series of Definitions Axioms and Theorems almost as rigorous [sic] and connected as if they were so many geometrical problems. One of the most important axioms is that as the quantity of any commodity, for instance plain food, which a man has to consume increases, so the utility or benefit derived from the last portion used decreases in degree ... And I assume that on average the *ratio of utility* is some continuous mathematical function of the quantity of commodity. This law of utility has in fact always been assumed by Pol. Economy under the more complex form and name of the Law of Supply and Demand. But once fairly stated in simple form it opens up the whole of the subject. Most of the conclusions are of course the old ones stated in a consistent form – but my definition of Capital and law of the Interest of Capital are as far as I have seen

quite new. I have no idea of letting these things lie by till somebody else has the advantage of them – and shall therefore try to publish them next Spring. (1973, pp. 410–11)

In the *Theory of Political Economy* he tells us that Bentham's ideas 'are adopted as the starting-point of the theory given in this work' (1911, p. xxvi). He takes the four Benthamite dimensions of pleasure and pain – intensity, duration, certainty, and propinquity – and proposes to treat them mathematically. Intensity and duration are intrinsic to a sensation, certainty and propinquity extrinsic, and so he takes the former to be the primary grounds defining 'quantity of feeling.' 'For clearly,' Jevons claims, 'every feeling must last some time, and ... while it lasts it may be more or less acute and intense' (1911, p. 34). The quantity of a feeling is the product of its intensity and duration. 'The whole magnitude would be found by multiplying the number of units of intensity into the number of units of duration. Pleasure and pain, then, are magnitudes possessing the two dimensions, just as an area or superficies possesses the two dimensions of length and breadth' (1871, p. 35). This account of the quantity of feeling clearly presupposes two units and two cardinal scales. Yet both are fantasies. Jevons himself recognizes both the problem of a unit and that of interpersonal comparisons.

As for interpersonal comparisons, he points out that 'every mind is ... inscrutable to every other mind ... The weighing of motives must always be confined to the bosom of the individual' (1911, p. 14). Feelings are commensurable only by each individual mind, so some interpersonal 'unit of intensity' would be impossible. But even then problems remain, so he proposes that economics can, for the most part, get on without requiring reference to units. 'We only employ units of measurement,' he tells us, 'in other things to facilitate the comparison of quantities; and if we can compare the quantities directly, we do not need the units. Now the mind of an individual is the balance which makes its own comparison, and is the final judge of quantities of feeling' (1871, p. 19), and since his 'theory turns upon those critical points where pleasures are nearly, if not quite, equal,' units may not be necessary (p. 20). Although the mathematics of his theory presupposes full cardinalization, Jevons is here indicating that certain crucial inferences depend upon only ordinal features. To this extent Jevons has moved a fair distance from the full cardinalization Bentham took for granted.

But he has in fact moved even further than this suggests. For

Jevons radically separates the economic from the moral order. According to him, the 'lower calculus' of the economist could be used without granting full consideration to the 'higher calculus of moral right and wrong'; economics considers only 'the lowest rank of feelings,' 'the ordinary wants of man' (1871, p. 32). Although moral feelings are ordinally related to the feelings of which economics treats, as higher to lower, there is no common unit to provide a standard of comparison between them. At this point there is, clearly, a real break with Bentham.

It was John Stuart Mill who, I would argue, made this break possible. So long as the moralists and the economists relied upon the sort of philosophical psychology to be found in the elder Mill's *Analysis*, there was no reason for supposing full cardinalization was impossible. For, in the absence of any empirical control on what could count as an 'analysis' of an idea or sensation, nothing could prevent one from finding in his 'analysis' what his philosophy disposed him a priori to find there. So, if one was disposed to think a cardinal scale possible, and to believe that a unit of pleasure existed, then in one's 'analysis' that is what one would find. But John Stuart Mill insisted that the concept of 'analysis' be clarified, and effected that clarification sufficiently for psychology to be transformed into an empirical science. *There are, he then argued, qualitative differences among pleasures that could not be reduced to quantities. These qualitative differences effect an ordinal ranking into higher and lower, but the higher remained incommensurable with the lower.*

Here, of course, we have claims which we have yet to justify. But if we can (as we propose) do the latter, then it will be clear that it was John Stuart Mill who prepared the way for replacing the empirically untenable idea of a cardinal scale of pleasures with the idea of pleasures being ranked merely ordinally. Thus, contrary to what writers such as Rauner (1961) argue, *it is not Bailey but John Stuart Mill who made the break with the Benthamite tradition that pointed the way, through Jevons, to contemporary theory of value in economic theory.*

However, if Mill goes part way towards the ordinal view of utility, he does not go all the way. Even in the notes to his father's *Analysis*, he accepts, as we shall see, the idea that the notion of 'quantity of pleasure' makes sense; it is just that, he argues, there are qualitative differences as well as quantitative, and that qualitatively different pleasures are incommensurable. However, this claim that there are qualitative differences among pleasures still permits qualitatively indistinguishable pleasures to be commensurable, comparable quantitatively. For example, physical pleasures of the sort dealt with by economics may all be commensurable quantitatively among themselves, but at the same time incommensurable with the qualitatively different and higher moral pleasures, which, just because they are higher, are preferred to, and therefore override and control, the economic pleasures. This is, of course, the position of John Stuart Mill, and also of Jevons.

We shall be pursuing the theme of qualitative differences directly, in the next chapter. But we might reasonably raise the question why John Stuart Mill did not proceed the whole distance towards the ordinal view of value. Why does he continue to assume the cardinal notion has validity, if only in restricted areas? Why, in particular, did he assume that the notion of quantitative differences made sense in the economic realm?

Two points are, I think, relevant. The first is that money does seem to provide an adequate, if indirect, test of value. Mill accepts this so far as one considers exchangeable value in a given static situation; for commodities in the frame of reference 'money is a complete measure of their value' (1871, p. 577). Marshall (1961, Bk. I, Ch. v, secs. 2–9) simply – but necessarily, given the problem – elaborates on Mill on this point. Monetary units provide the illusion of units of pleasure.

The second point to be made is that in dynamical considerations – no small matter for Mill, as it was no small matter for Ricardo – the notion of an absolute standard has a plausibility it does not have for the static situation.

The more recent developments of a theory of exchangeable value based upon only ordinal utilities have led to a real resistance to the Smith-Ricardo-Mill, that is, classical economic tradition, of 'real cost' as labour-time, or pains of exertion, or sacrifice. F.H. Knight concedes that the cost 'to an individual or society, of securing an income in the sense of his (or its) total aggregate of satisfaction does consist in the "pain" (or sacrifice of pleasure, if there be any difference, or both) involved in "production."' But he goes on: 'If the aggregate [income] is a fixed magnitude and the actual range of choice under consideration involves only its detailed composition, then the real "cost" of any particular small increment ... is the sacrifice of the competing increment which was actually given up' (1931, p. 185). This notion of cost as what was given up is the notion of 'cost' as 'opportunity cost.' So long as the assumption of more or less fixed aggregate holds, then the concept of 'cost' as 'opportunity cost' is indeed the significant concept. But if one is interested, as were Ricardo and Mill, in the *growth* of the aggregate, in the dynamics of economic change, then it is not so clear that the notion of 'cost' as the 'pain' or effort involved in 'production' lacks all sense. Let me refer to a discussion of the question of economic growth by Kenneth Boulding.

> In a society without capital, or with immortal equipment ... the thing which a society, like an individual, has to spend is the *time* of its members ... In a society with capital embodied in mortal goods – i.e., goods with a finite length of service life – the situation is complicated by the fact that such a society can spend currently beyond, or not up to, its 'means' by the process of decumulating or accumulating valuable goods. It still remains true, however, even in a society which has capital, that the *current* resources which are to be used consist in the 'time-income' at the disposal of its members, even though these current resources may not bear fruit until some future dates, and even though current wealth-income comes from resources which have been employed in the past. (1939, pp. 9–10)

Boulding noted that this view of resources as consisting, directly or indirectly, of 'man-hours' is close to the classical economists' – Ricardo's and Mill's – labour theory of value; but he went on to justify his emphasis on the grounds, with which we are familiar from Mill, that he was considering not 'the determination of prices, nor the distribution of income, but the *sources* of wealth' (p. 10). He then argued that it was perfectly legitimate 'to regard man-time as an original, homogeneous resource' (ibid.) and to introduce the factors which co-operate with man in the guise of 'coefficients of transformation of man-time into products' (ibid.). This technique does not 'debar us from considering the effects of an abundance or a scarcity of co-operating land or of co-operating equipment. The presence or absence of these co-operating factors can be reflected for our purposes perfectly adequately in the coefficients of transformation; when man is co-operating with large amounts of good land and equipment, or when his skill, energy and ability are high the coefficient of transformation of man-time into product is high – i.e., one man-hour will produce in a large quantity of goods and services' (ibid.). As for the term 'man-time price,' this is the 'number of man-hours necessary to produce a unit of commodity' (p. 11), and is, obviously, 'the reciprocal of the coefficient of transformation' (ibid.), that is, the number of units of a commodity produced by a man-hour. I introduce this reference not to justify Mill's position, or to defend its truth, but merely to indicate that in the context of trying to explain growth, the idea of 'cost' as 'pain' or 'man-hours' has continued far beyond Mill's time to present itself as a significant concept, or at least as a concept with respect to which it is *prima facie* plausible that it is significant, in the sense of being usable to state laws. Whether or not such considerations about the dynamics of society are correct, they do show why Mill, who was concerned with dynamics, might well wrongly (if it is that) suppose that a cardinalization of at least the economic values was possible.

However, this is perhaps to enter into more detail about John Stuart Mill's specific economic theories than is necessary for what we are about. For these purposes, which concern his philosophy of economics rather than his specific economic theories, what is important is that for Mill, and for the utilitarians in general, in contrast to Bailey, judgments of preference are with respect to mental states *alone*; they have no objective reference beyond those subjective states, nothing that could confer upon them some sort of objective validity. However, other aspects of the utilitarian position inherited by the younger Mill raised problems. Specifically, of course, I refer to the conflict between, on the one hand, the idea that economic behaviour is constrained by moral and institutional norms and that economics is a (relatively) autonomous science that takes for granted that men seek economic goods as ends, and, on the other hand, Bentham's thesis that 'Nature has placed mankind under the governance of two sovereign masters, *pain* and *pleasure*' (1789, Ch. 1, sec. 1). That is, how does Mill reconcile, what is necessary for his economic theory, the claim that men have non-hedonistic motives and the Benthamite utilitarian claim that the primary motives are hedonistic? This issue is the topic of the next chapter.

SEVEN

The Moral Sentiments

1 The Problem: Can the Moral Sentiments be Analysed?

When Bentham asserted that 'Nature has placed mankind under the governance of two sovereign masters, *pain* and *pleasure*,' and that it is these sensations alone that move men (1789, Ch. I, sec.1), he was accused by such critics as Macaulay (1829) of embracing the doctrine of psychological egoism, that men seek only to maximize their own pleasures. This criticism was neither new nor implausible.

The Newtonians emphasized the parallels between our moral knowledge and our knowledge of nature. We have seen Clarke argue that moral obligations are determined by relations among the Platonic ideas that constitute the a priori structure of the world. Richard Bentley is another who argues that just as the physical universe is subject to a certain order determined by God, so too are men subject to a moral order. In an important 'Sermon Preached before King George I' (1716–17), he argues that there are ties that have been 'established between all the matter of the universe, that the whole is linked together by mutual attraction of gravitation, working regularly and uniformly according to quantity and distance' (p. 266). He then goes on to suggest that one can generalize from the case of physical objects to the case of human beings. We discover that a harmony exists in the physical world, and this provides a reason for supposing that a similar harmony exists in the human world: 'What arrogance, therefore, for us, for us that probably make so small a figure in the great sum of creation, to think we only were made exempt from the universal law of service and dependence!' (p. 267). He adds that the new discoveries in science ought to teach us modesty, and then proceeds to develop his point:

let us now proceed from the natural world to the moral ... Our Creator has implanted in mankind such appetites and inclinations, such natural wants and exigencies, that they lead him spontaneously to the love of society and friendship, to the desire of government and community. Without society and government, man would be found in a worse condition than the very beasts of the field. That divine ray of reason, which is his privilege above the brutes, would only serve in that case to make him more sensible of his wants, and more uneasy and melancholic under them. (pp. 267–8)

Bentley then argues that this social feeling becomes as universal as the law of gravitation.

Certainly the nearer one can arrive to this universal charity, this benevolence to all the human race, the more he has of the divine character imprinted on his soul; for *God is love*, says that apostle; he delights in the happiness of all his creatures. To this public principle we owe our thanks for the inventors of sciences and arts; for the founders of kingdoms and first institutors of laws ... And if nature's still voice be listened to, this is really not only the noblest, but the pleasantest employment ... For the sweetness and felicity of life consists in duly exerting and employing those sociable passions of the soul, those natural inclinations to charity and compassion. (pp. 268–9)

This claim that there are social human impulses towards non-selfish benevolent actions was, of course, a Newtonian answer to the position of Hobbes who had argued that all human actions were intrinsically selfish, that there was no such thing as benevolent or generous action, and that the desire for society and government was to be derived from this selfish human nature rationally calculating what is in its long-term self-interest. The problem was that when Locke extended the 'historical plain method' of Newton to the case of the human mind, he seemed to undermine the possibility of giving this response to Hobbes. The same method seemed to undermine the possibility of a priori ethics. Moreover, when that method was taken in conjunction with the associationist theory of learning that it was used to defend, it seemed to argue against the very possibility of genuinely benevolent and generous action; it seemed indeed to support the Hobbesian view that the theologians, Newtonians included, were so concerned to refute.

Locke had given two explanations of our sense of duty. In either case he assumes that the end that men strive after is to attain pleasure and to avoid pain. 'What moves desire?' Locke asks, and answers, 'happiness, and that alone' (1700, II, xxi, 42). It is pleasure and pain that define good and evil: 'Things are good or evil, only in reference to pleasure or pain' (II, xx, 2). Thus, 'that which is properly good or bad, is nothing but barely pleasure or pain,' and 'things also that draw after them pleasure and pain, are considered as good and evil' (II, xxi, 63). Moral rules are patterns of behaviour that God has laid down in his wisdom and benevolence as conducive to our happiness:

> that God has given a rule whereby men should govern themselves, I think there is nobody so brutish as to deny. He has a right to do it; we are his creatures: he has goodness and wisdom to direct our actions to that which is best: and he has power to enforce it by rewards and punishments of infinite weight and duration in another life; for nobody can take us out of his hands. This is the only true touchstone of moral rectitude; and, by comparing them to this law, it is that men judge of the most considerable moral good or evil of their actions; that is, whether, as duties or sins, they are like to procure them happiness or misery from the hands of the Almighty. (II, xxviii, 8)

These moral rules enter into the definition or nominal essence of a morally ideal person. Moral principles can therefore be discovered by considering the relations that hold among those ideas which are our nominal essences of things (III, xi, 15–16). As we analyse our ideas, with the aim of giving their natural history in accordance with the empirical method, what we discover is that morality is a matter of the relations of our voluntary actions to the moral rules; the rule itself is a 'collection of several simple ideas,' and these define what it is to be a 'moral being.' We thus 'see how moral beings and notions are founded on, and terminated in, these simple ideas we have received from sensation or reflection' (II, xxviii, 14).

Locke gives two grounds for conformity to moral principles. The first is that because morality is a matter of relations among our ideas, it is demonstrable: 'I am bold to think that morality is capable of demonstration, as well as mathematics' (1700, III, xi, 16). This claim that morality is demonstrable on the basis of relations among ideas, shows clearly that, in effect, Locke's ideas are none other than Clarke's Platonic forms fallen into the mind.

In contrast, Locke is a sufficiently clear observer of mankind to note that, in fact, it is opinion that constitutes the views of virtue that most men have, and that these views vary from country to country (1700, II, xxviii, 10–11). There are various causes for the 'wrong judgments' that cause this deviation from the demonstrable ideal (II, xxi, 64). That is why God has further set up a system of rewards and punishments for securing the compliance of men with the moral law: 'if a Christian, who has the view of happiness and misery in another life, be asked why man must keep his word, he will give this as a reason: – because God, who has the power of eternal life and death, requires it' (I, ii, 5). This is the second ground that Locke advances for conforming to the rules of morality. It is, he thinks, the more important. When Molyneaux urged him to write a system of ethics demonstrated with mathematical certainty by reason alone, Locke excused himself on the grounds that 'the Gospel contains so perfect a body of ethics that reason may be excused from that inquiry, since she may find man's duty clearer and easier in revelation than in herself' (quoted in Locke, 1700, p. 65 n2). God's rules can therefore be known with certainty either by reason or by revelation, but for the most part it is revelation that does a better job of securing our conformity.

This view of morality was challenged by Thomas Burnet. In a pamphlet, *Remarks upon an Essay concerning Human Understanding* (1697), he argued that there was within man a higher source of morality beyond the fear of punishment, contrary to Locke's view that men were moved to do their duty through the threat of punishment of God. He charges that Locke obscures the 'moral attributes' of God, that is, the attributes of mercy, justice, holiness, and veracity, which lead men by *love* to obey His will (p. 8). Locke took up this point briefly in his *An Answer to Remarks upon an Essay concerning Human Understanding, &c.* (1697), which he attached to his first reply to Stillingfleet's attack on the *Essay*. He points out (p. 187) that Burnet had distorted the conception of God defended in the *Essay*, since he, in fact, holds the position that having demonstrated the existence of God as a wise, powerful, and benevolent being we can from this derive that he has the further qualities of being good, just and holy (cf. *Essay*, 1700, IV, x, 6). Locke then adds in his *Answer* the point that he made to Molyneaux, that we need not be overly concerned with attempting to demonstrate morality if we are assured that it is the 'law of God'; for then it must have 'all that reason and ground that a just and wise law can or ought to have' (Locke 1697, p. 189). Locke is no doubt correct here, that Burnet has failed to read him correctly. But Burnet has another point to make about morality that is important to note. It is that, on his view, morality is not a matter of reason but of intuition. 'This I am sure of, that the distinction, suppose of gratitude and ingratitude, fidelity and infidelity, ... and such others, is as sudden without any ratiocination, and as sensible and piercing, as the difference I feel from the scent of a rose, and of assa-foetida. 'Tis not like a theorem, which we come to know by the help of precedent demonstrations and postulations, but it rises as quick as any of our passions, or as laughter at the sight of a ridiculous accident or object' (Burnet 1697, p. 5).

Burnet is thus defending the view that Bentley wished to defend, that there is in the soul of man a tendency to benevolent and generous behaviour that provides a foundation for the social order that is more acceptable both to common sense and to theology than the Hobbesian appeals to mere self-interest. The important point to recognize is that Burnet bases his argument not on Bentley's appeal to an analogy to gravity, the law of universal attraction, but rather on a *Lockean appeal to experience*. In other words, an appeal is made to the 'historical plain method' in order to challenge what seems to be implied in Locke's use of that method, and in particular the associationist theory of learning the acceptance of which the method seems to argue for. Burnet repeats this appeal to experience in a set of *Third Remarks upon an Essay concerning Human Understanding* (1699), and extends it from moral to natural religion.

> Whether you will call this principle [of natural conscience], *knowledge*, or by any other name ... is indifferent to us; but 'tis a principle of distinguishing one thing from another in moral cases, without ratiocination; and is improveable into more distinct knowledge. We may illustrate this from our outward sensations. We can evidently distinguish *red* and *yellow* colours, and yet are at a loss how to define either of them, or to express their difference in words. And so in tastes, odours, sounds, and other sensible qualities. (p. 8)

We thus, according to Burnet, have intuition rather than reasoning as the basis of morality, and, assuming morality to be a matter of relations, as both Clarke and Locke held, this intuition grasps moral relations as directly and as clearly as sense grasps the differences among the various sensible qualities that are presented to one. Moreover, not only do we have an intuitive grasp of moral truths but we surely also, according to Burnet, have an intuitive grasp of God. If Locke were right, Burnet contends, then we would require 'long and obscure deductions' to reach a reasonable conception of God, something that is far above the capacities of the 'illiterate part of mankind (which is far the greatest part)' (1697, p. 4). He refers to Locke's denial of innate ideas, but surely, he suggests, the beneficent creator must have provided man with the capacity to achieve an intuitive grasp of the creator's being that is prior to any demonstration.

Burnet is in fact introducing a genuine problem here. Clarke and other Newtonians had attempted to construe morality as a matter of objective relations among things, parallel to the objective relations among things that were described by geometry, and parallel, or so they thought, to the causal relations that lead from every contingent being to the non-contingent or necessary being that is its ultimate cause. Now, as we have noted, Locke's adoption of the empirical method of Newton and his application of it to our ideas in the 'historical plain method' tended to weaken the appeal to that causal principle: the separability of our ideas that the method uncovered implied that we had no idea of a necessary being nor any idea of a necessary causal connection that could lead infallibly from a contingent being to one that is non-contingent. The point is that the critique of the causal principle to which Locke's method leads also yields a parallel critique for the claim that ethical propositions are necessary and demonstrable. Just as the causal principle is transformed into a contingent generalization about contingent beings, so we find moral rules similarly transformed. They cease to be necessary relations among things and become instead contingent rules about how to attain the good and avoid evil. But the 'historical plain method' reveals that our ideas of good and evil can be analysed into, respectively, ideas of pleasure and pain. Moral rules, therefore, become rules for attaining pleasure and avoiding pain, and more specifically rules about how to so relate ourselves to others that we maximize our own pleasure and minimize our own pain. Our moral sentiments, like the idea of God, also become contingent associations of ideas. Thus, 'the thought [which one] has of the delight which any present or absent thing is apt to produce in him ... [is] the idea we call *love*' (Locke 1700, II, xx, 4); in other words, the sentiment of *loving X* is analysable into *X produces pleasure* or, what is the same, into the *association of X with pleasure*. Similarly, hating X can be analysed into the association of X with pain. What Burnet is insisting upon is that this won't do. We in fact can distinguish, to use Burnet's example, gratitude and ingratitude without reference to their having to be *analysed* in any way: the recognition is *immediate* and 'as sensible and piercing,' as

Burnet says, 'as the difference I feel from the scent of a rose, and of assa-foetida.' The felt difference is one of simple characters and not one among complex characters that is to be discovered by analysis. We *know* what love is and it is *not*, or at least, *not simply* the same as 'productive of pleasure.' Locke's doctrine of analysis based upon the 'historical plain method' seems to have this consequence, and if it does then it is just wrong, contrary to the *phenomenological facts*. If the 'historical plain method' does lead to the conclusion that our moral sentiments are analysable, then it equally well requires that they *not* be analysable: we *do* have moral sentiments and these *cannot* be analysed in Locke's fashion into various ways in which objects become associated with pleasure and pain. We are immediately aware of these feelings, these moral sentiments, in consciousness, and immediately aware, too, of their simplicity and distinctness from mere feelings of pleasure. It is this *fact*, this *phenomenological fact*, that Locke appears to be denying and that Burnet is insisting upon.

This line of thought was developed by Locke's student Shaftes-bury, but in a way that attempted to remove it from the rationalist tradition and place it within the context of a philosophy of experience more attuned to the spirit of the age. This does not mean that it was fully compatible with the empiricist methodology of Newton and Locke, but only that it emphasized the link to experience rather than reason and that this cohered with the spirit of an age that had been alerted to the role of experience in cognition by Newton and Locke but had not yet appreciated the full implications that the empiricist methodology would have for natural religion.

Shaftesbury assumes, as we have seen, that the world is informed by a pattern of relations that give it definite form and structure. Right and wrong are established by this relational structure of the universe. Shaftesbury is thus arguing that there exists a moral order constituted by the relations of things in the world and the relations of man to his fellows and to the rest of the world. These provide an objective standard of right and wrong that lies beyond the appeal that Locke made either to actions being productive of pain or pleasure or to actions being ordained by God through revelation to be right or wrong. Shaftesbury is here siding with thinkers like Clarke and More against the claims of Locke. He was quite clear that he was disagreeing with his teacher. As he put it in one of his letters (1716):

Thus virtue, according to Mr Locke, has no other measure, law or rule, than *fashion* and *custom*: morality, justice, equity, depend only on *law* and *will*: and God indeed is a perfect *free agent* in this sense; that is *free to any thing, that is however ill*; for if he wills it, it will be made good; virtue may be vice, and vice virtue in its turn, if he pleases. And thus neither *right* nor *wrong*, *virtue* nor *vice* are anything in themselves; nor is there any trace or idea of them *naturally imprinted* on human minds. (3 June 1709)

He is making the same point, though carefully avoiding direct reference to Locke, when he writes in the *Characteristics* that 'if the mere will, decree, or law of God be said absolutely to constitute right and wrong, then are these latter words of no significancy at all' (1711, I, p. 264). Shaftesbury freely acknowledges the role that Locke has played in establishing a correct method for philosophy. In another of his *Letters by a Noble Lord to a Young Man at University* (1716), he writes that 'no one has done more towards the recalling of philosophy from barbarity, into use and practice of the world, and into the company of the better and politer sort; who might well be ashamed of it in its other dress. No one has opened a better or clearer way to reasoning' (24 February 1706). The trouble is that, as Burnet held, Locke has failed to recognize that the sense of obligation is unique and cannot be inferred from, or explained away in terms of, something else. 'Nor does the fear of hell or a thousand terrors of the Deity imply conscience, unless where there is an apprehension of what is wrong, odious, morally deformed, and ill-deserving. And where this is the case, there conscience must have effect, and punishment of necessity be apprehended, even though it not be expressly threatened' (ibid.).

And thus religious conscience supposes moral or natural conscience. And though the former be understood to carry with it the fear of divine punishment, it has its force however from the apprehended moral deformity and odiousness of any act with respect purely to the Divine Presence, and the natural veneration due to such a supposed being. For in such a presence the shame of villainy or vice must have its force, independently on that further apprehension of the magisterial capacity of such a being, and his dispensation of particular rewards or punishments in a future state (1711, I, pp. 305–6).

However, although Shaftesbury agrees with Clarke that morality is irreducible and that it is a matter of objective relations among things, he disagrees with Clarke on how we come to know the truths of morality. Clarke insisted that access to the objective relational standards of virtue and vice was by demonstrative reason, parallel to the way in which demonstrative reason makes known to us the truths of geometry. For Shaftesbury it is not reason that yields knowledge of these truths but *our experience of the world*, an experience that is of a piece with our sense experience of colours and shapes. But, if it is a matter of experience, it is also a unique kind of experience, as Burnet insisted. We in fact have, as we have seen Shaftesbury argue, a 'moral sense,' which is a faculty that apprehends the rightness or wrongness of actions immediately, without recourse to reasoning, neither the demonstrative reasoning of geometry nor the causal reasoning that is needed to determine which actions are and which are not productive of pleasure or pain.

Locke's position was not explicitly associationist. But the point of view was shortly to be restated by John Gay in straightforward associationist terms in his 'Dissertation' (1731). Gay adopts from Clarke and the other Newtonians the jargon of 'fitness' and 'unfitness' but construes this in utilitarian terms: an action is fit just in case that it contributes to the 'good of Mankind,' that is, the 'Happiness of Mankind' (p. xix). Wherever the end at which an action aims is 'the Happiness or another' then 'that Action is meritorious' (p. xxvi). But, in spite of this, Gay also holds that 'obligation is the necessity of doing or omitting any Action in order to be happy,' that is, as he goes on to put it, 'when there is such a relation between an Agent and any Action that the Agent cannot be happy without doing or omitting that Action, then the Agent is said to be *obliged* to do or omit that action' (p. xviii). In other words, psychological egoism is true; 'private Happiness' is our 'ultimate End' (p. xxv). This is reconciled with the notion that there are meritorious actions by distinguishing *particular* and *ultimate* ends (pp. xxv–xxvi). Although all actions are undertaken in order to bring about one's private happiness as the ultimate end, some also have that as their particular or proximate end, while others have private happiness as both the ultimate and particular ends; it is the former that are meritorious, the latter not. Things become the proximate ends of actions through a process of association; this in fact is the Lockean explanation that Gay offers of our moral sentiments, that is, Shaftesbury's notion of a moral sense. 'We first perceive or image some real Good, *i.e.* fitness to promote our Happiness in those things which we love and approve of. Hence ... we annex Pleasure to those things. Hence those things and Pleasures are so ty'd together and associated in our Minds, that one cannot present itself but the other will also occur. And the *Association* remains even after that which at first gave them the Connection is quite forgot, or perhaps does not exist, but the contrary' (p. xxxi). In this way, for example – Gay uses the example that Mill was later to use in his 'Utilitarianism' – money comes to be for the miser the end of various actions. Misers 'by dropping the intermediate Means between Money and Happiness, ... join Money and Happiness immediately together, and content themselves with the phantastical Pleasure of having it, and make that which was at first pursued only as a *Means*, be to them a real *End*, and what their real Happiness or Misery consists in' (ibid.). We can similarly explain in associationist terms our moral sentiments and public affections, though of course 'we do not always ... *make* this Association ourselves, but *learn* it from *others*' (p. xxxiii). There is, therefore, no need to assume that the 'Moral Sense, or ... public Affections are innate, or *implanted* in us: they are acquired either from our own *Observation* or the *Imitation* of others' (ibid.).

This pattern was to be repeated by James Mill in his *Analysis of the Phenomena of the Human Mind* (1825). The motives that are referred to as our 'moral sense' (II, Ch. xxiii) arise through a process of association: 'The man who does acts of Justice and Beneficence, anticipates the favourable disposition of mankind, as their natural effect.' These motives, therefore, 'are generated by the association of our own acts of Justice and Beneficence as cause with other men's acts of Justice and Beneficence as effects' (II, pp. 300–1).

But none of this is an advance upon Locke. The *desire for A as an end* is a complex mental phenomenon. This can be analysed. Specifically, it can be analysed into the association of the *idea of A* with the *feeling of pleasure*. This association has come to be because *A*s have in the past in our experience been productive of feelings of pleasure. Given the definitional model of analysis of Locke, the complex which is the desire is logically equivalent to the association of *A*s with feelings of pleasure. But the latter association is a causal inference. Moreover, this association of cause and effect is at the same time an association of means and end. Thus, saying that one has a *desire for A as an end* is logically equivalent to saying that one has a *desire for A as a means to feelings of pleasure*. In other words, upon the associationist account of motivation, all apparently non-egoistic motives turn out, given the Lockean model of analysis, to be after all egoistic. *Given the Lockean model of psychological analysis*, associationist psychology entails that psychological egoism is true. And because it entails this, it is of course seen by its critics as further entailing that no action is ever moral: all apparently virtuous actions are merely *apparently* virtuous, and are in fact done for selfish reasons. From the point of view of its critics, the associationist-utilitarian position destroys all morality, declaring that everyone is and ought to be amoral or even immoral.

There is, we see, considerable strength in the position that the Benthamites were committed to the immoral Hobbist position of psychological egoism. This was the essence of the criticism by Macaulay (1829) of Bentham's logic, and the essence of the charge of Sedgwick (1834) and Whewell (1845) that the associationist-utilitarian position is immoral. It was this charge of Hobbism to which John Stuart Mill wished to reply when he came to defend the utilitarian position. Thus, in his critique of the discussion of utilitarianism in Sedgwick (1834), the latter is accused of 'lumping up' the theory of utility with 'the theory, *if there be such a theory,* of the universal selfishness of mankind' (1835, p. 71; emphasis added). The reply to Hobbes that was made by both objectivists such as Butler and relativists such as Hume was to insist that people are, *as a matter of psychological fact,* moved by motives other than selfish ones. In particular, there are our moral sentiments, the dictates of conscience, which not only, at times at least, move us, but also, pretty often, function to control our other motives, for example, self-love or particular impulses. It is just this reply that John Stuart Mill also wishes to make. But he also wishes to defend the associationist account of the origins of our moral sentiments, that is, more or less the account that had been offered by Locke, by Gay, and by his father. But this associationist account of our moral sentiments seems to entail that in fact these other motives beyond the selfish do not exist. The argument of Burnet and Shaftesbury was to insist upon the phenomenological point that our moral sentiments are in fact different in kind from judgments of, say, prudence or self-love. Shaftesbury, to be followed on this point by Kames and Reid, inferred from the uniqueness of our moral sentiments that they could not have been acquired by a process of association and must therefore be innate. The younger Mill wishes to accept the phenomenological point of Burnet and Shaftesbury while also accepting the point of Gay and his father that our moral sentiments are learned, acquired through a process of association. The basis for this reconciliation is his doctrine of 'mental chemistry,' that is, the view that 'when a complex feeling is generated out of elements very numerous and various ... the resulting feeling always seems not only very unlike any one of the elements composing it, but very unlike the sum of those elements' (1869, p. 321). Conversely, he suggests, 'The reluctance of many persons to receive as correct [his father's] analysis of the sentiments of moral approbation and disapprobation, though a reluctance founded more on feeling than on reasoning, is accustomed to justify itself intellectually, by alleging the total unlikeness of those states of mind to the elementary one, from which, according to the theory, they are compounded' (ibid.).

Mill, like Bentham, agrees, of course, with the relativists. Indeed, like Bentham, he holds that 'pleasure, and freedom from pain, are the only things desirable as ends,' as he puts is in his 'Utilitarianism' (1861, p. 210), and this in turn means, he argues, that 'we have ... all the proof ... which it is possible to require, that happiness is a good' (1861, p. 234), where we are also told that 'By happiness is intended pleasure, and the absence of pain; by unhappiness, pain, and the privation of pleasure' (p. 210).[1] The 'proof' that Mill offers is not an ordinary proof – he signals its peculiarity in the title of the chapter in which it is presented: 'Of what sort of proof the principle of utility is susceptible.' Its essential thrust is this: 'good,' like 'ought,' 'desirable' (in its normative sense of 'worthy of desire'), and so on, is a term that is used to guide behaviour (cf. 1872a, VI, xii, 6–7), expressing not only the speaker's approbation of certain actions or motives but also, as in effect being in the imperative mood, enjoining others to adopt such behaviour. Since the linguistic function or point of using the term 'good' is to express one's having certain ends and to recommend the same as ends to others, and since, *as a matter of fact*, pleasure, and the absence of pain, are our only ends, it follows that it would be *pointless* to have 'good' apply to some end other than pleasure or the absence of pain. Pleasure, and the absence of pain, are therefore not simply desired but desirable, that is, worthy of desire. It is not our aim here to examine the soundness of this 'proof';[2] the point of mentioning it is, rather, the simple one of indicating that Mill does not conceive of his 'proof' as somehow establishing that pleasure and pain somehow have *objective value*: whatever the soundness of the 'proof,' Mill remains in ethics a relativist rather than an objectivist.

But, while Mill agrees with Bentham that pleasure, and the absence of pain, are the only ends, he at the same time wants to agree with Butler and Hume that our moral sentiments are not reducible to self-love, and that they in fact differ both in their *object* and *specifically*. In particular, he wants to insist, first, that we aim at virtuous behaviour for its own sake; the utilitarian doctrine maintains 'not only that virtue is to be desired, but that it is to be desired disinterestedly, for itself' (1861, p. 235). '[The utilitarians] not only place virtue at the very head of the things which are good as a means to the ultimate end, but they also recognize as a psychological fact the possibility of its being, to the individual, a good in itself ... and hold, that the mind is not in a right state ... not in the state most conducive to the general happiness, unless it does love virtue in this manner' (ibid.). Our moral sentiments thus differ from self-love in their *objects*. Mill wants to insist, second, that our moral sentiments differ specifically from such motives as self-love, and that motives which are specifically different in this way function to control other motives like those of self-love. It is, he insists, 'quite compatible with the principle of utility' to recognize that, as a matter of fact, 'some *kinds* of pleasure are more desirable and more valuable than others,' and it would be absurd, since quality enters into our estimation of all other things, that the 'estimation of pleasures should be supposed to depend on quantity alone' (p. 211). Our conscience is one of the 'higher faculties' the pleasures of which are qualitatively different from, and thereby preferable to, the pleasures of the lower faculties; 'no person of feeling and conscience would be selfish and base' (ibid.). Conscience controls the lower pleasures because men are maximizers of pleasures, and the pleasures of conscience are intrinsically, by virtue of their quality, preferable to quantities, most at least, of lower pleasures. Our moral sentiments are thus *specifically different* from and, by virtue of that difference, greater in their motivating power than self-love and therefore able to control the latter. Now, to say this about our moral sentiments is to characterize them as a sort of mental act that, in consequence of an idea ingredient in them, intend virtue as their object, and it is to characterize them in terms of a species ingredient in them that distinguishes them from other motives, and, indeed, from other sorts of mental act, for example, judgments. These mental acts are phenomenologically *simply unitary wholes*. Thus, they are not, say, inferences to the effect that the actions they intend are conducive to pleasure. As Mill puts it, to say that virtue is intended by such an act is to say that it is sought as an end and sought as 'part of pleasure' (p. 236), that is, as one of its species. Thus, G.E. Moore (1903, sec. 43) suggests that for Mill value judgments are judgments about means to pleasure and not about ends, a fact that Mill deceptively avoids admitting by confusedly holding that 'what is only a means to an end, is part of that end.' But this charge is quite mistaken: Mill clearly takes the value judgments to be about ends and not inferences concerning means to ends. And the object of the judgment is an end precisely because it is part of pleasure: what Mill holds is that there is an identity between 'to be desired as an end' and 'to be a part of pleasure.' This of course raises the further issue of how Mill proposes to establish this latter identity. We shall look at this in more detail in the next section, but the gist of Mill's answer is by now no doubt evident: it is established by psychological analysis, or, as Mill himself put it, by 'practised self-consciousness and self-observation, assisted by observation of others' (1861, p. 237).

It had, of course, been the claim of Kames and Reid that the existence of mental acts as phenomenologically simple unitary wholes implied (a) that they were innate, and (b) that, being simple, they must have a simple object, that is, simple non-natural objective property, to constitute the objective ground of virtue. In fact, as we have seen, Kames and Reid made this sort of claim not only with respect to value judgments but also with respect to perceptual judgments. Mill rejected these inferences in the case of perceptual judgments, as we saw in chapter 5. A perceptual judgment that is phenomenologically simple need not have a simple object; such simplicity is compatible with the act intending a perceptual object understood in the way defended by Berkeley and Hume as a pattern of sensible qualities. Moreover, that a mental act is phenomenologically simple does not imply that it is innate; and in fact, Mill argued, we have good reason to hold that our capacities to perceptually discriminate distance are learned.

Mill insists upon the same point in the case of our moral sentiments. These value judgments are phenomenologically simple unitary mental acts. This phenomenological simplicity implies neither that there is an objective ground for the value they ascribe to virtue nor that the judgments themselves are innate. As for whether there is an objective ground, Mill denies this when he affirms that such moral sentiments occur and proposes to defend the utilitarian moral thesis rationally but otherwise than 'solely in the way of intuition' (1861, p. 208). As for innateness, he allows that our moral sentiments have a variety of objects, of which the general welfare may be, but need not be, one. In particular, justice is often such an object. Far from being innate, as opponents such as Sedgwick and Whewell hold, or earlier critics such as Kames and Reid and Price held, and far from deriving from a moral sense, as peculiar and non-inferential as our senses of colour or taste, as Shaftesbury held, we in fact find our sense of justice taking quite different objects in different contexts: Mill lists six notions of what is just and unjust (1861, Ch. v), and this variety renders it implausible indeed that there is a special basis in the structure of the human system the function of which is to enable principles of justice to provide a firm foundation for morality. The alternative is, of course, that our moral sentiments are *acquired through learning*.

To be sure, such learning builds, as Hume earlier argued, upon the natural social feelings of mankind: the 'moral faculty, if not a part of our nature, is a natural outgrowth from it' (1861, p. 231). As for what we have called the principles of justice (respect for property) and contract (keeping promises), conformity to these becomes obligatory upon the utilitarian position for reasons similar to those given by

Hume, our intense non-moral interest in mankind conforming to them. Mill includes among those rules for which it is desirable that men be compelled to conform to them the rules 'which protect every individual being harmed by others, either directly or by being hindered in his freedom of pursuing his own good,' those which prevent anyone from 'wrongfully withholding from' another 'something which is his due,' and those which prevent someone from depriving another 'of some good which he had reasonable ground ... for counting upon' (p. 256). About these rules, he says, echoing Hume and Hobbes, 'it is their observance which alone preserves peace among human beings' (p. 255; cf. 1852, p. 192). Conformity to such rules is a necessary condition for maintaining those relationships among men that alone permit men to achieve almost anything desirable; these rules 'concern the essentials of human well-being more nearly ... than any other rules for the guidance of life,' for, 'if obedience to them were not the rule, and disobedience the exception, every one would see in every one else a probable enemy, against whom he must be perpetually guarding himself' (1861, p. 255). By virtue of the interest we all have in everyone's conforming to such rules, a natural learning process leads us all to develop certain *feelings* towards them, the moral sentiment that when such a rule is violated it is 'wrong' in the strong sense in which we 'imply that a person ought to be punished in some way or other for doing it' (p. 246). But conformity to these rules is not only *in fact* the object of our moral sentiments, and that higher faculty called conscience, but also *ought*, given the utilitarian moral standard, to be so desired as an end. For, these 'moral requirements, ... regarded collectively, stand higher in the scale of social utility, and are therefore of more paramount obligation, than any others' (p. 259).

Mill is therefore holding that our moral sentiments are phenomenologically simple unified wholes that (a) have specific objects other than self-love, that (b) are specifically different from other motives, and that, in virtue of that difference, (c) function to move men towards their objects rather than those of, say, self-love. Just *which object* our moral sentiments intend is determined by a process of learning, but a process that, in contrast, builds upon the natural social feelings of mankind. *That this is possible* is something that Mill has established against such thinkers as Kames and Reid when he rethought the notion of introspective analysis, and distinguished what was given phenomenologically from the analysis that was *recovered* by association and that, given the working hypotheses of the psychological theory, revealed the genetic antecedents. But *posse* does not imply *esse*, a point that Mill himself makes against some of the analyses proposed by his father (1872a, IV, iv, p. 3). However, to actually re-create in detail the causal processes by which our moral sentiments arise would require major detailed work in psychology. In fact, however, all that Mill needs in the context of the argument with the intuitionists and the innatists is to show that the following claim is true, *that there are processes of learning involving the association of pleasures and pains of which our moral sentiments, with their objects, and as qualitatively distinct, are the products*. And to establish this Mill needs only to establish the relatively modest claims that (1) the moral sentiments are learned – for this the observation of the fact that they are absent from children suffices – and that (2) this learning process involves the association of pleasures and pains – but for this too a modest amount of observation of others and of self-observation suffices. This relatively modest claim is in fact *evident on commonly available data*, if only one will recognize, in face of the prejudices of intuitionism and innatism, those data and their evidential worth. What was needed was not a detailed explanation, but simply an *explanation sketch* that could render the evidence plausible by showing *how possibly*, given the data, our moral sentiments are learned.[3] For such an 'how possibly' explanation it suffices to have the sort of hypothetical, not fully confirmed explanation sketches of such learning that his father provided.

In short, the answer to the question, how to reconcile the existence of non-hedonistic motives with the Benthamite claim that the primary motives are hedonistic, quickly becomes clear when one turns to James Mill's *Analysis*. The elder Mill emphasized that there is indeed a motive 'love of mankind' (James Mill, 1825 II: 278). This, which is 'the most ennobling' of all motives, is not innate, or even strong in most men. But in some it does exist, and in those cases it is a product of association, and, more specifically, those associations called 'education': 'it is only by a Philosophical Education, that men are early trained to the use of General Terms [such as 'Mankind'] and comprehensive Propositions; and have the means of forming those associations, on which the most ennobling of all the states of Human Consciousness depends' (ibid.). Central to the associations is the feeling of pleasure. Motives, such as the love of mankind, 'are formed by the association of our actions, not with pleasures immediately, but with the causes of them' (II: 265). In the chapter where these remarks occur, James Mill attempts to trace in detail how such motives as the love of mankind arise (II: ch. XXII, sec. 2). John Stuart Mill finds largely acceptable this account that describes how 'causes of pleasures and pains become so closely associated in thought with the pains and pleasures of which they are the causes, as not only to become themselves pleasurable or painful, but to become also, by their association with acts of our own by which they may be brought about, motives of the greatest strength' (1869 II: 278–9). As both father and son indicate, these considerations are not only of interest to psychology, but since they describe tools that education may employ, they are important also for ethics and politics (II: 272, 274f, 279n). In any case, it is clear even from this sketch of the Mills' theory of motivation how the reconciliation between disinterested moral acts and hedonism will occur.

James Mill of course goes into greater detail than this in his account of motives. Such details are the topics of the following sections. These sections proceed, however, not so much as exposition but as polemic, to show how John Stuart Mill's presentation of his ethics in 'Utilitarianism' can be defended against its many critics. The next section looks at the issue of our moral sentiments having objects other than self-love. The following section looks at the way Mill's view of people as maximizers of pleasure contrasts with that of economists. The final section examines Mill's views on the moral sentiments as qualitatively preferable pleasures; and it argues not only that the introduction of qualitative differences among pleasures is compatible with the utilitarian ethic, but more strongly that by introducing these differences of quality and rejecting the Benthamite notion of a quantitative scale of pleasures Mill places utilitarianism upon a much more secure foundation than had Bentham.

2   The Objects of the Moral Sentiments

We can begin to consider the variety of issues concerning John Stuart Mill's reconciliation of disinterested moral acts with hedonism through a consideration of two major criticisms of Mill's position. The first of these is Mill's equation of the 'desired' with the 'pleasant.' Mill declares (1861, pp. 237–8) that 'desiring a thing and finding it pleasant, aversion to it and thinking of it as painful, are phenomena entirely inseparable, or rather two parts of the same phenomenon.' Indeed, he continues, 'in strictness of language, [they are] two different modes of naming the same psychological fact,' so that 'to think of an object as desirable (unless for the sake of its consequences), and to think of it as pleasant, are one and the same thing.' However, at the same time he tells us (p. 237) that whether or not this is so is 'a question of fact and experience, dependent, like all similar questions, upon evidence,' where the appropriate evidence is provided by 'practised self-consciousness and self-observation, assisted by observation of others.' Mill, of course, holds that these sources of evidence do justify his claim – which, expressed in other terms, is the claim that 'mankind do desire nothing in itself but that which is a pleasure to them, or of which the absence is a pain' (ibid.), that is, the premiss of his famous 'proof' of the principle of utility that happiness and only happiness is desired as an end: 'there is in reality nothing desired except happiness' (ibid.). C.D. Broad, however, suggests that this argument for Mill's claim is 'obviously fallacious': 'If Mill's statement were true [that 'to desire' something and 'to find' that thing 'pleasant' are two ways of stating the same fact], there would be no more need of introspection to decide that than to decide that "to be rich" and "to be wealthy" are two different expressions for the same fact' (1930, p. 186). Mill was attempting to establish that, in some reasonable sense, the hedonistic psychology of the utilitarians was true. Broad is suggesting that Mill is arguing that his claim is 'true by definition.'[4] But, Broad replies, it is clearly *not* true by definition: 'to desire' something and 'to find' that thing 'pleasant' are *not* synonymous. And moreover, he indicates, Mill himself recognized this when he proposed to settle the issue by introspection. So Mill failed to establish psychological hedonism.

In any case, Broad argues, psychological hedonism is false, for we *do* desire things other than happiness (1930, pp. 64, 102). The same point has been made more recently by Williams: 'let us grant to utilitarianism that all worthwhile human projects must conduce, one way or another, to happiness. The point is that even if that is true, it does not follow, nor could it possibly be true, that those projects are themselves projects of pursuing happiness. One has to believe in, or at least want, or quite minimally, be content with, other things, for there to be anywhere that happiness can come from' (1973, p. 113). G.E. Moore had earlier made the same point (1903, p. 70). In fact, even the earliest critics of Mill had made this point. Thus, John Grote argues that action is not merely a means to enjoyment, as labour is to wealth; men have a love of action as well as a love of pleasure (1876, p. 293). In fact, he suggests, this is true even of the area of material concerns that are the domain of the science of economics: even economic progress is due as much to love of action as to love of wealth. 'They [states of higher civilization] exist, because along with love of enjoyment, the sole utilitarian motive, there exists in man an impulse to the exercise of his faculties' (p. 294). This point is equally true, Grote holds, for virtuous action: 'The interest of human action does not arise from its being, as the utilitarian would persuade us, simply action for happiness, but in its being ... a mutual action of moral beings for each other's happiness, and that under strong temptation for them to act each one for his own' (p. 75). This is the second criticism of Mill's position that we must consider, that he is a psychological hedonist who holds that only pleasure is desired or can be desired as an end, and that this claim is false because *in fact* men *do* desire other things as ends.

Now, far from disagreeing with this last, Mill accepts it! Mill does argue, on the one hand, that pleasure is the sole end that men have (1861, p. 210). But, on the other hand, men can also desire virtue as an end (p. 235). To be sure, it is not originally an end, but it can become so (ibid.). That is, the moral faculty is one that men can acquire (p. 230). Other things, too, can come to be sought as ends – money, power, fame (p. 237), music, and health (p. 235). However, these claims are often construed as marking a contradiction in Mill's thought. This is suggested, for example, by F.E.L. Priestley (1969, p. xiv), but it has been most forcefully put, perhaps, by G.E. Moore: 'these admissions are, of course, in naked and glaring contradiction with his argument that pleasure is the only thing desirable, because it is the only thing desired' (1903, p. 71).

The reply to Broad makes reference to the notion of *introspective analysis*, to which Mill himself refers when he speaks of 'practised self-conscious and self-observation' as the source of evidence for his claim that 'to desire' something and 'to find' that thing 'pleasant' name the same fact. The claim the younger Mill was making here had already been made by his father in his *Analysis*: 'The terms ... "idea of pleasure", and "desire", are but two names; the thing named, the state of consciousness, is one and the same' (J.S. Mill 1869, II: 192). This claim is established by an introspective analysis of what is involved in a desire (II: 191). The younger Mill does not wholly agree with his father's analysis – the analysis of 'desire' requires a further element that his father misses (of which, more in a moment) – but the main thrust is accepted (II: 194n). In any such analysis, as we know, one has, first, the phenomenological description D_P of the state to be analysed. In this case the description D_P is *desire*. And one has, second, the analytical description D_A. The analytical description of any desire D_A always includes the *idea of pleasure*. Moreover, nothing else when analysed contains the idea of pleasure. ('But what is a desire, other than the idea of something as good to have; good to have, being really nothing but desirable to have?' [1825 II: 191], the elder Mill puts it in the all-too-abrupt way so characteristic of his philosophical psychology –

but which at the same time is not necessarily wrong, or necessarily in conflict with the more empirical psychology that his son created.) Thus, *as required by the notion of introspective analysis, that the phenomenological description can be uniquely inferred from the analytical description, the 'idea of pleasure' that occurs in the analytical description uniquely correlates with the 'desire' that occurs in the phenomenological description.* Moreover, the working hypothesis of the psychology is that the elements described in the analytical vocabulary are the *genetic antecedents* of the state described in the phenomenological vocabulary. Thus, if the desire is the *desire for so-and-so* then this analysis into the *idea of pleasure* and the *idea of so-and-so*, and the desire for so-and-so is the product of an associative process that unites in consciousness the idea of pleasure and the idea of so-and-so (1869a, II: 190–1, 197–8).

Now, one and the same state of consciousness can be *named*, in the sense of *denoted*, by two terms that have, however, *different connotations*. Thus, a toothache may be denoted by 'the toothache in my left incisor' and also by 'the toothache treated by my dentist.' Clearly, it is a *matter of fact* and *not* one of mere definition, that these two terms denote or name the same state; for, clearly, that they name the same psychological state depends upon the *fact* that the properties connoted by the one term are instantiated in the very same state that instantiates the properties connoted by the other term. The point is that these two terms name the same state but that they do so is a matter of fact that can be established only by empirical evidence, not linguistic analysis. Similarly for those psychological states called 'desires.' The use of the term 'desire' is one way to denote such states; but such states may also be picked out uniquely by the term 'idea of pleasure.' That these two terms denote or name the same states is due to the correlation between *desire* and *idea of pleasure*. This correlation is one of fact, and it can be established to hold only by empirical evidence provided by systematic introspective analysis. Thus, contrary to what Broad suggested, Mill can quite consistently hold that 'desire' and 'idea of pleasure' name the same psychological states without this being a mere definitional tautology, to be established by linguistic analysis rather than empirical evidence.

This response to Broad leads into the reply to the second criticism of Mill, that he cannot reconcile the hedonism of the utilitarians with the fact that there are desires for objects other than pleasure. Mill himself proposed to resolve this contradiction by arguing that a desire for an object other than pleasure as an end is an *acquired* desire, one that is *the result of learning. The method of introspective analysis, and the working hypothesis of the psychology that the elements described in the analysis are the genetic antecedents of what is analysed, combine to yield a description of the associations that generate the acquired desires which intend objects other than pleasure, and which therefore move us towards those objects as ends.* Specifically, what we just saw was that, for both James and John Stuart Mill, a desire for so-and-so as an end is always the product of an associative process that unites the idea of so-and-so with the idea of pleasure. Moreover, the term 'desire so-and-so' will name the same state of consciousness as does 'the idea of so-and-so as pleasant.' *It is thus perfectly clear that Mill, by virtue of his learning theory, can quite consistently hold, on the one hand, the hedonist principle that whatever moves one is the thought of something pleasant, and also hold, on the other hand, that men are moved by ends other than pleasure.*

This suffices to reply to Moore's general statement of the second criticism of Mill that we are now considering. However, in order to reply to critics, such as Williams and Grote, who give a more detailed focus to their criticisms, it is necessary to fill in a few more features of the theory of motivation laid out by James and John Stuart Mill in the *Analysis.* In particular, we should lay out with greater accuracy the analysis the younger Mill actually proposes for *desire.* The analysis qualifies his father's bald identification of desire with the idea of pleasure – and also, therefore, the same bald identification of his own essay 'Utilitarianism.' However, as we shall see, the qualifications do not affect the thrust of the latter essay, and therefore, given the polemical purposes of that essay, were reasonably omitted.

The *Analysis* points out that there are regular connections between mental states and bodily states. Thus, anxiety disorders the digestion, fear causes tension in the intestines, and so on. Conversely, bodily states affect the mental. For example, eating food is accompanied by pleasurable sensations in the mouth (J.S. Mill 1869, 1: 101). Since causation *is* (well-supported) regular connection, it follows both that mind affects body and that body affects mind.

However, not only is there interaction but there are *specifically active mental elements.* Associationism is often charged with making the mind purely passive. The charge has been made against Hume, for example, by Bennett (1971, pp. 300–2). Coleridge made the charge against Hartley (1817, 1: 73, 76), and it has been repeated since (e.g., Willey 1940, pp. 152–4). It is a charge that is, however, wildly at variance with the truth,[5] as John Stuart Mill carefully pointed out:

no Hartleian could overlook the necessity, incumbent on any

theory of the mind, of accounting for our voluntary powers. Activity cannot possibly be generated from passive elements; a primitive active element must be found somewhere: and Hartley found it in the stimulative power of sensation over the muscles. All our muscular motions, according to him, were originally automatic, and excited by the stimulus of sensations; as, no doubt, many of them were and are. After a muscular contraction has been sufficiently often excited by a sensation, then, in Hartley's opinion, the idea or remembrance of the sensation acquires a similar power of exciting that same muscular contraction. Here is the first germ of volition: a muscular action excited by an idea. After this, every combination of associated ideas into which that idea or remembrance enters, and which, therefore, cannot be recalled without recalling it, obtains the power of recalling also the muscular motion which has come under its control. (1859, p. 354)

Hartley's point is, as we would expect, taken up by James Mill in his *Analysis* where he gives a general characterization of the 'active powers' of the mind as constituted by 'sensations and ideas ... considered as not merely existing, but also as exciting to action' (1825, II: 181). The sensations and ideas that become associated with actions have certain characteristics in common, to wit, they are either pleasures or pains (II: p. 184). Pleasurable and painful sensations are common to all the senses; there are pleasures and pains of the hearing, touch, taste, smell, and sight, and also of various internal senses (II: 185).

Desires are mental acts. Like cognitive acts, such as believings, they have ideas ingredient in them so that, as Brentano spoke, they *intend* or mean certain objects. Just as believings and rememberings differ intrinsically by virtue of those specific properties that make them believings and rememberings, that is, just as these are different *species* of mental act, so are desires another *species* of mental act. But besides thus differing intrinsically from other mental acts, desires also differ with respect to extrinsic causal properties: desires, in contrast to cognitive acts, have in common a causal tendency or function to move us to action. One must distinguish a desire from its object, from the exciting causes of that desire, and from collateral effects of satisfying it. Consider *hunger* (an example from Butler) and *revenge* (an example from Hume). When we are hungry, we experience certain sensations of our internal organs that are caused by lack of food. These are generally painful. They are the exciting cause of the desire we call hunger. This desire is an impulse to action. The action in this case is that of eating food. This action is also the object of the desire, the obtaining of which will satisfy the desire. As this object is attained, that is, as we eat, the impulse of hunger is gradually satisfied, and that is pleasant. If we are prevented from eating when we are hungry, and the desire remains unsatisfied, then this frustration of the impulse is unpleasant. The process of satisfying one's hunger has the collateral effect of producing sensations that may be pleasant or unpleasant according to the nature of the food and the tastes of the eater. The exciting cause of the desire we call hunger is: lack of food accompanied by unpleasant organic sensations; the object the obtaining of which will satisfy the desire is: eating food; the collateral effects are: pleasant, unpleasant, or indifferent sensations of tastes; the action it tends to bring about in us is: eating, which is the same as its object; and it is accompanied by the pleasure of satisfaction vs. the pain of frustration according to whether we achieve its object or not. Turn now to *revenge*. The exciting cause is: some real or imagined harm done to us; the object the obtaining of which will satisfy the desire is: our enemy's misery; the action it tends to bring about in us is: activity that will have as its causal consequence the misery of our enemy; it is accompanied by the pleasure of satisfaction or the pain of frustration according to whether we achieve its object or not; whether it has characteristic organic sensations as significant exciting causes and whether its satis- faction has characteristic pleasant or painful sensations as collateral effects are both doubtful.

Both the desire we call hunger and the desire we call revenge show egoistic hedonism – the claim that the only object of any desire is its owner's pleasure – to be false. One may be strongly motivated by self-love, the desire to maximize one's own pleasure narrowly under- stood. In that case one will attempt to attain the pleasure accompanying the satisfying of one's hunger. But one cannot attain the pleasure of satisfaction of the desire to eat food *unless that desire, with that object, exists*. Similarly, revenge has as its object the misery of one's enemy; and revenge would give one no pleasure when it is achieved if one did not want already to injure one's enemy, that is *unless that desire, with that object, exists*. What these examples make clear is that there are desires with objects other than one's own pleasure; and, indeed, they make clear that the desire to maximize one's own pleasure actually *presupposes* desires aiming at objects other than pleasure, for otherwise one could not have the pleasure of their satisfaction. However, we must also recognize that some desires have pleasure as their object. Thus, the gourmet does not eat so much from hunger as from the desire for the pleasant sensations that accompany eating food. And, of course, self-love has as its object the maximization of one's own pleasure.

The phenomenological facts we have just described, and to which we have appealed (with Butler and Hume) to show the falsity of egoistic hedonism, are clearly *facts*. Nor does John Stuart Mill deny them. In fact, he accepts them, as, for example, when he accepts that power, or money, or virtue can all be objects of desire. If the elder Mill at times wrote as if he denied those facts, and perhaps accepted egoistic hedonism, then that was his philosophical psychology at those times carrying speculation beyond empirical control to the point where it could deny obvious phenomenological facts.

There are two cases of pleasure and pain, then, that John Stuart Mill is concerned with. There is, on the one hand, the pleasure that accompanies the satisfaction of desires, including those desires that have objects other than pleasure. This is the sort of pleasure of which Mill is speaking when he says that to 'desire virtue' is to 'think of it in a pleasurable light, or of its absence in a painful one' (1861, p. 239). On the other hand, there are the pleasurable and painful sensations that begin the treatment of the 'active powers of the human mind' in James Mill's *Analysis*. Thus, when one writer contends that Mill uses 'pleasure' as 'a technical term for whatever anyone desires for its own sake' (Anon. 1960a, p. 268), he is wrong. A pleasant sensation is none the less pleasurable for its coming to one without its being desired. Holbrook, too, is wrong when he contrasts the 'sensation theory of pleasure,' which describes pleasures (and pains) as sensations, and the 'desire theory of pleasure,' which identifies pleasure with whatever is the object of desire (1988, pp. 56, 60). These are indeed two different views, but, contrary to Holbrook, they are not mutually exclusive, and any ethical theory that is, like Mill's, even remotely hedonist must take account of both.

For Mill there are definite connections between the two sorts of pleasure and pain; they do not stand isolated from each other. These are established by the associationist psychology. Specifically, introspective analysis establishes (Mill not implausibly claims) that desires have pleasant sensations as their genetic antecedents.

What James Mill proposed was that the state of desiring a certain object could be analysed (in the technical sense of 'analysis') into, *one*, an idea of that object; *two*, an idea of this object as future; and, *three*, the idea of pleasure associated with the object (1825, II: 193). Similarly, the state of having an aversion to an object is analysed into an idea of the object, an idea of this object as future, and an idea of this object as painful. John Stuart Mill objects in his notes that this is too simple. Desire is not just expectation of pleasure as his father asserts – that, rather, is hope; what has been omitted is that desire is inseparable from *will* (1869a, II: 194n). Now, ideas as well as sensations can cause muscular activity (II: 379). Thus, if the idea of the pleasure is produced then, given the association, this in turn produces the muscular action. Desire contains the idea of a pleasure. Hence, according to John Stuart Mill, 'desire ... is more than the idea of the pleasure desired, being, in truth, the initiatory state of Will. In what we call Desire there is, I think, always included a positive stimulation to action' (II: 194n), either to action having a definite thrust at obtaining the object of desire, or, at least, to a general disquiet and indefinite urge towards it. Similarly, in aversion there is a tendency to action of a kind that repels or avoids the painful object.

Motives are a complex case of desire. 'When the idea of Pleasure is associated with an action of our own as its cause; that is, contemplated as the consequent of a certain action of ours, and incapable of otherwise existing; or when the cause of a Pleasure is contemplated as the consequent of an action of ours, and not capable of otherwise existing; a peculiar state of mind is generated which, as it is a tendency to action, is properly denominated MOTIVE' (II: 258). Consider the simpler case first, in which an activity itself directly causes pleasant sensations, as, for example, eating food has pleasant sensations of taste as collateral effects (and also the removal of the painful sensations of hunger) (ibid.). The pleasant sensations are not only the 'consequent' of the activity, but are also 'incapable of otherwise existing.' Thus, the activity is not only sufficient but also necessary for those pleasant sensations; in the context, the activity is sufficient for the pleasant sensations, but also the latter, since the activity is necessary for them, are sufficient for the activity to occur. Now, if the sensation x is regularly followed by the sensation y, then two things will occur after the association is established: the sensation of x will be followed by the sensation of y, as before; and either the sensation of x or the idea of x can trigger the association and cause the idea of y to be present (II: 70). Suppose, then, that the activity of eating occurs. This activity will trigger the idea of the pleasant sensation as future, that is, will trigger the expectation (II: 196, 198n) of the pleasant sensations that are the collateral effects of eating. But then the activity will also cause those sensations. The activity thus creates the expectation and also the states that fulfil that expectation. Now, if x is necessary and sufficient for y, then in certain special cases it may be that not only will association establish that *x* will trigger the idea of *y*, but also that *the idea of y will trigger x. This will occur where x is a muscular activity. Where there is an association of this special sort between the idea of something pleasant and an activity, then we have a motive* (II: 258). In the simple case we are considering, the activity is necessary and sufficient for the pleasant sensations; and, as a consequence of the associative mechanisms, the idea of those pleasant sensations triggers the activity. The idea of the pleasant sensations produces the activity, which in turn produces, on the one hand, the expectation of such pleasant sensations and then, on the other hand, pleasant sensations that fulfil the expectation. *The idea of the pleasant sensations that causes the activity has as its object or intends that state of affairs which is the end that the motive aims through the activity to achieve* (II: 263). It is this point that Mill relies upon when he insists, as he does, that the virtuous 'love it [virtue] disinterestedly' and for such persons it 'is desired and cherished, not as a means to happiness, but as a part of their happiness' (1861, p. 235). When an object is desired as an end, it is thought of as pleasurable, and as part of happiness; while, when it is desired as a means, then it is *not* a 'part of one's happiness' in the relevant sense.

We can now turn to more complicated cases that the *Analysis* also envisages (J.S. Mill 1869, II: chs. 21 and 22). In these cases, the activity does not itself cause the pleasant sensations but rather some other object, for example, wealth (II: 267) or family (II: 273), with which pleasant sensations are regularly connected. Because the object regularly causes pleasant sensations, the idea of the former comes to be associated with the idea of the latter. These ideas generate – though, of course, they do not literally compose – the idea of the object as pleasurable. The activity is (in the context) the necessary and sufficient cause of the pleasurable object; that is, it is necessary and sufficient for the object, which is itself the cause of the pleasant sensations. Parallel to the patterns of the simpler case, the idea of something pleasurable can, as a result of the associative mechanisms, initiate activity. When it does, then it is a motive. The activity then creates the expectation of the pleasurable object, and produces, through a chain of further causes, the object itself and thereby the connected pleasure. The idea of the pleasurable object is one in which the idea of the object and the idea of the pleasure it causes are *not* distinguishable parts – they generate but do not compose the idea of the pleasurable object. Moreover, the idea that these metaphysical parts generate is the *idea of a pleasurable object*, not the *idea of an object that is a means to pleasant sensations*. In this way, objects other than pleasure can come to be motivating, not merely as means, but as ends. It is this idea of the pleasurable object rather than the idea of the object as the means to pleasure that initiates the activity; this idea intends the object as the end which the motive aims through the activity to achieve (II: 223n).

This sketch of Mill's psychological theory of motivation shows how he proposes – to some extent speculatively but no doubt with some plausibility – to reconcile the hedonism of his utilitarian forebears with the phenomenological fact that his critics emphasize, that people seek ends other than pleasure. More specifically, it shows how he proposed to establish, via the mechanisms of association, a connection between the pleasure of pleasant sensations, on the one hand, and the pleasure of satisfied desire, on the other.

A criticism Moore once proposed is immediately seen to be obviously wrong. Moore notes that Mill holds that money can be desired for its own sake and that, when it is, it is desired as part of happiness. 'Does Mill mean to say,' Moore asks, 'that "money," these actual coins, which he admits to be desired in and for themselves, are a part either of pleasure or of the absence of pain? Will he maintain that those coins themselves are in my mind, and actually part of my pleasant feelings? If this is to be said, all words are useless: nothing can possibly be distinguished from anything else; if these two things are not distinct, what on earth is? We shall hear next that this table is really and truly the same thing as this room' (1903, p. 21). But this is to take Mill's use of 'part' in the phrase 'part of pleasure' to mean 'real' or 'physical part.' And there is no reason so to read Mill. In fact, Mill goes out of his way to carefully explain, by means of the associationist psychology, what he means when he says that money – or virtue – can be 'part of' one's happiness. To be 'part of' in this sense is for a certain sort of association to be established between, on the one hand, that which is said to be a part and, on the other hand, feelings of pleasure. Since many things can come to be thus associated with pleasure, one can group them as various species within the genus of the intrinsically pleasurable. Money is such a species, for some at least; and so, for others, is virtue. Such a species is a part of the genus happiness as the species dog is part of the genus mammal. Moore's criticism is more that of a clever undergraduate than that of a thoughtful philosopher.

Moreover, with our now clear understanding of how Mill can consistently hold that what is sought for its own sake is sought as a part of happiness, we are in a position to reply to certain specific versions of what we called above the 'second criticism' of Mill's position, that he cannot reconcile the hedonism of the utilitarians with the fact that men desire as ends things other than pleasure, and, in particular, as Mill wished to emphasize, that men *can* seek virtue as an end and not (only) as a means, that men *can* disinterestedly seek virtue.

Thus, Williams, Grote, and others argue against Mill that not all human projects, even if they result in happiness, are projects of pursuing happiness. They thereby conclude that Mill's position, that happiness is indeed not always pursued as an end, cannot be reconciled with the hedonism of the utilitarians. This conclusion, we now see, does not follow. However, Mill argues from hedonism, the fact that men pursue pleasure and only pleasure, to the conclusion that happiness is the criterion of morality.[6] So Williams suggests (1973, p. 113) that utilitarianism as a *moral* system fails: Mill admits men pursue ends other than happiness, which therefore cannot be the sole criterion of morality. But this conclusion, too, does not follow. For, if men pursue, as ends, things besides happiness, then it is also true that they pursue these other ends only as *part of* happiness, and that happiness accompanies the achievement of those ends. Similarly, Grote (1876, p. 294) argues that even economic progress is often not due to the hedonistic motives proposed by the utilitarian philosophy but by a simple native impulse to exercise one's faculties. But this is to ignore that when one pursues as an end the exercise of one's faculties, then there is a real satisfaction in doing that. In such a case the performance of those activities is part of one's happiness. The learning theory of the *Analysis* quite easily, as we saw, can account (at least speculatively), through the operation of associative mechanisms, for activities coming to be performed for their own sake as part of one's happiness. Finally, Grote also argues (p. 75) that men seek virtue not as a means to happiness but for its own sake. But Mill's theory of learning can account for virtue becoming such an end, so Grote's point does not in any way refute Mill's utilitarianism.

A stronger point should be made, however. As a matter of phenomenological fact that is prior to any genetic account, including Mill's, pleasure is not only a quality of (some) sensations, there is also the pleasure *of satisfied desire*. Thus, even when men pursue virtue as an end, if that end is achieved then they feel the pleasure of satisfied desire (cf. Mill 1861, p. 228). If Williams, Grote, and so on, mean to deny this *fact* when they insist that men pursue ends other than happiness, then they are *just wrong*. And it is this point that Mill wishes to make when he says that, when men seek, as they do, ends other than happiness, they seek those ends as '*part of* their happiness' (1861, p. 235). Therefore Dryer, too, is wrong when he holds that 'if Mill can succeed in showing that virtue, or fame, or power, or money comes to be desired only as part of happiness, he can no longer hold that it is desired for its own sake' (1969, p. xvii). Misguided, too, is Bradley's complaint concerning happiness, that for Mill instead 'of pleasure it [happiness] has come to mean something like the life we prefer ... [and this] is to leave Hedonism altogether' (1927, p. 120). It may well be that Mill has abandoned a crude sensationalist hedonism of the sort proposed perhaps by Helvétius, but this is of little import. Mill's view remains non-trivial, and certainly non-tautologous, but it is, Bradley notwithstanding, also recognizably hedonistic in its emphasis that happiness and the satisfaction of human desires are ultimately ends not capable of being overridden by, or sacrificed to, some abstract claims of, say, justice or religious dogma, as intuitionist of his day – and ours – insist.

When Mill asserts that men seek only happiness, what he is asserting is that men seek to satisfy their desires, whatever ends those desires aim at, and that when a desire is satisfied one has the pleasure of satisfied desire. And when Mill asserts this, what he is saying is just common-sense fact. It is because Mill is asserting no more than this common sense that he does not hesitate to speak of men seeking not pleasure or happiness but satisfaction (1861, p. 231). Since the term 'pleasure' is so strongly associated with the idea of crude hedonism of the egoistic sort, Mill not only follows Bentham in generally substituting the term 'happiness' when he defends the utilitarian morality, but moves still further yet to the even more neutral term 'satisfaction.'[7]

Furthermore, when Mill holds that the principle of utility enjoins one to maximize human happiness, he holds that it enjoins one to provide the 'ingredients of happiness,' which 'are very various, and each of them ... desirable in itself' (1861, p. 235), which in turn means that it enjoins one to provide maximal satisfaction to men, that is, to satisfy their desires as much as is possible. Dryer is thus correct when he asserts that Mill's principle that one maximize happiness is 'not incompatible with the view that something should be done if and only if it would bring about a greater fulfillment of human wants than would any alternative'; but he is wrong when he goes on to say that Mill's principle 'is incompatible with the view that something should be done because it would have this result' (1969, p. lxix) for that is precisely what Mill's principle *does* enjoin.

3 Men as Maximizers: Economics and Morality

According to Mill, then, people seek to maximize their satisfactions.

His position is that for each man there is a preference order among his pleasures; this preference order cannot be fully cardinalized, some pleasures remain quantitatively incommensurable; but men are none the less *maximizers*, each man seeking that pleasure which is highest on his preference scale. Having moral motives, enjoying aesthetic pleasures, being bound by custom, disdaining the pleasures of the senses are compatible with man being a maximizer, seeking what constitutes his greatest pleasure.

This position is fully compatible with there being an economic realm, where men prefer a greater gain to a lesser, a realm that is circumscribed by moral and institutional norms where gain is not an operative motive. What is required, of course, is a distinction between 'gain' understood as referring to an increase of material goods, and 'gain' understood as referring to an increase of preferred pleasures. In rejecting as immoral certain ways of making economic gains one thereby gains the satisfaction of having done one's duty.

This sort of distinction comes out neatly, if only implicitly, in the following remark by Malinowski: '[The Trobriander] is not guided primarily by the desire to satisfy his wants, but by a very complex and traditional set of forces, duties and obligations, beliefs in magic, social ambitions and vanities. He wants, if he is a *man*, to achieve social distinction as a *good gardener* and a good worker in general' (1922, p. 62; his italics). In this first sentence man is not motivated by his wants, while in the second he is. This is non-contradictory only if we read 'wants' in the first sentence as meaning something different from 'wants' in the second sentence. The first use refers to economic wants, the second to the 'higher' wants of morality, institutional norms, custom, and so on; and the claim is that the latter constrain the former. The same point has more recently been made by Firth: 'Situations continually tend to arise ... in which some sacrifice of economic benefits is judged necessary to maintain or raise one's social status, or to help give reality to social ideals which one thinks are important' (1952, p. 153). Of course, from the purely formal point of view in which economizing consists of allocating scarce resources among alternative ends so as to maximize one's goods, this distinction between economic and non-economic motives does not arise. A person might well sacrifice, say, some produce from his garden and therefore a full stomach in order to secure an added measure of social status. From the formal point of view, from the point of view of men as maximizers, the person is not choosing something non-economic over something economic. Rather, he is allocating his resources between satisfying his hunger or want for food and satisfying his want, no doubt thought of as a more noble want, for status, accepting somewhat less nourishment for the sake of having somewhat more social status (cf. Robbins 1935, pp. 1–23). None the less, there *is* a distinction to be drawn. Polanyi put it this way, in distinguishing the 'substantive' meaning and the 'formal' meaning of 'economic':

> The substantive meaning of economic derives from man's dependence for his living upon nature and his fellows. It refers to the interchange with his natural and social environment, in so far as this results in supplying him with the means of material want satisfaction.
>
> The formal meaning of economic derives from the logical character of the means-end relationship, as apparent in such words as 'economical' or 'economizing'. It refers to a definite situation of choice, namely, that between different uses of means induced by an insufficiency of those means. If we call the rules governing choice of means the logic of rational action, then we may denote this variant of logic, with an improvised term, as formal economics.
> (1957, p. 243)

Mill, of course, proposes so to define 'political economy' that that science deals only with substantive economics: 'What is now commonly understood by the term "Political Economy" ... does not treat of the whole of man's nature ... It is concerned with him solely as a being who desires to possess wealth, and who is capable of judging of the comparative efficacy of means for obtaining the end. It predicts only such of the phenomena of the social state as take place in consequence of the pursuit of wealth. It makes entire abstraction of every other human passion or motive' (1844, p. 321). Robbins (1935), in contrast, proposes to define 'economics' to coincide with formal economics. Since Mill holds that men are maximizers, and since choice under conditions of scarce resources is hardly restricted to the realm dealt with by substantive economics, Mill would no doubt agree with Robbins that formal economics is appropriate for describing and explaining human behaviour in a range of situations well beyond the economic in the narrower, substantive, sense. In fact, Mill could not but regard that as evidence for his claim that the basic laws of economics are, in the final analysis, laws of psychology, no different in kind from the laws that describe the function – and learning – of motives other than the pursuit of wealth. None the less, he would argue, within the realm covered by formal economics – and, of course, how far formal economics accurately describes human behaviour, is a *matter of fact* – there is a subrealm that is relatively autonomous, to wit, the realm of substantive economics, what Mill calls 'political economy,' and this relative autonomy justifies our treating it as a distinct science in its own right. How far this is a useful abstraction is a *matter of fact*, as is the point at which one will have to move to psychology and sociology to remove the imperfections with which economics, as only *relatively* autonomous, is inevitably saddled.

On these matters, then, there is no real disagreement between Mill and Robbins. In particular, what is the present point, he agrees with Robbins that the notion of men as maximizers applies to all human motives, and not just to those that are economic in the narrower sense. Robbins in fact takes this notion to be so much a part of common sense as to make it self-evident, true a priori.[8] With the latter Mill would in no way agree: that men are maximizers, even in the purely economic realm, is for Mill an *empirical law*. But he would go this far with Robbins, to claim as common-sense facts the theses that men seek to maximize their satisfactions – their pleasures, if one wishes to speak in the older way, and in the way that links up with Mill's psychology of learning – and that among the satisfactions that enter into calculations are those of morality, aesthetics, and so on, that is, the 'nobler' satisfactions.

If Mill's claim that whatever is desired as an end is desired as part of happiness is, though non-trivial, a piece of common sense, then what is the role of the argument from learning? Why does Mill feel he must argue for a piece of obvious common sense? The answer is clear enough: in spite of the common-sense nature of the claim, many have denied it. For example, Grote argues, as we saw, that action for a moral ideal always requires self-sacrifice (1876, p. 73), and that this counts against the utilitarian claim that men always pursue happiness. But this ignores that fact that felt satisfaction accompanies the disinterested doing of one's duty, so that one does, after all, pursue it as 'part of happiness' in Mill's sense; and, moreover, it ignores the fact that this felt satisfaction outweighs the pain of the sacrifice. Again, James Martineau holds that, for the utilitarian, morality is always sought as a means for sense pleasure, never as an end (1886, II: 304–5). He is prepared to grant that through association things other than pleasure can indeed come to be sought for their own sakes as part of happiness (II: 316), but morality is not one of these: conscience provides a felt standard which is not manufactured in the subject (II: 100); it therefore is not the product of an associative process, nor is it sought as part of happiness. Pleasure derives from our this-worldly nature, apparently, but conscience derives from God. Again, to thus distinguish between pleasure and conscience ignores the felt satisfaction that accompanies conscientious action, and makes it true that pursuing the latter is to pursue it as part of happiness. As Mill says, 'the ultimate sanction ... of *all* morality (external motives apart) [is] a subjective feeling in our own minds' (1861, p. 229). The common-sense position, that when virtue is sought as an end then it is pursued as part of happiness, is compatible with one's holding either that 'the feeling of duty is innate or [that it is] implanted' (p. 230). However, to defend this common sense against those who hold that 'moral obligation [is] a transcendental fact' (p. 229), and to show that feelings of obligation *can* come to be attached to the end proposed by the utilitarian principle, Mill proposes to offer the empirical evidence derived from the introspective analysis of sentiments of moral obligation. It is in Chapter III of 'Utilitarianism' that Mill argues that the sense of duty can come, through learning, to function as the internal sanction for the principle of utility (pp. 230ff), and in Chapter IV he defends the common-sense view that in aiming at virtue as an end one aims at it as part of one's happiness (p. 235). Many philosophers, and especially moral philosophers, have denied what is obvious common sense. In order to argue against *these* philosophers Mill proposes to ask them to go through the process of introspective analysis to uncover the empirical evidence that will lay bare the causal antecedents. These causal antecedents produce the feeling that virtue is part of one's happiness. Understanding the causal connection, then, one will recognize that what the antecedents produce will be a part of pleasure. But what those antecedents produce is the sense of moral obligation. So, in this way, one will come to understand that one's feelings of moral obligation are not only learned but aim at virtue as a part of happiness. An understanding in terms of the associative mechanisms of the causal antecedents of a desire will lead one to recognize that the effects of those causes are part of happiness; but the sense of duty is among the effects of those causes; hence, one will recognize that what one aims at out of a sense of duty is aimed at as a part of happiness. It follows that there are not several criteria of morality, as the opponents of utilitarianism propose, namely, happiness and whatever else that is desired as an end, but only one as the utilitarian proposes, namely, happiness, but happiness in all its parts including virtue.

Furthermore, through the associative processes revealed through introspective analysis we can identify the means, a bit more fully discussed in the *Analysis* (J.S. Mill 1869, II: 230ff), namely, mental culture (1861, p. 216), that is available for causing new objects to become part of one's happiness, so that one comes to seek them for their own sake, for example, art, politics, history (p. 216), and also, of course, life as a moral or virtuous person (p. 217; 1869, II: 280ff).[9]

A variation on the criticisms of Mill that we have been considering is given by Williams. Actions, he suggests, are always valuable only for their consequences, not intrinsically and for their own sake (1973, p. 84). However, actions as such can be performed joyously; doing them can be intrinsically pleasurable. Here, then, there are pleasures that, since they are not consequences of actions, cannot be taken into account in the utilitarian calculation of what is right and wrong (p. 84). The utilitarian principle of choosing that action that has the maximally pleasurable consequences is inconsistent with the goal of maximizing human happiness. But this is really only a quibble. In the first place, Mill as we have seen can (speculatively at least) account for actions becoming parts of one's happiness. In the second place, if an action is intrinsically pleasurable, then that pleasure, which makes it part of one's happiness, should be taken into account as among the pleasures produced by the action. At least, it should be so taken into account on Mill's view anyway, if not the version of utilitarianism that Williams chooses to criticize. Actions may produce happiness in two ways: they may function as a *means to* other states, which are themselves intrinsically pleasurable; or they may produce the pleasure that makes them *part of* one's happiness. Only the former sort of production counts as consequences, in William's sense, but both sorts of production are relevant, for Mill at least, to the utilitarian calculation. One may suspect that Williams is not wholly concerned to be fair to the utilitarian.

Mill, then, has a clear case against those who argue against both his psychology and his ethics on the ground that men seek ends other than pleasure. Accepting this *fact*, he can defend economics as partially autonomous, independent of hedonics, and circumscribed by institutional and moral constraints. At the same time he can also defend the claim central to the utilitarian ethics that men seek as an end their own happiness, that is, their own happiness in all its parts.

4 The Moral Sentiments as Higher Pleasures

In the notes of the younger Mill to his father's *Analysis* concerning these derivative laws of psychology that explain how, through association with pleasure, we acquire attachments to persons and acquire love of things to which we have not native or innate attachment or love, he tells us: 'This portion of the laws of human nature is the more important to psychology, as they show how it is possible that the moral sentiments, the feelings of duty, and of moral approbation and disapprobation, may be no original elements of our nature, any may yet be capable of being not only more intense and more powerful than any of the elements out of which they may have been formed, but may also, in the maturity, be perfectly disinterested' (1869, II: 233n). We have examined in detail the issue of how men can come to aim disinterestedly at goals such as virtue. We must now turn to the other issue raised by Mill, that of *intensity*. For, intensity accounts for our preferring these higher pleasures, and explains how such motives can function, as Butler correctly insisted they do function, to control other desires. But unlike Butler, the Mills insisted that one must go beyond functions to deeper, less imperfect, causal explanations to account for why we have the specific deliverances of conscience that we have and why they have the controlling power or authority that they have. Sparshott wrote: 'It does seem difficult to deny that if one asks a person, "Why did you eat those strawberries?", the answer, "Because I like them" calls for no elaboration, whereas the answer, "Because I don't like them" does' (1958, p. 284). Now, if the questioner's 'Why?' is simply a request for a motive, that is, for, as one says, the reason for one's action, or, what is the same more accurately put, for a functional explanation of one's action in terms of motives, then of course 'Because I like them' calls for no further elaboration. It does not follow, however, that that is the end of the matter, that no further elaboration is possible or reasonable to seek. For, beyond functions there are less imperfect, causal explanations. James Mill once put the point this way. Sir James Mackintosh, following Butler, held that 'No gratification can indeed be imagined without a previous desire.' The elder Mill quotes this, and remarks: 'The prediction must be reversed, in order to make sense of it. *There can be no desire without a previous gratification.* There can be no desire, without an idea of the pleasure desired. But there can be no idea, without a previous sensation' (1835, p. 77). How, then, can we account causally for our various motives having the *intensities* that they have, which determine how they function to produce and control behaviour? This answer, of course, is in terms of association. In his *Analysis*, James Mill points out that, although every pleasure is desirable, and every motive a tendency to action, not every motive actually produces action (J.S. Mill 1869, II: 258). 'The reason is,' he tells us, 'the existence of other motives which prevent it.' As an example he considers the case of a man tempted to commit adultery with his friend's wife. If he does not do it, that is, does not act to achieve the pleasure such an act will produce, then that is because there are other motives that are stronger, to wit, the pains associated with the act – the pains of the wronged husband, the moral indignation of others, the future feelings of guilt (II: 258–9). The younger Mill agrees: 'the one or the other motive will prevail, according as *the pleasurable or the painful association* is the more powerful' (II: 262n; italics added). It is the *history of association* that causally accounts for the intensity of motives, and this association in particular consists in *the association of pain and pleasure*.

Critics of Mill such as John Grote argue that virtuous action is not simply action undertaken as a means to happiness (1876, p. 75), and further that there is always an element of sacrifice (pp. 73, 75), that is, a conflict with other, often self-regarding, motives. Mill not only agrees with the former, but also with the latter: 'one can best serve the happiness of others,' he tells us, 'by the absolute sacrifice of his own' (1861, p. 271). However – and this is the point – in cultivating the disinterested pursuit of virtue, one is giving oneself 'the best prospect of realizing such happiness as is attainable'; for, living up to that standard as best one can, in a world of chance and often outrageous fortune, can, as much for oneself as for the Stoic, be 'one of the sources of satisfaction accessible to [one]' (pp. 217–18). However, Mill, unlike intuitionists such as Grote, will not admit that sacrifice is, by itself, good; it is good only if it actually contributes to an overall increase of human happiness (1861, p. 218). St Simon Stylites shows indeed what men *can* do, but surely not what they *should* do (p. 217). None the less, even the pillar saints did what they did because of the satisfaction they gained from such self-sacrifice. For them, as in the case of all disinterested action, there was a conflict of motives, and the stronger motive won out. And this strength or intensity, as with that of any motive, is a result of a previous history of association.

The strength of a motive is a function of two factors. As the younger Mill puts it in the *Analysis*: 'What makes one or the other more powerful, is (conformably to the general laws of association) partly the intensity of the pleasurable or painful ideas in themselves, and partly the frequency of the repetition of their past conjunction with the act, either in experience or in thought' (1869, II: 262n). It is the latter of these two factors that makes education possible, as both Mills emphasize (II: 259, 262n). A good education will ensure that the strongest motives are those that aim at the good.[10]

But the *intensity* of the pleasure is also relevant to the strength of the motive, and it is this aspect to which we must now attend.

Some pleasures are more intense than others; moreover, the more intense are *preferred* to the less intense (1861, p. 211). In saying this, John Stuart Mill was, of course, following Bentham (1789, Ch. iv, sec. ii). Now, Bentham assumes that pleasures can always be *summed*, so that each pleasure is a certain *quantity* relative to others (Ch. iv, sec v, no. 5). There is, he suggests, a discernible unit of pleasure: 'The limit of the quantity of a pleasure in respect of intensity on the side of diminution is a state of insensibility: the degree of intensity possessed by that pleasure which is the faintest of any that can be distinguished to be pleasure, may be represented by unity: Such a degree of intensity is in every day's experience' (1770s, p. 4 [33]). The younger Mill, however, insists that in ranking pleasures according to preference, the 'estimation' does not 'depend on quantity alone' and 'quality is [to be] considered as well as quantity' (1861, p. 211). Or, as he once put it in his journal, 'The only true or definite rule of conduct or standard of morality is the greatest happiness, but there is needed first a philosophical estimate of happiness. Quality as well as quantity of happiness is to be considered; less of a higher kind is preferable to more of a lower' (1854, p. 381). These qualitatively preferable pleasures have different sources than do the pleasures enjoyed by swine (1861, p. 210); they derive from emotional and intellectual experience rather than physical experience: 'the pleasures derived from the higher faculties [are] preferable in *kind* ... to those of which the animal nature, disjoined from the higher faculties, is susceptible' (p. 213). Many who have accepted that claim that only pleasure is desirable have argued that the preferability of the pleasures of the higher faculties derives from their *extrinsic* properties: they are more permanent, they are usually attained at less cost, and so on. Mill agrees that these factors are certainly relevant, but besides these extrinsic grounds for preferring the pleasures of the higher faculties, these pleasures are *also intrinsically* preferable.

> Utilitarian writers in general have placed the superiority of mental over bodily pleasures chiefly in the greater permanency, safety, uncostliness, etc., of the former – that is, in their circumstantial advantages rather than their intrinsic nature. And on all these points utilitarians have fully proved their case: but they might have taken the other, and, as it may be called, higher ground, with entire consistence. It is quite compatible with the principle of utility to

recognize the fact, that some *kinds* are more desirable and more valuable than others. It would be absurd that while, in estimating all other things, quality is considered as well as quantity, the estimation of pleasures should be supposed to depend on quantity alone. (pp. 210–11)

It is in these intrinsically preferable higher pleasures that a cultivated mind finds an inexhaustible source of satisfaction that alone can yield genuine fulfilment (p. 216). An adequate utilitarianism must take into account these intrinsic, or qualitative differences among pleasures.[11]

In making this point, Mill has been accused quite simply of being inconsistent. As Ewing put it, 'Mill tried indeed to reconcile his utilitarianism with the admission that a lesser pleasure might rationally be preferred to a greater on the grounds of the superior quality of the former, but it is generally, and I think rightly, agreed among philosophers that he failed to escape inconsistency' (1965, p. 42). Taylor makes a similar point about Mill's introduction of the notion of a qualitative distinction among pleasures: 'The claim is just incoherent ... [I]f pleasure is the only thing good for its own sake and is the standard by which other things are deemed good, as hedonism declares, then no pleasure can be inherently better than others. Pleasures can in this case differ only in quantity ... they cannot differ in their quality of goodness' (1970, p. 94). And here is what Garner and Rosen say: 'If two things vary in their desirability, there must be some factor (not itself without value) that makes the difference. If so, and if pleasure alone is valuable, only an addition of pleasure could bring about an increase in the value of anything. Bentham accepts this but Mill does not, and therefore Mill is sometimes criticized as being inconsistent' (1967, p. 153). Sosa (1969) argues that Mill is not inconsistent, but only because he (Sosa) also argues, implausibly enough, that Mill never did give up the view that the only criterion for something being preferred is that it produces a greater quantity of pleasure.

The objection seems to be this. Mill claims that a difference of pleasure provides a basis for determining the relative value of higher- and lower-quality pleasures. But pleasure is supposed to be a simple, undefinable quality. If it is simple, then how can there be differences in *kind* among its instances? Or conversely, if there are differences in kind, then is not Mill introducing something over and above the simple quality of pleasure associated with two objects to determine their relative value?

We can approach the issue of whether this objection is sound by approaching the distinction that Mill makes from an aspect of it to which Mill also draws our attention.

What Mill tells us is that the pleasures that are higher in quality are 'intellectual' or 'mental' whereas the pleasures that are lower in quality are 'sensual' and arise from our 'animal nature' (1861, pp. 210–11). What Mill is claiming is that these two different sorts of pleasure have a different 'feel' to them.

Now, Mill is not alone in claiming a distinction between 'sensual' and 'mental' pleasures. Thus, Hospers (1961, pp. 111ff) develops a distinction between pleasure$_1$ and pleasure$_2$. Pleasure$_1$ is a non-localized agreeable feeling, while pleasure$_2$ is a localized agreeable feeling. (A similar distinction is made among disagreeable feelings.) 'We may speak of pleasure – call it pleasure$_1$ – in the sense of a pleasurable state of consciousness, one with "positive hedonic tone." It seems to be impossible to define it further, for the term refers to an experience which, like so many experiences, no words are adequate to describe. We can only cite typical circumstances under which the experience occurs: we may derive this kind of pleasure from such sources as a refreshing swim, from reading a good book, from grappling with a philosophical problem, from creating a work of art, or from talking with congenial persons' (pp. 111–12). Other sources of non-localized pleasure that Hospers mentions include 'good books, symphony concerts, and doing one's duty' and also 'the pleasures of worshipping God' (p. 113). In none of these cases are we inclined to locate the pleasure in a specific part of the body; the pleasure does not have a precise physical locus but is rather a general sense of well-being. Pleasure$_2$, in contrast, is located in a precise part of the body. 'There are pleasurable sensations, such as those of being tickled, stroked, and rubbed; since these pleasures have a definite bodily location, here it makes sense to ask, "*Where* do you feel the pleasure?" – whereas it does not make sense to ask, "Where do you feel the pleasure you get from reading a good book?"' (p. 112). The opposite of pleasure$_2$ is pain$_2$, that is, a localized pain, such as a toothache, a burn on the arm, a bruise on the toe, heartburn. And the opposite of pleasure$_1$ is non-localized pain$_1$, the displeasure we feel, for example, 'from hearing bad news, from situations involving distress, anger, terror, jealousy' (p. 113). One could add to this list such moods as those of despair, loneliness, boredom, and melancholy, as Edwards (1975, p. 276) points out.[12] Edwards also rightly distinguishes non-localized feeling from universally localized feeling (ibid.); the former has no physical locus, whereas the latter is felt to be present 'all over.' Fatigue and chill are universally localized discomforts. When one drinks there are taste and gastric pleasures that are localized, but the pleasure of drunkenness itself is something felt 'all over.'

Gilbert Ryle once made much the same distinction as Hospers:

> To say that a person has been enjoying digging is not to say that he has been both digging and doing or experiencing something else ... it is to say that he dug with his whole heart in his task, i.e., that he dug, wanting to dig and not wanting to do anything else (or nothing) instead ... to enjoy doing something, to want to do it and not to want to do anything else, are different ways of phrasing the same thing.
>
> (It should be mentioned that 'pain' in the sense in which I have a pain in my stomach, is not the opposite of 'pleasure.' In this sense, a pain is a sensation of a special sort, which we ordinarily dislike having.) (1949, p. 108)

Oddly enough, while Ryle thus notes localized pain and contrasts this localization to the absence of a physical locus in the case of pleasures of the sort he mentions, he suggests that there are no localized pleasures: 'We can tell the doctor where it hurts and whether it is a throbbing, a stabbing or a burning pain; but we cannot tell him, nor does he ask, where it pleases us, or whether it is a pulsating or steady pleasure. Most of the questions which can be asked about aches, tickles, and other sensations or feelings cannot be asked about our likings and dislikings, our enjoyings and detestings. In a word, pleasure is not a sensation at all, and therefore not a sensation on one scale with an ache or twinge' (1960, p. 58). But similarly anyone who has ever had a gentle massage will know that there are localized bodily pleasures; and so will anyone who has eaten a good meal and drunk good wine and experienced the purely local gustatory, olfactory, and gastric satisfactions thereof. When we are sexually aroused we *can* locate where it feels good, to wit, in the genital zones. As for asking *where* it feels good, while Ryle may never have asked such questions, at least at Oxford in the 1940s, it is surely entirely appropriate for Masters and Johnson to ask, or one's sex partner during foreplay. Moreover, the adjectives Ryle eschews are also appropriate: the localized pleasures of gentle massage are *steady* while those of an orgasm are *pulsating*. Sexual relations produce many localized pleasures. They also often give rise to a generalized sense of well-being – pleasure$_I$ in Hospers's sense – but not always; at least, that is one interpretation that one can give to the popular saying that 'sex without love is meaningless.'

Hospers's (and, in effect, Ryle's) distinction between pleasure₁ and pleasure₂ does not directly address the issue of qualitative distinctions among pleasures. But it does help us, I think, to comprehend what Mill has in mind when he characterizes the lower pleasures as 'bodily' or 'physical' or 'sensory,' whereas the higher pleasures are 'mental' or 'non-sensory.' With this distinction in hand, one can raise the *causal* question of the relations between the higher and the lower pleasures. The localized pleasures of eating tend to give rise to a generalized feeling of well-being, as do those of sex. In contrast, the localized pains of disease and injury tend to create generalized feelings of despair and hopelessness. One tries to counteract the depression of an injured person by making him comfortable, stroking him gently, and so on. More generally, Mill proposes, as we know, that the higher pleasures all have lower pleasures as their genetic antecedents, the higher arising from the former through a process of association. For the moment, however, these causal questions are not before us, but only the issue of whether Mill's qualitative hedonism is consistent.

Sidgwick, like Mill before him, takes pleasure to be what is desirable – 'meaning by "desirable" not necessarily "what ought to be desired" but what would be desired, with strength proportioned to the degree of desirability, if it were judged attainable by voluntary action, supposing the desires to possess a perfect forecast, emotional as well as intellectual, of the state of attainment of fruition' (1907, p. 111). Sidgwick proposes 'to define Pleasure – when we are considering its "strict value" for the purposes of quantitative comparison – as a feeling which, when experienced by intelligent beings, is at least implicitly apprehended as desirable or – in the case of comparison – preferable (p. 127). However, Sidgwick suggests, contrary to Mill, judgments of preference are always quantitative: to say that pleasure x is preferable to pleasure y is to say that pleasure x is a greater quantity of the same sort of pleasure as pleasure y; in fact, there are not different *sorts* or *kinds* of pleasure. As Sidgwick put it, 'distinctions of *quality* that Mill and others urge may ... be admitted as grounds of preference, but only insofar as they can be resolved into distinctions of quantity' (p. 121). Sidgwick did not believe Mill intended this, and therefore thought that Mill was trying to do the impossible. Elsewhere he (Sidgwick) remarked that 'it is hard to see in what sense a man who of two alternative pleasures chooses the less pleasant on the grounds of its superiority in quality can be affirmed to take the "*greatest*" happiness or pleasure as his standard of preference' (1931, p. 247). Martineau, too, held that qualitative preference is unintelligible without degrees, that is, quality (1886, II: 328); as did Bradley, who tells us that 'apart from degree, there is no comparison, no estimation, no higher and lower at all' (1927, p. 118). A similar point was made by Grote: 'A consistent utilitarian can scarcely hold the difference of *quality* in pleasures in *any* sense: for if they differ otherwise than in what, speaking largely, may be called *quantity*, they are not mutually comparable, and in determining as to the preferability of one pleasure to another, we must then be guided by some considerations not contained in the idea or experience of the pleasure itself' (1870, p. 52).

But it is hard to understand why this objection is even plausible. It supposes that there can be no ordering of objects unless there is a cardinalization of that scale. However, there are clear examples in which this is not so. For example, as Dahl (1973, p. 47) suggests, not every use of 'more' can be paraphrased as 'greater amount of' or 'greater quantity of,' as when we say that Jones is more graceful than Smith: it is not implied in this case that there is a greater quantity of gracefulness that Jones has. Or, since Mill treats pleasure as a sensory element, consider the parallel case of sensory (phenomenal) colours. These are ordered on the spectrum from reds through yellows to blues and violets, though there is no question of a unit or any question of a quantitative measure of the distance between two colours. These properties are comparable in respect of being colours, though they remain quantitatively incomparable. The (phenomenal) colours form, as Helmholtz (1878) pointed out, a *sensory modality*, a modality being constituted by the fact that the properties in it are connected to each other by a relation that generates an order among them. As we saw earlier (chapter 4), sensations are, for purposes of psychology, more properly classified in terms of the modalities in which they occur than in terms of their causes. Neither Mill saw this clearly. But it is this point that the younger Mill is getting at in his discussion of pleasures: pleasures not only can be classified in terms of their causes (physical, mental) and other external characteristics (e.g., localized, non-localized), but also independently of such extrinsic features, as forming a sensory modality structured by a *preference relation*. But this relation, like pleasure itself, links up with motivation. When one pleasure is preferred to another, it is, *as a matter of psychological fact*, the former that moves one to act; it is this that gives the substance of the metaphor that the pleasure that moves one is the 'stronger'; and it is also the substance of the idea that we are moved by the pleasure that, among the alternatives, constitutes the 'greatest' happiness. What this implies, in short, is that there is nothing inconsistent in Mill's (quite reasonable) proposal that pleasures can be arranged in an order of greater and lesser, even where they are not quantitatively comparable.

From what has been said about Mill's theory of motives, it is clear enough what Mill has in mind. 'Pleasure,' like 'colour,' is a *determinable* concept with several *determinate* species under it.[13] These species are simple but differ qualitatively, and may be ranked in orders according to the quality, for example, colours ordered in the spectrum, pleasures ordered according to preferability.

This account of pleasure as a determinable characteristic is in fact pretty plausible to common sense. The distinction between localized and non-localized pleasures is, no doubt, one of *locus*, but once this distinction is grasped it is also evident that the pleasant and unpleasant feelings themselves are *just not qualitatively the same*: they do *not* differ only in intensity and duration. The agreeable feeling that is obtained from making a breakthrough scientific discovery or from reading a Jane Austen novel is simply not the same *kind* of feeling as the localized pleasant feelings that one obtains from bathing one's feet in warm water or from masturbation: it is *not* a matter of intensity and duration alone. The grief at the loss of a beloved relative or pet is not the same *kind* of feeling as one has when one has a toothache or a scald. We in fact have a fairly impoverished vocabulary to describe the subtle variations in these feelings; that is why we must so often use metaphors, or refer to the causes, or use metaphors based on causes (e.g., 'stabbing') when we attempt to describe these feelings. So when G.E. Moore says the following he is simply flying in the face of common sense: 'If you say "pleasure" you must mean "pleasure": you must mean some one thing common to all different "pleasures" some one thing, which may exist in different degrees, but which cannot differ in kind' (1903, p. 80). It is of course true that if you say 'colour' you must mean 'colour,' that is, something common to all colours, or, if you wish, with Moore, all 'colours.' This is, of course, 'one thing,' namely, the property of being a colour. But what has this property are *the various colours*. From the fact that these share a certain property it simply does not follow that these differ only in degree, that is, that there are no qualitative differences among them such that the relations that order them are not quantitative (do not yield a cardinal ordering). Equally as inappropriate as Moore's is the following remark of Edwards (1975, p. 273), that 'the notions of "pleasure" or "pain" are in a sense ambiguous notions which refer to a wide range of agreeable or disagreeable feelings which are qualitatively distinct. The words have a variety of referents rather than a single referent.' The word 'colour' is not ambiguous even though it 'refers' to all the − qualitatively distinct − colours; it is not ambiguous because there is in fact a common property − that of being a colour − which is shared by all colours. Similarly, the word 'pleasure' is not ambiguous even though there are many qualitatively distinct pleasures, that is, even though that term 'refers' to all the (qualitatively distinct) pleasures. And just as the various colours are ordered in *their* modality by certain relations, so the various pleasures are ordered, Mill claims, in *their* modality by the relation of preference.

Mill, of course, argues that these feelings of pleasure, with their intrinsic qualitative differences, and their preference ordering, are connected to our motives and desires. Specifically, whenever one attains a desired object one thereby attains, too, the pleasure associated with the latter. From what we have now seen, it is clear that, for Mill, and also quite plausibly, this pleasure may fit either one of two cases. (1) It may be a pleasure of the same determinate kind as the pleasures into which it can be introspectively analysed, and which constitute, according to the working hypothesis of the theory, its genetic antecedents. It differs only in quantity from the 'parts' into which it is analysed. The fact that it is preferred to the latter has its *foundation*[14] in this *quantitative difference*. (2) It may be a pleasure of a different determinate kind from the pleasures into which it is analysed and which constitute its genetic antecedents. The fact that it is preferred to each of the latter, and to the sum of the latter, has its *foundation* in this *qualitative difference*. In spite of Bentham's speculative psychology that proposes such qualitative differences are reducible to quantitative differences, *phenomenology requires* one to recognize that irreducible qualitative differences are a *fact*.

Moreover, there is nothing inconsistent in holding that the genetic causes − the lower pleasures − have effects − the higher pleasures − that are unlike those causes. As chemical processes show, there is no reason why effects should be qualitatively like their causes; is water like hydrogen and oxygen? This is the point that Mill came to understand during his mental crisis, and appeared more generally in his rethinking of the notion of introspective analysis. It was a point he insisted upon in the discussion of perception. It is a point he now makes again with respect to the moral sentiments, and suggests that failure to respect this point may well lie behind those who argue that our moral faculties are innate and unlearned. After observing that the moral sentiments are

totally unlike the elementary sensations into which they are introspectively analysed and which constitute their genetic antecedents – as (he
also notes) holds also for the love of money for which, he elsewhere
points out, 'no one thinks it necessary to suppose an original and
inherent love' (1869, II: 234) – Mill observes

> In the case, then, of the moral sentiments, we have, on the one
> hand, a *vera causa* or set of causes, having a positive tendency to
> generate a sentiment of love for certain actions, and of aversion for
> certain others; and on the other hand, those sentiments of love and
> aversion, actually produced. This coincidence between the senti-
> ments and a power adequate to produce them, goes far towards
> proving causation. That the sentiments are not obviously like the
> causes, is no reason for postulating another cause, in the shape of
> an original principle of our nature. (II: 321–2)

Mill's position, that there are qualitatively different higher pleasures, must carefully be distinguished from the superficially similar
position of Hutcheson. The latter also holds, as we saw, that pleasures
are qualitatively distinct. But, for Hutcheson, the distinction between
higher and lower is a *moral* distinction. 'We are conscious,' he tells us, 'in
our state of mature years, that the happiness of our friends, our
families or our country are incomparably nobler objects of our pursuit,
and administer proportionably a nobler pleasure than the toys which
abundantly entertained us when we had experienced nothing better'
(1755, P 478). He expresses this as the claim that 'in comparing
pleasures of different kinds ... we have an immediate sense of dignity, a
perfection, or beatifick quality in some kinds' (P 476). He recommended that we estimate the value of a pleasure by, taken jointly, their
'dignity and duration: dignity denoting the excellence of the kind
where those of different kinds are compared; and the intenseness of
the sensations, when we compare those of the same kind' (P 477). In his
view, any quantity of pleasure of a higher kind is superior to all
quantities of every lower kind; no 'intense sensations of the lower kinds
with sufficient duration may compleat our happiness' (ibid.). Hutcheson even proposed that the 'superior orders in this world probably
experience all the sensations of the lower orders, and can judge of
them. But the inferior do not experience the enjoyment of the
inferiors' (P 478). These remarks sound indeed like Mill, so much so
that Martineau says that Hutcheson's 'anticipation of J.S. Mill's
well-known doctrine respecting the dimensions of pleasure [is] here

very striking, extending almost to the words of the exposition' (1886, II: 550).

Other philosophers also have suggested Mill is adopting something like Hutcheson's position, making difference in quality an evaluative distinction which then turns out, of course, to be inconsistent both with Mill's claim that the maximization of utility is the sole criterion for moral evaluation, and with Mill's claim that judgments of preferability are purely matter-of-fact judgments, that is, of simple experience. Thus, Grote asserts that 'the word "higher" ... evidently involves something in the nature of idealism' (1870, p. 49), a value judgment that cannot be established by experience (p. 51) and must be made by reference to a standard external to the pleasures (p. 53). Bradley argues similarly that Mill 'abandons·the greatest amount of pleasure principle' since 'the "higher" pleasure here is not the more intense pleasure; it is not the pleasure connected with the maximum of pleasure on the whole without distinction of kind. It is the preferable kind of pleasure'; and concludes that 'higher then ... has no meaning at all unless we go to something *outside* pleasure,' thereby accusing Mill of implicitly using a normative notion of quality (1927, p. 119). Moore, too, for similar reasons, objects to Mill's use of 'higher' and 'superior' (1903, p. 78). Abelson put the objection this way: 'But like Epicurus' preference to "natural" over "unnatural" pleasures, Mill's criterion of quality introduces a standard of value other than pleasure, by which pleasure itself can be evaluated, and thus contradicts the principle of utility, that pleasure is the single standard of good' (1967, p. 97). Hospers expresses the same objection: 'this "qualitative" principle of Mill's is a blunder: partly because if something is (in the long run) *less* pleasurable and yet better, then one has already deserted pleasure as the sole criterion of desirability' (1961, p. 59). Bronaugh has recently argued that, for Mill, all pleasures are intrinsically the same save for degrees of intensity, that is, quantity (1974, p. 323), and that the more intense pleasures are qualitatively superior only in a normative sense, relative to a standard of excellence established by the principle of utility (pp. 324–5).[15] A somewhat similar proposal has been made earlier by Seth, who argued that the 'so-called difference of quality will be found to resolve itself (so far as pleasure is concerned) into a difference of quantity *for the higher nature*' (1911, p. 125). A similar position is that of Urban, who holds that, 'in Mill's theory, the *standard* is taken from some sphere other than pleasure itself' and that, 'although [Mill] still speaks of the good as pleasure, the qualitative differences in the good are determined by the nature of the *self* for whom the pleasure *is* a pleasure. A higher self of more "dignity" determines the quality of one experience, a lower self of less dignity the quality of another' (1930, pp. 86–7). Finally, we might note that Sidgwick, while not attributing it to Mill, adopts a closely related position when he argues that 'When ... we judge of the preferable quality (as "elevation" or "refinement") of a state of consciousness as distinct from its pleasantness ... it is not really the feeling that is preferred, but something in the mental or physical conditions or relations under which it arises' (1907, p. 128). A similar tack is taken by Sosa who argues that a pleasure's quality is determined by that which is its 'immediate source' where anything that Mill would say is a 'part of happiness' is an immediate source of pleasure (1969, pp. 171–2); that some such sources are associated with greater quantities of pleasure than others (p. 171n), among which, in particular, are the higher faculties (pp. 165–6); and that the latter sources are, by the principle of utility, also morally the most valuable, with the quantity of pleasure of which they are the immediate sources for the subject contributing significantly to that value, sufficiently when added to the other consequences to tip the scale from bad to good (pp. 170, 172).

Now, with many of the points that these critics make against his position, Mill agrees! The qualitatively higher feelings are described as 'nobler' (1861, p. 213), and those who feel them are described as 'superior' (p. 212). Mill clearly takes these in a *moral* sense. For, it is precisely such motives that can lead men to the sort of self-sacrifice that so often is to the benefit of mankind in general (p. 218). As James Mill points out, one *wants* the pleasures to be associated with acts that are morally valuable: 'the business of a good education is to make the associations and the values correspond' (J.S. Mill 1869 II: 259). But, besides all this, the younger Mill *also* argues that 'the superiority of mental over bodily pleasures' does *not* lie 'in their circumstantial advantages' but 'rather in their *intrinsic* nature' (1861, p. 210; italics added). All the views just canvassed locate qualitative differences in *extrinsic* features of the pleasures, which is in straight contradiction to Mill's claim that the qualitative differences are intrinsic.

Moreover, the views that locate qualitative differences as *solely* normative differences clearly are at variance with the structure of Mill's essay. In the first place, while Mill holds that the higher pleasures are indeed morally superior, he also holds that the judgment that a pleasure is higher is itself *solely a factual judgment*. As he says, 'On a question which is the best worth having of two pleasures ... *apart from its moral attributes and from its consequences*, the judgement of those who are qualified by knowledge of both, or, if they differ, that of the majority among them, must be admitted as final' (1861, p. 213; italics added). (We shall say more of this test below.) In the second place, if the notion of a 'higher' pleasure were a value judgment then Mill would, at the point where the discussion occurs in Chapter II of 'Utilitarianism,' be *justifying* value-claims rather than, as the chapter title reports, simply stating 'What Utilitarianism is.' Such justification does *not* appear in Mill's essay until Chapter IV where he investigates 'Of What Sort of Proof the Principle of Utility is Susceptible.' Qualitative differences among pleasures, then, are both intrinsic properties of the pleasures and also non-normative.

But what, really, is the issue? Can sensations be qualitatively different from each other and yet fall within the same genus? Clearly the answer is affirmative. For, sensations can be qualitatively different in being red and green but none the less fall within the same genus of being coloured, and indeed are different precisely in respect of being coloured. Similarly, then, two sensations can be qualitatively different and yet both be pleasures and differ precisely in respect of being pleasures. Can qualitatively different sensations within the same genus be placed in an order? Again the answer is clearly affirmative. For, coloured sensations can be ordered on the spectrum. Similarly, pleasurable sensations can be ordered as to preference, or the relative capacity to move to action. Can the fact that one prefers some qualitatively different pleasures to others seriously compromise any claim to be a hedonist? Once again, the answer is clear, in this case clearly negative. It is hard to understand how these things can really be questioned. In fact, the points would seem to be sheer common sense. That being so, it would seem that the only issue that remains is whether Mill can consistently claim that such qualitatively superior pleasures as our moral feelings or our sense of beauty are not innate, while the only pleasures to which we natively respond are the lower, sensual pleasures. That is, is Mill's common-sense claim about qualitative differences among pleasures compatible with Mill's learning theory? Nor is this a purely abstract issue in psychology. For, if the higher pleasures cannot be accounted for by Mill's psychology, then that will provide some support, at least, for the claim that our moral feelings, that is, the higher pleasures, are innate, with all the support which that gives to intuitionism.

But the answer to this last question, too, is clear: that there are pleasures qualitatively different from their genetic predecessors is clearly compatible with Mill's psychology. Mill gives an indication of how this goes quite explicitly in 'Utilitarianism,' where, discussing justice, he tells us: 'Our notion ... of the claim we have on our fellow creatures to join in making safe for us the very groundwork of our existence, gathers feelings around it so much more intense than those concerned in any of the more common cases of utility, *that the difference in degree (as in often the case in psychology) becomes a real difference in kind*' (1861, p. 251; italics added). As he indicates in this passage, we can find help if we turn to his psychological studies, that is, his notes to his father's *Analysis*. With reference to this very point, though in connection with another feeling that is also unlike its antecedents, he tells us:

> When a complex feeling is generated out of elements very numerous and various, and in a corresponding degree indeterminate and vague, but so blended together by a close association, the effect of a long series of experiences, as to have become inseparable, the resulting feeling always seems not only very unlike any of the elements composing it, but very unlike the sum of those elements. The pleasure of acquiring, or of consciously possessing, a sum of money (supposed not be desired for application to some specific purpose,) is a feeling to our consciousness, very different from the pleasure of protection against hunger and cold, the pleasure of ease and rest from labour, the pleasure of receiving consideration from our fellow-creatures, and the other miscellaneous pleasures, the association with which is admitted to be the real and only source of the pleasure of processing money. (1869, II: 321n)

This is simply the point that we have recognized previously that in psychology the 'deductive method' of research, in which wholes are always the sums of their parts, is not applicable. Rather than the mode of combination being mechanical, where wholes are simply sums of parts, it is *chemical*. There is nothing incoherent in the assertion that the chemical mode of combination is characteristic of psychology. Nor does it render the normal rules of the logic of science inoperative. In his notes to the *Analysis*, Bain notes that quantities are not so clear in psychological as in physical phenomena, and that one therefore cannot use the deductive method as in physics – we 'cannot show, by casting a sum, that the assigned constituents of a compound exactly amount to the whole' – and so 'to evade this source of uncertainty we are thrown back upon the Experimental Canons, or the Four Methods' (II: 303n).[16] There is absolutely no reason, then, why Mill cannot quite consistently hold that pleasurable sensations have as their genetic consequences pleasures that are unlike and preferable to those antecedents.

What one finds amazing is that none of the writers at whom we have looked ever saw fit to turn to Mill's psychology for a discussion and elaboration by Mill himself of the notion that quantitative differences can become qualitative. Is it too much to ask writers to familiarize themselves with the writings of the philosophers whom they criticize?

There is one case of qualitative emergence that the Mills look at in detail. This was the case of beauty, which, many insisted, was, like morality, a pleasure qualitatively different from, and intrinsically superior *in a normative* sense to, the lower pleasures. John Stuart Mill quotes, in his notes to the *Analysis*, from his father's *Fragment of Mackintosh*: 'The beautiful is that which excites in us the emotion of beauty, a state of mind with which we are acquainted by experience. This state of mind has been successfully analyzed, and shown to consist of a train of pleasurable ideas, awakened in us by a beautiful object' (1869, II: 316n). Coleridge objected to this position, that beauty is not *merely* the agreeable. John Stuart Mill accepts this objection. But he rejects Coleridge's further conclusion that beauty does not arise from association (II: 252n). It is the innatist moral-sense position of Hutcheson, for example, that the Mills were concerned to deny. Hutcheson held that 'we immediately perceive the difference in kind [between the pleasure of things that are beautiful and the lower pleasures], and that the dignity of enjoyment from fine poetry, painting, or from knowledge is superior to the pleasures of the palate, were they never so delicate,' just as 'we immediately discern moral good to be superior in kind and dignity to all others which are perceived by the other perceptive powers' (1755, p. 472). The position was, of course, akin to that of Diderot. It was this which the Mills were concerned to deny, without, however, denying that beauty was a pleasure qualitatively distinct from its genetic antecedents, without denying that it was preferable in a descriptive sense to lower pleasures, and without denying that its enjoyment was nobler in a moral sense. To be sure, 'associations of commonplace and every-day pleasures' occur in states of consciousness that arise when contemplating objects of Nature and Art; these are 'agreeable' (II: 253). 'But besides these there are other elements, constituting the beauty, properly speaking, of the [objects] which appeal to other, and what we are accustomed, not without meaning, to call the higher parts of our nature; which give a stronger stimulus and a deeper delight to the imagination, because the ideas they call up are such as in themselves act on the imagination with greater force' (II: 253n). Mill points out how complex are the associative processes that give rise to the aesthetic pleasures: 'Of all our feelings, our acquired pleasures and pains, especially our pleasures, are the most complex; resulting from the whole of our nature and of our past lives, and involving, consequently, a greater multitude and variety of associations than any other phenomena of the human mind. And among our various pleasures, the aesthetic are without doubt the most complex' (II: 254n). The point was illustrated by the example of appreciating music. 'That the full physical pleasure of a tune is often not experienced at the first hearing, is a consequence of the fact, that the pleasure depends on succession, and therefore on the coexistence of each note with the remembrance of a sufficient number of the previous notes to constitute melody: a remembrance which, of course, is not possessed in perfection, until after a number of repetitions proportioned to the complexity and to the unfamiliar character of their combination' (II: 242n). What pleasures an object evokes in an observer on a given occasion will thus depend upon the history of each observer prior to observing the object on that occasion. Different persons will have different pleasures evoked by the same object, and the same object will evoke different pleasures on different occasions. Of course, these differences will often be subtle. Moreover, 'there are some ingredients which are universally, or almost universally, present, when the emotions have their characteristic peculiarity; and to which they seem to be mainly indebted for the extraordinary power with which they act on the minds which have the greatest susceptibility to them' (II: 254n). The younger Mill gives unity, repose, and symmetry as examples of such ingredients, and then refers the reader to Ruskin's *Modern Painters* for a more detailed discussion of these nearly universal parts of beauty. But, details aside, it is these ingredients that make aesthetic pleasures *qualitatively distinct from but superior to the pleasures from which they arise*: ingredients, such as unity,

> all represent to us some valuable or delightful attribute, in a completeness and perfection of which our experience presents us with no example, and which therefore stimulates the active power of the imagination to rise above known reality, into a more attractive or a more majestic world. This does not happen with what we call our lower pleasures. To them there is a fixed limit at which they have a stop: or if, in any particular case, they do acquire, by association, a power of stirring up ideas greater than them-selves, and stimulate the imagination to enlarge its conceptions to the dimensions of those ideas, we then feel that the lower pleasure has, exceptionally, risen into the region of the aesthetic, and has

superadded to itself an element of pleasure of a character and quality not belonging to its own nature. (II: 255n)

This general picture is equally appropriate for the emergent qualitative differences that render our moral feelings preferable to the lower pleasures.

How far, then, has the younger Mill moved us from the original Benthamite position?

We can perhaps answer this question by noticing some remarks that Mill's student Alexander Bain made about Mill's distinction between the quantity and quality of pleasure. Bain criticizes the distinction and adds that the only differences that the utilitarian should admit among pleasures, besides differences of quantity, are those of moral dignity. In stating this, Bain was developing a position that was later to be worked out in more detail by Seth, who, as we saw above, argued that difference of quality could be nothing more than 'difference of quantity for the higher nature' (1911, p. 125). If we turn, however, from these remarks to what Bain has to say in his psychological works about the notion of quantity when applied to pleasure or pain, then we find that Bain's remarks about qualitative differences among pleasures can be construed quite differently, as agreeing in effect with the younger Mill against Bentham. Bain, like Mill, criticizes the notion that all pleasures (or pains) can be put on a cardinal scale in which differences can all, in principle at least, be measured with reference to a single unit of pleasure (or pain).

Bain attempts to explain Mill's view of the qualitative differences among pleasures in terms of an estimation of dignity: 'Few human beings would consent to become beasts, or fools, or base, in consideration of a greater allowance of pleasure. Inseparable from the estimation of pleasure is a *sense of dignity*, which determines a preference among enjoyments' (1880a, p. 288; his italics). And for him as for Seth, this sense of dignity is a *moral* distinction, as he explains elsewhere in a critical study of Mill (1882). Nor is it even an intrinsic moral distinction, as Hutcheson had held; it is, rather, an extrinsic one, based upon the principle of utility. Mill was in error when he argued otherwise, that there is an *intrinsic non-moral* relation of preferability among qualitatively distinct pleasures.

He [Mill] courageously faces the difficulty [that regarding pleasure as the sole object of desire or pursuit is a doctrine worthy only of swine] by pronouncing in favour of a difference in *kind* or *quality* among pleasures .... My own decided opinion is, that he ought to have resolved all the so-called nobler pleasures into the one single circumstance of including, with the agent's pleasure, the pleasure of others. This is the only position that a supporter of Utility can hold to. There is a superiority attaching to some pleasures that are still exclusively self-regarding, namely, their amount as compared with the exhaustion of the nervous power; the pleasures of music and of scenery are higher than those of stimulating drugs. But the superiority that makes a distinction of *quality*, that rises clearly and effectually above the swinish level, is the superiority of the gratifications that take our fellow-beings along with us: such are the pleasures of affection, of benevolence, of duty. To have met opponents upon this ground alone would have been the proper undertaking for the object Mill had in view. It surprises me that he has not ventured upon such a mode of resolving pleasures ... Apart from moral attributes and consequences, I do not see a difference of quality at all; and, when these are taken into account, the difference is sufficient to call forth any amount of admiring preference. A man's actions are noble if they arrest misery or diffuse happiness around him: they are not noble if they are not directly or indirectly altruistic; they are essentially of the swinish type. (1882, pp. 113–14)

Bain agrees with Mill that desires may have objects other than one's own pleasure; in particular, they may have the pleasure of others as well as that of oneself, that is, the general welfare, as their object. If they do, then it is *that* which makes those desires preferable, that is, morally preferable, to other desires. But, while these nobler desires differ in their objects from less noble desires, they do not differ *specifically* and *non-morally*; they do not have an intrinsic or specific difference apart from their objects that functions to make them, so far as those who experience them are concerned, preferable in a non-moral sense to other, say the solely self-regarding, desires. Mill was wrong to hold that there were such intrinsic qualitative differences.

   Now, Mill was arguing that there are qualitative differences that cannot be reduced to quantitative differences *in the way that the earlier generation of utilitarians, following Bentham, had proposed.* How, precisely, did they attempt this reduction? Bentham proposes that there are seven 'circumstances' that have to be considered when one measures the value of a pleasure or a pain. With respect to a single individual, there are four such circumstances: the intensity, the duration, the certainty (or uncertainty), and the propinquity (or remoteness) (1789, Ch. IV, secs. 2, 3). When calculating the value with respect to a number of persons, one includes three further circumstances: the fecundity (the chance it has of being followed by sensations of the same kind, pleasure if it is a pleasure, pain if it is a pain), the purity (the chance it has of not being followed by sensations of the opposite kind), and the extent (the number of persons to whom it extends or who are affected by it) (Ch. IV, secs. 3–5). Strictly speaking, it is the first two circumstances that form the basis of the calculation; these give the 'magnitude' of the pleasure or pain. The others build upon these. The certainty is measured by degrees of belief or probability. Propinquity allows for the discounting of time (1822, p. 540, col. 2). Fecundity, purity, and extent are easily included on top of these (1789, Ch. IV, sec. 5; 1822, sec. 3). As for the magnitude of a pleasure, Bentham says this:

> The *magnitude* – the *greatness* – of a pleasure, is composed of its *intensity* and its *duration*; to obtain it, supposing its intensity represented by a certain number of degrees, you multiply that number by the number expressive of the moments or atoms of time contained in its duration. Suppose two pleasures have the same degree of intensity, – give to the second twice the duration of the first, the second is twice as *great* as the first.
>
> Just so it is with pains: and thence with exemptions from pains. (1822, p. 540, col. 1)

The greatness of a pleasure is obtained, Bentham insists, by multiplying the numbers that express its intensity and its duration. Donner (1983, p. 491) suggests that Bentham did not recognize that defining greatness as this product needed defending, since in fact there are an infinite number of ways in which intensity and duration can be weighed relative to each other and put into a single scale. But Bentham was at least partially aware of this problem, offering a justification of the claim that the scales should be multiplied rather than added when the single scale of 'greatness' was formed, and arguing, too, implicitly at least, that the two dimensions of intensity and duration should be given equal weight. We find this is an unpublished manuscript from the 1770s written before the publication of the *Principles of Morals and Legislation* (1789).[17] In this manuscript Bentham tells us: 'The numbers expressive of the intensity of a pleasure and those expressive of its duration, are to be multiplied together, not merely added. For supposing the pleasure to continue all along at the same degree of intensity, every degree of intensity it possesses is carried through every degree of duration: and *vice-versa* every degree of duration is extended over every degree of intensity. Accordingly if of two pleasures, the one be *three* times as intense as the other, and likewise continues three times as long, it is not six times only as great, but nine times' (1770s, p. 6 [40]).

For this calculation to work, units that can be added and multiplied are required for each of the dimensions. Duration, on the face of it at least, seems to present no problem, since units of time are readily available. But intensity is another matter. It is sometimes asserted, for example by Donner (1983, p. 483), that Bentham gives no explanation of how units of intensity are to obtained. But this is not so. In the 1770s manuscript, Bentham explained it thus: 'The limit of the quantity of a pleasure in respect of intensity on the side of diminution is a state of insensibility: the degree of intensity possessed by that pleasure which is the faintest of any that can be distinguished to be pleasure, may be represented by unity: Such a degree of intensity is in every day's experience. According as any pleasures are perceived to be more and more intense they may be represented by higher and higher numbers: but there is no fixing on any particular degree of intensity as being the highest of which a pleasure is susceptible' (1770s, p. 4 [33]). Where there is no noticeable difference the two pleasures (or pains) are to be reckoned equal. 'If of the two pleasures a man knowing what they are would as lief enjoy the one as the other, they must be reputed equal. There is a reason for supposing them equal, and there is none for supposing them unequal. If of two pains a man had as lief escape the one as the other, such two pains must be reputed equal. If of two sensations, a pain and a pleasure, a man had as lief enjoy the pleasure and suffer the pain, as not enjoy the one and not suffer the latter, such pleasure and pain must be reputed *equal*, or as we may say in this case, *equivalent*' (p. 11 [36]). This procedure for defining equality among pleasures is reminiscent of the 'indifference mappings' of modern economists, except that for Bentham the scale has a unit, that is, is a cardinal scale, while for contemporary economists the scale is ordinal. The point is that what Bentham is suggesting in these passages is the use of what later were to be called 'just noticeable differences' (jnds) not only for measuring the equality of pleasures and pains, but also for establishing a unit: the unit of pleasure (or pain) was 'the degree of intensity possessed by that pleasure which is the faintest of any that can be distinguished to be pleasure.' Bentham had thought carefully about this, for he applied the same idea to the measurement of time: 'The limit of the quantity of pleasure in respect of duration is the least portion of duration that can be distinguished: suppose a moment. If then a moment be taken for the least portion of time that is distinguishable, it is certain that no pleasure, to exist at all, can last for less than a moment. Such a degree of duration is within every day's experience. But there is no fixing upon any particular number of moments as being the greatest during which any pleasure can continue' (p. 5 [33]). This idea that Bentham introduces, to employ the just noticeable difference to establish a scale of measurement for sensations, was later rediscovered by G.T. Fechner who gave a detailed account of the jnd in his *Elemente der Psychophysik* (1860); and it was only later that F.Y. Edgeworth was to use the idea – that of a 'minimum sensible,' as he called it – in economics, in his *Mathematical Psychics: An Essay on the Application of Mathematics to the Moral Sciences* (1881). Bentham's idea may not ultimately work – if this is what Donner means when she says that Bentham did not deal with the issue, then she is surely correct. But she seems to be making the stronger claim that Bentham was not even aware of the problem. What the 1770s manuscript establishes is that he was indeed aware of the issue, and moreover, as the work of Fechner and Edgeworth makes clear, the solution he proposed is not simply silly. But even if the idea is not simply silly, it remains a question of fact whether all pleasures can be put on a single scale with the only differences those of intensity as reckoned by numbers of units. What the younger Mill argued was that, given the phenomenological facts, and those of the mental chemistry of the laws of association, this was simply *not* the fact of the matter: there are qualitative differences that imply that not all pleasures (or pains) are commensurate on a single cardinal scale with a single unit of pleasure. It is this claim that Bain challenged – or, rather, seemed to challenge. But did he really?

To answer this question we must turn to what Bain had to say about the scale of pleasure. This is very revealing of the distance that psychology had moved – had been moved by the younger Mill – from the position of Bentham and the early utilitarians. Bain writes:

> Of two pleasures, two pains, two emotions, closely succeeding each other, we can pronounce one to be the stronger within a certain limit of delicacy ... The discrimination ... is not very delicate, if we take as a standard the delicacy of these senses – sight and hearing, for example, as regards things seen and heard. From the zero of indifference, up to the highest known pitch of agreeable warmth,

as in the bath, no one would venture to interpolate twenty gradations; perhaps eight or ten would be the utmost that we could practically bear in mind. Not much superior would be the discrimination of the pleasure of a taste, a relish, or an odour, or the pain of their opposites. In our rough estimates, we usually jump from one extreme to another in four or five leaps. In object properties on the other hand, we can (apart from artificial means) interpolate many times that number of stages; visible magnitude, visible form, shades of colour, intensity and pitch of sounds, can be discriminated into hundreds of graduations; the length of a line, the sharpness of a bend, the brightness of a tint, are appreciated and remembered with far greater nicety than a mode of pleasure and pain. (1880b, p. 27)

Where for Bentham the scale of pleasure and pain is established by finding a unit that yields a cardinal ordering, for Bain the scale does not depend upon the discovery of a unit. On Bain's account, indifference judgments establish the scale but do not yield a unit. For Bain, the best that one can obtain is an ordering of greater and less with four or perhaps five steps from the lowest to the highest. That is, for Bain in contrast to Bentham, the idea of establishing a cardinal ordering of pleasures and pains has completely disappeared. All that remains is the notion that pleasures and pains can be put in a rough ordering of greater and less. But this, of course, is precisely what John Stuart Mill was insisting upon when he insisted that there were qualitative differences among pleasures that could not be reduced to quantitative differences. Bain is simply taking for granted the case that Mill made against the Benthamites; it does not occur to Bain that one could go beyond the obvious phenomenological data to which he, following Mill, appeals, to a cardinal ordering that somehow one knows a priori must be there. Bentham, and James Mill, knew that it *must* be there, and found it – as Bentham insisted about the unit, 'such a [minimal] degree of intensity is in every day's experience' (1770s, p. 4 [33]). John Stuart Mill had clearly effected a revolution in psychology. In Bentham, the a priori needs of philosophy could ride roughshod over phenomenology and determine what the psychologist *must* find in his analyses. In Bain, there is no question but that psychology must take for its data what it empirically finds: if the facts won't yield a unit of intensity and a cardinal scale, then there simply is no such scale. And so, for Bain, all one finds are pleasures (or pains) ranked ordinally in a scale of greater and less. Thus, pleasures (and pains) differ, but not quantitatively as Bentham held; and since they do not differ quantitatively, but none the less differ, they therefore differ only qualitatively, as Mill held. Bain's position, then, is one in which pleasures (and pains) differ only qualitatively and stand in a preference relation that ranks them on a scale of more and less.

But so far has the younger Mill moved psychology that Bain is unable to recognize how far his position is from that of Bentham. For the younger Mill the claim that one can establish only an ordinal scale of preferences is sufficient to refute the idea that pleasures can be ordered qualitatively. But for Mill's successor Bain, the claim that one can establish an ordinal scale of preferences is simply all there is to the idea of a 'quantity of pleasure.' This shift in what the psychologist Bain means by 'quantity of pleasure' marks the real effect that John Stuart Mill had in transforming psychology from a branch of a priori philosophy to an empirical science. At the same time, it meant that Bain was never really able to understand Mill's point about qualitative differences among pleasures. From his point of view, to 'quantify' pleasure is simply to establish an ordinal scale. So when he reads Mill as asserting that there are qualitative differences which prevent the establishing of a quantitative order, he understands this as saying that no preference order can be established among different kinds of pleasure. This is indeed as absurd as Bain's comments imply. Except that this was not the point that the younger Mill was making. The targets at which Mill was aiming were Bentham and his associates, who held that there was not only an order of preferences but that there was a single unit of intensity that could be discovered and could yield a single cardinal scale. It is just this that explains why Bain, as sympathetic as he was to his teacher John Stuart Mill, was none the less led to advance (1882) the same invalid criticism of Mill that Seth (1911) was later to make. Such had been the change in the climate of psychology that Bain was simply unable to recognize that he himself was accepting the real point that Mill was making against the older generation of utilitarians.

If we accept Mill's point that there is no unit of pleasure (or pain) that will do the job that Bentham asks of it, then we recognize a real difficulty in the earlier utilitarianism. Bentham's ethics depend upon there being a unit; such a unit cannot be found – it is the creation of a priori metaphysics, rather than something that people could really use in calculations. Bentham's ethics thus leads inevitably to a moral scepticism. Not without reason, one early writer argued that Bentham's thinking was banal, and concluded that 'We can see nothing but the quackery – the absurd affectation of mathematical exactness in a matter which does not admit of it' (Legaré, 1845, II: 468).[18] Others, for example John Plamenatz (1949, p. 73), have made the same sort of point. It is evident in fact in Bentham's own moral reasonings. Thus, in the *Principles of Morals and Legislation* (1789), while he holds that pleasure and pain are 'names of homogeneous real entities' (1789, Ch. IV, sec. 6, note), and assumes pleasures and pains are commensurable on a single scale, he none the less also gives (Ch. V) an elaborate classification of the 'several sorts of pains and pleasures' (ibid., sec. 1). As Wesley Mitchell pointed out (1918, p. 173), this is a pattern that is repeated throughout the essay: Bentham's tool is classification, not calculation. Whatever the topic – pleasures, pains, motives, dispositions, 'cases unmeet for punishment,' offences – one discovers an elaborate classification into kinds, that is, *qualitative distinctions*. When one does find comparisons of degree, that is, supposedly quantitative comparisons, these are in fact limited to judgments of greater and lesser – and even these are for the most part limited to comparisons within the same kind. All this is clear in the following passage in which Bentham himself seems to realize how limited is his method of comparing quantities:

> punishments of different kinds are in very few instances uniformly greater one than another; especially when the lowest degrees of that which is ordinarily the greater, are compared with the highest degrees of that which is ordinarily the less: in other words, punishments of different kinds are in few instances uniformly commensurable. The only certain and universal means of making two lots of punishment perfectly commensurable, is by making the lesser an ingredient in the composition of the greater. This may be done in two ways. 1. By adding to the lesser punishment another quantity of punishment of the same kind. 2. By adding to it another quantity of a different kind. (1789, Ch. XVII, sec. 6)

While Bentham himself does not make the detailed calculations that his ethical theory asserts to be possible, he does not fail to exhort others to undertake just those calculations: 'The value of the punishment,' the magistrate is exhorted, 'must not be less in any case than what is sufficient to outweigh that of the profit of the offence' (Ch. XVI, sec. 8). His readers can be excused for taking such exhortation less than seriously. The utilitarian ethic could be an effective vehicle for arguing the case for reform only after the illusion that one could proceed by calculation was dispelled. It was the task of John Stuart Mill to end that illusion, an illusion that could be sustained in the face of the facts only through an a priori determination that it is so. Once the illusion was gone, utilitarianism could be taken seriously.

Bentham did at certain points try to do better. This was by offering an *indirect measure* of the degrees of pleasure (or pain) in terms of *money*.

> The magnitude of a pleasure, supposing it present, being given, – the value of it, if not present, is diminished by whatever it falls short of being present, even though its certainty be supposed entire. *Pleasure itself not being ponderable or measurable, to form an estimate of this diminution, take the general source, and thence representative, of pleasure, viz., money.* Take accordingly two sums of the same magnitude, say twenty pounds, the one sum receivable immediately, the other not till at the end of [10] years from present time, interest of money being (suppose) at 5 percent. – the value of the second sum will be but half that of the first; namely, ten pounds: in the same case, therefore, will be the value of two equal pleasures receivable at those several times. Just so it is with pains: and thence with exemptions from pains. (1822, p. 540, col. 2; italics added)

Bentham held this view from the beginning to the end of his career. Thus, in the 1770s manuscript Bentham writes: 'As pleasure is given by giving money, so is pain by taking it away. This latter fact stands equally uncontroverted, and is equally a matter of experience with the former ... *caeteris paribus* the [quantity of] money is the direct and proper measure and the only proper measure of that sort of pain which is produced by means of money' (1770s, p. 11 [35]); and again: 'If then between two pleasures, the one produced by the possession of money, the other not, a man had as lief enjoy the one as the other, such pleasures are to be reputed equal. But the pleasure produced by the possession of money is *as* the quantity of money that produced it: money is therefore the measure of this pleasure. But the other pleasure is equal to this: the other pleasure thereof is as the money that produces this: therefore money is also the measure of that other pleasure. It is the same between pain and pain; as also between pain and pleasure' (pp. 11–12 [36]).

Bentham is here adopting the same principle as Ricardo did in economics, that of measuring pleasures and pains indirectly by means of money. But Ricardo limited himself to the domain of economics or of political economy, the domain that Mill was later to call the 'business part of the social arrangements' (1838, p. 99). Bentham, in contrast, extends it to the whole of our life. This extension makes the proposal significant for the understanding of Bentham, since it shows that the monetary calculations are understood by Bentham to mirror fairly exactly the calculations of the felecific (and dolorific) calculus. Bentham is in fact maintaining that the whole of our life is governed by calculations of the sort found in the business part of life. It was this extension of the idea of calculation from part to all of our life that the younger Mill was to reject when he insisted that there were qualitative distinctions among pleasures that placed limits upon the role that the calculation of pluses and minuses could play in our life.

But that general point aside, the proposal will not do, not even in the limited realm of economics, as Ricardo already recognized, for the reason that value of money changes over time: the unit of money does not always buy the same unit of pleasure. In addition Bentham noticed a further reason why his proposal won't do, a reason the significance of which would not be fully understood until after Jevons and the marginalist revolution in economics. This reason why money wouldn't do as a measure of pleasure and pain is the fact of the diminishing marginal utility of money. Consider, Bentham asks us, the monarch with a million pounds a year and a labourer with twenty pounds: 'The quantity of pleasure in the breast of the monarch will naturally be greater than the quantity in the breast of the labourer ... But ... by how many times greater? Fifty thousand times? This is assuredly more than any man would take upon himself to say. A thousand times, then? – a hundred? – ten times? – five times? – twice? – which of all these shall be the number? ... For the monarch's, taking all purposes together, *five times* the labourer's seems a very large, not to say an excessive allowance: even *twice*, a liberal one' (1822, p. 541, col. 1). And so, in the end, while Bentham used money as the measure of value, he did so knowing that it could not do the job that he required of it.[19] The cardinal scale of pleasure and pain that Bentham's utilitarianism required remained an illusion; the turn to money could only postpone a short while the recognition of the illusion.

In fact, since the existence of the unit and the cardinal scale was dictated by a priori considerations, there could be no empirical check. It follows that, so far as the facts are concerned, anything could be reckoned at any value. So far as the facts are concerned, subjective whim would dictate what would be counted for how much. Of course, that subjective whim will be disguised as a supposed objective fact.

Except that, that 'fact' will be one that is imposed upon the data by an a priori psychology that claims to be empirical science. It was the younger Mill who was to make all this clear when he thought through for the first time the method of introspective analysis in psychology.

The present point, however, is that Bentham's insistence that there is a unit and cardinal scale of pleasure and pain has the consequence that his own ethics is in fact as subjective, in the sense of 'relative,' and arbitrary as those of, for example, Whewell or Sedgwick, who appealed to our moral intuitions. These philosophers in effect appealed, as Bentham put it, to 'the principle of sympathy and antipathy' (1789, Ch. II, sec. 2), which is the principle 'which approves or disapproves of certain actions ... merely because a man finds himself disposed to approve or disapprove them' (Ch. II, sec. 11). But this is not really a principle: it provides no objective standards to guide us in how to assign our feelings of moral approval and disapproval: 'this is rather a principle in name than in reality: it is not a positive principle of itself, so much as a term employed to signify the negation of all principle. What one expects to find in a principle is something that points out some external consideration, as a means of guiding the internal sentiments of approbation and disapprobation: this expectation is but ill fulfilled by a proposition, which does neither more nor less than hold up each of these sentiments as a ground and standard for itself' (Ch. II, sec. 12). This quite sound criticism of intuitionist theories in ethics applies, unfortunately, we now see, just as much to Bentham's own ethical system.

Donner has emphasized how the demand for a cardinal scale for the intensity of pleasures and pains prevented Bentham from achieving the objective standard at which he aimed (1983, pp. 490ff). She has also correctly pointed out that when Mill abandons the quest for a unit of pleasure, and introduces qualitative distinctions, the source of subjectivity or relativity in Bentham's theory is eliminated. That is, what controls the scale of preference among pleasures and pains is not subjective whim imposed a priori upon the psychological data but rather – simply the facts, the facts as explained by the method of introspective analysis. By accepting the phenomenological fact of qualitative distinctions among pleasures rather than insisting a priori that this fact could be reduced to others one felt to be more congenial, John Stuart Mill succeeded in restoring objectivity to the utilitarian principle.

Unfortunately, Donner blurs this point in with another that Mill makes in the same context. This is the issue of the 'competent judge' that Mill introduces in his discussion in 'Utilitarianism' (1861, p. 213). In Donner's view, objectivity is attained by John Stuart Mill when he as it were 'operationalizes' (1983, p. 492) the scale of pleasure by having competent judges establish the scale of preferability among pleasures. Holbrook has made a somewhat similar point. 'We cannot test the theory' that one pleasure is preferable to another, he tells us,

> by putting together an actual tribunal because no one is free from prejudice in this area. Juries taken from different times and places will give very different evaluations of pleasures. Most people are incapable of making unprejudiced evaluations in this area because a great part of their cultural backgrounds is based upon the sanction and prohibition of certain types of pleasurable activities, and these prejudices are deeply imbedded. A jury of traditional Christians is likely to place a high value on [the pleasures of] Bible study and a low value on [the pleasures of] 'exploring one's sexuality.' A different jury will arrive at very different values. Mill's solution ... is that if the judges differ then the decision of the majority is taken. (1988, p. 99)

Now, the role of the 'competent judge' is indeed important in Mill's utilitarianism. But Donner is wrong to think that objectivity is attained only when they are introduced, and that Mill's insistence upon qualitative distinctions among pleasures is of a piece with the introduction of competent judges as a way of operationalizing preferences. Holbrook is closer to the truth, when he suggests that the role of the judges is to eliminate prejudice. But even this is not accurate. And it is certainly not true that the majority vote is introduced by Mill as a way of solving an otherwise unresolvable problem of ineliminable prejudice. Three points must be made. (1) The subjective element in Bentham's utilitarianism is eliminated when Mill introduces the notion of qualitative distinctions among pleasures; the move to objectivity is not dependent upon introducing the notion of a 'competent judge.' (2) 'Operationalizing' the scale of preferences can be done quite independently of Mill's notion of a 'competent judge.' (3) The 'competent judges' are introduced by Mill primarily in the context of moral education and social reform.

Let us address these points in turn.

The first point should, by now, be clear enough. The element of subjectivity enters Bentham's system because judgments of relative preference are determined by factually arbitrary considerations disguised as the results of psychological analysis rather than by the simple psychological facts, that is, *the objective facts about what a person's relative preferences are.* John Stuart Mill made this move to objectivity possible when he rethought and clarified the notion of introspective analysis. This securing of objectivity does not presuppose that there is a special role for 'competent judges.' Moreover, contrary to what Holbrook seems to hold, there is in the case of mental facts such as those about our preferences among pleasures no special problem concerning prejudice. Prejudice can warp our judgments of fact in any area. Since mental facts do not form a special case here, they do not need a special solution. In particular, we do not need for mental facts the special device of taking a majority vote to decide what the facts are since we can never get an unprejudiced view of them, no more than we need, or use, that device for, say, claims about UFOs. The problem of prejudice is overcome, not by taking a majority vote, but by cultivating, as Mill says (1861, p. 214), the habits of self-consciousness and self-observation.

Second, when Donner refers to the role of judges as that of 'operationalizing' the scale of pleasures and pains, she clearly has in mind the problem of *making public* the facts of relative preference (1983, p. 486). These facts of relative preference are *mental* facts, and, as such, are private. We none the less share these facts, by expressing them in our overt behaviour, including our verbal behaviour. We shall have more to say about this aspect of classical (and contemporary) psychology in the next chapter. Mill does not spend much time on this sort of problem, not even in his major work on psychology, that is, the notes to this father's *Analysis*. Bain dealt with it more fully. He considers the problem posed by our 'inability to compare notes on psychological states': 'The only solution of the difficulty is ... – accept identical objective marks, as showing identical subjective [i.e., private mental] states. The same expression, behaviour, &c., under the same circumstances must be held as evidence of the same feelings. The collective manifestations are to be taken as the ultimate test of another man's mind' (1880b, p. 38). Bain proceeds to discuss the various sorts of behaviour that are relevant. He mentions 'emotional signs,' which include 'all the outward gestures, movements, exclamations, and other symptoms, excluding the voluntary conduct.' Of particular importance here are what Bain calls 'critical manifestations': 'the point of intensity of pain that makes a child cry, or puts one into a fright, or a rage, is very expressive.' In addition, 'conduct, or pursuit and avoidance, is a distinct head, and is a criterion of pleasure and pain, less liable to concealment than the emotional expression.' Finally, 'the occupation of the Thoughts is the intellectual test; most valuable as an independent testimony, and as a check upon others'; this test finds its expression in 'the Spontaneous Testimony of the individual, completed by Interrogation' (pp. 39–40). The sharing of information about the relative preferability of different pleasures clearly presupposes this sort of exercise of making our private mental states public through our behaviour, including verbal behaviour. The point to be made in this context is that this sort of 'operationalizing,' to use Donner's phrase, of our mental states has nothing to do with their objectivity – the facts of our inner mental life are as objectively there in the world as are any other facts; it has to do, rather, with their publicity, a very different issue. Donner is mistaken to think that Mill's decision of competent judges is introduced in order to secure the objectivity of judgments of relative preference.

But why, precisely, does Mill introduce this topic, to which Donner and Holbrook, quite correctly, draw our attention? And why does Mill link the appeal to 'competent judges' to a final decision being made by a majority vote, as Holbrook in particular stresses? This brings us to the third point.

Mill introduces the issue in the context of a person's gaining advice about the relative preferability of two pleasures. This sort of advice is particularly relevant in those cases where one has not experienced one of the pleasures. In order to judge of two qualitatively different pleasures that one is preferable to the other, one must experience both pleasures (1861, p. 211). Where both pleasures have been experienced, our judgments will generally be safe. Yet even here error is possible: in such cases subtle differences might be missed by one who lacks the 'habits of self-consciousness and self-observation' (p. 214). But more important, we often wish to make such judgments of relative preferability when we have *not* experienced both pleasures. This would be the case if we were wondering whether it was worth our while to cultivate certain faculties; would the resultant pleasure be sufficiently preferable to compensate for the effort of cultivation? Or again, in estimating the moral worth of our actions it is necessary to take into account whether they will bring about situations others prefer, in which case it might be that we will have to judge that certain pleasures are preferable to other pleasures and therefore are what others do indeed prefer even though we have not experienced those pleasures.

In such circumstances, says Mill, one must rely upon the 'verdict' of 'competent judges' (1861, p. 213), to wit, those who *have* experienced both pleasures and who *also* have the habits of self-consciousness and self-observation (p. 214).

Now, as Dahl (1973, p. 44) has pointed out, there is nothing in this sort or reliance upon expert judgments that is in principle paradoxical or problematic. If a person is little acquainted with wines, yet wished to pick out a good one, he is well-advised to rely upon the preferences of wine-tasting experts. These experts provide him with a way of picking out good wines. They can, however, do this only if there are differences between good and bad wines, differences of such things as bouquet, body, acidity, dryness, which the experts, through their developed gustatory and olfactory senses, can discriminate. What makes the oenologist an expert is just his capacity, acquired through learning, to distinguish just those differences that separate wines into the good, the bad, and the indifferent. What Mill is suggesting is that experts can play a similar role in judging the preferability of pleasures, that, even if we are not acquainted with, or able ourselves to discriminate those differences, we can find for ourselves a guide to their relative preferability in the judgment of certain experts, 'pleasure-experts' if you wish, or, perhaps, 'hedonologists.'

But, if there is nothing in principle wrong with this criterion, and certainly nothing inconsistent in Mill's introducing the notion, none the less even on Mill's own terms there are problems in practice that imply that even an appeal to the 'pleasure-experts' can never yield full certainty. For, as we noted above in the case of aesthetic pleasure, the whole history of an individual is relevant to determining precisely what intensity and quality of pleasure one feels. It is not the object alone that is the cause of the pleasure, but the object *plus* history. As a consequence, the same object in the context of different histories may excite slightly different pleasures in different persons. There are moreover individual differences to be taken into account. Thus, two competent judges, while not misjudging their own cases, may well disagree about the preferability of the pleasure an object excites in them, their own cases actually differing as a consequence of their different histories or of their individual differences. How, then, are we to judge about whether we ought to cultivate a pleasure when there is a disagreement between two competent judges from whom alone we can obtain a verdict?

Well, as Mill points out in his discussion of beauty, there are ingredients in the higher pleasures that are 'universally, or almost universally, present when the emotions have their characteristic peculiarity' (1869, II: 254n). As a consequence, different preference judgments about the pleasures excited by an object may largely be attributed to different histories or to individual differences rather than to features of the object. Owing to their histories or to their individual differences, some persons will judge one excited pleasure to be preferable to a second, while those who differ in these respects will judge the second to be preferable. But since the impact of individual differences or of differences in the histories will be minor compared to the impact of the more universal ingredients, we may expect *overall* that, in a group of *competent* judges, *statistically* the *majority* will agree, and, moreover, if one has oneself not yet experienced the relevant pleasures, one may none the less also expect it to be *very likely* that upon appropriate cultivation of one's faculties one would agree with the majority. Mill therefore quite reasonably concludes that 'on a question which is the best worth having of two pleasures, or which of two modes of existence is the most grateful to the feelings, apart from its moral attributes and from its consequences, the judgment of those who are qualified by knowledge of both, or, *if they differ, that of the majority among them*, must be admitted as final' (1861, p. 213; italics added).

This argument clearly assumes that persons who have the same history, that is, who have undergone the same learning processes, will have acquired the same associations, and will therefore have the same pleasure – the same with respect to quality and intensity – from the same object. All the difficulties associated with interpersonal comparisons arise here, but we should note that the assumption is plausible enough *provided that we accept, as Mill does, the deterministic principle of 'same cause, same effect'* – as Bain put it, 'The same expression, behaviour, &c., under the same circumstances must be held as evidence of the same feelings' (1880b, p. 38). Mill's position, then, is more plausible than its often hasty dismissal, for example, by Jevons (1890, pp. 284–5), would suggest. However, to pursue these issues would take us much farther afield than we can here go. The point here is the simple one that the role that Mill assigns to his 'competent judges' is not that of securing objectivity of moral judgments, as Donner (1983) has claimed.

Classical psychology, so long as the notion of introspective analysis remained unclarified, always tended to slide into arbitrariness, as philosophical theories imposed a priori upon the facts certain structures that are not really there. John Stuart Mill clarified the notion of introspective analysis and thereby enforced a strict adherence to the empirical facts. He thereby eliminated from psychology the ever-present threat of subjectivity that had previously infected that science. But once claims in psychology were subjected to empirical control, the old style of utilitarianism had also to be revised. That old style had depended upon the claim that one could quantify pleasures and pains and order them on a single cardinal scale. Once the notion of introspective analysis was clarified, the existence of such a scale could no longer be defended: careful introspective analysis, controlled not by theories but by the facts alone, could not discover that pleasures (or pains) were all of a single kind differing only in increments of the unit of intensity. All that introspective analysis reveals is that there are qualitatively distinct pleasures that can be placed on a scale of preferences that is at best ordinal. This was the point that John Stuart Mill made against the Benthamites when he insisted that utilitarianism must acknowledge qualitative differences among pleasures. In this way the subjectivism and arbitrariness, the defects of the intuitionist position, that threatened Bentham's form of utilitarianism, were exorcised. The utilitarian role could thus provide for Mill, as it could not for Bentham, an objective test for right and wrong. The moral basis of the Benthamite program of social reform was radically insecure; Mill's move transformed that basis into a secure foundation.

In principle one could easily incorporate Mill's point about qualitative differences without any radical changes in Bentham's calculus. There are, let us say, two qualitatively different orders of pleasure. Suppose that one kind is superior to the other. If one adopts the position of Hutcheson that no 'intense sensations of the lower kinds with sufficient duration may compleat our happiness' (1755, P 477), so that any quantity of pleasure of the higher kind is superior to all quantities of the lower kind, then one has a position different from that of Bentham. For, Bentham insists that there is a single scale, while the Hutchesonian position implies that there is no single quantitative ordering; for the latter there is, instead of a single scale, a sort of 'gappy' ordering in which different parts of the scale will be incommensurable with each other. On the Hutchesonian idea, the lower pleasures can be ranked quantitatively relative to each other, and the higher pleasures can be ranked quantitatively relative to each other, but comparisons between the two orders are merely those of greater and less rather than quantitative. The difficulty with this view is not that it is impossible, but rather that it seems false. There are indeed differences of a qualitative sort between pleasures, as Hutcheson and Mill insist. The pleasures of our moral sense are superior to those of, say, taste. Hutcheson's claim, that any quantity, however small, of a superior pleasure is preferable to any quantity of a lower pleasure, however large, flies in the face of the fact that, for better or for worse, slight moral scruples are often outweighed by the prospect of great material gain. The claims of conscience are often submerged by the desire for wealth. This domination of higher by lower pleasures may be *bad*, and indeed it no doubt often is. But it is none the less a *psychological fact*, and it is the latter fact, not its being regrettable, that is here significant. For, the claim that Hutcheson is making must be one of fact, and that factual claim is clearly wrong, upon the least reflection. In other words, it turns out that some quantity of the lower pleasure can outweigh some quantity of the higher pleasure, despite the overall superiority of the higher to the lower. But if there is such an overlap, then there will be a certain quantity of the lower pleasure – say, a quantity that is X times the lower unit u_L – that just matches such and such a quantity of the higher pleasure – say, a quantity that is Y times the higher unit u_H. But this means that

$$Xu_L = Yu_H$$

or in other words that

$$u_H = (Y/X)u_L$$

The unit on the scale of higher pleasures will thus be expressible in terms of the unit on the scale of lower pleasures, and the two qualitatively different portions of the scale will be fully commensurable. Thus, as long as there is overlap between the higher and the lower pleasures the overall utilitarian calculus goes forward without a hitch, just as Bentham thought it would. In this sense, it is perfectly possible to accept the claim that there are qualitative differences among pleasures and also accept the full utilitarian calculus as Bentham conceived it.[20]

Yet Mill rejected more than this. He rejected the very idea that the calculations of the sort found in the 'business part of the social arrangements' (1838, p. 99) could be extended to the whole of life. In his earliest essay on Bentham, he complains that Bentham 'supposes mankind to be swayed by only a part of the inducements which really actuate them; but of that part he imagines them to be much cooler and more thoughtful calculators than they really are' (1833, p. 17). Mill criticizes Bentham's psychology. Bentham's list of motives, or 'springs of action,' is one 'from which some of the most important are left out'; it wrongly emphasizes the idea that 'all our acts are determined by pains and pleasures *in prospect*'; it implies that all motivation is a calculus of 'consequences' and thereby omits many important motives, including 'conscience, or the feeling of duty'; Bentham's list of motives, insofar as it omits 'the moral sense,' is inferior to Hartley's (1833, pp. 12–13). He put the same point a little later in this way: 'Whatever can be understood or whatever done without reference to moral influences, his [Bentham's] philosophy is equal to; where those influences require to be taken into account, it is at fault. He committed the mistake of supposing that the business part of human affairs was the whole of them; all at least that the legislator and the moralist had to do with. Not that he disregarded moral influences when he perceived them; but his want of imagination, small experience of human feelings of the filiation and connexion of feelings with one another, made this rarely the case' (1838, pp. 99–100). Mill thus separates the area where calculation is appropriate and the area where it is not; the latter includes the motives associated with the moral sense. But the latter area is that which 'Utilitarianism' ascribes to the qualitatively superior pleasures. The qualitative distinctions among pleasures, while they determine an order of greater and less, do not enter into the sort of scale that is appropriate for the lower pleasures, those of the business part of life. There is therefore for John Stuart Mill no possibility of there being a single cardinal scale of pleasures and pains of the sort envisaged by the earlier generation of utilitarians as represented by Bentham. Careful psychological analysis, the 'habits of self-consciousness and self-observation' (1861, p. 214), eliminated the notion of ranking all pleasures on the basis of a single unit of intensity.[21]

Thus passed the illusion of a generation of ethical theorists and social reformers. Utilitarian theory was freed from the subjectivism and relativity implicit in the illusion of the unit of intensity. And in place of the illusion of a cardinal scale of pleasures and pains, the doctrine was given all that it needed, namely, a notion of maximization based on an ordinal scale determined by the empirical psychological facts about our preferences. John Stuart Mill thus left utilitarianism standing on a much more solid foundation than Bentham had done. This was Mill's major achievement in ethical theory. It was achieved through his recognition of the role of qualitative differences among pleasures and pains. And this he could not have achieved had he not carefully rethought the notion of introspective analysis, to transform it from a method that could, at the behest of a priori metaphysics, run roughshod over the empirical facts into a legitimate method of empirical research in psychology.

EIGHT

Whatever Happened to Classical Psychology?

1 Introduction: The Idea of an Objective Science of Psychology

Until the twentieth century, psychology consisted largely of the introspective psychology practised by the Mills and refined and developed experimentally by their successors, such as John Stuart Mill's student Alexander Bain in Britain, and especially the German workers who succeeded the founder of the first laboratory for experimentation in psychology, Wilhelm Wundt. While this development of introspective psychology was going on, there were also, partly independently of, and partly in concert with psychology, rapid developments in the science of physiology,[1] and its relevance to psychology was becoming ever more evident. John Stuart Mill himself acknowledged the relevance of physiology to psychology in his *Logic* (1872a, VI, iv, 2, 4), and had in an essay on Bain's psychology complimented the latter on his giving physiology greater emphasis than psychologists previously had done (1859). In his own practice, however, the younger Mill had little to do with that side of psychology; the notes to his father's *Analysis* remain determinedly introspective. It was especially with Wundt, who wedded British introspectionism with the Continental tradition deriving from Descartes's physiological speculations, that physiological concerns became as important in psychological research as introspective analysis.[2] Mill himself distinguished between data obtained by introspection, that is, by 'practised self-consciousness and self-observation,' and data obtained by 'observation of others' (1861, p. 237). Since data of the latter sort are public, let us call them 'objective,' and data of the former sort 'subjective.' This distinction between the public and the private is common-sensical, and while it does raise a variety of philosophical problems, we can here take the distinction for granted, and need not attempt to solve, or even discuss, those problems.[3] We should note, however, that this sense of 'objective' in which it means 'intersubjective' is different from that sense of 'objective' in which the objective is contrasted to the subjective in the sense of the relative. For, the report of a subjective state – for example, 'I am now feeling a pain' – is as objectively true as a statement of objective data – for example, 'This is a chair' – that is, neither the statement of subjective data nor the statement of objective data is relative in the way in which value judgments are relative. Note, though, that a statement that one has a certain value or is making a certain value judgment, for example, 'I morally approve of so-and-so,' is, upon the relativist account of values, an objective (vs. relative) statement about subjective (vs. objective) facts. The present point is that for the classical psychologists, from James Mill through his son to Wilhelm Wundt and then beyond, the laws that psychology aimed to discover were for the purpose of explaining the subjective part of our life. To be sure, among the laws that they proposed as part of psychology were some that included, where relevant, not only subjective factors among the variables but also objective factors. But the objective factors were included only to the extent that they were required in order to explain the subjective; the aim remained that of explaining the subjective.

What happened in the twentieth century was the disappearance of the subjective from psychology. The data are now of three sorts: environmental, physiological, and behavioural. All are objective. The laws psychology aims to discover mention variables of these three sorts, but not subjective factors. And the laws are for the purpose of explaining not mental events, that is, not our subjective experience, but rather our behaviour. The science of the subjective that was the concern of classical psychology has been replaced by the objectivist science of behaviourism.

This change is perhaps not so radical a one as the bald statement suggests. After all, our subjective states often find expression in our behaviour. For example, that we are in pain finds expression behaviourally in infants in crying and wincing, and in adults trained to a greater stoicism it finds expression as a *disposition* (not always actualized) to wince; while our conscious awareness of pain finds expression in the verbal behaviour of saying 'I am in pain' or at least in the *disposition* to say 'I am in pain.' One can here use the effect (behaviour, including the disposition to certain behaviour) to refer to the cause (the mental state). In this way, talking about behaviour can be an indirect way of talking about subjective experience. Moreover, of course, to eschew talking about subjective experience is not to deny either its existence or, for many contexts other than science, its vital significance. None the less, once all this is said, the shift from classical psychology to behaviourism is still one that is dramatic indeed.

John Stuart Mill pointed out that our sensations are preceded by physiological processes. 'The laws of this portion of our nature – the varieties of our sensations and the physical conditions on which they proximately depend – manifestly belong to the province of Physiology' (1872a, p. 850). But, while this is undoubtedly true of sensations, it is a further issue whether it is true of other mental (subjective) phenomena. On Mill's view, while it is *possible* that other mental phenomena are similarly dependent upon physical states, whether this possibility is fact is a question for which the data are not yet all in:

> Whether the remainder of our mental states are similarly dependent on physical conditions, is one of the *vexatae questiones* in the science of human nature. It is still disputed whether our thoughts, emotions, and volitions are generated through the intervention of material mechanism; whether we have organs of thought' and of emotion in the same sense in which we have organs of sensation. Many eminent physiologists hold the affirmative. These contend that a thought (for example) is as much the result of nervous agency as a sensation; that some particular state of our nervous system, in particular of that central portion of it called the brain, invariably precedes, and is pre-supposed by, every state of our consciousness ... On this theory the uniformities of succession among states of mind would be mere derivative uniformities, resulting from the laws of succession of the bodily states which cause them. There would be no original mental laws ... and mental science would be a mere branch, though the brightest and most recondite branch, of the science of Physiology. (1872a, p. 850)

Mill in this context (ibid.) mentions Comte as one who held that the physiological was the *only* way to approach psychology. This notion is rejected by Mill, who elsewhere, in his essay 'Auguste Comte and Positivism' (1865), saw this, along with Comte's political attitudes, as one of the serious, and disastrous, limitations of French positivism. Comte is criticized for giving psychology no place in his grand classification of the sciences; Comte's failure to take psychology seriously as a mental science is not a 'mere hiatus' in his system, but 'the parent of serious errors in his attempt to create a Social Science' (1865,

p. 298). Comte, we are told, 'always speaks of it [psychology] with contempt,' and reduces it, in fact, to a branch of physiology, totally rejecting introspection or 'psychological observation properly so called ... internal consciousness' (p. 296). Comte relies, as his 'Organon for the study of "the moral and intellectual functions,"' upon Gall's phrenology, which already at that time was thoroughly discredited as a science. In the *Logic*, Mill points out that the claim that every mental state has a 'nervous state' as 'its immediate and proximate cause,' if not yet sufficiently supported by inductive evidence to be worthy of assertion as a statement of law, is at least thought by many 'eminent physiologists' to be worthy of 'affirmation' as a 'theory'; though it 'cannot hitherto be said to be proved,' it is none the less 'extremely probable' (1872a, p. 851). But while this abstract theory, that *there are* such physiological causes, is worthy of affirmation, we do not yet have instantial evidence for its truth. For, while we may well have reason to believe that there are such physiological causes, we do not know (then or now) *specifically* what those states of the nervous system are: we are as yet 'wholly ignorant of the characteristics of these nervous states' (ibid.).[4] We are therefore in no position to deduce the laws of succession of mental phenomena from those of physiology, and 'all real knowledge of them [the laws of mental phenomena] must continue, for a long time at least, if not always, to be sought in the direct study, by observation and experiment, of the mental successions themselves' (ibid.). Comte shows no knowledge of, and makes no use of, the work of Hartley, Brown, and James Mill, and still less does he notice that the real progress in psychology has come not from Gall but from Bain and Herbert Spencer (1865, p. 298). As Mill sees it, this failure is a real, and error-producing, gap in Comte's scheme to create a social science.

However, even if Mill did not think a purely objective science of man was, in his day, something that it was feasible to attempt to practise, he none the less suggests that it is a possibility that is not merely logical but one for which there is sufficient tentative evidence that renders it at least plausible as an account of human nature and of the relation of mind to body.

What Mill has in mind is clear enough. For each sort of mental state MS there is a corresponding sort of bodily, or, as Mill says, nervous state NS such that whenever there is a certain MS_1, then, and only then, there is a certain NS_1, that is,

(*) MS_1 if and only if NS_1

Clearly, then, with a set of such laws linking each mental state to a corresponding bodily state it will always be possible, in principle at least, for any law of succession of mental states

(1) Whenever MS_1 then MS_2

to effect a "translation" into a purely objective law about bodily states

(2) MS_1 if and only if NS_1
    MS_2 if and only if NS_2

hence

(3) whenever NS_1 then NS_2

In this way, given such laws as (*), laws about subjective phenomena can all be 'translated' into laws about objective states. If such 'translation' is possible, then all reference to the subjective is in principle eliminable, and the science of man can be stated in purely objective terms. Conversely, of course, if we have the law of physiology (3) and the laws (2) connecting body to mind, then it is also possible, as Mill says, to treat the laws (1) about mental, or subjective, states as laws derivative from, and explained by, the objective laws of physiology, together, of course, with the laws that connect body to mind. What the existence of such laws as (*) establishes is that there is a *parallelism* between mind and body. What Mill is claiming, then, quite correctly, is that, *if the parallelistic hypothesis is true, then the subjective side of man can be reduced to and explained by the purely objective side, and a wholly objective science of man is possible.*

It should be emphasized, however, that to say this is not to say that the subjective is somehow eliminated. The 'translation' from the subjective to the objective is effected by the *laws* (*) of parallelism. These are, let us emphasize, *laws*, not conventions or definitions. As laws they are synthetic, matter-of-fact generalizations describing the regular coexistence of logically independent, or, as Mill says, 'distinguishable,' facts; and where we have 'distinguishable sensations or other feelings of our nature' the laws that relate these feelings to other things as causes are 'ultimate laws' that cannot be deduced from and thereby 'resolved into other and more general ones' (1872a, III, xiv, 1, 2). On Mill's account, then, *the possibility of an objective science of man does not entail the disappearance of the subjective.*

Mill, however, having allowed the *plausibility* of the parallelistic hypothesis, and therefore of the notion of an objective science of man, does not, as we have seen, think it at all worthwhile to pursue psychology as a purely objective study. For, even if the evidence we have for the hypothesis were strong, which in his day, perhaps, it was not, it remains that one had still not discovered the *specific* character of the bodily states that are parallel to the mental states. One could not, therefore, treat psychological laws of succession as derivative from the laws of physiology. The laws of psychology, then, had to continue to be studies directly, in their own right, by observation and experiment.

Within half a century this sober judgment had been overturned, the subjective had disappeared from psychology, and that science was being pursued in a purely objective fashion. What happened?

It is the purpose of this chapter to answer this question. What made it possible in the first place was that scientists became convinced of the truth of parallelism. The next section discusses parallelism and the evidence that convinced Mill's successors, such as Bain, that this hypothesis, in spite of a variety of problems that philosophers tried to raise, is true. After that, however, in the following section, we show that the research program of classical psychology can be restated in objective terms. That this is possible should not surprise us: after all, the truth of the parallelistic hypothesis will ensure that every statement of classical psychology about a subjective state has a translation in objectivist terms. Thus, *if behaviourism broadly understood is the thesis that an objective science of man is possible then there is nothing incompatible between behaviourism and introspective psychology.* In other words, there is no reason in principle why introspective psychology should not have continued its program of research within the behaviourist framework for psychology that emerged early in the twentieth century. Yet in the end that research program died out. The final section of the chapter discusses why this happened.

2   Parallelism[5]

Consider the following model of a causally closed system which has certain further states running parallel to part of it. The example is far-fetched, but for that very reason is useful in making the relevant points.

The causally closed system is the solar system. Assume that Newton's explanation of the motions of the planets in it is sound. We have ten objects, the nine planets and the sun. The (complete) set of relevant variables consists of the masses (m), positions (p), and velocities (v) of the ten objects. The system is closed. A possible state of the system consists of each of the relevant variables taking on a specific value. There is a process law such that, given any state of the system (actual or possible), all other states (that it does, or would, have) can be deduced. Thus, given the process law, one state determines all other states; any one state *causally determines* all other states. The system is thus (causally) *closed*, (causally) *complete*, and (causally) *deterministic*.

Now let us suppose, contrary to fact, that colour (c) is a further variable, and that *colours are correlated to velocities*, that is, that for each velocity v_i, there corresponds one and only one colour, c_i, such that an object has the velocity v_i if an only if it has the colour c_i:

(+) v_i if and only if c_i

Like the laws (*) that state mind-body parallelism, the (supposed) laws (+) state a parallelism between colour and velocity.

The system of masses, positions, and velocities – call this the 'physical system' – is closed, complete, and deterministic; the system consisting of the colours is not.

There are laws of succession among the colours. Given the laws of the parallelism, these laws about the colour system are deducible from, and in this sense reducible to, the laws for the physical system. However, such reduction *does not eliminate* the colours; the laws (+) are laws, not definitions, and relate distinguishable variables. The parallelism does mean, however, that one can give an explanation of the physical system in terms of a process law, that is, as we saw in chapter 2, an explanation that meets the ideal explanation, without mentioning colours. Thus, in order to explain, and even to fully explain, the physical system and its process, one *need* not refer to the events in the colour system.

In contrast, given the process law for the physical system and the laws of the parallelism, there will be derivative laws relating colours to physical variables. For example, suppose that it is a law of succession among velocities that

(a) Whenever v_1 then v_2

Then, given the law of parallelism that

(b) c_1 if and only if v_1

it is also a law of succession that

(c) Whenever c_1 then v_2

Although we do not *need* to cite colour events in order to explain events in the physical system, we *can* so refer *if we wish*: laws such as (c) yield perfectly good explanations for physical events.

Let us say that, if we *do not need* to take into account a variable if we are to explain events in a system, then that variable does *not interact* with the variables that describe those events. In our little contrary-to-fact example, colour does not interact with velocity; however, mass and position do interact with velocity.

Suppose that besides the laws (a), (b), and (c), we also have the laws

(a') Whenever v_k then v_l

(b') c_k if and only if v_k

(c') Whenever c_k then v_l

Suppose that there is a planet that in fact has the colour c_k. In that case, its next velocity will be v_l, as law (c') implies. If the planet has colour c_k, then it does not have the colour c_l. But the law permits us to infer[6] the contrary-to-fact conditional that

If the planet were c_r then it would be v_l

Thus, although colour does not interact, it remains true that a planet's colour *makes a difference* to the velocity of that planet. Generalizing, let us say that, if we have two sorts of variable *f* and *g* and laws that permit us to assert the counterfactual conditional that

If *f* were different then *g* would be different

then (variable) *f makes a difference to* (the variable) *g*. Finally, let us say that if *f* makes a difference to *g* then *f* is *(causally) productive of g*.[7] Thus, velocity is causally productive of velocity in the physical system that we are considering. But since colour makes a difference to velocity, it too is causally productive of velocity. Colour, however, does not interact. Thus, *even if we have a system with a variable that does not interact with certain others, there may none the less be laws, in particular laws of parallelism, which entail that that non-interacting variable is causally productive of states of the system as defined by the other variables.*

One complication is worth developing. Let us suppose that the laws of parallelism are not one-to-one as we have assumed, but one-to-many:

(β) c_i if and only if: either v_m or v_n

Suppose also that we have the laws for the physical system

(d) Whenever v_m then v_p
     Whenever v_n then v_q

and the further parallelistic laws

(β') $\begin{array}{l} c_j \text{ if and only if: either } v_p \text{ or } v_r \\ c_k \text{ if and only if: either } v_q \text{ or } v_s \end{array}$

This leads us to the laws

(e) $\begin{array}{l} \text{Whenever } c_i \text{ then either } v_p \text{ or } v_q \\ \text{Whenever } c_i \text{ then either } c_j \text{ or } c_k \end{array}$

Notice that both these laws predict not a determinate value for the variable but a disjunctive or *determinable* value; this means that these laws are gappy or imperfect relative to the laws (d) that make *determinate* predictions.[8] Thus, where a parallelistic connection is one-to-many from reduced to reducing variables then it is possible that when we reduce the one set of laws by means of the parallelistic connections (β), (β'), *we reduce a set of imperfect laws to another set that is less imperfect.* Whether this will actually occur will depend, of course, upon all three sorts of laws: the parallelistic laws, the reduced laws, and the reducing laws.

Let us now apply some lessons from this model to the mind-body case. What holds for the colour-velocity parallelism in the model applies, clearly, to the mind-body parallelism also.

Assume to begin with that the mental events of our subjective experience are law-governed. Although some philosophers deny this in the name of free will, John Stuart Mill was not one of them (1872a, VI, ii). Mill's view of causation is Hume's: objectively there is nothing to causation, or, more generally, lawfulness, than regularity. And among our free choices, there are regularities. There are those who, when offered a choice of soft drinks, invariably choose a cola: the choice is none the less free for its being invariably the same. Regularity, that is, causation, is not, in short, contrary to free choice. Nor, therefore, is it at odds with our moral system in which people are held to be morally responsible for, and hence subject to rewards and punishments in respect of, actions that result from their free choices. What is contrary to free choice and moral responsibility is, as Mill points out, not causal determination but coercion, that is, an external force that deters us from choosing to do what we prefer to do. Indeed, the whole point of education and moral training, and of self-cultivation too, is to so shape our preferences as to determine our future free choices. It may at times be true that a certain degree of regularity in our choices is evidence of rigidity and a lack of creativity; but creativity itself is subject to laws. For, creativity is nothing other than learning how to respond in appropriate ways to new sorts of situations, and is therefore subject to the same general laws of learning that constitute the basic laws of human nature. From the point of view of the spectator there is no reason whatsoever why a novel response of a person being observed should not be predicable, that is, subsumable under a regularity, and therefore caused.[9] Let us take it as given, then, that mental events – our sensations, perceptions, desires, aversions, loves, hates, volitions, and all – are throughout subject to law.

Now, it is common sense that our preferences determine our volitions and that our volitions in turn determine our actions. These are regularities that we all know to be true, and that have the status of laws. On the basis of these laws we know that, when we freely choose, if our preferences were different we would choose differently, and if our choices were different our actions would be different. We know, moreover, sufficient laws about the physical world to know that if our actions were different, various other events in the world would be different. The claim that our choices and our actions make no difference to the course of events is *fatalism*. Fatalism is, of course, true in certain cases. Thus, in respect of what will happen if we step out a window twelve storeys above the ground, fatalism is the correct view – our choices and actions will make no difference to whether we are subject to gravity and to whether we will hit the ground; in general, our being subject to the law of gravity is one point where we are entitled to be fatalistic. But as a general thesis about all choices and all actions fatalism is, we know, false. Thus, as we put it above, since they make a difference, our choices are (often) causally productive of our actions and our actions are (often) causally productive of further consequences. This is common sense, and it is this common sense that is at the core of the practice, central to our system of morality, of holding people morally responsible for actions that result from their free choices and for the consequences, or at least the reasonably anticipated consequences, of those actions.

John Stuart Mill, as we saw, suggested that parallelism is, quite plausibly, the correct description of the relation between mind and body. The discussion of the fiction of the coloured planets makes clear the following four points. First, *upon the parallelistic hypothesis, mind does not interact with body.* Second, it is therefore *possible to explain all human behaviour by laws that refer only to objective facts.* However, third, *to say that an objective science of human behaviour is in this sense possible is not to deny either the existence or the importance for many purposes of the subjective side of human nature.* Moreover, fourth *the parallelistic hypothesis and its consequence that mind does not interact with body is compatible with maintaining the common-sense position that mind makes a difference to body and with the common practice of ascribing moral responsibility.*

The doctrine that body is causally productive of mind, but that mind is not causally productive of body, is often called 'epiphenomenalism.' We see that parallelism is *not* a version of epiphenomenalism in this sense. To be sure, upon the parallelistic hypothesis, mind and body do not interact. Moreover, the mental process cannot be causally complete and closed, whereas the physical process can. None the less, parallelism squares, as epiphenomenalism by definition does not, with the common-sense claim that our preferences and our choices are causally productive of (the bodily events which are) our actions. Parallelism must, therefore, *not* be identified with epiphenomenalism.[10]

Mill took it as clear that man was able to shape his own nature. We have noted above, following Donner (1983), the emphasis that Mill gives to the idea of cultivating our higher nature. Mill, in other words, accepted that mind is causally productive of changes in matter. Thus, in accepting parallelism he also rejected epiphenomenalism. Later thinkers such as T.H. Huxley (1874) were not so careful, however, and suggested that the mind-body relation can be best understood in epiphenomenalistic terms. Other thinkers and scientists were unwilling to go so far, and accepted the common sense of parallelism while rejecting epiphenomenalism on the Millian ground that mind is in fact causally productive of changes in the material world.

Among these was William B. Carpenter, the great British physiologist, who did important work in comparative anatomy but also extended his physiological researches to consider, as the title of one of his books has it, the *Principles of Human Physiology: With Their Chief Application to Psychology, Pathology, Therapeutics, Hygiene, and Forensic Medicine* (1855), and who was later to write *Principles of Mental Physiology, with Their Applications to the Training and Discipline of the Mind, and the Study of Its Morbid Conditions* (1890). Carpenter expressed the parallelistic position by asking us to consider 'that mortal contest which [fable tells us] was once carried-on by two knights respecting the material of a shield which they saw from opposite sides, the one maintaining it to be made of gold, the other of silver, and each proving to be in the right as regarded the half seen by himself' (1855, p. 547). The 'materialists' and the 'spiritualists' are like these two knights, each getting half the picture right but ignoring the other half, and ignoring too what he elsewhere refers to as the 'intimacy of that *nexus* between Mental and Bodily activity' (1890, p. 696). There is a moral, he thinks, that is to be drawn.

...the moral of this fable, as regards our present enquiry, is, that as the entire shield was really made-up of a gold-half and a silver-half *which joined each other at midway,* so the Mind and the Brain, notwithstanding those differences in *properties* which place them in different philosophical categories, are so intimately blended in their *actions,* that more valuable information is to be gained by seeking for it at the points of contact, that can be obtained by the prosecution of those older methods of research, in which Mind has been studied by Metaphysicians altogether without reference to its material instruments, whilst the Brain has been dissected by Anatomists and analyzed by Chemists, as if they expected to map-out the course of Thought, or to weigh or measure the intensity of Emotion. (1855, p. 547)

At the same time, Carpenter clearly distinguishes parallelism from epiphenomenalism, accepting the former and rejecting the latter. Epiphenomenalism had been proposed by T.H. Huxley who argued that we are nothing but 'parts of the great series of causes and effects which, in unbroken continuity, composes that which is, and has been, and shall be – the sum of existence' (1874, p. 577). On this view, Carpenter suggests, people are automata, with no duty, no obligations, no responsibility (1890, p. xlvi). But this position is absurd, so Carpenter rejects the epiphenomenalism of Huxley (1890, p. xlviii). What he objects to is the materialist claim that 'the highest elevation of Man's *physical* nature is to be attained by due attention to all the conditions which favour his *physical* development,' where this is taken to imply that man's 'fancied power of self-direction [is] altogether a delusion' and that 'the notions of *duty* or *responsibility* have no real foundation, Man's character being formed *for* him, and not *by* him' (1855, p. 548). For it is in fact evident that this position is false; man 'really possesses *a self-determining power,* which can rise above all the promptings of external suggestion, and can, to a certain extent, mould external circumstances to its own requirements, instead of being completely subjugated by them' (p. 549). This is clear from 'the direct testimony of Consciousness, in regard not only to the existence of this Volitional power, but also to the Self-determination of the Ego in the exercise of it' (1890, p. xxiv). It was Carpenter's – and Mill's – parallelism rather than Huxley's epiphenomenalism that was to become the working hypothesis of the practising psychologist and physiologist.

Parallelism is compatible with our ordinary common-sense view that mind makes a difference, and with our ordinary practice of ascribing moral responsibility. Any position that is to be reckoned at all plausible must meet this condition. But, of course, *interactionism* meets this condition also. On this latter position, no explanation of our bodily states and of our actions can be complete unless mental variables are taken into account. Interactionism is compatible with scientific determinism, and, if properly circumscribed, with the ascription of moral responsibility.[11] The difference between parallelism and interactionism lies in the fact that on the former view the physical system is causally closed whereas on the latter it is not.

It is this last that convinced *scientists* that parallelism was *in fact* the correct account of the mind-body relation. Descartes had wanted to defend interactionism but also the sufficiency of materialistic explanations for the material world. The latter was the motive force behind his physiological speculations about the bodily processes underlying the passions. Descartes thought that he could reconcile interactionism with the causal closure of the material world by having mind affect only the direction and not the speed of the (material) animal spirits in the brain. It is, however, not the product of mass and speed that is conserved, as Descartes thought, but momentum, the product of mass and velocity, where velocity is speed in a certain direction. Descartes's proposal therefore results in violations of the law of conservation of momentum. Since the latter law is well confirmed, Descartes's version of interactionism was quickly rejected. For those who accepted his speculative view that all physical phenomena could be reduced to mechanical processes in which the law of conservation of momentum held – that is, an atomism in which all causation is by collision of material particles – then the result was soon a picture of man, for example, that of La Mettrie in his *L'Homme machine*, in which mind does not interact with body. It was obvious to most, however, that the physics which the materialists needed to secure their picture of man was in fact almost wholly speculative. There were many physical processes besides the mechanical, for example, chemical or physiological, for which the reduction either to each other or to mechanistic atomism was in no way confirmed or even plausible theory, but pure speculation. The mechanical therefore was hardly considered to form a closed system, and if other factors such as the chemical or the physiological interacted with the mechanical, so that, for example, momentum was not in general conserved, then there was no reason to suppose that the mental, too, could not interact: common sense tended to support it, and science did not exclude it.

As both defenders of parallelism, such as Bain (1873, p. 195), Carpenter (1855, p. 696), and Wundt (1902, pp. 360ff), and its critics, such as Ward (1915, pp. 330f, 355ff), indicate, the crucial turning-point in favour of that hypothesis was the acceptance after the mid-nineteenth century of the law of the conservation of energy, what Carpenter (1855, p. 696) referred to as the 'Convertibility of the Physical Forces.' What this law asserts is that in every physical process there is a characteristic sort of energy, this energy has a mechanical equivalent, each form of energy can be transformed into the others, and the total energy of a causally closed system is conserved. But, while we can define the concept of energy for physical systems, which are *extended* (Bain 1873, p. 123), mental phenomena are impalpable (Ward 1915, p. 331) in the sense of being *unextended, and existing in time alone* (Bain pp. 135ff; Carpenter 1855, p. 552). A perceiving, for example, occurs at a time, and, indeed, even has some temporal duration, but it is not spatially extended, nor, though it is associated with a particular body, is it even at a place. 'When, as in pure feeling ... we change from the object attitude to the subject attitude, we have undergone a change not to be expressed by place; the fact is not properly described by the transition from the *external* to the *internal*, for that is still a change in the region of the extended. The only adequate expression is a CHANGE OF STATE ... By various theologians, heaven has been spoken of as not a place, but a *state*; and this is the only phrase that I can find suitable to describe the vast, though familiar and easy, transition from the material or extended, to the immaterial or unextended side of our being' (Bain 1873, pp. 136–7). The point is that, if all energy has a mechanical equivalent, and can be transformed into that equivalent, then the transformation must occur *at a place*. But, if the transformation occurs at a place, then the energy must be *localized* at that place (Bain, p. 195; Ward 1915, p. 173). Since mind is not localized, the law of conservation of energy is incompatible with mind interacting with the body. We must therefore be expected to fail in any attempt to discover, in the physiological processes that underlie our subjective experiences, a point at which the physical state is insufficient for its successor and at which mental states must be invoked in order to give an adequate causal account. And in any case, independently of the law of conservation of energy, we have, on the basis of inductive evidence, no reason to suppose that there are causal gaps in the physiological processes underlying thought that can be closed only by introducing mental states as relevant variables (Bain, p. 131). That is, in short, all evidence points to physical processes being closed relative to the mental: given the evidence of physics and physiology, *mind does not interact with body*. The only way to reconcile this with the common sense that mind does make a difference is to accept the parallelistic hypothesis. The data that support the common sense that mental states are causally productive of bodily states, together with the data that support the non-interaction of mind and body, *jointly confirm the parallelistic hypothesis*.

The objections that were raised were more often philosophical than scientific. Both materialists and idealists raised the problem of how two sorts of things so different as mind and body could possibly interact (cf. Bain 1873, pp. 188–9, 195; Ward 1915, pp. 472f). On the empiricist account of science of John Stuart Mill this turns out to be no real problem at all. For, given the Humean account of laws, which Mill accepts, according to which causation, objectively considered, consists in regularity or constant conjunction, the problem of mind-body interaction dissolves. As Hume himself remarked, the problem arises only when one assumes that there is in things besides regularity some unanalysable power that is supposed to yield a necessary connection between cause and effect. 'That their motion [i.e., when we "apply our limbs to their proper use and office"] follows the command of the will is a matter of common experience, like other natural events: But the power or energy by which this is effected, like that of other natural events, is unknown and inconceivable' (1777, p. 67). If, as Descartes held, the property of being mental excludes the property of being material, so that nothing can be both mental and material, it is indeed difficult to understand how a power in one side could so necessarily tie that substance to the other as to impose a change on that second substance, which, however, with equal necessity excludes the first: Descartes is insisting that the two substances are so unlike as to exclude each other and also insisting that far from excluding each other they are necessarily tied together. Epiphenomenalism, restricting causal power to the material, is often, as, for example, perhaps in Hobbes (1651) and perhaps in Huxley (1874), a response to this problem; but in denying that mental states can be causally productive of bodily states it conflicts with common sense. Indeed, insofar as the Cartesian position makes, as Hume says, an insolvable mystery of the mind-body connection, it too conflicts with common sense. But so long as one rejects the idea that causation involves a necessary connection, there is no problem: two kinds of substance or process can exclude each other while yet having events in the one kind constantly conjoined to events in the other kind. Science, restricting itself to the search for matter-of-fact regularities, has no problem with the fact that mental states are causally productive of bodily states. Nor, in particular, does parallelism have any difficulty with that fact.

It is sometimes suggested that to insist upon a distinction of mind and body and then to affirm a parallelism between them is to leave the conjunction as a mere correlation unexplained by any deeper connection; but science of course wishes to go beyond correlation to causation, and so parallelism is simply bad science (cf. Ward 1915, pp. 317ff). This insisting that science go beyond correlation, is, however, unfair to the Humean position on causation. It suggests that when the Humean restricts himself to regularities, he abandons the search for causes to restrict himself to correlations. There is, however, a common-sense distinction between correlation and causation, and it is wrong to suggest that the Humean ignores it. To the contrary, he accepts it, and then goes on to explain the difference between the two, not as a difference between a regularity and a necessary connection, but as a difference between two different kinds of regularity.[12] As Mill (1872, III, v, 6) makes clear, the distinction between correlation and causation is essentially one between a conditioned regularity and an unconditioned regularity. So the Humean does *not* ignore the difference between correlation and causation and, indeed, insists upon proceeding beyond the former to the latter, that is, from the conditioned to the unconditioned, since such a development moves science from the more to the less imperfect, or, in other words, from a weaker to a stronger explanation. The ideal would be ultimately to derive all correlations from what, in chapter 2, we called process laws. It may turn out, however, that there are regularities of coexistence that cannot be deduced from process laws (cf Mill 1872a, III, xxii, 3). In that case they remain as regularities irreducible to causal regularities. The laws of geometry are of this sort. So are the laws that, upon the parallelistic hypothesis, describe the mind-body relationship. This ultimacy is a *matter of fact*. It may well be that in a neater world that fit more nearly our ideals of scientific explanation there would be no such 'nomological danglers'; but there is no reason a priori to expect that the world conforms exactly to what, ideally, we would like it to be. The world is what it is, and if there are in it laws that are 'nomological danglers' that, too, is a fact. If such laws are in fact ultimate, the parallelist, when he recognizes that fact cannot be criticized for failing to seek a 'deeper' explanation; so to criticize him is to ask him to wish away what is unalterable fact.[13]

Many of the arguments against parallelism turned upon its apparent exclusion of mind from a place in determining what happens in the world. But most often they turned, as in Ward's case, upon rejecting the idea of causation as regularity. The notion was that if the connection is one of mere regularity then there is no causal impact of mind on body, and the mental events are mere epiphenomena to the events in the causally complete and closed physical universe; in which case, of course, there is no question of holding people morally responsible for their actions: 'the naturalists ... say ... : The physical world is a complete whole in itself, and goes along altogether by itself ... The very same laws fundamentally, that determine the varying motion of the solar system, bring together from the four corners of the earth the molecules that from time to time join in the dance we know as the brain of a Dante creating immortal verse, or as the brain of a Borgia teeming with unheard crimes. And finally we must say: The presence of mental epiphenomena is as irrelevant and immaterial to the one result as is their absence to the other' (Ward 1915, p. 353). But this is simply wrong if one accepts both parallelism and the Humean account of causation. On the parallelistic hypothesis, the physical world may well be causally closed and complete. Certainly at least, mind does not interact; that, after all, is the point of parallelism. But to say this is also, as we have seen, and as Ward does not recognize, compatible with holding that mental events make a difference to, and are causally productive of, physical events, allowing, therefore, that people can be held morally responsible for their actions.

It is equally unfair of Ward to object against Wundt's position (1893) on parallelism, that it begins 'by formulating parallelism with causal independence, and yet in the end subordinating the physical series to the psychical,' since it accepts the doctrine 'that the soul shapes the body' and assigns 'to voluntary impulses the rôle of *primum movens* in organic development' (1915, p. 324). This is not the place to deal with Wundt in detail. Suffice it to say that he rejects both the metaphysical dualism of substances of the Cartesian sort and also epiphenomenalistic materialism, and takes parallelism to be confined to the claim that there are matter-of-fact regularities connecting mind and body, or, as it was then put, *psychosis* and *neurosis*. But on such a parallelism, it is possible to 'translate' all mentalistic laws into physical laws. This is all that there is to Wundt's claims about how the states of our soul, that is, our preferences through our volitions, shape our organic development and about how they all have, in principle, 'translations' into physicalistic language. He can, therefore, quite legitimately claim, as we have argued, that mind *does make a difference* to what happens in the physical world, even if it does not interact. Ward's criticism of Wundt is thus simply mistaken.

The problems that were raised with parallelism tended to be in this way mostly philosophical and, in fact, mostly turning upon the way parallelism supposedly eliminated the causal power of mind over body and thereby also the practice of morality. Since science seeks, as John Stuart Mill argued, nothing more than knowledge of laws as matter-of-fact regularities, it follows that these objections fell on deaf ears: it was obvious that, so far as concerns the purposes of science, parallelism and the causal capacity of mind to make a difference are quite compatible. As even so vehement a critic as Ward admitted (1915, pp. 387, 606), that for the practising psychologist, in the methodology of the discipline, parallelism became the working hypothesis.

That being so, it became part of the working assumptions of psychology that an objective science of man is possible. This raises certain obvious questions. First, what would such a science look like? And second, what would the role of classical psychology be in such a science? It is to these questions that we turn in the next section.

3 Behaviourisms and Classical Psychology

For John Stuart Mill, an objective science of man seems to be possible but is certainly not practicable. Upon his view, even if one accepts the parallelistic hypothesis, the 'translation' of the laws of our subjective experience into objective terms would have to be a 'translation' into the language of the physiology of the central nervous system. But the prospect of actually identifying the brain states that are tied by the laws of coexistence of the parallelism to mental states was slim indeed; even today it is clear that there is a long way to go. It is evident, then, that if psychology has become objective but is also to continue to study the same things that it always studied – sensations, ideas, perceptions, desires, and so on – then another way of 'translating' the subjective into objective terms is needed.

The way out of this is to consider expressions of mental states in behaviour, or, at least, in dispositions to behaviour. Thus, for example, my experiencing of pain is accompanied by a disposition to assert 'I am in pain' if appropriately prompted, and, conversely, having learned the language, that is, the rules for the use of 'I am in pain,' the behavioural disposition that is appropriately prompted then I assert 'I am in pain' is present. In general, our mental states are expressed in tendencies to sorts of behaviour that are characteristic of those mental states, often enough, of course, verbal behaviour. We saw earlier, in the preceding chapter, that Bain had emphasized this idea. Concerning our knowledge of 'subjective states' in others, he suggests that we 'accept identical objective marks, as showing identical subjective states. The same expression, behaviour, &c., under the same circumstances must be held as evidence of the same feelings' (1880b, p. 38). In particular, he noted that in this context 'What we have termed *critical* manifestations are of great interest. The point of intensity of pain that makes a child cry, or puts one into a fright, or a rage, is very expressive, and great stress is naturally put upon all these ebullitions or outbursts' (p. 40).

The point here is that our mental states not only run parallel to brain states but also parallel to dispositions to behave in certain ways. These dispositions are, of course, very often actualized, given the appropriate environmental prompting. If ES is the appropriate environmental state, and BS is the behavioural state which the environmental prompt evokes, then the disposition is:

if ES then BS

and we have a law for the mental state MS_1:

(**) MS_1 if and only if: if ES_1 then BS_1

Given the parallelism of mental states MS and brain states NS as represented in our little model by the law

(*) MS_1 if and only if NS_1

then we also have a parallelism of behavioural dispositions to internal states of the organism:

(***) NS_1 if and only if: if ES_1 then BS_1

If we have a law of succession for mental states

(1) Whenever MS_1, then MS_2

then the laws of parallelism for mental states – brain states give us the law of succession for the process in the central nervous system that runs parallel to the process described by (1):

(2) Whenever NS_1 then NS_2

Then the laws (**) and (***) that describe how mental states find expression in characteristic behaviour give the law of succession for behaviour states, or, at least, dispositions:

(3) Whenever a person is so disposed that if ES_1, then BS_1, then that person is also so disposed that if ES_2 then BS_2.

Laws such as (**) provide one with a means for 'translating' laws about our subjective states into laws about behaviour. Since we have greater access to behaviour and to the environment that evokes that behaviour, it follows that the 'translation' of the statements of mentalistic psychology into the language of behaviour offers a better chance than does 'translation' into the language of physiology for science being able in practice, and not just in principle, to undertake research in psychology in a wholly objective way.

There is, however, behaviour and there is behaviour. Something more is needed than even the principle of 'translation' into the language of behaviour before an objective science of man becomes possible. To see what this is we shall consider an example that will permit us to make a number of relevant points.

Some remarks about the law (***) are in order first, however.

If we make more explicit the sort of thing intended by (***) then what we have is:

(λ_1) For any person, that person is in NS if and only if, if he is in ES then he is in BS.

This logically entails a law that describes how the environment causally evokes the behavioural response:

(λ_2) For any person, if that person is in ES then he is in BS if and only if he is in NS.

But if one does not know the brain states that run parallel to the mental states and cannot discover the physiological law (3), then it follows that, equally, one cannot discover the behavioural laws such as (λ_2) since they also mention brain states NS.

Now, it might occur to one here to, for the time being, simply ignore the brain states NS. That is, as a first step one would settle upon discovering a law such as

(λ_3) For any person, if that person is in ES then he is in BS

which correlates environmental states and behavioural states, but omits the internal states that causally link those two ends of the process. (λ_3) would omit parts of the process, and would therefore be gappy and imperfect. But imperfect knowledge is still knowledge, and to discover laws such as (λ_3) would be a first step, at least, towards a later discovery of less imperfect knowledge that would take into account the as-yet-inaccessible physiological variables that intervene between the environmental state, that is, the stimulus S, and the behavioural state, that is, the response R. It is this notion, of course, that is embodied in the famous formula of behaviourism that the response is a function of the stimulus:

$$(f_1)\ R = f(S)$$

and that it is the job of psychology, in the immediate future at least, to discover laws of this sort.

Unfortunately, generalizations like (λ_3) are almost invariably false, and to characterize psychology as the search for laws of the sort (f_1) is invariably misleading. For, again consider the example of experiencing pain: in that case (λ_3) states that everyone in a certain environment, that is, subject to a certain stimulus, will respond with the assertion 'I am in pain'; but that is false, since one will so express the feeling of pain only if *previously* one has learned English. The relevant law is not represented by a schema such as (λ_3) but, if LS represents an environmental context that constitutes a *learning situation*, by something such as

(λ_4) For any person, if that person is in LS at t_0 then, and only then, for any later time t, if that person is in ES then he is in BS.

(λ_5) For any person, if that person is in LS at t_0, then, and only then, that person is in NS at any subsequent time.

But this state NS is the one that underlies the behavioural disposition. For, from (λ_4) and (λ_5) we can deduce (λ_1):

For any person, if that person is in NS, then, and only then, if that person is in ES then he is in BS.

The law (λ_4) is itself the 'translation' into behavioural language of the mentalistic *law of learning*.

(λ_6) For any person if that person is in LS at t_0 then, and only then, for any later time t, that person is in mental state MS.

The 'translation' is effected by the law (**) connecting our subjective states to their expression in behaviour. (λ_6) is a schema for, say, learning by association: if one has experienced a constant conjunction of (say) f and g by t_0, then subsequently one will have the mental state that consists of the idea of f being associated with the idea of g.

If the law (λ_4) is *historical* in the sense that in order to predict BS one must know not only the present stimulus ES but also the *previous history* LS,[14] (λ_1) is not in that way historical. The state NS that is caused by LS is a physiological state by which *traces* from the past are carried into the present. Since (λ_4) follows from (λ_1) and (λ_5), it follows that we have reduced the historical law (λ_4) to the non-historical law (λ_1) by the *discovery* of the role of trace variables indicated by the law (λ_5). If one focuses upon behaviour, then the laws are as a matter of fact almost all historical. In particular, the behavioural laws of learning are historical. But this does not surprise: it merely reflects the historical nature of the mentalistic laws of learning, for example, the laws of association proposed by the classical psychologists. But such historical laws can be reduced to non-historical laws of physiology, provided trace variables can be discovered. However, whether or not trace variables exist is a matter of fact.

It should be noted that there is nothing about historical laws that is incompatible with empiricism or determinism;[15] John Stuart Mill himself emphasized the relevance of a person's history to his mental life (1872a, VI, IV, 4). Contrary to some,[16] then, the so-called historicity of man is quite compatible with the empiricist philosophy of science of the sort defended by John Stuart Mill, and, in fact, the psychology of the latter already, in the laws of learning by association that it proposes, recognizes this historicity.

The example we are about to consider illustrates this historicity of man, and shows, too, how that historicity can be accommodated within a psychology of the sort described by the empiricist. The example is that of an infant and a candle flame, and was already old when William James used it. A candle flame twinkles. An infant is placed in front of it. Attracted by the brightness of the flame, the infant reaches out to touch it – and is painfully burned. A while later the infant is placed before a candle flame again. This time it recoils, for it perceives the candle as dangerous and consequently withdraws in fear.

This example shows once again the inappropriateness of the formula (f_1):

$$R = f(S)$$

since the same S, the candle flame, evokes one R the first time it is presented, namely, the motion of the infant towards the flame, and a very different R, namely, the motion of withdrawal, the second time it is present. The difference between the first presentation and the second consists in the fact that the response to the first presentation has a certain effect, namely, that the infant was burned and experienced pain. The response is thus not a function of the stimulus (S) alone, but also of the history (H) of the person.[17] Indeed, there are also relevant physiological factors (P), for example, the infant isn't blind, as Mill pointed out, and further still, as Mill also pointed out, those factors psychologists call individual differences (I). The accurate way to schematize the form that the behavioural laws of psychology take on is thus not (f_1) but, as Bergmann and Spence (1941) pointed out,

(f_2) $R = f(S, H, P, I)$

One way this point is often expressed – it was expressed this way above – is that the response depends upon how the subject 'perceives' the situation. The second response of the infant is different from the first because the infant perceives the stimulus differently the second time. What has happened? Upon the associationist account, the experience of the candle flame has been followed by the experience of pain, and this conjunction, together with the special reinforcing capacity of pleasure and pain, has the consequence that the idea of a candle flame comes to have associated with it the idea of pain. This in turn causes the subject, when it responds to the sensations caused by the candle flame, to perceive the latter as having the property of causing pain. One may not agree with the associationist theory of learning that the classical psychologists proposed, but the example makes clear what is for our present purposes most important, namely, that it is the *history* of the subject that accounts for that subject 'perceiving' a stimulus differently at different times. This fact, that the subject responds differently according to how it perceives the stimulus, is represented in the formula (f_2) by the factors H; to say that a subject 'perceives' the stimulus in a certain way amounts to saying that the subject has had a certain history. The gestalt psychologist Kurt Lewis (in, for example, 1926, 1936) emphasized that people respond differentially according to different perceptual structures (which he misleadingly referred to as 'topological'). But he thought that this was somehow incompatible with behaviourism; he never understood the point we have just made, that this difference in the way the subject perceives a situation amounts in behavioural terms simply to a difference in history. Others continue to restate the old Lewinian theme,[18] so it is no doubt worth having the behaviourist reply once again.

A second important point that the candle example makes clear is that *behaviour has effects on subsequent behaviour*. In the example, the reaching of the infant for the candle flame brings about sensations of pain, and this modifies the response to the same stimulus: subsequently the behaviour is not motion towards, but withdrawal from, the candle. Upon the psychological theories of the Mills, as we know, the association of pain with the idea of a candle flame yields a motive for avoiding candle flames, and this motive in turn produces bodily motions that carry the infant away from the flame.

Bishop Butler was concerned to sketch the effects of such feelings as our moral sentiments upon our mental life. But he did not proceed from there to search for *causes* – deflected, of course, by the providential teleology that led both him and so many others to neglect the scientific task of searching for causes as well as effects. James Mill, in the *Analysis*, undertook this further task that Butler neglected. But the younger Mill cautioned that if one should not neglect the search for causes by focusing on functions, equally one should, in searching for causes, not neglect the investigation of effects (1872a, VI, IV, 3). What our example shows is that *behaviour also has functions* in our mental life. *For this reason, psychology, as the science of mental life, cannot restrict itself to the subjective, but must take into account behaviour and its effects on our mental life.* Even if psychology does not attempt to become what is in principle possible, a science of objective data, it turns out that it cannot neglect behaviour.

John Stuart Mill's principled warning that psychologists must look at effects did not especially move them to what that in reality implied, namely, study behaviour. To be sure, some students were prepared to argue for the introduction of more objective material into the science than had hitherto been the case. Thus, the physiologist William B. Carpenter argued that 'it is much to be desired that a systematic study should be made, by those whose mental training and habits of scientific research qualify them for the task, of that wide and almost unexplored domain, which comprehends the whole range, not only of what may be termed *Mental Physiology*, but also of *Mental Pathology*, and, in addition, the *Comparative Psychology* of the lower Animals, and the *History of Development* of the Human Mind, from the earliest manifestation of its powers' (1885, p. 547n). This is not yet to emphasize behaviour, however, though it does point the way for psychology to move from the limited subject-matter that it had as the science of consciousness to the far broader range that was later to be included in its subject-matter. What provided the immediate thrust towards the study of behaviour was neither psychology itself nor physiology but rather the work of Darwin.[19]

The example of the candle and the infant illustrates the relevant point here also. The withdrawal response is the behavioural expression of *fear*. More generally, fear is expressed in the tendency or disposition to withdraw. Adults, of course, learn to control that response. In them the environmental stimulus will evoke the response only in the absence of efforts at self-control. The latter, in other words, comes to be one of the conditions under which that S evokes that R; it, too, is the result of history (H). Sometimes, though, the environmental stimulus will evoke the withdrawal response in spite of efforts at self-control; just when an environmental stimulus can overcome such efforts will also be a function of the person's history. These are the sorts of details for which an adequate learning theory must generate explanations. Throughout, however, the behavioural expression of the emotion of fear is the disposition to withdraw; that is the 'translation' of the language describing the subjective emotion into the objective language of behaviour. *Biologically this response has a certain function in ensuring the survival of the organism.* This biological function is that of protecting the organism from danger. We all recall the catch-phrase of Darwinism: 'the survival of the fittest.' The *fitness* of an organism is constituted by the various tendencies, dispositions, and capacities that it has and that enable it so to respond to its environment that it survives and reproduces. The emotion of fear directed towards an object in the environment that is perceived as dangerous, or, what amounts to the same, the tendency to respond to a dangerous object by withdrawing from it, has, it is obvious, survival value, and it therefore contributes to the biological fitness of the organism. *From the viewpoint of Darwinian theory, then, what is important is not so much the subjective state as its behavioural expression*, since it is the latter that has the biological function of contributing towards the survival and reproduction of the organism. *The impact of Darwinism was to shift attention away from the subjective to the objective aspects of persons, and, more specifically, not so much to the physiological correlates of subjective states but to the behavioural expressions of the latter.* We all recall Darwin's own interest in the expression of emotions in animals (1872); and these concerns of Darwinian biology had a dramatic impact in psychology (cf. Boring 1957, pp. 471–2). Here as elsewhere one is entitled to speak of a 'Darwinian revolution.'

From the viewpoint of Darwinian theory what is important about the infant's bodily movement is its function, that is, the effects which it tends to bring about. The intrinsic characteristic is in fact of little importance. A variety of bodily movements will, in the context, have the same effect. What is important from the biological perspective is that *one* of the motions of this sort occur but not which one specifically. That is, what is important is that it be true of the organism that:

(*r*) *there is* a *bodily motion* which has the *effect* of protecting the organism from the danger of the stimulus

(*r*) is a term or phrase referring to a characteristic of organisms. This characteristic is, we should note *first*, a *determinable* characteristic. A determinable characteristic, such as being coloured, is true of an object just in case *there is any one of a range* of specific characteristics present in the object. The determinable characteristic to which (*r*) refers is present in an organism just in case *there is* a specific character of a certain generic sort (viz., a bodily motion) which the organism has; but to predicate (*r*) of an organism is not to say specifically what determinate character it is that is present in the organism. The characteristic to which (*r*) refers is, we should note *second*, a *functional* characteristic, that is, one that holds of an object just in case the specific characteristics of the object, whatever they may be, bring about certain effects.

Now, let *s* refer to the characteristic of a stimulus of being dangerous. Note that to say of a stimulus that it is dangerous is also to ascribe to the stimulus a characteristic that is determinable and functional. Then the disposition that is the behavioural expression of the emotion of fear is:

if *s* then *r*

What is true of this example is true almost invariably: *the descriptions of stimuli and responses that are at once relevant to both biology and the expression of subjective experience are determinable and functional.*

Responses can also be classified in terms of their *causes*. Thus, if we consider the *mark* 'red,' this is said to *mean, or refer to,* the property of things, namely, the colour red, that tends to evoke its application, that is, tends to cause it to be applied to red things. However, not all meaning is referential meaning. Thus, words such as 'ought' have *imperatival meaning* because their use in such contexts as 'ought: you do A' tends to evoke your doing A; that is, imperatival meaning is a matter of *effects*. Linguistic items are classified as the same, or as having the same meaning, if they play the *same linguistic role*,[20] where the role of an item consists in the regularities, tendencies, and dispositions that characterize its use. These connections include world-word transitions, word-word transitions and word-world transitions. Among the important aspects of the linguistic role of an expression is the causal role of rule expressions which, with their imperatival force, govern the use of an expression.[21] Within the general framework, more specific sorts of meaning can be defined, for example, *referential meaning* in terms of world-word connections (language-entry transitions), and imperatival or, more generally, *emotive meaning* in terms of word-world connections (language-exit transitions).

In looking upon behaviour as the expression of subjective states, language plays a crucial role. The fear of something such-and-such that expresses itself in the tendency to withdraw also expresses itself, in those who have learned English, in the tendency to say 'I am afraid of that such-and-such,' where it is not just the sounds that constitute the response, but those sounds *qua* having a certain role, that is, a certain *meaning*. The perception of something such-and-such as dangerous appears behaviourally not only as summarizing a certain specific sort of history but also as the tendency to say 'I see a dangerous such-and-such' where, again, it is not just the sounds that constitute the response but the sounds *qua* having a certain *meaning*.

Let us distinguish between the response characterized in micro terms (call it the 'micro response') and the response characterized in macro terms (call it the 'macro response'). In the infant-and-candle example, the movement of the bodily part characterized in its full specificity is the response characterized in micro terms. The same response characterized determinably and in terms of its function as a protective response is the response characterized in macro terms. Similarly let us distinguish between the distal stimulus and the proximate stimulus. A physical object or other feature of the environment characterized in determinable and functional terms is the distal stimulus. But it actually affects the organism only when it produces, through some causal process or other, an impact upon the sensory apparatus of the organism; this impact on the sense organs of the organism is the proximate stimulus.

John Stuart Mill, as we saw, when he conceived of purely objective psychology, did so in terms of physiology. This means that, insofar as he thought of psychology in stimulus-response terms, he did so in terms of the proximate stimulus and the micro response. That, however, is to exclude a consideration of behaviour in those terms – that of the distal stimulus and the macro response – that must be used if one is to achieve a 'translation' of our subjective experience into a behaviouristic language. And only if one proceeds with a behaviouristic psychology will one in practice, as opposed to merely in principle, be able to pursue a research program in psychology in purely objective terms. Mill therefore thinks of an objective psychology in terms that preclude any practical program of purely objective research. In Mill's terms, the only practical program would be mentalistic. It was the Darwinian revolution that led psychologists to focus on the sorts of stimuli and the sorts of behavioural responses that alone made an objective psychology a practical proposal.

Bain had already started to move in the direction of an objective science of man: he was more than willing to introduce the physiological into his psychology – in that sense, his psychology moved beyond the purely mentalistic: he was, moreover, also happy enough to accept the truth and general principles of the theory of evolution (cf. 1880b, pp. 47ff); and, most important, he was prepared to introduce the sorts of distinctions, between macro and micro responses, between distal and proximate stimuli, that were crucial to the impact of Darwin upon psychology. Thus, in considering sensation on its physical side, Bain distinguishes between 'the mode of action on a sensitive surface' and 'the outward manifestations or diffused wave of effects' (1880b, p. 3), which is, in effect, the distinction between the micro response and the macro response. Again, he distinguishes between the 'seat of the feeling,' which is a 'sensitive mass, which *can* be affected by irritants external to it, and which yields nearly the same effects in the case of a purely internal stimulus' (1868, p. 103), thus distinguishing between the proximate stimulus, the irritation of the sensitive mass, and the distal stimulus, the external cause, when it exists, of that irritation. However, while Bain does introduce these distinctions and discussions, they have in fact little impact upon the outline of his psychology, which remains thoroughly Millian in its outline – Millian, but supplemented with a little more physiology, and a whiff of evolution around the edges. Insofar as Bain moves towards the idea of an objective psychology, he more or less follows Mill; what he in fact introduces into his psychology is purely physiological (cf. 1868, pp. 59ff, 104ff), precisely the sort of objective correlates of subjective states that Mill talked about. And when Bain thought of evolution, he thought of inheritance rather than survival. When he discusses the evolution of mind, the main topic is instincts, and he is mainly concerned to establish that neither the capacity to perceive distance nor our moral sentiments are innate; they are, rather, he insists on the basis of sound evidence, learned (cf. 1880b, pp. 54, 55). The point is not the truth of what Bain here argues – his argument is reasonable enough – but rather that his discussions are rooted in the earlier controversies with Kames and Reid. There is colouring from the new theory of evolution, but little substance. So, although there is in Bain a move towards a science of man that could be objective, it is still largely the objective science that Mill contemplated, one that involves a physiological reduction, rather than the behaviour-istic science that would be the ultimate product of the Darwinian revolution.

Let us explore this notion of an objective behaviouristic science of man a bit farther. In fact we must distinguish three sorts of behaviour-ism. To see this, begin with an example.

A tree is a complex patterned set of perceptual events; the pattern is one of laws that establish not only what will follow, but also what would follow were the context to be different. Through a process of learning we come to be able to judge of an entity that we are experiencing that 'this is a tree.' This perceptual judgment is *not* an inference, but a simple unified mental act in which the entity is non-inferentially judged to be a tree. We have examined John Stuart Mill's discussion of perceptual judgments above, in chapter 5. What holds for the perception of physical objects holds also for the perception of behaviour and the perception of meaning, linguistic meaning in particular. Behaviour, understood in macro terms, since it is defined in terms of its causes and effects, is also a lawful pattern. We perceive such patterns in simple judgments. Thus, we perceive that the second response of the infant is one of fear. This, too, is not an inference but a simple perceptual judgment; as with the perception of physical objects, the capacity to make such judgments is acquired. Finally, auditorily (with speech) and visually (with writing) we perceive (linguistic) meanings of various sounds and marks that are given to us in sense experience. Again it is not an inference but a simple perceptual judgment; and again, as with the perception of ordinary physical objects, the capacity to make such judgments is acquired. In each case, *one perceives the pattern in a simple judgment as a unity and not, as when one becomes aware of a pattern by inference, as a structure with a wealth of distinguishable parts.* Moreover, *in each case one perceives the pattern without knowing how one perceives it*; the perceiving is evoked by often uncon-scious cues, and the capacity so to perceive is the result of learning processes that are, when one is perceiving, certainly not present to one in consciousness.

And now we must, following Bergmann (1956), distinguish among sorts of behaviourism. There is, first, *metaphysical behaviourism*. On this view, minds or subjective states simply do not exist. J.B. Watson tended to profess this view (1913; cf. 1924), but once having asserted the non-existence of mental states such as emotions he goes on a few paragraphs later to propose to identify these mental states with certain bodily states. One cannot 'identify' x with y, however, unless x exists.

And moreover, as the tentative nature of Watson's 'identification' makes clear, the 'identity' between the mental and the physical states is clearly a contingent one; a distinguishability is therefore implied between the two states that one is supposed to be identifying. And such a distinguishability is all that such a one as John Stuart Mill insists upon to secure the distinction he needs between mind and body. In the end, metaphysical behaviourism is, as Broad put it (1923, pp. 6, 623), a silly view: whatever problems subjective states pose for philosophers their existence is patent.

The second sort of behaviourism is *physicalistic behaviourism*. On this view, psychology can be not only an objective science but one in which all the concepts are defined in terms of the concepts that we apply to non-living matter. Terms that we use to describe the macro response, for example, when we say that the response is one of fear, or when we say that her response consisted in her replying 'Yes, please,' and terms that we use to describe the distal stimulus, for example, when we say that what evoked her response was his offering some tea, are terms that do *not* occur in the science of inanimate objects; they are characteristically psychological. However, these terms apply to events by virtue of certain patterns of cause and effect into which those events fall. That is, these terms are *definable* by means of the laws that describe these patterns. In principle one might want to suggest that there are emergent qualities of behaviour that cannot thus be reduced to the qualities of inanimate matter. Yet is does not seem that there are such. What is different about behaviour does not lie in its own special qualities but in the subjective states that cause the behaviour. Those do indeed involve emergent qualities not reducible to those inanimate matter, as John Stuart Mill correctly held; but, given the parallelistic hypothesis, that is quite compatible with holding that on the side of the behaviour there are no such emergent qualities, only complex patterns of physical, including physiological and bodily, events, all fully describable by the terms we apply to inanimate matter. Physicalistic behaviourism is therefore true; it is, in effect, a consequence of accepting the parallelistic hypothesis.

But truth is one thing, practice is another. Though the concepts we apply to behaviour are in principle all definable physicalistically, by means of the terms that apply to inanimate matter, they are *not* all so defined, nor do we know how to define them. For, we do not know what are the lawful patterns that define, for example, linguistic roles, that is, meanings. *To be sure, we can on the basis of perception apply these concepts; but we do so without knowing how we apply them, that is, in particular, without being able to trace inferentially the lawful patterns that justify their use, and that, if we could specify them, would yield physicalistic definitions of those concepts.* The point is that the stimulus and the response that are relevant to psychology are the distal stimulus and the macro response; a psychology that is to be both objective and practical must refer to these. But the terms that we use in ordinary discourse and on the basis of perception to describe the distal stimulus and the macro response are not in practice definable physicalistically. A behaviourism that attempted to define all its terms physicalistically is therefore *not yet possible in practice.* In other words, *physicalistic behaviourism does not yield a program of practical research.*

It is, however, possible to take for granted our ordinary ways of describing the distal stimulus and the macro response, and to search for laws which relate these in conformity with the general pattern (f_2): $R = f(S, H, P, I)$. This third sort of behaviourism is not physicalistic but *methodological.* Unlike the former *it makes possible a practical research program in an objective science of man.*

We should note here also what behaviourism is *not.* One: behaviourism is not a theory, or at least, beyond the parallelistic hypothesis itself, behaviourism is not a theory. That is, it is not a particular set of laws. It is no set of laws at all, but rather the claim that the laws of psychology can all be stated in objective terms.

Moreover, two, it is not something that could be called 's-R theory.' Since behaviourism is not a theory, it is in particular not an 's-R theory.' But even the phrase 's-R theory' is a misnomer. To say that psychology seeks to discover 's-R connections' is, in one sense, to say nothing more than that psychology seeks to discover cause and effect relations, that is, that psychology is a science. To suppose that one could have a *scientific* psychology that did *not* proceed in 's-R' terms is simple confusion. However, one can contrast different sorts of laws psychology can study. Thus, those who design IQ tests attempt to establish correlations between responses to tests and responses to learning situations, to use the former to predict the latter, that is, to predict performance in schools. They also attempt to establish correlations between responses to one sort of test and responses to other sorts of tests. Here it is responses that are correlated, and one may refer to the laws as 'R-R' (response-response) laws.[22] These may indeed be contrasted to 's-R' laws. To search for R-R laws is, clearly, to search for correlations among effects; to search for s-R laws is to go beyond this correlation of effects to search for causes and common causes. *Thus, it is to pass from the more to the less imperfect.* In other words, *to insist that the laws in psychology are of the* S-R *form, rather than, say,* R-R, *is to insist that the ideal of scientific explanation that holds for physics holds also for psychology.* Once again, to suppose that one could have a scientific psychology that did not proceed in this way in 's-R' terms is simple confusion.

Furthermore, three, behaviourism, as the claim that psychology can be objective, commits one to no specific theory of learning. Learning may proceed only by simple association (that is, what is now called classical conditioning, of the sort studied by Pavlov) or pleasure and pain may also play a role in learning (that is, reinforcement may play a role in learning, as John Stuart Mill proposed, and as Skinner has explored in detail); both theories are compatible with behaviourism, and the decision between them, or other alternatives, is to be made on the basis of objective data.

Finally, four, we must note that among the alternative learning theories are various versions of innatism. Indeed, on *any* view, *some* behavioural responses are innate. The only question is not whether there is an innate component but how much. For us the point is, once again, that behaviourism, as the view that psychology can be objective, is compatible with any or all behaviour being innate; and how much is innate is not a philosophical problem but one of science, to be settled by observation and experiment.[23]

What, then, does the research program of classical psychology look like from the viewpoint of methodological behaviourism?[24]

Classical psychology gives descriptions of subjective states. Thus, for example, if the psychologist is experiencing a red sensation, then he describes this by saying something like 'this is red.' The red sensation is a subjective state. What does this amount to behaviourally? That is, how is it expressed in behaviour? The evident answer is that it finds expression in the verbal behaviour of saying 'this is red.' That is, the behavioural state that is parallel to the subjective state of experiencing a red sensation is the disposition

(d_1) if in the appropriate set, then says 'this is red'

This provides the definition for the behavioural concept

(d_2) sensing-red

Note that in (d_2) the marks 'red' are part of a unitary phrase; they are no more separable in it than they are in the phrase (word) 'bred.' Given that we have the parallelistic connection

(e) experiencing a red sensation if and only if sensing-red

the marks 'red' in the unitary phrase 'sensing-red' indeed function linguistically as a piece of code reminding us of the parallel mental or subjective state that is the cause of that behavioural state. None the less, for the purposes of objective psychology, the subjective states mentioned in (e), and signalled by the code, are to be ignored. It is for that reason, and for those purposes, that there is no red in sensing-red.

Now, as we have seen in exploring the notion of introspective analysis in chapter 3, experiments in classical psychology are of the following sort. The subject of the experiment is presented with a certain sensory stimulus, say, a red circle within a green circle, or two pitches one higher than the other by a third. Then, first, the subject is given the phenomenological set and he responds with the phenomenological description, and, second, the subject is given the analytical set and he responds with the analytical description. The aim is to find correlations that enable one to infer the first response from the second. The claim that such correlations exist is a claim that *there* are certain laws; this claim is the abstract generic law that we earlier called (L$_1$). Thus, what (L$_1$) asserts is the existence of laws correlating one sort of response with another. Thus, *from the viewpoint of methodological behaviourism, what introspective analysis aims to discover is a set of* R-R *correlations*. Then, as a further working hypothesis of classical psychology, there is the assumption, which we earlier called the law (L$_2$), that the terms of the second response refer to the features of the stimulus and other factors in the subject's history that are the causal antecedents of disposition to give the phenomenological description of the stimulus. Here one must of course assume the viewpoint of methodological behaviourism, and take the meanings of the verbal responses for granted if this is to be a practicable research program that proceeds on an objective basis. But, given that, then it is evident that it is a purely factual matter, to be tested by observation and experiment, how much of our past history of learning can be recovered by means of the verbal responses given under the analytical set.

We may therefore conclude that *there is nothing in the research program of classical psychology that is incompatible with behaviourism*. The question we must return to, therefore, is this: when psychology turned away from the subjective to become a purely objective science, why did it also do what it did not have to do, namely, turn away also from the research program of classical psychology? The answer to this question, which is the question of whatever happened to classical psychology, is not, we have seen, the simple answer, that it was overthrown by behaviourism, since its research program is compatible with behaviourism. The next section attempts to answer our question.

4   The Demise of Structuralism

The thrust from physics associated with the discovery of the law of the conservation of energy convinced psychologists of the truth of parallelism and therefore of the possibility of a purely objective science of man. But so long as the objective counterparts of the subjective states were located within the confines of the skin of the organism, there could be little push to replace in practice the mentalistic science of classical psychology by an objective science. It was Darwin with his concern with the impact of the environment on the organism and with the sorts of response the organism makes to that environment, or, more generally, his concern with fitness for survival, who created among psychologists an interest in investigating the connections between distal stimuli and macro responses. With respect to the latter sort of connection, a research program could be carried out in practice. The result was methodological behaviourism. Sometimes the push towards objectivity was sufficiently strong that psychologists felt driven to secure it by defending metaphysical behaviourism. Such a one was John B. Watson, but even he recognized the practical necessity of methodological behaviourism, when he pointed out the necessity of using the 'linguistic method' in psychology, for example, using interviewing techniques, which takes meaning for granted (1924, pp. 6, 286). The main thrust in psychology, however, was not to move to such silly ideological extremes, but simply to ignore subjective states. By the 1920s this had already become part of the textbook tradition in psychology.[25]

Not only did methodological behaviourism provide the possibility for an objective research program in psychology, but there was moreover a theory capable of guiding such research ready to hand. Broadly there was the Darwinian theory of evolution by natural selection. Within this context, the capacity to learn was clearly adaptive; it made an organism fitter for survival. So the translation of the associationist theory of learning of the classical psychologists provided a ready-made framework with which to begin. Indeed, once it was stated in objective terms it could be applied to animals as well as people. Psychology thus became a discipline that studied animals as well as men.[26] But Darwinian theory also created a new concern for aspects of psychology previously neglected. The philosophical psychology of James Mill had insisted that the higher mental processes of the will and the intellect were part of the proper subject-matter of psychology, and they received their explanation-sketch in the *Analysis*. But when psychology became experimental with Wundt, psychology largely devoted itself in practice to the study of sensation and perception. The research techniques developed for that research simply could not be applied to the higher mental processes.[27] However, these higher processes clearly had adaptive value. A biologically oriented psychology had therefore to take such processes seriously. There was in consequence an impulse to break out of the confines of sensation and perception to which the research techniques tended to restrict psychologists,[28] and to investigate new methods, new sorts of experiment, in terms of which psychologists could begin to deal with these other topics the importance of which they had come to see. Here, too, in short, the Darwinian revolution provided an impulse for psychologists to break out of the confines of classical associationism as they had inherited it from the Mills on the one hand and from Wilhelm Wundt on the other.

All this came together in the American functionalism of, for example, Angell (1907). The whole biological orientation led these psychologists to emphasize the broader causal context. They began to think in 's-r,' that is, causal, terms rather than in the restricted 'r-r' terms of classical psychology. The functionalists recognized the legitimacy of the sort of research that the classical psychologists following Wundt, were pursuing. (The leader in the United States of the latter sort of research was Titchener at Cornell.) But they insisted that it was but a small part of psychology. And with this went a broad concern for introducing into psychology subject-matters (e.g., animal psychology) that could be treated only objectively. The impulse to objectivity was massive, and since physics insisted that it was possible, it soon became the dominant point of view. The animal psychologist John B. Watson provided a footnote to the broad movement of American functionalism when he insisted that all concepts in psychology be objective. With that footnote, functionalism became behaviourism.[29] By the 1930s the remaining structuralists, as those who carried on the classical tradition had come to be called, were reformulating even psychophysics in objectivist terms.[30]

The point remains, however, that within this context there is nothing illegitimate in the r-r research of the classical psychologists. Indeed, research of this sort continued to be pursued in a variety of areas. Mental testing was one such area. Social psychologists continued such research also. The aim was to discover how the subject responded (R_t) to a stimulus given differences in how that stimulus is perceived. Such psychologists understood different ways in which the stimulus is perceived not so much as a way of summarizing past history but as expressing itself in a disposition to verbal behaviour of the sort 'I perceive it as a such-and-such' (R_2). Such verbal reports are analogous to the phenomenological descriptions of the classical psychologists, and it is not surprising that the psychologists who pursued this sort of research often took their inspiration from the Gestalt psychologists or even the philosophical movement also called 'phenomenological' that was founded by Edmund Husserl. But in any case, the verbal reports that express how the subject perceives the stimulus are another sort of response (R_2). What these psychologists were investigating, then, were connections between the two responses, (R_1) and (R_2), that is, they were searching after r-r laws.[31] This tradition has been revived more recently as 'cognitive psychology,' which, by studying such laws, aims to get access to certain features at least of the higher mental processes. The earlier social psychologists sometimes, as in the case of Kurt Lewin, did not recognize the compatibility of their concerns with (methodological) behaviourism, or even the limited validity of their concerns if one looks at psychology as concerned not merely with correlating effects but also with causes, that is, if one looks at psychology from the viewpoint of the ideal of scientific explanation. Cognitive psychologists today also often share these limitations with Lewin. Be this as it may, however, the point is that in a variety of areas the search for r-r laws continues to be a legitimate enterprise within the broad context of methodological behaviourism.

Why did it turn out, then, that the classical program of introspective analysis, now reconceptualized as a search for certain r-r laws, disappeared? What happened to this paradigm?

There were two aspects to the classical paradigm, the law (L_1) that asserts that the phenomenological description (response) can be inferred from the analytical description (response), and the law (L_2) that asserts that the elements uncovered in the analytical description (the terms that appear in the second response) are (describe) the genetic antecedents of the mental state described in the phenomeno-logical description (i.e., the antecedents of the disposition to give the first response). It was the law (L_1) that characterized the research program of introspective analysis narrowly considered. It was the law (L_2) that connected the results of introspective research with the learning theory of associationism. As we saw, (L_1) could be accepted while (L_2) was denied. Indeed, as we saw, John Stuart Mill himself was prepared to uncouple the two laws. For Mill, the 'law of obliviscence' meant that the genetic connections were often more complicated than could be traced out by any process of introspective analysis. Mill himself, as we saw, struggled, within the narrow confines of his simplistic physiology of perception, to find other means by which to explore learning processes. But one could effectively in practice explore learning by means other than introspective analysis only after one had moved towards a psychology that thought, not as Mill did in terms of the proximate stimulus and the macro response, but rather in terms of the distal stimulus and the macro response. That is, one could explore learning by means other than introspective analysis only after the Darwinian revolution had made the viewpoint of methodological behaviourism acceptable in psychology. What quickly became apparent was that there was far more to learning than introspective analysis could ever dream to uncover. Freud was driven to the techniques of free association pursued at great length (as contrasted to the constrained association of introspective analysis, which was conducted in brief intervals in a laboratory), in order to discover how the present choices of an individual are determined in a complicated way by his past. The exploration of the role of reinforcement in learning led to a systematic study of the way in which apparently small differences in the schedule of reinforcement could have profound effects on learning. And so on: one could multiply the examples at length. The point is that cumulatively this sort of research fairly quickly led to the abandonment of (L_2) and any pretence that introspective analysis could reveal much about learning.[32]

As a consequence, research by means of introspective analysis ceased to be seen as having much relevance to the explanation of learning, and such research came to be guided by (L_1) alone; its concern ceased to be learning and became only structure. And so in its last stages it became the school of 'structuralism.'[33]

But even as structuralism it became a program that not only turned out to be sterile but in the end discovered its own inutility.

What structuralism aimed to discover were the elements of the mental chemistry; that is, in terms of methodological behaviourism, the minimal vocabulary needed for the analytic descriptions.

As Wundt and his students pursued their research, it became evident that no simple or single list of elements was possible. There was, in the first place, distortion by theory. Wundt held that all relations are analysable into non-relational elements, specifically into elements of feeling. But as the Wundtians pursued the master's program, it turned out that every relation had to have its own elementary feeling. The resulting one-to-one correlation of phenomenological relations to elementary feelings tended to conflict in an obvious way with the notion of *analysis*. But it also led Wundt and his students to discover a host of subtly different elementary feelings that other psychologists found themselves simply unable to distinguish. As one commentator has put it, 'The data emerging from Wundtian studies – whether back at Leipzig or at Titchener's laboratory at Cornell – did not behave the way scientific data are supposed to. Even the most comfortable subject, try as he may, had trouble "introspecting" identically on separate occasions' (Robinson 1981, p. 404). It became pretty clear that the theory was forcing the observations, that is, that 'observations' were being reported, not because they were genuine, but because they were needed to confirm the theory.[34]

Even where theory did not lead to distortions, it became evident, as introspective analysis was pursued systematically by a larger number of people, that what was analysable by one person was not so by another, what was an element for one person was not so for another. Individual differences made a difference.[35] Titchener attempted to meet the problem by holding that what psychology aimed to explain was the 'generalized mind.'[36] He in effect proposed to use statistical techniques to as it were average away the variations due to individual differences. But the resulting correlations, precisely because of the statistical feature, were imperfect, and a concern for the fuller causal picture, such as that generated by Darwinism, together with an interest in variation which the latter also created, was bound to lead scientists to attempt to replace the imperfect laws of the 'generalized mind' with a systematic investigation of the individual differences that Wundt attempted more or less, for the sake of his program, to wish away.[37] It is not surprising, therefore, to find out that many of Wundt's American students, while they analysed as Wundt wished them to while they were in Leipzig, when they returned to the United States and founded their own laboratories, pursued in their research an interest in individual differences.[38] Given the causal role of individual differences, it became evident that controversies about the list of mental elements were largely sterile, and that the interest of science in causal explanations could be more usefully served by pursuing other lines of research than that of introspective analysis. As Kuhn has pointed out, it is just such a sterility of results that leads scientists to abandon an old paradigm and to search for a new one; this is what happened in psychology.[39]

In fact, not only were the results sterile, but the program, in pursuing its research, discovered that, as a matter of fact, it could not be anything other than sterile. Although psychology had since before James Mill claimed to deal with higher mental processes, the program of systematic experiment initiated by Wundt focused on sensation and perception. It was Oswald Külpe and his students at Würzburg who first turned their attention to the systematic study of the higher processes, for example, the intellectual process of problem-solving.

Consider what is in the consciousness of a person who knows English when hearing the *sound* 'tree,' and compare it to what is in the consciousness of one who does *not* know English when hearing that sound. There will be similar sensory contents, but in addition the *meaning* of the word will be in the mind of the English-speaker and not in the mind of the non-English-speaker. Such meanings were, of course, none other than the mental acts that Brentano insisted, from a phenomenological perspective, were part of the subject-matter of psychology, and to which John Stuart Mill had earlier directed the attention of psychologists. What Külpe and his students soon concluded was that these non-sensory contents could not be introspectively decomposed, and had, therefore, to be included among the elements. Titchener held that these meanings could be analysed contextually into patterns of sensory contents, but given another fact systematically described by the Würzburgers, namely, the fact that the same meaning can be carried by different sensory contents, and different meanings by the same sensory contents, Titchener convinced no one but himself, and it became evident to all but the committed that Külpe had the best of the controversy:[40] meanings, non-sensory contents, had to be included among the elements. What this result implied, however, was that the same thing was appearing in both the phenomenological description and the analytical description, and to say this is to say that analysis is incapable of revealing any structure in the conscious states that occur in higher mental processes. If you are interested in structure – and with the demise of (L_2) that was all that those who practised introspective analysis *could* be interested in, since structure is by definition what the method reveals – and you then discover by the method that there is no structure to be revealed, the method has been suddenly revealed to be a research tool without a use. *Analysis revealed that it was in many significant cases incapable of yielding an analysis; it thereby discovered its own inutility as a research method.*

In the light of the result of the Würzburg experiments that the non-sensory feature that was given phenomenologically in the state to be analysed reappeared in the analysis as a non-sensory content, one can understand what had happened in Wundt's attempts to analyse relations into feelings of a kinaesthetic sort. What happened, as we noted above, was that Wundt began to find, in one-to-one correlation with relations, feelings that no one else could find.[41] In effect, these special 'feelings' were none other than the relations themselves reappearing in the analysis but misleadingly relabelled in a way that could save a too-dogmatically held theory. In other words, the relation was appearing both phenomenologically and in the analysis. What Wundt had discovered, though he disguised it from himself, was what John Stuart Mill had been prepared to grant, that at least some relations were incapable of introspective analysis. It was, of course, the Gestalters who made this fact, that relations could not be analysed, explicit. The Gestalters and the Würzburgers are thus of a piece in showing the methodological limitations of classical psychology. But many, such as John Stuart Mill himself, and Herbert Spencer as well as late thinkers such as von Ehrenfels and Stumpf,[42] had been prepared to grant the Gestalters' point long before Wundt had turned the claim that relations were analysable from an hypothesis to be tested into an ideology to be imposed. In spite of their shrillness, the Gestalters merely emphasized what most knew, and the rest suspected. Their impact was therefore less on psychology proper than their image in literary circles and the semi-popular press would give one to believe, and it was certainly less than that of the Würzburgers who genuinely discovered to be unanalysable what everyone hitherto had thought could be analysed.

But this is not the end of the Würzburg contribution to the demise of classical psychology and the disappearance of the method of introspective analysis. An even more surprising discovery of these psychologists was that in such higher mental processes as problem-solving *much of the work occurred unconsciously*. The Würzburgers had to invent new techniques for systematically observing the very transient and impalpable states that are before the mind in the higher proces-ses.[43] But this they did, and what careful observation revealed was that, when a person is given a problem to solve, for example, to sum a set of figures, the solution appears before consciousness prior to, and in fact in the absence of, any awareness of the calculating process.[44] This discovery of the unconscious by the Würzburgers is of a piece in the history of psychology with its discovery in another context by Freud.[45] The point is that *if the higher mental processes occur in large part unconsciously then techniques involving the observation of conscious-ness, including that of introspective analysis, are useless tools for research into the nature of these processes.* Under the impact of Darwin, the higher mental processes, because they are biologically adaptive, came to be a subject that psychologists hoped to explore, but when scientists came to apply the method of analysis to this area that had come to be a major concern, here again, *analysis revealed its own inutility as a research method*.

These results obtained by the analytic method, which revealed the inutility and inefficacy of that very same method, had the further result that the school of structuralism, that is, the school that used the method of introspective analysis, quickly came to play a constantly diminishing role in psychology; in other words, *the research program of classical psychology gradually petered out and disappeared from psychology*.

So to describe the demise of classical psychology, however, is misleading. The method did indeed provide data that supported a variety of hypotheses. If it turned out that the method could not be applied in areas psychologists came to want to explore, and could not be extended to deal in detail with areas where it did apply, neither of these things either invalidated the data the method did supply or challenged, in its broad outlines at least, the theoretical framework those data tended to confirm. These data and these hypotheses therefore remained, to be absorbed into the main stream of behaviourist psychology, while the school and the research program that generated them disappeared.

With the Mills, psychology was still a more or less armchair discipline. But in the nineteenth century several small laboratories became annexed to this enterprise. At first it was in laboratories of physics, medicine, and astronomy that procedures were developed by which researchers could observe, count, measure, or categorize various features of human sensation, reaction time, memory, and word association. Boring, in his *History of Experimental Psychology* (1957), has described the origins of these procedures and how they were collected together to form the working tools of the first Laboratory of Psychology that Wundt founded at Leipzig in 1879. Boring analysed 109 papers in Wundt's journal, the *Philosophischen Studien*, and has outlined the work that was undertaken in the Leipzig laboratory (pp. 339–43). There were studies of absolute and difference limens in the several sensory modalities; studies of sensory phenomena such as colour contrast, illusions, auditory beats, taste categories, and so on; studies of simple and complex reaction times; studies of word association and rote memory; and a miscellaneous group of introspective studies concerning the role of attentional and emotional factors in thought. The research was directed at topics in psychology for which there were research tools available. This meant, in effect, that it was largely limited to the problems of sensation, and largely ignored the higher mental process, even though, of course, the latter were treated speculatively and in a non-experimental way much as the Mills had earlier treated them.

The guiding theory was associationism, not essentially different from the classical version of the *Analysis of the Phenomena of the Human Mind*. But there was no *more specific* theory than associationism developed to capture the detailed results of the research of Wundt and Titchener until Boring's *The Physical Dimensions of Consciousness* (1933). This book aimed at providing an analysis of the dimensions of conscious experience that fit with the three relevant kinds of data: introspective, physiological, and physical. Fechner (1860) had taken the dimensions of the world that were found in physics, and had attempted to discover mathematical functions that related these to the dimensions of sensation. The assumption was that the dimensions of sensation simply paralleled those of physics. This was an empirical assumption that might well be false. And in fact the upshot of the Wundt-Titchener research established that falsity. Boring sets out to bring these results together in a picture of the dimensions of our experience of physical things that does equal justice to the results of physics, of the physiology of the senses, and of introspection; he aims at drawing a map that captures the domains of both sensation and physics. The dimensions that he proposes for such a map would be intensity, extensity, protensity, and quality.

If Boring's attempt were successful, subsequent research would have found its place within this map, this theoretical structure. It would, in fact, have functioned as a paradigm for ongoing research. But it was not to be. Boring's 1933 theory provided a structure for a world of research that was no longer being undertaken. The Wundt-Titchener program, as an organized one, had largely disappeared, and Boring's theory was of little interest to any but a handful of practising psychologists (cf. White 1977, p. 68). The techniques that were central to the Wundtian laboratory were tools that enabled knowledge of certain lower mental processes, such as sensation, reaction time, and association, to be developed in a systematic way. But there were pressures, largely resulting from the Darwinian revolution, to take a broader view of what could constitute the subject-matter of psychology. The techniques of introspective psychology showed themselves to be incapable of dealing with these other topics. The result was the displacement of introspection from the centre of psychology to a peripheral interest. And so today even so-called cognitive psychology proceeds behaviouristically rather than introspectively (cf. Spiker 1977, pp. 98ff).

Meanwhile, the investigative procedures that proved themselves to be useful in the Wundtian laboratories continue to be used by psychologists. As White has put it: 'Reports of the death of the Wundtian laboratory have been somewhat exaggerated ... Most of the procedures of the Wundtian laboratory – the psychophysical procedures, the studies of sensory phenomena, the studies of simple and complex reaction time, the studies of association and rote memory – all survive nicely today, technologically upgraded, analyzed in different ways, but all present and in use in diverse contemporary laboratories' (1977, p. 72). The data, the research techniques, the hypotheses where relevant, of introspective psychology have remained, as we have said, to be absorbed into the mainstream of behaviourist psychology, while the school and the research program that generated them has disappeared.

Whatever happened, then, to classical psychology? Well, on the one hand, its method revealed its own inutility and so ceased to be used. But, on the other hand, the data and the theories that those data supported continue to exist, suitably modified and improved by later research, as part of the accumulated knowledge of psychology.

Now, John Stuart Mill used classical psychology to draw certain conclusions with respect to the science of economics and in moral philosophy. Are these conclusions invalidated by the demise of classical psychology? What we have just seen is that the answer to this question depends upon the nature of the conclusions. If they are claims that do not stand independently of the method of introspective analysis, then more likely than not they will be invalid. But if they are claims that have empirical support that is not intrinsically dependent upon that method, then they will stand.

In the area of moral philosophy, Mill argued, against the cruder utilitarians and with such thinkers as Butler, that the value judgments of morality are distinct both specifically and in their objects, and that in their specific difference they render their objects qualitatively preferable to the objects of, say, self-interest. These points are phenomenological; they therefore stand independently of any psychological theory. The older generation of utilitarians had challenged these phenomenological claims on the basis of their version of psychological analysis. The qualitatively distinct pleasures could all be reduced to quantitative differences among bundles of homogeneous pleasures (and pains). Mill defended the phenomenological facts by clarifying the notion of introspective analysis. What this clarification implied was that a philosopher could no longer pretend to find in the empirical facts entities that he surmised a priori to be there: the data were left to be what they are presented as. To insist that what is given phenomenologically is what it is and not something else does not presuppose introspective psychology, either in theory or in practice. Mill's point here therefore does not presuppose the success of the method of introspective analysis – except in this sense, that he could defend his so insisting against the contrary claims of Bentham and his father only by showing that these thinkers had proceeded on the basis of an *inadequate* account of introspective analysis. The point that Mill defended by his appeal to introspective analysis was that the phenomenological facts about our values and the qualitative differences among our pleasures did not entail an innatist account of value. Mill was defending these claims against the suggestions of the older generation of utilitarians that they did not exist. But precisely those same phenomenological facts had been used by such thinkers as Kames and Reid to infer an innatist account of our moral sense. Mill argued to the contrary, on the basis of data obtained by introspective analysis, that our moral sentiments were learned, and, more specifically, were the products of processes of association.

Developments in psychology were to challenge this associationist account of learning; more dramatically, they were to challenge the utility of the method of introspective analysis. No one denied the importance of pleasure and pain in motivating action, but the associationist account was often judged not to be the whole story. As William James was to put it, 'So widespread and searching is this influence of pleasures and pains upon our movements that a premature philosophy has decided that these are our only spurs to action, and that wherever they seem to be absent, it is only because they are so far on among the 'remoter' images that prompt the action that they are overlooked.' But, James continues, 'This is a great mistake ... Important as the influence of pleasures and pains upon our movements, they are far from being our only stimuli. With the manifestations of instinct and emotional expression, for example, they have absolutely nothing to do. Who smiles for the pleasure of the smiling, or frowns for the pleasure of the frown? Who blushes to escape the discomfort of not blushing?' (1890, II: 550). The impulsive quality of mental states is a primitive notion, a simply unanalysable quality. Some states of mind have it in high degree, others in low degree. Pleasures and pains have it in high degree, but it is not a property exclusively of such states; perceptions can also have it, for example. How creatures have come to be impelled towards certain objects, and other creatures towards other objects, is 'a problem for evolutionary history to explain'; and 'those persons obey a curiously narrow teleological superstition who think themselves bound to interpret [all impulsions] in every instance as effects of the secret solicitancy of pleasure and repugnancy of pain' (1890, II: 551).

James clearly has the British utilitarians in mind (he mentions [1890, II: 551n] Bain); and equally clearly he sees himself as challenging their view that men are maximizers, and aim to maximize pleasure. If James's criticisms are on the mark, then the newer psychology would indeed be challenging John Stuart Mill's position at a crucial point. For it is essential to both Mill's utilitarian ethic and to his economics, as well as to his justification of the radical reformers' program, that men always act to maximize their pleasure, that is, that psychological hedonism is true.

However, a careful examination of James's claims shows that James in fact does not challenge psychological hedonism. His discussion does challenge the associationist learning theory as a way of explaining the role of pleasure and desire. James's theory derives much more from Darwin than it does from associationism, though to be sure he is careful to allow a significant role for learning by reinforcement. Moreover, James wants to insist, as we saw him put it above, that pleasure and pain are not the only 'spurs to action'; people have other ends than pleasure and the avoidance of pain, and moreover these other spurs to action, our emotions and so forth, can all be qualitatively distinguished from each other. On these latter points, however, the younger Mill would agree. After all, what he was insisting upon against the older generation of utilitarians was that our various desires are all specifically different from one another and that they have objects (for example, money or virtue) that are not pleasure (or the avoidance of pain), and that, by virtue of being such objects, are sought for their own sake. But Mill also held that this was compatible with psychological hedonism, since these other objects, when they are sought for their own sakes, are sought as 'parts of happiness.' Mill held that this was so because he also held that, when these other objects of desire are attained, one experiences the pleasure of satisfied desire. Because pleasure in fact always accompanies the satisfaction of a desire, Mill can hold that men seek to maximize their happiness and that they seek objects other than pleasure and the avoidance of pain.

This issue, then, is what role James ascribes to pleasure and pain? Does he deny that when a desire is satisfied we experience the pleasure of satisfied desire?

What is immediately clear is that James is not denying that the satisfaction of desire yields pleasure, and its frustration pain. Pleasure and pain are not the *objects* of these desires and aversions; but when those objects are achieved or avoided, pleasure and pain are felt. These pleasures and pains are explained in terms of their function. 'If a movement feels agreeable, we repeat and repeat it as long as the pleasure lasts. If it hurts us, our muscular contractions at the instant stop. So complete is the inhibition in this latter case that it is almost impossible for a man to cut or mutilate himself slowly and deliberately – his hand invincibly refusing to bring on the pain' (1890, ii: 550). The function is that determined by Darwin's evolutionary theory: survival. The pain that accompanies actions that are harmful and dangerous induces us not to perform such actions; the pleasure that accompanies acts that have survival values induces us to continue performing such acts. Learning via a process such as that described by Mill can account for why many acts come to be performed for their own sakes.

Objects and thought of objects start our action, but the pleasures and pains that 'action brings modify its course and regulate it; and later the thoughts of the pleasures and pains acquire themselves impulsive and inhibitive power ... as present pleasures are tremendous reinforcers, and present pains tremendous inhibitors of whatever action leads to them, so the thought of pleasures and pains takes rank amongst the thoughts which have most impulsive and inhibitive power' (ii: 549–50). However, not all our actions derive from a process of reinforcement, many are sheer matters of habit, for example, all our daily routines, such as dressing or breathing. In these cases there is mere ideo-motor action, unaccompanied by pleasure or pain. In actions of others sorts, there is pleasure and pain, but actions of these sorts are prompted not by learned motives but by certain innate instincts and emotions. In these latter sorts of case, the connection of pleasure and pain with actions of those sorts has been established not by association but by mechanisms that are prior to association, namely, the mechanisms of natural selection and of evolutionary history. These biological mechanisms have established in the history of the species these primitive connections of pleasure and pain with certain forms of action as innate structures of the human mind (ii: 552ff).

Now, it is not clear whether Mill would feel compelled to disagree with this. It is clear that, for Mill, what is innate and what is a matter of learning is a *matter of fact*, to be discovered empirically. That there was more that was innate than Mill himself thought might have surprised him, but, if the evidence was there, he would not have disagreed with it. James does not deny that men are maximizers of pleasure; if we find that a certain sort of action is pleasurable we continue to perform acts of that sort precisely because they are pleasurable. *This thesis of psychological hedonism, that men are maximizers of pleasure, which Mill shares with the later psychology of James that was influenced by Darwin, is the only thesis that Mill needs in order to defend his utilitarian ethics and his work in economics.* The psychology that emerged under the impact of Darwin therefore seems to pose no real problems at this point, at least, for Mill's claims in ethics and economics.

The challenge to the associationist theory of learning could, however, have effected Mill's critique of ethical intuitionism, the theories of Sedgwick and Whewell, of Kames and Reid. After all, Mill based this critique on the data supposedly discovered by introspective analysis, data that supposedly established that our moral sentiments are all acquired by learning through a process of association. If one rejects that learning theory, or at least supplements that theory with large doses of innatism based on considerations drawn from evolutionary theory, then could it not be argued that moral principles are after all innate? If it could so be argued then the resulting innatism would have the considerable virtue of being based upon sound science rather than the divine teleology in which Kames and Reid, for example, had placed it.

This is certainly a *possibility*. There is not much of a real threat, however. Bain is prepared to allow that there could be inheritance of acquired characteristics, subject to at least three conditions. These are that the characteristic is (1) simple, (2) incessantly iterated, and (3) intensely interesting (1880b, p. 53). These conditions, he supposes, bring about the fixity in the animal that is necessary for there to be any possibility of hereditary transmission. On this basis Bain is prepared to allow that various reflex actions, such as eating and breathing, are innate, 'descended to us from our progenitors in the animal series' (p. 54). Bain is also prepared to allow that our capacity to distinguish spatial relations is innate. These are complex, compared to reflex actions, but they do satisfy the conditions of iteration and interest (pp. 54–5). So Bain is prepared to join Spencer (1902, II: 188–9) in contemplating the possibility that some of our abilities in space perception are innate. But 'if the notions involved in Space are, of all important mental products, the most favourably situated for being bequeathed from one generation to another, the Moral Sentiment is about least favourably situated for transmission by inheritance' (1880b, p. 55). While we are constantly involved with space, we are only intermittently involved with matters moral; although space perception is complex relative to reflex action, it is none the less simplicity itself relative to our moral notions; as for interest, the fact is that good moral habits often do conflict with interest, and this counts strongly against their becoming sufficiently habitual or fixed in individuals for them to be transmissible by inheritance (pp. 55–6). These make it antecedently improbable that our ideas of moral right and wrong, our moral sentiments, are inherited. Moreover, the posterior probabilities are also small. Careful examination of the development of moral ideas in children gives no support for the notion that they are inherited. Bain does allow that 'certain powers belonging to us at birth indispensable to the growth of our moral feelings; which powers, one or all, may have been developed through the cumulative experience of past generations' (p. 57). But, Bain says, 'Looking at the early impressions connected with the outer world, I allow that they possess a degree of precocity that experience or education can hardly account for; looking at the early moral impressions, I do not feel the same difficulty' (p. 56). On this point James agrees. A feeling of necessity attaches to our moral principles, but a careful examination shows that this sense of necessity arises from experience (1890, II: 672ff). So James agrees with Bain – and Mill – that the intuitionists are wrong in thinking that the deliverances of our moral sentiments are innate and derive from a transcendental source (II: 617).

Mill argued the same point against Kames and Reid, against Sedgwick, and against Whewell. His argument was placed in the framework established by his associationist theory of learning and the data provided by introspective analysis in support of the claim that moral sentiments are products of processes of association. But in fact the empirical evidence that he advances does not depend in any serious ways upon the details of that theory, or upon the method of introspective analysis being generally valid. What Mill does provide in support of his claim that the moral sentiments are learned is – empirical evidence. To be sure, much of this was obtained by self-observation and introspective analysis. But these were by no means the exclusive source. The point is that, on the basis of the empirical evidence provided by Mill, one could safely say that, after a process of experiencing pleasant (and unpleasant) effects, often enough deliberately instituted as rewards (and punishments), people come to experience as pleasant (or painful) activities and ends that had not originally been so, and in so experiencing them they are pursuing them for their own sake. Not even James ventured to disagree with this. It is a position that has been refined, and developed in significant detail, by psychologists, and appears today, reformulated in behaviourist terms, under the guise of reinforcement theories of learning. Mill's psychological account of the origins of our moral sentiments has simply been absorbed into the mainstream of psychology. And the conclusion that Mill drew from that account, that the phenomenology of value does not entail innatism, remains unscathed, however much Mill's way of *stating* the psychology has been transformed.

We may conclude, then, that the basic points that Mill wished to defend in the realm of ethical theory, while expressed by Mill himself in a way that took for granted associationism and the introspective method, are in fact not themselves challenged by the developments in psychology as it shifted from introspectionism and structuralism to behaviourism.

Turn now to economics.

In this area Mill's points were these, that our economic preferences are learned in a way that is to be explained by psychology, that the economic preferences are subordinate in an ordinal scale of values to our moral values (the latter are qualitatively superior), and that the hardships of accumulation through labour are relevant to the theory of economic development. Economics continues, as Mill proposed, to take economic preferences for granted. But this means, as Mill recognized and as economists too often today do not recognize, that as a science of man economics is of limited scope, that is, its law are only conditioned regularities, and a fuller science must move to remove such imperfections by fitting economics into the picture of man that psychology yields. Subjective preferences have been replaced by an objectivist account of value in the axioms of revealed preference.[46] This does not, however, mean that those preferences are unlearned. At most it implies that the psychology that explains those patterns of behaviour must itself be a behaviourist psychology; but *that* does not invalidate Mill's point. The doctrine of revealed preference is, moreover, compatible with there being revealed in behaviour a preference, superior to economics preferences, for what we would call moral behaviour, that is, behaviour in conformity to the principles of justice, contract, and allegiance. And finally, it is compatible with the hardships of labour being among the revealed preferences, so that this, too, can be incorporated into the theory of economic development, if, as Mill thought, it is indeed a relevant variable.

In short, the appeals that Mill made in moral philosophy and in the philosophy of economics to psychology remain valid, unchallenged by the demise of the classical psychology that Mill practised, or, rather, by its absorption into the broad stream of behaviourist psychology.

Conclusion

There are a number of conclusions at which we have arrived, both historical and systematic.

Historical

The major historical point that we have made is that any interpretation of some particular aspect of John Stuart Mill's philosophy – for example, his moral philosophy or his philosophy of economics – cannot neglect to take into account both his philosophy of science and his psychology. We have found that Mill's views on psychology presuppose his views on scientific explanation, and also in particular the distinction between the mechanical and the chemical modes of the composition of causes. It is the latter that turns out to give him the logical handle for rethinking the psychology that he inherited from his father and for transforming the notion of analysis from a metaphysical or logical notion into what is clearly a tool for empirical research. This enabled Mill to provide effective replies to such critics as Reid or Whewell who attacked at once Berkeley's account of perception, which seemed on the whole to Mill to be true, and the utilitarian theory of motivation, which also seemed on the whole to Mill to be correct.

We have found that an adequate reading of Mill's moral philosophy, and, in particular, such disputed points as pleasure or happiness being the only end and the defence of the quality/quantity distinction among pleasure, presupposes an understanding of Mill's views on psychology and the philosophy of psychology. It turns out that, though Mill has come in for heavy criticism since the publication of 'Utilitarianism' (1861), the critics have almost invariably written in apparent ignorance of the context of psychological theory that Mill took for granted, and employed when needed. As a consequence the critics have failed to see that Mill in fact regularly has available fully adequate responses to their objections.

Most critics have failed to recognize that John Stuart Mill can be defended in his views on psychological hedonism and on the qualitative differences among pleasures. They have therefore failed to recognize the further point that in his defences of these views the younger Mill places them on far firmer foundations that they had had in the works of Bentham or James Mill. The 'quantitative hedonism' of the latter incorporated an element of subjectivism that denied to it the status of a secure moral standard. When the younger Mill denied this quantitative hedonism by affirming the role of qualitative differences among pleasures he was able to give the utilitarian principle that status of a moral standard that it had lacked in Bentham.

More generally, we have seen that what is true of any great philosopher not surprisingly turns out to be true of John Stuart Mill, that no part of his views can be understood apart from the whole.

Systematic

We have looked at the use Mill made of the method of introspective analysis in three areas: perception, economics, and moral philosophy.

Perception

As for perception, Mill's views are now largely of historical interest only. The area is still one of psychological research, though now transformed by the shift to behaviourism and more recently by notions of information-processing. As Galileo's physics takes its place suitably transformed in the present theory of physics, so Mill's account of perception takes its place suitably transformed in the present theory, or, perhaps, theories, of psychology.

Economics

In economics, two major points we found Mill making were, first, that the science should concern itself not merely with the workings of the market but also with the theory of economic development and, second, that economics is by its nature an imperfect science the laws of which are conditioned by other variables, for example, moral factors – political might also be included – and which must, ultimately, be located as derivative from the laws of learning of psychology. In short, all economics must in the end be political economy. If one thinks of the sort of theory – general equilibrium theory – and some of the philosophy – for example, Milton Friedman's positivism, or, rather 'positivism' – that dominates so much of professional economics these days, then these two points of John Stuart Mill have compelling continuing relevance; economists would do well to take them to heart; their science, and the place of their science in society, would both be the better for it.[1]

Moral Philosophy

It is in moral philosophy, however, that Mill's message is perhaps most seriously neglected. His argument here was against the intuitionists, who claimed a final sort of moral authority for the moral sentiments they felt. Mill challenged such claims to authority by arguing that our moral sentiments, in both their objects and their motivating strength, are almost all learned. Our merely having the sentiments we have therefore confers upon them no moral authority or importance whatever. To the contrary, so to elevate them to authority is itself a value judgment that anyone who thinks rationally about such things will inevitably be led to challenge.

Now let us look at the methodology used by two recent major works in moral and political philosophy, both of which defend principles of justice that are at variance with utilitarianism. These are Nozick's *Anarchy, State and Utopia* (1974) and Rawls's *A Theory of Justice* (1971).

Nozick argues: 'The minimal state is the most extensive state that can be justified. Any state more extensive violates peoples right' (1974, p. 149). The minimal state has the sole function of protecting the rights of its citizens (pp. 12, 28–9). These rights are constituted at bottom by the rights to be undisturbed by others in, as it was traditionally put by Locke, one's life, health, liberty, and possessions (p. 10). The right of possession includes the right of possession of what one has appropriated from the common (p. 150), subject to the proviso that such appropriation makes no one else worse off (p. 178), and the right to transfer, that is, dispose of as one wills, one's possessions, including the transfer of one's rights of possession to another (p. 150). The possessions to which one has a right include those that one is entitled to by original acquisition or by transfer, or has acquired through the operation of a further principle that functions to correct past violations of rights (p. 152). Since the minimal state exists to protect rights, it is wrong for the state to attempt to redistribute goods in a society, however well meaning are the reasons, by methods of, for example, taxation by which some are made involuntarily to transfer to others goods to which they (the former) have a right by original acquisition or transfer (pp. 167ff).

Rawls disagrees. The good life is not possible without social co-operation; the good life of each is in fact the joint product of the co-operation of all (1971, p. 15). Some do in practice, for various reasons, acquire more goods than others, but since these cannot be obtained save by the co-operation of all, the others have an equal *prima facie* claim to those goods. However, all inequality, for example, of wealth or authority, cannot be eliminated (p. 103); but such inequalities are *just* provided that 'they result in compensating benefits for everyone, and in particular for the least advantaged members of society' (p. 14).

These views are at variance with each other and with the utilitarianism of John Stuart Mill. They are two among the several conceptions of justice that we find our moral sentiments leading us to approve. Mill, of course, has already pointed out that we have several such conceptions of justice (1861, pp. 241ff) and that, for these to serve the moral function of providing a guide to behaviour in the settling of disputes, a further criterion is needed to decide among them and to decide their limits of applicability. The criterion he proposes is, of course, the utilitarian. But Nozick and Rawls each claim final moral validity for their schemes, each against the other and both against utilitarianism. And it is how those who hold these positions propose to defend them that concerns us here.

If we look at Nozick, we discover that he takes the notion of rights, and of rights of original possession and transfer – essentially what we earlier called the principles of justice and of contract – as does Mill, to be principles that constrain all actions and prevent our so acting on other ends that we would violate these principles (Nozick 1974, pp. 28–35; Mill 1861, p. 255ff). But then these specific constraints are traced back to the 'root ideas ... that there are different individuals with separate lives and so no one may be sacrificed for others' (1974, p. 33). But why *ought* these specific rights to be those that define the inviolate person? We receive no answer, beyond that this is so: this is what our moral sentiments, or intuitions, are.

Suppose some of my possessions *are* taken from me, contrary to what Nozick's intuitions take to be my rights, and these goods are transferred to others to improve their lot. 'What happens is that something is done to him for the sake of others ... To use a person in this way does not sufficiently respect and take account of the fact that he is a separate person, that his is the only life he has. *He* does not get some overbalancing good from his sacrifice, and no one is entitled to force this upon him – least of all a state of government that claims his allegiance (as other individuals do not) and that therefore scrupulously must be *neutral* between its citizens' (1974, p. 33).

It is perhaps not surprising that someone in a society in which capitalism and economic individualism are dominant ideologies will have the moral sentiment that inviolable personhood and indeed 'the only life [a person] has' is defined by his rights of property and transfer. But what gives those moral sentiments moral authority?

Other sentiments are clearly possible, for example, those of Rawls. Why should one, not so in harmony with the ideology of capitalism as is Nozick, not have different moral sentiments? Some, at least, have the contrary moral sentiment that it is *right* that their property be sacrificed to improve the lot of others, with no compensation, in terms of property, to themselves. Some, at least, have the moral sentiment that it is *right and legitimate* that the government towards which they *feel* allegiance *should* effect a redistributive transfer from the better off to the less better off with no compensation of a property sort for the former. Why are these moral sentiments unjustified and those of Nozick justified? Nozick gives no answer: he simply makes the assumption that it is *his* intuitions that have moral authority.

But, of course, if Rawls is correct then it is his views that are correct. How does he propose to defend them?

Rawls's account of the fundamental principle of justice is defended by the claim that it fulfils two conditions sufficient to justify any such theory (1971, pp. 182, 6). The first of these conditions is that such a theory must be *capable* of serving as the 'public moral basis of society' (p. 182), and in particular it must comport with general facts of psychology and moral learning (pp. 145; cf pp. 8, 175–83, 245–6). With this criterion Mill would not disagree. Indeed this is the basis of his argument that happiness is the criterion of morality,[2] which is the first step in his 'proof' of utility in 'Utilitarianism.'[3]

The second Rawlsian condition is that such a theory must characterize 'our considered judgments in reflective equilibrium' (1971, p. 182); that is, applying the theory must lead us to make the same judgments 'which we now make intuitively and in which we have the greatest confidence' (pp. 19–20; cf. pp. 48ff, 318). It can be argued that Rawls's theory does not meet this second condition;[4] a follower of Nozick might well so respond, as might a follower of Milton Friedman.

But be that as it may, one should note that these conditions are far different from those imposed on a *scientific* theory, and so to appropriate the term 'theory' to describe the principle of justice that Rawls defends is to do little more than to dignify it illicitly with the sort of prestige and status that attaches to scientific theories.

But further, the second condition states that one can defend a principle of justice by showing that it accords with the strongest among our unexamined moral convictions. Rawls's principle of justice is therefore justified because it fits the strongest among the moral sentiments that he (Rawls) feels. But why should Rawls's moral sentiments have *authority* against those of Nozick? In the end, Rawls's appeal, like that of Nozick, is based on the assumption that it is his own moral intuitions that have authority.[5]

In either case this is to do no more than Whewell did when he, much earlier (1845), made such intuitions the touchstone of any acceptable moral principle. Mill was scathing in his criticism of this appeal of Whewell: 'His *Elements of Morality* could be nothing better than a classification and systematizing of the opinions which he found prevailing among those who had been educated according to the approved method of his own country; or, let us rather say, an apparatus for converting those prevailing opinions, on matters of morality, into reasons for themselves' (1852, p. 169). Nor is it merely a matter of bad reasoning: it is also socially pernicious.[6] 'The contest between the morality which appeals to an external standard, and that which grounds itself on internal conviction, is the contest of progressive morality against stationary – of reason and argument against the deification of mere opinion and habit. The doctrine that the existing order of things is the natural order, and that, being natural, all innovation upon it is criminal, is as vicious in morals, as it is now at last admitted to be in physics, and in society and government' (p. 179). Mill makes a similar point against Sedgwick (1834), who, like Whewell (a close colleague of Sedgwick), had appealed to our basic moral judgments as the criterion of morality:

> we may remark that, upon the truth or falseness of the doctrine of a moral sense, it depends whether morality is a fixed or progressive body of doctrine. If it be true that man has a sense given to him to determine what is right and wrong, it follows that his moral judgments and feelings cannot be susceptible of any improvement; such as they are they ought to remain. The question, what mankind in general ought to think and feel on the subject of their duty, must

be determined by observing what, when no interest or passion can be seen to bias them, they think and feel already. According to the theory of utility, on the contrary, the question, what is our duty, is as open to discussion as any other question. Moral doctrines are no more to be received without evidence, nor to be sifted less carefully, than any other doctrines. An appeal lies, as on all other subjects, from a received opinion, however generally entertained, to the decision of cultivated reason. The weakness of human intellect, and all the other infirmities of our nature, are considered to interfere as much with the rectitude of our judgments on morality, as on any other of our concerns; and changes as great are anticipated in our opinions on that subject, as on every other, both from the progress of intelligence from more authentic and enlarged experience, and from alternatives in the condition of the human race, requiring altered rules of conduct. (1834, pp. 73–4)

We have seen at length that Mill was fully justified in his rejection of the arguments of the intuitionists and the arguments of the defenders of moral sense. Mill's argument took as its basis his theories of psychology, and, in particular, his claim that our moral sentiments could be analysed into associations of ideas with feelings of pleasure, that is, as we would now put it after the behaviourist turn, the claim that our moral feelings are internalized principles learned in a process involving reinforcement and, more specifically, patterns of rewards and punishment. This claim of Mill's is entirely sound. Mill's critique of the intuitionists thus applies equally to Rawls and Nozick. The common view that these philosophers, the former in particular, have effected a devastating challenge to utilitarianism is simply untenable: Rawls and Nozick have erected structures without foundations, and, like any such structure, they are not worth the sand upon which they are built. We may conclude that Mill's work in moral philosophy is as devastatingly relevant to its critics as it was in Mill's own day. The critics today, as then, continue to proclaim dogmatically the moral authority of their own sentiments, and ignore Mill's psychological critique of their positions. They do so at their own risk, the risk of being refuted as mere dogmatists. Meanwhile Mill continues to stand superior to them both in depth of intellect and in moral sensibility and sensitivity to the claims of others.[7] This conclusion, which is both historical and systematic, is, perhaps, our most significant.

Notes

Introduction

1 For a detailed history, see Halévy (1901).
2 Mill argues that happiness is desirable in the normative sense in Chapter
  IV of his 'Utilitarianism' (1861). I have discussed the logical structure
  of Mill's proof of this point in Wilson (1982c), where it is shown that the
  standard objections to Mill's inference from *desired* to *desirable* are without
  substance.
3 Cf. Coleridge (1817), I: 73, 76, and, in the same idealist tradition, Blanshard (1961), pp. 26f. Similar points are made by Willey (1940), pp.
  152–4, and Bennett (1971), pp. 300–2.
4 I have argued this in detail in Wilson (1979b). It is also much of the point
  of chapter 7, below.
5 Cf. Robson (1968), pp. 119ff, 134ff, 148ff. Berger (1984), p. 21, and
  Robson (1968), p. 133, make rather more of Mill's tentativeness than
  is necessary; the principle that the capacity to respond sympathetically to
  others is learned is a scientific *hypothesis* about which very little, and
  certainly no conclusive, evidence is available, and Mill therefore cannot
  but treat it as tentative.
6 Donner (1983) also emphasizes this point.

Chapter 1

1 This *crise morale* is described in Norton (1982) and in Mintz (1962).
2 There was, of course, the furious reaction of Anglican divines,
  emphasizing the naturalness of morality and the innate nature of our
  capacities for moral judgment. This tradition culminated in Shaftesbury
  and Hutcheson. For this broader context, see Crane (1932; 1934).

By far the most subtle of these critiques, however, and the most philosophically interesting, is that of Hume in Book III of the *Treatise* (1739).

3 Cf. Cudworth, *Treatise on External and Immutable Morality* (1731), p. 125.

4 Cf. Hume, *Treatise* (1739), Book III, Part III, section iii, and Book III, Part I, section i.

5 In his *Analogy of Religion* (1736), Butler takes it for granted that the argument from design is accepted by the deists.

6 Cf. the passage quoted above, p. 25.

7 For criticism of Hume's argument, cf. Harrison (1976), and for a defence Mackie (1980).

8 Elsewhere Hutcheson puts the inference from adaptation to God in this way. It is, he says, 'in our own nature' that we discern 'a universal Mind, watchful for the Whole,' a mind that has designed our faculties and the world 'with a view to a general good *End*,' that is, so that those faculties operate in harmony in the world and provide us with the information (moral, physical, aesthetic) that is needed for our well-being' (1742, reprint ed., p. 180). Once the existence of a wise, powerful, and benevolent God has thus been inferred, we can appeal to this being and his faculties to explain our own. Thus, our innate dispositions and native capacities have been 'fixed for us by the AUTHOR of our nature, subservient to the interest of the *System*' that he has created (p. 118).

9 For the outline of such a defence, cf. Mackie (1980).

10 This is the point of G.E. Moore's 'Open Question'; cf. his *Principia Ethica* (1903), Chapter I.

11 For greater detail, and the Cartesian context, cf. Watson (1966).

12 I have examined the demise of the substance account of explanation in Wilson (1969b; 1986b).

13 For an extended discussion of this pattern of argument, based on a 'Principle of Acquaintance,' cf. Wilson (1970; also 1983a).

14 For analysis of Hume's argument here, cf. Wilson (1989a; 1982d; 1989c).

15 For analysis of this pattern in Berkeley, cf. Allaire (1963), Cummins (1963), and Hausman (1984).

16 For discussion of Berkeley's claim to be a realist, cf. Luce (1945).

17 For a detailed discussion of Hume's analysis and argument, cf. Wilson (1989a).

18 This argument of Hume's is analysed in Wilson (1985b). If the argument of Wilson (1982c) is correct, then there is a clear connection with Mill's proof that happiness is desirable.

19 Berkeley is quite clear on this; cf. (1734, PP 30, 34, 36).

20 This argument is discussed in detail in Cummins (1963).

21 Cf. Luce (1945) for a clear statement of the realist interpretation of Berkeley.

22 This point is discussed in Árdal (1977).

23 Berkeley, in *The Principles*, refers to these qualities as 'ideas,' an injudicious choice of terminology that he corrects in the *Three Dialogues between Hylas and Philonus*.

24 I skirt the Molyneaux problem.

25 Berkeley's connections with Malebranche are discussed in Luce (1934), Hume's connections in Jones (1982) and J. Wright (1983).

26 The connection of Berkeley to Malebranche is explored in detail in Luce (1934); cf p. 46.

27 All references are to this second edition. The first two editions were published anonymously. There was a third edition with Kames's signature in 1779. Kames was replying in part to Hume. While Hume was likely not convinced, he did approve of the way Kames went about his task; cf. Hume's letter to Michael Ramsey, 22 June 1751 (1932, I: 162).

28 The Gestalt psychologists were later to make the same point, that since certain mental states were not inferences, they were therefore (non-sensory) contents. In making this point, they were preceded by the Würzburg psychologists, led by Külpe (cf. Boring 1957, p. 593). But the Würzburgers followed Mill in not drawing the further conclusion of innateness. The Gestalters, in contrast, followed Kames and Reid in making this illegitimate inference.

29 Compare the lines of Blake: 'I touch the sky with my finger / Distance is nothing but a fantasy.'

30 Cf. Russell's *Principles of Mathematics* (1903) for a metaphysical defence of relations against monadistic and monistic attempts to analyse them into non-relational qualities. See also Weinberg's essay 'Relation' in his collection of important studies (1965) and Wilson (1969a). Russell employs his account of relations in the analysis of perceptual objects as patterns of sensible qualities in his 'Ultimate Constituents of Matter' (1915).

31 Cf. Norton (1982), pp. 189ff. Norton scruples at saying that Reid was 'profoundly' influenced by Kames.

32 On Hume's account of causation, cf. Wilson (1979b).

33 The extent to which this connects Reid's position to the similar Cartesian position is discussed in Vernier (1976) and Marcil-Lacoste (1975). See also Sommerville (1987), Cummins (1974), and Wolterstorff (1987).

34 This history is discussed in Waldman (1959).

35 F.E.L. Priestley (1969) claims that J.S. Mill 'dismisses the calculus of pain

over pleasure' (p. xli) when he (Mill) argues that quality which cannot be 'reduced' (Priestley's term) to quantity is a moral criterion. But Priestley unfortunately does not say why the addition of quality amounts to dismissing the calculus. Why could one not still have a *calculus*? Priestley doesn't explain. Why must a calculus involve a *reduction* of the qualitative to the quantitative? Priestley does not explain. Priestley simply characterizes the difference between Bentham and J.S. Mill through an employment of such terms as 'reduction' and 'calculus,' with no attempt either to analyse these concepts or to understand what is involved in the difference.

36 Priestley (1969, p. xl) simply dismisses the notion that one could have a *calculus* even with the introduction of qualitative over and above quantitative distinctions. But why should the notion of a calculus be restricted to relations establishing a cardinal order? Why can we not have calculi for other, perhaps weaker, perhaps stronger, relational structures? But one of course *can* have such calculi. Priestley has clearly not studied, or at least not understood, abstract algebra, where such structures are routinely studied – or, for that matter, modern economics, which has established that the theorems of economics do not need to assume a cardinal ordering of preferences, that a weaker ordinal structure will do. Such an ignoring of mathematics and science is, perhaps, typical of 'humanists' such as Priestley for whom an 'understanding' of what Mill is about can be derived from comparisons with religious reformers and from the use of such metaphors as 'conversion.' But this is quite insufficient for a genuinely sympathetic understanding for such a one as John Stuart Mill who has a breadth of vision that is not narrowly humanistic but extends to include the sciences, including the science of psychology. Indeed, the notion that one can obtain a genuinely humane vision of man without a serious study of scientific psychology, a notion all too characteristic of those who like to call themselves humanists, is just silly. But more specifically it also prevents Priestley from recognizing the important role that Wordsworth and his poetry played in the younger Mill coming to an adequate understanding of the introspective method in scientific psychology. For the latter, see Wilson (1989b).

37 Wordsworth's relationship with the associationist–utilitarian tradition, and its significance for the younger Mill, are explored in Wilson (1989b).

Chapter 2

1 The classic discussion is that of Hempel and Oppenheim (1965). For a

defence of the covering law model against a variety of recent criticisms, cf. Wilson (1969b; 1985a; 1986a).

2 For discussion, cf. Brodbeck (1960) and Wilson (1985a).

3 On the notion of function, cf. Bergmann (1962); also Wilson (forthcoming b).

4 Cf. E.G. Boring, *A History of Experimental Psychology* (1957), for details. This extremely valuable history can be usefully read for most of the topics that we discuss, as well as for relevant background and for its full bibliography.

5 On the notion of an abstractive generic theory and its relevance for the philosophy of science, cf. Wilson (1986b).

6 For discussion of the formal logic of these inference patterns, cf. G.H. von Wright (1965).

7 For further discussion of the logic of Mill's inference, cf. Wilson (1982b; 1986b).

8 As I argue in Wilson (1983d, 1986b), there are connections between Mill's account of science and that of Thomas Kuhn in his *Structure of Scientific Revolutions* (1970).

9 The best discussion of the notion of a composition law is in Bergmann, *Philosophy of Science* (1957), Chapter Three. See also Madden (1962) for a discussion specific to issues in the philosophy of psychology.

10 Cf. Bergmann (1957) and Madden (1962) for detailed discussions of Gestalt psychology.

11 For discussion of these psychologists, cf. Grossmann (1983).

12 Some recent thinkers have forgotten these lessons about relations; cf. Wilson (1984).

13 For a discussion of this notion, cf. Addis (1975).

Chapter 3

1 In this terminology, we follow that of Bergmann (1952). This use of the term 'phenomenology' does not, of course, make specific reference to Husserl; it follows, rather, the normal use that psychologists made of it before Husserl managed to appropriate the term for his own special, and metaphysically idiosyncratic, type of analysis. The location of phenomenology, in the broad, non-Husserlian sense, in late nineteenth- and early twentieth-century psychology can be found described in detail in Boring (1957), pp. 601–4.

2 There was a controversy concerning the essences or 'real definitions' of substances into which we need not go but which forms the context of Locke's discussions of nominal definitions and of substances; cf. Wilson (1986a).

3 For a more extended discussion of this point, cf. Wilson (1965).
4 See also Wilson (1979b; 1985a; 1986b).
5 For greater detail, and some other aspects of Hume's introspective psychology, cf. Wilson (1989d).
6 Cf. Wilson (1985a), Chapter One.
7 Cf. Weinberg's essay 'Abstraction,' in his important book (1965).
8 For greater detail, cf. Wilson (1979b; 1983c).
9 This suggestion can be found in James's *Principles of Psychology* (1890).
10 Some philosophers, such as Hume (1739), argued that association could be based on *similarity* as well as contiguity (cf. Wilson 1989d). James Mill attempted to reduce association by resemblance to contiguity (1825, I: 106ff); John Stuart Mill asserts that this is 'the least successful attempt at generalisation' in the work (1869, I: 111n). It was a continuing issue for psychologists, however; Wundt, for example, agreed in effect with the elder Mill (cf. 1902, pp. 270–1).
11 These developments are neatly discussed in Boring (1957), pp. 404ff.
12 Cf. also Mill (1859a), p. 349: 'There can be no positive proof that oxygen, or any other body, is a simple substance. The sole proof that can be given is, that no one has hitherto succeeded in decomposing it. And nothing can positively prove that any particular one of the constituents of the mind is ultimate. We can only presume it to be such, from the ill success of every attempt to resolve it into simpler elements.'

Chapter 4

1 For more on these patterns of confirmation in Mill, cf. Wilson (1982b, 1985a).
2 On this notion of significance, cf. Bergmann, *Philosophy of Science* (1957), Chapter One. See also Wilson (1967).
3 For more detail, see Wilson (1982a).
4 See Wilson (1985a).
5 This supposition must be true if the definite description is to be successful, and capable of use in making true statements of scientific law.
6 Cf. Wilson (1986b), Chapter One.
7 Mill's use of 'introspective' in this context is not the current use, nor is it the one we use.
8 For a good discussion of Whewell's views, cf. Butts (1969).
9 Cf. Russell (1903), Weinberg (1965), and Wilson (1969a; 1970).
10 It is 'empiricism' in *this* sense, of a psychological theory of learning, opposed to nativism or innatism, that Chomsky attacks. There is nothing in his discussions that at all touches empiricism as a philosophy of

science. Like a long line of nativists, Chomsky misses this point. He would have done well to read Mill, or Herbert Spencer, who were perfectly clear on all this.

Chapter 5

1 And it is a matter of fact; cf. Wilson (1985d; also 1985c).
2 The first crucial distinction was that between sensation and idea, discussed in the preceding chapter.
3 On this point about Reid, cf. Boring (1942), pp. 13–14, Boring (1957), pp. 205–6, and Pastore (1971), pp. 114–20. See also Wolterstorff (1987).
4 For further discussion of Brown, cf. Boring (1942), p. 14, and Boring (1957), pp. 207–9.
5 Cf. Allaire (1963), Cummins (1963), and Hausman (1984).
6 Cf. Wilson (1970; 1989a).
7 Bergmann developed this point in his philosophy of mind; cf. his seminal essay (1960) and Grossmann (1959). See also Wilson (1983a) and Addis (1982, 1986).
8 For a discussion of some central aspects of these problems, cf. Lewis (1965).
9 For discussion, cf. Bergmann (1955), Grossmann (1959), Sellars (1964), and Wilson (1983a).
10 For Hume's view, cf. Wilson (1979b).
11 On this point, cf. Bergmann (1960).
12 For more on this important point, cf. Wilson (1979b; 1983c).
13 See chapter 2, above. Also G.H. von Wright (1965) and Wilson (1982b).
14 Other, more contemporary, uses of such examples are also disposed of, with equal ease; cf. Wilson (1985a).
15 Hume also recognizes that one can draw conclusions about causes from a single experiment; cf. *Treatise* (1739), p. 104. Hume's discussion makes clear that he intends the same analysis of such an inference as we are about to supply for Ducasse; cf. Wilson (1979a).
16 Patterns of *ex post facto* explanation are familiar in science and in everyday life; cf. Wilson (1985a; 1986b).
17 See, for example, Gibson (1982), Essay 4.2.
18 Concerning representationalism in this context, cf. Grossmann (1959) and Wilson (1970).
19 On this point, cf. Boring (1942), pp. 25–6.
20 See chapter 2, above, especially note 13.
21 On this point, cf. Pastore (1971), pp. 270–1, 284ff.

22 For such detail, cf. Boring (1942), pp. 83–90, 95f, 245–56, 260–2. Boring (1942) also contains further bibliographic references.
23 On Titchener's view, cf. Bergmann (1955).
24 For the development of the Würzburger position against Titchener, cf. Humphrey (1951).
25 On this point, cf. Boring (1942), pp. 17–18, 31–3.

Chapter 6

1 This is not to say that these are *all* the required principles; but conformity to at least these is required.
2 Compare the discussion in Rosenberg (1976), and, from a different perspective, Addis (1975).
3 Mill quite reasonably accepted this principle; cf. Wilson (1982c).
4 For the argument in detail for this attribution, cf. Rauner (1961), Appendix III.
5 For a discussion of the possible influence of Bentham on Ricardo's economic thought, cf. S. Hollander (1979).
6 On this notion of significance, cf. Bergmann (1957), Chapter One, and Wilson (1967).
7 On this point, cf. Cassels (1935), p. 87.
8 Or rather, if explanation and justification are to be pursued beyond the innateness claim, then it would be, as for Kames and Reid, in both perception and ethics, by reference to a providential teleology.
9 This point is made in Wilson (1967).

Chapter 7

1 Dryer spells out how this requires us to interpret the principle of utility.
2 On Mill's proof, cf. Hall (1964) and Wilson (1982c; 1983b; 1985b).
3 For the notion of 'how possibly' explanations, cf. Dray (1957), pp. 164–6, and Wilson (1985a). The latter argues that this notion is fully compatible with the empiricist 'covering law model' or 'deductive-nomological model' of explanation that John Stuart Mill developed and defended.
4 A similar point is suggested in Holbrook (1988), p. 65, at least upon what he calls the 'desire theory of pleasure,' in which "pleasure" is either what is desired or what would be desired, given the proper situation' (p. 62). Broad's argument certainly works against this position. But that is neither here nor there, since this 'desire theory of pleasure' is certainly not Mill's view.
5 I have argued this point in detail in Wilson (1979b).

6 I discuss this argument in detail in Wilson (1982c).

7 Priestley (1969), p. xli, makes more of this terminological shift than is necessary. Mill's views may, as Priestley suggests, be 'broader' than Bentham's, but on every *crucial* point he is with Bentham and against Richard Price, Reid, Sedgwick, and Whewell.

8 Robins's view is discussed in Rosenberg (1976).

9 The role of such mental culture is emphasized in the important essay of Wendy Donner (1983).

10 Again, the role of such mental culture is spelled out in Donner (1983).

11 It can, I think, be argued that the ancestors of the utilitarians, from Hume back to Epicurus, understood the role of qualitative differences among pleasures. The same could be said for Bentham and James Mill – as the younger Mill did on occasion say of them. But they all lacked what the younger Mill had, namely, a philosophy of science adequate enough to allow that the higher pleasures are a consequence of learning.

12 Edwards, in his later essay (1979), deals with these points in much the same way as he did in his earlier one (1975).

13 A similar point has been made by Narveson (1967), pp. 75–82. See also Dahl (1973), and Edwards (1979), pp. 86ff. Holbrook (1988), pp. 86–9, does not understand this simple point.

14 Recall the discussion of relation in chapter 4, section 4, above.

15 Compare the discussion in Donner (1983).

16 Mill thinks that the Deductive Method applies to political economy, but in this he is mistaken (cf. Wilson 1983b). It follows that Bain's remark also applies to the social sciences.

17 Halévy (1901, vol. 1) suggested a later date, posterior to the publication of the *Principles of Morals and Legislation*; but the earlier dating is demonstrated in Goldworth (1979).

18 Cited in Goldworth (1979), p. 13

19 For further discussion of this aspect of Bentham's thought, see Wesley Mitchell (1918).

20 Priestley (1969) fails to recognize that the claims of Mill and Bentham are in this way compatible; contrary to what Priestley claims, the mere presence of qualitative distinctions among pleasures would not have prevented John Stuart Mill from developing a quantitative ethics on the model of Bentham. The disagreement between Mill and Bentham cuts to a deeper level than Priestley's texbook-level account can conceive.

21 We now know, of course, that using the device invented by von Neumann and Morgenstern, any ordinal scale of preferences can be cardinalized. But this method does not depend upon the illusion of a unit of inten-

sity; it is not at all the sort of cardinalization that Bentham and his immediate disciples had in mind.

Chapter 8

1 A good first history of physiology can be found in T.S. Hall (1975).
2 Cf. Boring (1957), pp. 157ff, 316ff, for the lines from Descartes to Wundt.
3 For a discussion of these issues, cf. Wilson (1974).
4 Cf. Mill (1859), p. 348: 'if it be materialism to endeavour to ascertain the material conditions of our mental operations, all theories of the mind which have any pretension to comprehensiveness must be materialistic ... [T]hat our mental operations have material conditions, can be denied by no one who acknowledges, what all now admit, that the mind employs the brain as its material organ ... Unhappily, the knowledge hitherto obtainable on this subject [the detailed connexions between mental manifestations and cerebral or nervous states] has been very limited in amount; but when we consider, for example, the case of all our stronger emotions, and the disturbances of almost every part of our physical frame, which is occasioned in these cases by a mere mental idea, no rational person can doubt the closeness of the connexion between the functions of the nervous system and the phenomena of mind, nor can think any exposition of the mind satisfactory, into which that connexion does not enter as a prominent feature.'
5 For the best discussion of parallelism see Addis (1965, 1975, 1982). The discussion in C.A. Strong (1903) is still good, if redolent of the views of the late nineteenth century. See also Bergmann (1956; 1957). Parallelism by itself is a relatively weak notion. There are stronger versions of the thesis, for example, the double-aspect view of Bain (1873), or the panpsychism of Strong (1903), or the contingent identity of some more recent philosophers such as Feigl (1958) (on the last named, cf. Brodbeck [1966]). These stronger claims raise many important issues, but this is not the place to pursue them. The point is: each of these stronger claims entails the weaker thesis of parallelism, to which we may restrict ourselves.
6 For a discussion of the logic of such counterfactual inference along the lines first laid down by Hume, and followed by Mill, cf. Wilson (1986b). For Hume, see Wilson (1979b).
7 There are many simplifications being made here concerning the notion of causation. For more on the analysis of this latter concept, cf. Wilson (1985a; also 1986b).
8 On this point, cf. Wilson (1985a; 1986b).

9 See Bergmann (1957), Chapter Three, and Addis (1975).

10 Textbooks such as Shaffer's (1968) continue to make this crude identification. It is unfortunate that, for whatever reason, textbooks are so often written by those who have not thought the issues through clearly enough. That is how philosophical myths are perpetuated.

11 Addis (1965) shows how interactionism, unless it is properly restricted, leads to a scepticism with regard to other minds. Parallelism, he establishes, does not have this problem.

12 For discussion of the correlation/causation distinction, cf. Wilson (1985a; 1986b).

13 The phrase 'nomological dangler' is Feigl's; cf. his monograph (1958).

14 The logic of historical laws in psychology is discussed in Bergmann (1957), Chapter Two, and, with special reference to Freud, in his important essay (1940).

15 The mathematics of such laws – integro-differential equations – was worked out by Volterra (1930).

16 The existentialist and phenomenologist philosophers make much of the so-called historicity of man, suggesting that this distinguishes people from stones, and makes the notion of natural science as applied to stones inapplicable to man. Disdaining science, those philosophers are simply ignorant of the fact that in physics laws are historical in just the way that man is said by philosophers to be 'historical.' Their case therefore collapses. Both Hume and Mill recognize the 'historical' nature of man – the laws of learning are 'historical' laws – but quite correctly insisted that these are none the less *laws* of human phenomena, and that the method appropriate for their discovery is the same method as that used in natural sciences such as physics.

17 The response to a poem on its second reading is very different from the response on its first reading.

18 How often is it that one sees the suggestion (cf. Bennett, 1971) that one cannot explain the meaning of 'salt-shaker' by reference to the disposition to use 'salt-shaker' in the presence of a salt-shaker because often people are not so disposed! Quick allusions to set, history, and stimulus conditions remove the problem immediately.

19 For details, cf. Boring (1957), Chapter 20.

20 Cf. W. Sellars (1954; 1964).

21 Cf. Sellars (1954) and Wilson (1975).

22 Cf. Bergmann and Spence (1941).

23 Since some thinkers, for example, Chomsky, tend to confuse *behaviourism* with reinforcement *theories of learning*, the point just made is worth emphasizing, as is the further point, again contrary to Chomsky, that the

issue is scientific, not ideological. On the connection between behaviourism and logical positivism, see Smith (1986) and Addis (1989). The important point that what is now called 'cognitive psychology' practises methodological behaviourism is made in Spiker (1977, pp. 98ff).

24 On this point, cf. Bergmann (1952).

25 Cf. the textbook of Harvey Carr (1925). Carr was Angell's successor at Chicago.

26 For the beginnings of animal psychology, cf. Boring (1957), pp. 472ff; for the connections of this with the emergence of behaviourism, cf. Boakes (1984).

27 On this point, cf. Boring (1957), pp. 338–9, 386ff, 401ff.

28 Kuhn (1970) has emphasized how developments in research techniques can, like breakthroughs in theory, lead to profound changes in science.

29 On this footnote, Cf. Bergmann (1956).

30 Cf. Pratt (1939), Boring (1941), and Bergmann and Spence (1944).

31 Cf. Bergmann and Spence (1941).

32 The title of Watson's thesis at Chicago in 1903 was 'Animal Education: The Psychical Development of the White Rat,' that of Thorndyke's at Columbia in 1898 was 'Animal Intelligence: An Experimental Study of the Associative Processes in Animals.' These titles alone give a flavour of how psychology was developing.

33 The term is Titchener's, but he got it from James; cf. Boring (1957), p. 555.

34 As Boring puts, 'it is impossible to resist the impression that these feelings [of Wundt's theory], responsible to nothing but the will of their master, prevented many problems from coming to the fore, like the problem of meaning' (1957, p. 330).

35 This was Galton's major contribution; cf. Boring (1957), p. 485.

36 The point came out in a controversy between Baldwin (1895, 1896) and Titchener (1895, 1896) over reaction times. The practised observers of the Leipzig laboratory registered that sensorial reaction is longer, by about 1/10 second, than muscular reaction. Titchener defended this result. Baldwin found a difference in the other direction, however, with unpractised observers. Baldwin argued that Titchener was refusing to open his eyes to a fact of nature; while Titchener argued that science is concerned only with the laws of the generalized mind, that practice in adopting an attitude makes it possible to exhibit the laws of the generalized mind for those attitudes, and that a statement that deviations are a matter of individual differences is not a statement of law unless those differences can be shown to result from certain definite conditions. See Boring (1957), pp. 413–14.

37 One early (1896) study by the functionalist J.R. Angell (with A.W. Moore) on reaction times (cf. note 36, above) was an attempt to bring Baldwin and Titchener, that is, individual differences and the generalized mind, together in a single framework – a sort of Hegelian synthesis, as Boring (1957, p. 555) suggests.

38 As Boring (1957, p. 507) puts it: 'The Americans travelled to Leipzig to learn about the new psychology from Wundt; they came back fired with enthusiasm for physiological psychology and experimental laboratories; they got their universities to let them give the new courses and have the new laboratories; they extolled their German inspiration; and then, with surprisingly little comment on what they were doing and probably little awareness of it, they changed the pattern of psychological activity from the description of the generalized mind to the assessment of personal capacities in the successful adjustment of the individual to his environment. The apparatus was Wundt's, but the inspiration was Galton's.'

39 Cf. Kuhn (1970), Section VII.

40 For details, cf. Humphrey (1951). For an example of the impact of research into imageless thoughts on the practice of psychology, see Washburn (1916), Ch. X.

41 Cf. Bergmann (1952).

42 These thinkers are discussed in detail in Grossmann (1983).

43 Cf. Boring (1957), pp. 402–6.

44 Cf. Humphrey (1951) for details.

45 Cf. Boring (1957), pp. 639–41, 715ff.

46 Cf. Samuelson (1938; 1948) for a discussion of revealed preference.

Conclusion

1 For more on this line of thought, from very different perspectives, cf. Bladen (1974) and Rosenberg (1976).

2 Cf. Wilson (1982c).

3 This 'practical' side of Mill's thought receives its due emphasis in Robson (1968).

4 As, for example, in D. Copp (1974).

5 R.M. Hare (1973) also argues that Rawls is committed to a sort of intuitionist foundationalism that is inherently conservative. For an alternative reading, see M.P. DePaul (1986).

6 See also M. Goldinger (1976).

7 To thus argue that intuitionists then and now are constructing edifices without foundations is not to say that Mill's celebrated defence of the

utilitarian principle (in Chapter IV of 'Utilitarianism') is wholly sound. I
have argued elsewhere (1983b) that it is not, though I have also
argued (1982c) that it is not as defective as is usually thought. Mill
at the very least recognizes, as Nozick and Rawls do not, that moral
principles require a justification that goes beyond a mere appeal to our
moral 'intuitions.' In the end, if Mill's 'proof' of the principle of utility
is unsound, then he may be no better off than Nozick and Rawls, but he
will have at least established that he is the better philosopher since
he was aware of the problems where they are not. That is, perhaps,
a reasonable achievement.

References

Abelson, R. 1967. Art: 'History of Ethics.' *The Encyclopedia of Philosophy*, vol. 3, ed. P. Edwards. New York: Collier Macmillan

Addis, L. 1965. 'Ryle's Ontology of Mind.' In L. Addis and D. Lewis (1965)

– 1975. *The Logic of Society*. Minneapolis: University of Minnesota Press

– 1982. 'Behaviorism and the Philosophy of the Act.' *Noûs, 16*: 399–420

– 1986. 'Pains and Other Secondary Mental Entities.' *Philosophy and Phenomenological Research, 47*: 59–74

– 1989. Review of L.D. Smith, *Behaviorism and Logical Positivism. Synthèse, 78*: 345–56

Addis, L., and D. Lewis. 1965. *Moore and Ryle: Two Ontologists*. The Hague: Nijhoff

Allaire, E.B. 1963. 'Berkeley's Idealism.' *Theoria, 29*: 229–44

Angell, J.R. 1907. 'The Province of Functional Psychology.' *Psychological Review, 14*: 61–9

Anonymous. 1826. 'On the Nature, Measures, and Causes of Value.' *Westminster Review, 5* (Jan. 1826): 157–72

– 1960a. Article 'John Stuart Mill.' In J.O. Urmson (1960)

– 1960b. Article 'Utilitarianism.' In J.O. Urmson (1960)

Árdal, P. 1977. 'Convention and Value.' In G.P. Morice, ed., *David Hume: Bicentenary Papers*, 51–68. Edinburgh: University of Edinburgh Press

Bailey, S. 1825. *A Critical Dissertation on the Nature, Measures and Causes of Value*. London: R. Hunter. London School of Economics Reprints, 1931

– 1826. *A Letter to a Political Economist*. London: R. Hunter

– 1842. *A Review of Berkeley's Theory of Vision, designed to show the unsoundness of that celebrated speculation*. London: Ridgeway

– 1843. *A Letter to a Philosopher in Reply to Some Recent Attempts to Vindicate Berkeley's Theory of Vision*. London: Ridgeway

– 1855–63. *Letters on the Philosophy of the Human Mind*. London: Longman, Brown, Green and Longmans

Bain, A. 1868. *The Senses and the Intellect*. Third edition. London: Longmans, Green, and Co.
- 1869. Notes to James Mill's (1825) *Analysis of the Phenomena of the Human Mind*
- 1873. *Mind and Body*. Second edition. London: Henry S. King & Co.
- 1880a. *Moral Science: A Compendium of Ethics*. New York: D. Appleton and Co.
- 1880b. *The Emotions and the Will*. Third edition. London: Longmans, Green, and Co.
- 1882. *John Stuart Mill. A Criticism: With Personal Recollections*. London: Longmans, Green, and Co.
Baldwin, J.M. 1895. 'Types of Reaction.' *Psychological Review*, 2: 259–73
- 1896. 'The "Type-Theory" of Reaction.' *Mind*, n.s. 5: 81–90
Bennett, J. 1971. *Locke, Berkeley, Hume*. London: Oxford University Press
Bentham, J. 1770s. Bentham Manuscripts, University College, London. U.C. xxvii; excerpted in part in A. Goldworth (1979). Page references are to the Goldworth paper, followed in parentheses by the page reference to the manuscript U.C. xxvii in the University College Bentham collection.
- 1789. *Principles of Morals and Legislation*. Oxford: Clarendon Press 1907
- 1822. *Codification Proposal Addressed by Jeremy Bentham to All Nations Professing Liberal Opinions*. In J. Bowring, ed., *The Works of Jeremy Bentham*. New York: Russell and Russell 1962
Bentley, Richard. 1716–17. 'A Sermon Preached before King George I.' In his *Works*, vol. III. London: Francis Macpherson 1838
Berger, F. 1984. *Happiness, Justice, and Freedom*. Berkeley: University of California Press
Bergmann, G. 1940. 'On Some Methodological Problems of Psychology.' *Philosophy of Science*, 7: 205–19
- 1952. 'The Problem of Relations in Classical Psychology.' In his *The Metaphysics of Logical Positivism*, 277–99. New York: Longmans, Green, & Co. 1954
- 1955. 'Intentionality.' In his *Meaning and Existence*, 3–38. Madison, Wis.: University of Wisconsin Press 1959
- 1956. 'The Contribution of John B. Watson.' *Psychological Review*, 63: 265–76
- 1957. *Philosophy of Science*. Madison, Wis.: University of Wisconsin Press
- 1960. 'Acts.' In his *Logic and Reality*, 3–44. Madison, Wis.: University of Wisconsin Press 1964
- 1962. 'Purpose, Function and Scientific Explanation.' *Acta Sociologica*, 5: 225–38
Bergmann, G., and K.W. Spence. 1941. 'Operationism and Theory in Psychology.' *Psychological Review*, 48: 1–14

- 1944. 'The Logic of Psychophysical Measurement.' *Psychological Review*, 51: 1–24
Berkeley, G. 1709. *An Essay towards a New Theory of Vision*. In *The Works*, ed. A.A. Luce and T.E. Jessop. Edinburgh: Nelson 1948–57. References are to the numbered paragraphs of this work.
- 1734. *A Treatise concerning the Principles of Human Knowledge*. In *The Works*, ed. A.A. Luce and T.E. Jessop. Edinburgh: Nelson 1948–57. References are to the numbered paragraphs of this work.
Bladen, V. 1965. 'Introduction' to J.S. Mill, *The Principles of Political Economy*, vols. II and III of *The Collected Works of J.S. Mill*, ed. J. Robson. Toronto: University of Toronto Press
- 1974. *From Adam Smith to Maynard Keynes*. Toronto: University of Toronto Press
Blanshard, B. 1961. 'The Case for Determinism.' In S. Hook, ed., *Determinism and Freedom*. New York: Collier
Boakes, R. 1984. *From Darwinism to Behaviourism*. London: Cambridge University Press
Boring, E.G. 1933. *The Physical Dimensions of Consciousness*. New York: Century
- 1939. 'The Psychophysics of Color Tolerance (three color attributes as functions of two stimulus variables).' *American Journal of Psychology*, 52: 384–94
- 1941. 'An Operational Restatement of G.E. Müller's Psychophysical Axioms.' *Psychological Review*, 48: 457–64
- 1942. *Sensation and Perception in the History of Experimental Psychology*. New York: D. Appleton-Century Co.
- 1957. *A History of Experimental Psychology*. Second edition. New York: Appleton-Century-Crofts
Boulding, K. 1939. 'Equilibrium and Wealth.' *Canadian Journal of Economics and Political Science*, 1: 1–18
Bradley, F.H. 1927. *Ethical Studies*. Second edition. Oxford: Clarendon Press
Brandt, Richard B. 1979. *A Theory of the Good and the Right*. Oxford: Clarendon Press
Brentano, F. 1874. *Psychologie vom empirischen Standpunkte*. Leipzig: Duncker and Humbolt
Broad, C.D. 1925. *Mind and Its Place in Nature*. London: Routledge and Kegan Paul
- 1930. *Five Types of Ethical Theory*. London: Routledge and Kegan Paul
Brodbeck, M. 1960. 'Explanation, Prediction, and "Imperfect" Knowledge.' In Brodbeck (1968), 363–98
- 1966. 'Mental and Physical: Identity vs. Sameness.' In P.K. Feyerabend and G. Maxwell, eds. *Mind, Matter and Method*. Minneapolis: University of Minnesota Press

– ed. 1968. *Readings in the Philosophy of the Social Sciences*. New York: Macmillan

Bronaugh, R.N. 1974. 'The Utility of Quality: An Understanding of Mill.' *Canadian Journal of Philosophy, 4*: 317–26

Brown, T. 1820. *Lectures on the Philosophy of the Human Mind*. Edinburgh: William Tait 1828

Burnet, Thomas 1697. *Remarks upon an Essay concerning Humane Understanding. In a Letter Address'd to the Author*. London: M. Wotton

– 1699. *Third Remarks upon an Essay concerning Humane Understanding*. London: M. Wotton

Butler, J. 1736. *The Analogy of Religion*. In *The Works*, ed. Rt Hon. W.E. Gladstone. Two volumes. Oxford: Oxford University Press 1897

– 1749. *Fifteen Sermons*. Fourth edition. Reprinted (in part) in D.D. Raphael (1969), vol. I. References are to numbered paragraphs in the latter.

Butts, R. 1968. 'Introduction' to R. Butts, ed., *William Whewell's Theory of Scientific Method*. Pittsburgh: University of Pittsburgh Press

Carpenter, William B. 1855. *Principles of Human Physiology*. Fifth edition. London: John Churchill

– 1890. *Principles of Mental Physiology*. Fourth edition. New York: D. Appleton and Co.

Carr, Harvey 1925. *Psychology*. New York: Longmans

Cassels, J. 1935. 'A Re-interpretation of Ricardo on Value.' In J.H. Rima, ed., *Readings in the History of Economic Theory*. New York: Holt, Rinehart, and Winston 1970

Clarke, S. 1705. *Discourse upon Natural Religion*. Reprinted (in part) in L.A. Selby-Bigge (1897), vol. II. References are to the latter.

– 1740. *Dissertation of the Nature of Virtue*. Third edition. Reprinted (in part) in D.D. Raphael (1969), vol. I. References are to numbered paragraphs in the latter.

Coleridge, S.T. 1817. *Biographia Literaria*, ed. J. Shawcross. Two volumes. London: Oxford University Press 1907

– 1818. 'On Method.' In *The Portable Coleridge*, ed. I.A. Richards. New York: Viking Press 1961

Copp, D. 1974. 'Justice and the Difference Principle.' *Canadian Journal of Philosophy, 4*: 229–40

Crane, R.S. 1932. 'Reviews of Alderman, W.E., "Shaftesbury and The Doctrine of Benevolence" and Alderman, W.E., "Shaftesbury and the Doctrine of Moral Sense in the Eighteenth Century".' *Philological Quarterly, 11*: 203–6

– 1934. 'Suggestions toward a Genealogy of the "Man of Feeling".' *English Literary History, 1*: 205–30

Crousaz, J.P. de. 1724. *A New Treatise on the Art of Thinking*. London: Tho. Woodward

Cudworth, R. 1731. *Treatise on Eternal and Immutable Morality*. Reprinted (in part) in D.D. Raphael (1969), vol. I. Page references are to the latter.

Cummins, P. 1963. 'Perceptual Relativity and Ideas in the Mind.' *Philosophy and Phenomenological Research, 24*: 202–14

– 1974. 'Reid's Realism.' *Journal of the History of Philosophy, 12*: 317–40

Dahl, Norman. 1973. 'Is Mill's Hedonism Inconsistent?' In N. Rescher, ed., *Studies in Ethics*. American Philosophical Quarterly Monograph Series, no. 7. Oxford: Basil Blackwell

Darwin, C. 1873. *The Expression of Emotions in Man and Animals*. New York: D. Appleton

Datan, N., and H.W. Reese, eds. 1977. *Life-Span and Developmental Psychology*. New York: Academic Press

DePaul, M.P. 1986. 'Reflective Equilibrium and Foundationalism.' *American Philosophical Quarterly, 23*: 59–70

Descartes, R. 1637. *La Dioptique*. In his *Oeuvres*, ed. C. Adam and P. Tannery, vol. VI. New ed. C.N.R.S. Paris: J. Vrin 1973

Diderot, D. 1748. *Mémoires sur différents sujets de mathématiques*. In D. Diderot, *Ouevres complètes*, tome second. Paris: Société Encyclopédique Française et le Club Français de Livre 1969

– 1752a. Article 'Beau' in *l'Encyclopédie*. Published alone in 1772 as 'Traité du beau' and in 1778 as 'Recherches philosophiques sur l'origine et la nature du beau.' In D. Diderot, *Oeuvres complètes*, tome second. Paris: Société Encyclopédique Française et le Club Français de Livre 1969

– 1752b. Article 'Juste' in *l'Encyclopédie*. In D. Diderot, *Oeuvres complètes*, tome quinzième. Paris: Garnier Frères 1876

Dobb, M. 1973. *Theories of Value and Distribution since Adam Smith*. London: Cambridge University Press

Donner, W. 1983. 'John Stuart Mill's Concept of Utility.' *Dialogue, 22*: 479–94

Dray, W. 1957. *Laws and Explanation in History*. London: Oxford University Press

Dryer, D.P. 1969. 'Mill's Utilitarianism.' In J.S. Mill, *Essays on Ethics, Religion and Society*, vol. X of *The Collected Works of John Stuart Mill*, ed. J. Robson. Toronto: University of Toronto Press

Ducasse, C.J. 1951. *Nature, Mind and Death*. LaSalle, Ill.: Open Court

Edgeworth, F.Y. 1881. *Mathematical Psychics: An Essay on the Application of Mathematics to the Moral Sciences*. London: C.K. Paul

Edwards, Rem. 1975. 'Do Pleasures and Pains Differ Qualitatively?' *Journal of Value Inquiry, 9*: 270–81

– 1979. *Pleasures and Pains*. Ithaca, NY: Cornell University Press

Ehrenfels, C. von. 1890. 'Über Gestaltqualitäten.' *Vierteljahrsschrift für wissenschaftliche Philosophie, 14*: 249–92

Ellis, W.D. 1938. *A Sourcebook of Gestalt Psychology*. New York: Harcourt Brace

Epstein, W. 1961. *Varieties of Perceptual Learning*. New York: McGraw-Hill

Ewing, A.C. 1965. *Ethics*. London: English Universities Press

Fechner, G.T. 1860. *Elements of Psychophysics*. Trans. H.E. Adler. New York: Holt, Rinehart and Winston 1966

Feigl, H. 1958. 'The "Mental" and the "Physical".' In H. Feigl et al., eds., *Minnesota Studies in the Philosophy of Science*, vol. ii. Minneapolis: University of Minnesota Press

Firth, R. 1952. *The Elements of Social Organization*. Second edition. London: Walts

Garner, R., and B. Rosen. 1967. *Moral Philosophy*. New York: Macmillan

Gay, John. 1731. *A Dissertation concerning the Fundamental Principle and Immediate Criterion of Virtue*. Prefixed to William King, *Essay on the Origin of Evil*. London and Cambridge: W. Thurlbourn

Gibson, J.J. 1982. *Reasons for Realism: Selected Essays of James J. Gibson*. Hillsdale, NJ: L. Erlbaum

Goldinger, M. 1976. 'Mill's Attack on Moral Conservatism.' *Midwest Studies in Philosophy*, *1*: 61–8

Goldworth, A. 1979. 'Jeremy Bentham: On the Measurement of Subjective States,' *Bentham Newsletter*, no. 2: 3–17

Gray, A. 1931. *The Development of Economic Doctrine*. London: Longmans, Green and Co.

Grossmann, R. 1959. *The Structure of Mind*. Madison, Wis.: University of Wisconsin Press

– 1983. *The Categorial Structure of the World*. Bloomington, Ind.: Indiana University Press

Grote, J. 1870. *An Examination of the Utilitarian Philosophy*. Cambridge: Deighton, Bell and Co.

– 1876. *A Treatise on Moral Ideals*. Cambridge: Deighton, Bell and Co.

Halévy, E. 1901. *La Formation du Radicalisme Philosophique*. Paris: Ancienne Librairie Germer Baillière

Hall, E.W. 1964. 'The "Proof" of Utility in Bentham and Mill.' In his *Categorial Analysis*, ed. E.M. Adams. Chapel Hill: University of North Carolina Press

Hall, T.S. 1975. *History of General Physiology*. Two volumes. Chicago: Phoenix Books, University of Chicago Press

Hare, R.M. 1973. 'Rawls' Theory of Justice I.' *The Philosophical Quarterly*, *23*: 144–55

Harrison, J. 1976. *Hume's Moral Epistemology*. London: Oxford University Press

Hausman, A. 1984. 'Adhering to Inherence.' *Canadian Journal of Philosophy*, *14*: 421–43

Helmholtz, H. von. 1878. *Die Thatsachen in der Wahrnemung*. Berlin: August Hirschwald

Hempel, C.G., and P. Oppenheim. 1965. 'Studies in the Logic of Explanation.' In C.G. Hempel, *Aspects of Scientific Explanation and Other Essays*. New York: The Free Press

Herrnstein, R.J., and E.G. Boring. 1966. *A Source Book in the History of Psychology*. Cambridge, Mass.: Harvard University Press

Hobbes, T. 1651. *Leviathan*. Reprinted (in part) in D.D. Raphael (1969), vol. I. References are to numbered paragraphs in the latter.

Holbrook, Daniel. 1988. *Qualitative Utilitarianism*. Lanham, Md: University Press of America

Hollander, S. 1979. 'The Role of Bentham in the Early Development of Ricardian Theory: A Speculative Essay,' *Bentham Newsletter*, no. 3: 2–17

Horne Tooke, J. 1798. *The Diversions of Purley*. Reprint. Menston, England: The Scolar Press 1968

Hospers, J. 1961. *Human Conduct*. New York: Harcourt Brace Jovanovich

Hume, D. 1739. *Treatise of Human Nature*, ed. L.A. Selby-Bigge. London: Oxford University Press 1888

– 1777. *Enquiries concerning the Human Understanding and concerning the Principles of Morals*, ed. L.A. Selby-Bigge. Second edition. Oxford: Clarendon Press 1902

– 1932. *Letters*, ed. J.T.Y. Grieg. Two volumes. Oxford: Clarendon Press

Humphrey, G. 1951. *Thinking*. London: Methuen

Hunter, J.F.M. 1987. 'Seeing Dimensionally.' *Canadian Journal of Philosophy*, *17*: 553–66

Hutcheson, F. 1726. *An Inquiry concerning the Original of Our Ideas of Virtue or Moral Good*. Second edition. Reprinted (in part) in L.A. Selby-Biggte (1897), vol. I. References are to numbered paragraphs in the latter.

– 1742. *An Essay on the Nature and Conduct of the Passions and Affections. With Illustrations on the Moral Sense*. Third edition. Reprint. Gainesville: Scholars' Facsimiles and Reprints 1969. Reprinted (in part) in D.D. Raphael (1969), vol. I. Unless otherwise noted, references are to the numbered paragraphs of the latter.

– 1755. *A System of Moral Philosophy*. Reprinted (in part) in L.A. Selby-Bigge (1897), vol. I. References are to numbered paragraphs in the latter.

Huxley, T.H. 1874. 'On the Hypothesis that Animals Are Automata, and Its History.' *The Fortnightly Review*, n.s. 22: 555–80

Ittelson, W.S. 1960. *Visual Space Perception*. New York: Springer

James, W. 1890. *Principles of Psychology*. Two volumes. New York: Holt

Jevons, W.S. 1871. *The Theory of Political Economy*. London and New York: Macmillan and Co.

– 1911. *The Theory of Political Economy*. Fourth edition. Ed. H.S. Jevons. London: Macmillan

– 1973. *Papers and Correspondence*, vol. 2. London: Macmillan

Johnson, W.E. 1913. 'The Pure Theory of Utility Curves.' *Economic Journal*, 23: 483–513

Jones, P. 1982. *Hume's Sentiments*. Edinburgh: University of Edinburgh Press

Kames, Henry Home, Lord. 1758. *Essays on the Principles of Morality and Natural Religion*. Second edition. London: C. Hitch & L. Hawes, R. & J. Dodsley, J. Rivington & J. Fletcher, and J. Richardson

Knight, F.H. 1931. 'Professor Fisher's Interest Theory: A Case in Point.' *Journal of Political Economy, 39*: 176–212

Köhler, W. 1920. *Die physischen Gestalten in Ruhe und im stationären Zustand*. Translated in part in W.D. Ellis (1938). Page references are to the latter.

– 1922. 'Some Gestalt Problems.' In W.D. Ellis (1938)

Kuhn, T. 1970. *The Structure of Scientific Revolutions*. Second edition. Chicago: University of Chicago Press

Lakatos, I. 1970. 'Falsifiability and the Methodology of Scientific Research Programmes.' In I. Lakatos and A. Musgrave, eds., *Criticism and the Growth of Knowledge*. London: Cambridge University Press

Lazarsfeld, A. 1958. 'Evidence and Inference in Social Research.' In M. Brodbeck (1968), 608–34

Legaré, Hugh Swinton. 1845. 'Jeremy Bentham and the Utilitarians,' in vol. II of the *Writings of Hugh Swinton Legaré*, two volumes. Charleston, SC: Burges and James

Lehrer, K. 1987. 'Beyond Impressions and Ideas: Hume vs. Reid.' *Monist, 70*: 383–97

– 1989. 'Conception without Representation – Justification without Inference: Reid's Theory.' *Noûs, 23*: 145–54

Lewin, K. 1926. 'Will and Needs.' In W.D. Ellis (1938)

– 1936. *Principles of Topological Psychology*, trans. F. and G.M. Heider. New York: McGraw-Hill

Lewis, D. 1965. 'Moore's Realism.' In L. Addis and D. Lewis (1965)

Lively, J., and J. Rees, eds. 1978. *Utilitarian Logic and Politics*. London: Oxford University Press

Locke, John. 1697. *An Answer to Remarks upon an Essay concerning Human Understanding, &c*. In vol. III of *The Works of John Locke*, Twelfth edition. Nine volumes. London: C. & J. Rivington, T. Egerton, J. Cuthell, 1824

– 1700. *An Essay concerning Human Understanding*. Fourth edition. Ed. A.C. Fraser. Oxford: Clarendon Press 1894; reprinted New York: Dover 1959. Unless otherwise noted references are to book, chapter, and section.

Luce, A.A. 1934. *Berkeley and Malebranche*. London: Oxford University Press

– 1945. *Berkeley's Immaterialism*. London: Nelson

Macaulay, T.B. 1829. 'Mill's Essay on Government: Utilitarian Logic and Politics.' In J. Lively and J. Rees (1978)

Mach, E. 1886. *Beiträge zur Analyse der Empfindungen*. Prague: Gustav Fischer

Mackie, J.L. 1965. 'Causes and Conditions.' *American Philosophical Quarterly*, 2: 245–64

– 1980. *Hume's Moral Theory*. London: Routledge and Kegan Paul

Madden, E.H. 1962. *Philosophical Problems of Psychology*. New York: Odyssey Press

Malebranche, N. 1674–5. *De la Recherche de la Vérité*, ed. G. Rodis-Lewis. Three volumes. In the *Oeuvres complètes*, ed. André Robinet. Paris: J. Vrin 1958–68

Malinowski, B. 1922. *Argonauts of the Western Pacific*. London: Routledge 1961

de Mandeville, B. 1723. *Fable of the Bees, or private vices, public benefits*. Second edition, including *An Enquiry into the Origin of Moral Virtue*, ed. F.B. Kaye. London: Oxford University Press 1957

Marcil-Lacoste, L. 1975. 'Dieu, garante de veracité, ou Reid critique de Descartes.' *Dialogue, 14*: 584–605

Marr, David. 1982. *Vision*. San Francisco: W.H. Freeman

Marshall, A. 1925. 'Mr. Mill's Theory of Value.' In A.C. Pigou, ed., *Memorials of Alfred Marshall*, ed. A.C. Pigou. London: Macmillan and Co.

– 1961. *Principles of Economics*. Variorum edition. Ed. C.W. Guilleband. London: Macmillan

Martineau, J. 1886. *Types of Ethical Theory*. Second edition. Two volumes. Oxford: Clarendon Press

Mill, James. 1818. 'Essay on Education.' In W.H. Burston, ed., *James Mill on Education*. London: Cambridge University Press 1969

– 1820. *An Essay on Government*. In J. Lively and J. Rees (1978)

– 1824. *Elements of Political Economy*. Second edition. London: Baldwin, Cradock, and Joy

– 1825. *Analysis of the Phenomena of the Human Mind*, ed. John Stuart Mill, with additional notes by A. Bain, A. Findlater, G. Grote, and J.S. Mill. London: Longmans, Green, Reader, and Dyer

– 1835. *A Fragment on Mackintosh*. London: Baldwin and Cradock

Mill, J.S. 1833. 'Remarks on Bentham's Philosophy.' In his *Essays on Ethics, Religion and Society*, vol. x of *The Collected Works of John Stuart Mill*, ed. J. Robson. Toronto: University of Toronto Press 1969

– 1838. 'Sedgwick's Discourse.' In his *Essays on Ethics, Religion and Society*, vol. x of *The Collected Works of John Stuart Mill*, ed. J. Robson. Toronto: University of Toronto Press 1969

– 1840. 'Coleridge.' In his *Essays on Ethics, Religion and Society*, vol. x of *The Collected Works of John Stuart Mill*, ed. J. Robson. Toronto: University of Toronto Press 1969

- 1842–3. 'Bailey on Berkeley's Theory of Vision.' In his *Essays on Philosophy and the Classics*, vol. XI of *The Collected Works of John Stuart Mill*, ed. J. Robson. Toronto: University of Toronto Press 1978
- 1844. 'On the Definition of Political Economy and the Method of Investigation Proper to It.' In his *Essays in Economics and Society*, vol. IV of *The Collected Works of John Stuart Mill*, ed. J. Robson. Toronto: University of Toronto Press 1967
- 1852. 'Whewell on Moral Philosophy.' In his *Essays on Ethics, Religion and Society*, vol. X of *The Collected Works of John Stuart Mill*, ed. J. Robson. Toronto: University of Toronto Press 1969
- 1859a. 'Bain's Psychology.' In his *Essays on Philosophy and the Classics*, vol. XI of *The Collected Works of John Stuart Mill*, ed. J. Robson. Toronto: University of Toronto Press 1978
- 1859b. 'On Liberty.' In *Essays on Politics and Society*, vol. XVIII of *The Collected Works of John Stuart Mill*, ed. J. Robson. Toronto: University of Toronto Press 1977
- 1861. 'Utilitarianism.' In his *Essays on Ethics, Religion and Society*, vol. X of *The Collected Works of John Stuart Mill*, ed. J. Robson. Toronto: University of Toronto Press 1969
- 1865. 'Auguste Comte and Positivism.' In his *Essays on Ethics, Religion and Society*, vol. X of *The Collected Works of John Stuart Mill*, ed. J. Robson. Toronto: University of Toronto Press 1969
- 1869. 'Notes to James Mill's *Analysis of the Phenomena of the Human Mind*.' In James Mill (1825)
- 1871. *The Principles of Political Economy*, vols. II and III of *The Collected Works of John Stuart Mill*, ed. J. Robson. Toronto: University of Toronto Press 1966
- 1872a. *A System of Logic*, vols. VII and VIII of *The Collected Works of John Stuart Mill*, ed. J. Robson. Toronto: University of Toronto Press 1974. Unless otherwise noted references are to book, chapter, and section.
- 1872b. *An Examination of Sir William Hamilton's Philosophy*, vol. IX of *The Collected Works of John Stuart Mill*, ed. J. Robson. Toronto: University of Toronto Press 1979
- 1873. *Autobiography*. In his *Autobiography and Literary Essays*, vol. I of *The Collected Works of John Stuart Mill*, ed. J. Robson. Toronto: University of Toronto Press 1981

Mintz, S.I. 1962. *The Hunting of Leviathan*. Cambridge: Cambridge University Press

Mitchell, Wesley. 1918. 'Bentham's Felicific Calculus.' *Political Science Quarterly*, *33*: reprinted in B. Parekh (1974), 168–88. Page references are to the latter.

Moore, G.E. 1903. *Principia Ethica*. London: Cambridge University Press

Narveson, J. 1967. *Morality and Utility*. Baltimore, Md: The Johns Hopkins Press

Norton, D.F. 1982. *David Hume: Common-Sense Moralist, Sceptical Metaphysician*. Princeton: Princeton University Press

– 1985. 'Hutcheson's Moral Realism.' *Journal of the History of Philosophy*, 23: 397–418

Nozick, R. 1974. *Anarchy, State and Utopia*. New York: Basic Books

Pappas, G. 1989. 'Sensation and Perception in Reid.' *Noûs*, 23: 155–67

Parekh, B. 1974. *Jeremy Bentham: Ten Critical Essays*. London: Frank Cass

Pastore, N. 1971. *Selective History of Theories of Visual Perception*. New York: Oxford University Press

Plamenatz, J. 1949. *Mill's Utilitarianism, Reprinted with a Study of the English Utilitarians*. Oxford: Oxford University Press

Polanyi, K. 1957. *Trade and Market in the Early Empires*, ed. Polanyi, C. Arensberg, and H. Pearson. New York: Free Press

Pratt, C.C. 1939. *The Logic of Modern Psychology*. New York: Macmillan

Price, Richard. 1787. *A Review of the Principal Questions in Morals*. Third edition. Reprinted (in part) in D.D. Raphael (1969), vol. II. References are to the numbered paragraphs in the latter.

Priestley, F.E.L. 1969. 'Introduction' to J.S. Mill, *Essays on Ethics, Religion and Society*, vol. x of *The Collected Works of John Stuart Mill*, ed. J. Robson. Toronto: University of Toronto Press

Ramsey, F.P. 1931. *The Foundations of Mathematics and Other Logical Essays*. New York: Harcourt Brace

Raphael, D.D. 1969. *British Moralists 1650–1800*. Two volumes. London: Oxford University Press

Rauner, R. 1961. *Samuel Bailey and the Classical Theory of Value*. Cambridge, Mass.: Harvard University Press

Rawls, J. 1971. *A Theory of Justice*. Cambridge, Mass.: Belknap Press

Reid, T. 1785a. *Inquiry into the Human Mind*. In *The Works*, ed. W. Hamilton. Third edition. Edinburgh: MacLachlan and Stewart 1852

– 1785b. *Essays on the Intellectual Powers of Man*. In *The Works*, ed. W. Hamilton. Third edition. Edinburgh: MacLachlan and Stewart 1852

– 1788. *Essays on the Active Powers of the Human Mind*. In *The Works*, ed. W. Hamilton. Third edition. Edinburgh: MacLachlan and Stewart 1852

Ricardo, D. 1821. *On the Principles of the Political Economy of Taxation*, vol. I of the *Works and Correspondence of David Ricardo*, ed. P. Sraffa. London: Cambridge University Press 1951. This is a reprint of the third edition of 1821.

Robbins, L. 1935. *An Essay on the Nature and Significance of Economic Science*. Second edition. London: Macmillan

Robinson, Daniel N. 1981. *Intellectual History of Psychology*. New York: Macmillan

Robson, J. 1968. *The Improvement of Mankind*. Toronto: University of Toronto Press

Rosenberg, A. 1976. *Microeconomic Laws*. Pittsburgh: University of Pittsburgh Press

Russell, B. 1903. *Principles of Mathematics*. Cambridge: Cambridge University Press

- 1915. 'The Ultimate Constituents of Matter.' *The Monist*, 25: 399–417

Ryle, Gilbert. 1949. *The Concept of Mind*. New York: Barnes and Noble

- 1960. *Dilemmas*. Cambridge: Cambridge University Press

Samuelson, P. 1938. 'A Note on the Pure Theory of Consumer's Behavior.' In his *Collected Scientific Papers*, vol. 1: 2–14. Boston: MIT Press 1966

- 1948. 'Consumption Theory in Terms of Revealed Preference.' In his *Collected Scientific Papers*, vol. 1: 64–74. Boston: MIT Press 1966

Schumpeter, J. 1954. *A History of Economic Analysis*. New York: Oxford University Press

Sedgwick, A. 1834. *A Discourse on the Studies of the University*. Third edition. London: Parker

Sellars, W. 1954. 'Some Reflections on Language Games.' In his *Science, Perception and Reality*, chapter 11. London: Routledge and Kegan Paul 1963

- 1964. 'Notes on Intentionality.' In his *Philosophical Perspectives*, 308–20. Springfield, Ill.: Charles C. Thomas 1967

Seth, James 1911. *A Study of Ethical Principles*. New York: Scribner

Shaffer, J. 1968. *Philosophy of Mind*. Englewood Cliffs, NJ: Prentice-Hall

Shaftesbury, Anthony Ashley Cooper, Earl of. 1711. *Characteristics of Men, Manners, Opinions, Times*, ed. J.M. Robertson, with an Introduction by S. Grean. Two volumes in one. Indianapolis, Ind.: Bobbs-Merrill 1964

- 1716. *Several Letters, Written by a Noble Lord to a Young Man at the University*. London: J. Roberts

- 1900. *The Life, Unpublished Letters, and Philosophical Regimen of Anthony Ashley Cooper, Earl of Shaftesbury*, ed. B. Rand. London and New York: Sonnenshein

Sidgwick, H. 1907. *The Methods of Ethics*. Seventh edition. London: Macmillan

- 1931. *Outlines of the History of Ethics for English Readers*. London: Macmillan

Smith, Adam. 1776. *Inquiry into the Nature and Causes of The Wealth of Nations*, ed. E. Canaan. New York: Modern Library 1937

Smith, L.D. 1986. *Behaviorism and Logical Positivism: A Reassessment*. Stanford: Stanford University Press

Sommerville, J. 1987. 'Reid's Conception of Common Sense.' *Monist*, 70: 418–29

Sosa, E. 1969. 'Mill's *Utilitarianism*.' In J. Smith and E. Sosa, eds., *Mill's 'Utilitarianism.'* Belmont, Calif.: Wadsworth Publishing Co.

Sparshott, F.E. 1958. *An Enquiry into Goodness and Related Concepts*. Toronto: University of Toronto Press

– 1978. 'Introduction' to J.S. Mill, *Essays on Philosophy and the Classics*, vol. XI of *The Collected Works of John Stuart Mill*, ed. J. Robson. Toronto: University of Toronto Press

Spencer, H. 1902. *Principles of Psychology*. Two volumes. New York: D. Appleton

Spiker, Charles C. 1977. 'Behaviorism, Cognitive Psychology, and The Active Organism.' In N. Datan and H.W. Reese (1977), Chapter 4

Stecker, R. 1987. 'Thomas Reid on the Moral Sense.' *Monist, 70*: 452–64

Stevens, S.S. 1934a. 'The Volume and Intensity of Tones.' *American Journal of Psychology, 46*: 397–408

– 1934b. 'Tonal Density.' *Journal of Experimental Psychology, 17*: 585–92

Stigler, G.J. 1955. 'Originality in Scientific Progress.' *Economica*, n.s. 22: 293–302

Strong, C.A. 1903. *Why the Mind Has a Body*. New York: Macmillan

Stumpf, C. 1873. *Über den psychologischen Ursprung der Raumvorstellung*. Leipzig: S. Hirzel

– 1883, 1890. *Tonpsychologie*. Two volumes. Leipzig: S. Hirzel

Taylor, R. 1970. *Good and Evil*. New York: Macmillan

Titchener, E.B. 1895. 'The Type-Theory of Simple Reactions.' *Mind*, n.s. 4: 506–14

– 1896. 'The "Type-Theory" of Simple Reaction.' *Mind*, n.s. 5: 236–41

– 1909. *Lectures on the Experimental Psychology of Thought-Processes*. New York: Macmillan

– 1909–10. *A Textbook of Psychology*. New York: Macmillan

– 1929. *Systematic Psychology: Prolegomena*. New York: Macmillan

Tucker, Abraham. 1768. *The Light of Nature Pursued*. Fifth edition. Two volumes. London: Charles Daly 1840

Urban, W.M. 1930. *Fundamentals of Ethics*. New York: Henry Holt and Co.

Urmson, J.O., ed. 1960. *The Concise Encyclopedia of Western Philosophy and Philosophers*. London: Hutchison

Vernier, D. 1976. 'Thomas Reid on the Foundations of Knowledge and his Answer to Skepticism.' In S.F. Barker and T.L. Beauchamp, eds., *Thomas Reid*, 14–24. Philadelphia: Philosophical Monographs

Volterra, V. 1930. *Theory of Functionals and of Integral and Integro-differential Equations*, ed. L. Fantappie; trans. M. Long. London: Blackie

Waldman, T. 1959. 'Origins of the Legal Doctrine of Reasonable Doubt.' *Journal of the History of Ideas, 20*: 299–316

Ward, J. 1915. *Naturalism and Agnosticism*. Fourth edition. London: A. and C. Black

Warren, Howard C. 1921. *A History of the Association Psychology from Hartley to Lewes*. Baltimore: Charles Scribner's Sons

Washburn, Margaret Floy. 1916. *Movement and Mental Imagery*. Boston: Houghton Mifflin

Watson, J.B. 1913. 'Image and Affection in Behavior.' *Journal of Philosophy, 10*: 421–8

– 1924. *Behaviorism*. New York: W.H. Norton and Co. 1930

Watson, R. 1966. *The Downfall of Cartesianism*. The Hague: Nijhoff

Weinberg, J. 1965. *Abstraction, Relation, and Induction*. Madison, Wis.: University of Wisconsin Press

Wertheimer, M. 1922. 'Untersuchungen zur Lehre von der Gestalt.' Translated in part in W.D. Ellis (1938). Page references are to the latter.

– 1923. 'Untersuchungen zur Lehre von der Gestalt.' Translated in part in R.J. Herrnstein and E.G. Boring (1966). Page references are to the latter.

– 1925. 'Über Gestalttheorie.' Translated in W.D. Ellis (1938). Page references are to the latter.

Whewell, W. 1845. *The Elements of Morality, including Polity*. New York: Harper

White, Sheldon H. 1977. 'Social Proof Structures: The Dialectic of Method and Theory in the Work of Psychology.' In N. Datan and H.W. Reese (1977), Chapter 3

Wicksteed, P.H. 1933. *The Common Sense of Political Economy*, ed. L. Robbins. Two volumes. London: G. Routledge 1945

Willey, B. 1940. *The Eighteenth Century Background*. New York: Columbia University Press

Williams, B. 1973. 'A Critique of Utilitarianism.' In J.J.C. Smart and B. Williams, *Utilitarianism For and Against*. London: Cambridge University Press

Wilson, F. 1965. 'Implicit Definition Once Again.' *Journal of Philosophy, 62*: 364–74

– 1967. 'Definition and Discovery.' *British Journal for the Philosophy of Science, 18*: 287–303 and *19*: 43–56

– 1969a. 'Weinberg's Refutation of Nominalism.' *Dialogue, 8*: 460–74

– 1969b. 'Explanation in Aristotle, Newton and Toulmin.' *Philosophy of Science, 36*: 291–310 and 400–28

– 1970. 'Acquaintance, Ontology and Knowledge.' *The New Scholasticism, 54*: 1–48

– 1974. 'Why I Do Not Experience Your Pain.' In M. Gram and E.D. Klemke, eds., *The Ontological Turn*. Iowa City: University of Iowa Press

- 1975. 'Marras on Sellars on Thought and Language.' *Philosophical Studies, 28*: 91–102
- 1979a. 'Hume and Ducasse on Causal Inference from a Single Experiment.' *Philosophical Studies, 35*: 305–9
- 1979b. 'Hume's Theory of Mental Activity.' In D.F. Norton, N. Capaldi, and W. Robison, eds., *McGill Hume Studies*, 101– 20. San Diego: Austin Hill Press
- 1982a. 'A Note on Hempel on the Logic of Reduction.' *International Logic Review, 13*: 17–29
- 1982b. 'Mill on the Operation of Discovering and Proving General Propositions.' *Mill News Letter, 17*: 1–18
- 1982c. 'Mill's Proof that Happiness Is the Criterion of Morality.' *Journal of Business Ethics, 1*: 59–72
- 1982d. 'Is There a Prussian Hume?' *Hume Studies, 8*: 1–18
- 1983a. 'Effability, Ontology, and Method.' *Philosophy Research Archives, 9*: 419–70
- 1983b. 'Mill's "Proof" of Utility and the Composition of Causes.' *Journal of Business Ethics, 2*: 135–58
- 1983c. 'Hume's Defence of Causal Inference.' *Dialogue, 22*: 661–94
- 1983d. 'Kuhn and Goodman: Revolutionary vs. Conservative Science.' *Philosophical Studies, 44*: 369–80
- 1984. 'Critical Review of J. Katz, *Language and Other Abstract Objects*.' *Canadian Journal of Philosophy, 14*: 663–73
- 1985a. *Explanation, Causation, and Deduction*. Dordrecht, Holland: D. Reidel
- 1985b. 'Hume's Cognitive Stoicism.' *Hume Studies*, 1985 Supplement: 521–68
- 1985c. 'Addis on Analysing Disposition Concepts.' *Inquiry, 28*: 247–72
- 1985d. 'Dispositions Defined: Harré and Madden on Defining Disposition Concepts.' *Philosophy of Science, 52*: 591– 607
- 1986a. 'The Lockean Revolution in the Theory of Science.' In G. Moyal and S. Tweyman, eds., *Early Modern Philosophy*. Delman, NY: Caravan Books
- 1986b. *Laws and Other Worlds*. Dordrecht, Holland: D. Reidel
- 1989a. 'Was Hume a Sceptic with Regard to the Senses?' *Journal of the History of Philosophy, 27*: 49–73
- 1989b. 'Wordsworth and the Culture of Science.' *Centennial Review, 33*: 322–92
- 1989c. 'Hume's Fictional Continuant.' *History of Philosophy Quarterly, 6*: 171–88
- 1989d. 'Abstract Ideas and Other Rules of Language.' Presented to the Conference on Ideas in 17th and 18th Century Philosophy, University of Iowa, Iowa City, April

- forthcoming a. *Empiricism and Darwin's Science*. Dordrecht, Holland: D. Reidel
- forthcoming b. 'The Logic of Multi-track Dispositions.' Copies available from the author
Winkler, K.P. 1985. 'Hutcheson's Alleged Realism.' *Journal of the History of Philosophy, 23*: 179–94
Wolterstorff, N. 1987. 'Hume and Reid.' *Monist, 70*: 398–417
Wright, G.H. von. 1965. *The Logical Problem of Induction*. Second edition. London: Blackwell
Wright, J. 1983. *The Sceptical Realism of David Hume*. Minneapolis: University of Minnesota Press
Wundt, W. 1893. 'Über Psychische Causalität und das Princip der psycho-physischen Parallelismus.' *Philosophische Studien*, x: 1–124
- 1902. *Outlines of Psychology*. Trans. C.H. Judd. New York: G.E. Stechert and Co.

Index of Names

Byron, George Gordon, Lord, 82

Carpenter, W.B., 304f, 307, 317
Carr, Harvey, 362
Cassels, J., 208, 213f, 358
Chomsky, N., 356, 357, 361
Christ, J., 77
Clarke, S., 20, 24–9, 31f, 35f, 45ff, 211, 224ff, 228f, 231
Coleridge, S., 73, 77, 145f, 244, 273, 351
Comte, A., 296f
Copp, D., 363
Crane, R.S., 351
Crousaz, J.P. de, 102
Cudworth, R., 24, 352
Cummins, P., 352, 353, 357

Dahl, N., 265, 289, 359
Darwin, C., 317, 318, 321, 327, 330, 331, 333, 335, 338ff
Democritus, 147
DePaul, M.P., 363
Descartes, R., 51f, 57ff, 63, 87, 103, 294, 306, 308, 310, 352, 353, 359
Diderot, D., 210f, 273
Dobb, M., 204
Donner, Wendy, ix, 17, 285–90, 351, 359
Dray, W., 358
Dryer, D.P., 9ff, 251f
Ducasse, C.J., 173ff, 357

Edgeworth, F.Y., 279
Edwards, R., 262f, 266, 359
Ehrenfels, C. von, 93, 95, 333
Epicurus, 147, 269
Epstein, W., 186
Ewing, A.C., 261

Fechner, G.T., 279

Feigl, H., 360, 361
Freud, S., 330, 333, 361
Friedman, M., 345, 347

Galileo Galilei, 183, 344
Gall, F.J., 297
Galton, F., 362, 363
Garner, R., 261
Gay, John, 232f, 234
George, King, the First, 224
Gibson, J.J., 178, 357
God, 24, 28, 32f, 40ff, 47, 49f, 64ff, 70, 224–31, 352, 358
Goldringer, M., 363
Goldworth, A., 359
Gray, A., 193
de Groot, Hans, ix
Grossmann, R., 355, 357, 363
Grote, J., 241f, 244, 251, 255, 259, 265, 269

Halévy, E., 351, 359
Hall, E.W., 358
Hall, T.S., 360
Hamilton, Sir William, 171, 172, 180, 182, 186, 187ff, 190
Hare, R.M., 363
Harrison, J., 352
Hartley, D., 109, 138, 169, 244f, 292f, 297
Hausman, A., 352, 357
Hegel, G.W.F., 213
Helmholtz, H. von, 140, 265
Hempel, C.G., 354
Heraclitus, 147
Hobbes, T., 20, 21–4, 26f, 29f, 40, 44, 45f, 59, 71, 102, 209, 211, 225, 234, 237, 308
Holbrook, D., 247, 286, 288, 358, 359
Hollander, S., 358
Horne Tooke, J., 100, 108

Index of Subjects

activity, mental, 12, 244ff, 351
allegiance, 4ff, 21–4, 35, 191, 223, 225
analysis. *See* introspection
assocationism, 10ff, 12, 63f, 89f,
  101–26, 127–51, 154–71,
  199ff, 232ff, 243ff, 248ff, 255ff,
  258f, 264, 267, 273f, 315ff,
  337ff, 340ff, 354, 356; historical
  laws in, 315f

beauty, sense of, 210f, 273ff
behaviour, 311–36; as subject-matter
  of psychology, 317ff
behaviourism. *See* psychology,
  behaviourist
benevolence, 33ff, 228, 233; compared to gravity, 224f, 228

causation
– contrasted with correlation, 309
– determinism, 302ff; compatible
  with free will, 302
– regularity view of, 47, 63, 70,
  102ff, 105, 302, 308, 360; denied, 46, 70, 106, 153, 173–8; importance for psychology, 308
composition: chemical, 17, 97ff, 110,
  116, 120f, 122f, 124ff, 138, 179,

184f, 234, 267, 272, 330, 343; mechanical, 17, 91f, 116f, 122f,
  272, 343, 359; of causes, 90–9,
  116f
contract, 4ff, 21–4, 35, 191, 223,
  225, 237f, 346ff
conventions: in ethics, 44, 56; in perception, 56
cultivation, self, 4, 12, 76, 80–3, 259,
  359

duty. *See* virtue

economics
– classical, ix, 3ff, 12, 17, 18f, 152,
  191–223, 254ff, 342; laws of
  distribution, 200, 208; statics and
  dynamics in, 195ff, 203–23
– developmental, 191–223, 345
– imperfect explanations in, 195,
  199–201, 223, 254, 342, 344
– marginalist, 3, 192, 218f, 284
– a relatively autonomous science,
  198f, 223, 254f
education, 4, 12, 15, 73–8, 78–83,
  239f, 270; *see also* cultivation,
  self
egoism, psychological, 3ff, 13ff, 17,

20, 21–4, 27, 30, 33, 37, 59, 74,
191, 200, 214f, 225, 233, 234, 252;
see also rationality, economic
epiphenomenalism, 304ff, 308, 310,
361; *see also* psychology,
parallelism
energy, conservation of, 307, 327
evolution, Darwin's theory of, 317,
321, 327, 333, 335, 339, 340;
and learning, 327f, 337f, 340
explanation, 84–90, 343, 352, 354f,
358
– causal, 43, 47f, 86f, 256, 258, 268
– functional, 43, 65, 70, 86, 113, 236,
254, 259f, 317, 318f, 339
– historical laws in, 314ff, 361; compatible with determinism, 315
– imperfect, 44, 85f, 113, 195, 302
– S-R, 314ff, 324
– theoretical, 87f

faculties, higher, 73ff, 82, 139, 229,
237ff, 255ff, 262ff, 273ff, 327–
36; introspective method does not
apply to, 139, 255ff, 330–6

God. *See* teleology, divine

happiness. *See* pleasure
hedonism, psychological, 13ff, 202,
223, 239ff, 241ff, 250ff, 256f,
257–93, 338, 340, 344; in economics, 197f, 202, 253ff; *see also*
motivation

idea, 132–8; (vs. sensation), *see*
sensation
idealism, 54f, 169, 352
innatism. *See* nativism
intersubjective, 7f
introspection, 11, 15, 16f, 18f, 20, 46,
48, 61, 78–83, 98f, 100–26,

128, 138, 141, 144ff, 153, 154–71,
179ff, 188ff, 241ff, 256, 267,
285, 290f, 293, 294–336, 337,
340ff, 343
– and behaviourism, 326f
– and higher faculties, 328–36, 363
– compatible with simplicity of the
analysed, 61, 66, 70, 83, 97, 49,
98f, 117, 121, 125, 141f, 153, 159,
178–83, 267; *see also* composition, chemical
– definitional model of, 100–7, 114,
118, 120, 123, 133ff, 136
– dispositional model of, 106–26,
137f, 169f
intuitionism, ethical, 12, 45f, 49, 71,
117f, 203, 228, 271, 285, 340,
363; contemporary, 345–9; *see also*
nativism

justice, 346ff; *see also* property
just noticeable differences, 278f

labour, pain of, 194; *see also* value,
labour theory of
learning, 10, 18, 63f, 98, 104, 114,
137, 142, 150, 187, 199ff, 239ff,
243, 271ff, 289, 315ff, 337ff,
340ff, 344, 351, 356, 361; and
evolution, 327, 340; *see also*
associationism

meaning, context theory of, 160f,
187f, 332ff
method, scientific, 71, 84–90, 113f,
132–8, 172, 175f, 188f, 190, 225,
230f, 272, 293, 343
morality. *See* virtue
motivation, 4ff, 12f, 35, 42, 76f, 81ff,
114, 137, 192, 194–5, 197ff,
226, 239ff, 244–52, 266, 267,

292f, 317, 343, 344; maximizing, 252–7, 293, 339, 340

nativism, 43, 70, 86, 106f, 154f, 188f, 200, 203, 205, 233, 337ff, 351, 352, 356, 358, 361; and behaviourism, 325; in ethics, 12, 20, 30ff, 37, 48ff, 62–4, 70, 200, 237, 256, 258, 268, 271, 340f; in perception, 18, 60–5, 67ff, 70, 149f, 154–8, 177f, 178–83, 237, 340f

objectivity
– ethical, 6ff, 12, 20, 35ff, 39, 45–51, 71f, 203f, 211, 223, 228, 230f, 235, 256; moral standards, 285–90; see also intuitionism
– = intersubjective, 7, 295
– in economics, 342
– in scientific psychology, 294–336; compatible with existence of subjectives, 298, 303
objects, perceptual
– non-substantialist account of, 52ff, 55ff, 152f, 155ff, 167–71f; causal beliefs involved in, 173f
– substance account of, 51ff, 55f, 60–2, 66f, 166f, 172, 237
oblivescence, law of, 141, 329

perception, 152–90, 162–71, 307, 343, 357
– as inference, 54, 62, 64, 178, 180, 322, 352
– not representational, 161f, 357
– of distance, ix, 57ff, 69, 150, 153, 154–71, 179ff, 182, 203
– of spatial relations, 56f, 63f, 69, 144–51, 153, 163f, 170, 178, 185, 195

– simple and unanalysable, 47, 60ff, 70, 97ff, 152, 170f, 176ff, 179ff, 237, 322; can be learned, 67, 70, 98, 148, 178, 237, 322
– simple objects of, 60f, 67, 70
– (vs. sensation), 128, 161–71
– see also objects, perceptual
philosophic radicals, 4f, 8, 11, 13, 17, 24, 51, 59, 77, 84, 152, 191ff, 196, 199, 276
pleasure, 9, 14ff, 16, 114, 202, 224–93, 337–42, 359
– cardinal vs. ordinal scale of, 216–20, 223, 253, 275–90, 354, 359
– kinds of, 260f, 262ff, 265–75
– parts of, 9ff, 236, 242, 250f, 256, 267
– quantity/quality distinction, 19, 38–40, 77, 117f, 137, 190, 191f, 213, 216ff, 220, 221, 253, 265–75, 275–90, 293, 336, 343f, 354, 359
– higher (vs. lower), 83, 200f, 221, 253, 255, 257–93, 336; generated by lower, 259f, 264, 271f; unanalysable into lower, 73, 77, 83, 262, 293, 336
– See also hedonism, psychological; motivation; psychology: physiological processes in; value
poetry, 80ff
preference. See relations, of preference
promises. See contract
property, 4ff, 21–4, 35, 191, 200, 223, 225, 233, 237f, 345f, 347
psychology, 354, 357
– behaviourist, 19, 115f, 134, 139, 295, 311–42, 344, 349, 361; and classical psychology, 325f, 341f; and economics, 343, 344;